MW00657724

Many Mouths

This compelling study explores food programs initiated by the British government across two centuries, from the workhouses of the 1830s to the postwar Welfare State. Challenging the assumption that state ideologies and practices were progressive and based primarily on scientific advances in nutrition, Nadja Durbach examines the political, economic, social, and cultural circumstances that led the state to feed some of its subjects but not others. Durbach follows food policies from their conception to their implementation through case studies involving paupers, prisoners, famine victims, POWs, schoolchildren, wartime civilians, and pregnant women and toddlers. She explores what government food meant to those who devised, executed, used, and sometimes refused these social services. *Many Mouths* seeks to understand the social, economic, and political theories that influenced these feeding schemes, within their changing historical contexts. It thus offers fresh insights into how both the administrators and the intended recipients of government food programs realized, interpreted, and made meaning out of these exchanges, and the complex relationship between the body, the state, and the citizen.

Nadja Durbach is a historian of modern Britain at the University of Utah, where her work focuses on the history of the body, particularly in relationship to the modern state. Her research interests include anti-vaccinationism in the nineteenth century, the Victorian and Edwardian freak show, and the history of state-feeding. Nadja has received grants from the John Simon Guggenheim Foundation and the American Philosophical Society. She is also the author of *Bodily Matters: The Anti-Vaccination Movement in England, 1853–1907* (2005) and *Spectacle of Deformity: Freak Shows and Modern British Culture* (2010).

Many Mouths

*The Politics of Food in Britain from
the Workhouse to the Welfare State*

Nadja Durbach

University of Utah

CAMBRIDGE
UNIVERSITY PRESS

CAMBRIDGE
UNIVERSITY PRESS

University Printing House, Cambridge CB2 8BS, United Kingdom

One Liberty Plaza, 20th Floor, New York, NY 10006, USA

477 Williamstown Road, Port Melbourne, VIC 3207, Australia

314–321, 3rd Floor, Plot 3, Splendor Forum, Jasola District Centre,
New Delhi – 110025, India

79 Anson Road, #06-04/06, Singapore 079906

Cambridge University Press is part of the University of Cambridge.

It furthers the University's mission by disseminating knowledge in the
pursuit of education, learning, and research at the highest international
levels of excellence.

www.cambridge.org
Information on this title: www.cambridge.org/9781108483834
DOI: 10.1017/9781108594189

© Nadja Durbach 2020

This publication is in copyright. Subject to statutory exception
and to the provisions of relevant collective licensing agreements,
no reproduction of any part may take place without the written
permission of Cambridge University Press.

First published 2020

Printed in the United Kingdom by TJ International Ltd, Padstow Cornwall

A catalogue record for this publication is available from the British Library.

Library of Congress Cataloging-in-Publication Data
Names: Durbach, Nadja, 1971- author.
Title: Many mouths : the politics of food in Britain from the workhouse to
the welfare state / Nadja Durbach, University of Utah.
Description: Cambridge, United Kingdom ; New York : Cambridge University
Press, 2020. | Includes bibliographical references and index.
Identifiers: LCCN 2019043912 | ISBN 9781108483834 (hardback) | ISBN
9781108705202 (ebook)
Subjects: LCSH: Nutrition policy--Great Britain--History. | Food--Great
Britain--History. | Food consumption--England--History.
Classification: LCC TX360.G7 D87 2020 | DDC 363.8/5610941--dc23
LC record available at https://lccn.loc.gov/2019043912

ISBN 978-1-108-48383-4 Hardback

Cambridge University Press has no responsibility for the persistence or
accuracy of URLs for external or third-party internet websites referred to in
this publication and does not guarantee that any content on such websites is,
or will remain, accurate or appropriate.

To Miles and Finn

Contents

Figures

Acknowledgments

I am extremely grateful to the funding agencies that believed in this project and provided me with the time and research monies to complete this book. I received generous support from the John Simon Guggenheim Memorial Foundation, the American Philosophical Society, and the University of Utah's University Research Committee Awards and Faculty Fellowships, as well as the College of Humanities International Travel Grant program.

This is a deeply archival book, and I am profoundly indebted to the archivists and librarians who helped me with this research. The staff at The National Archives, United Kingdom, went above and beyond to provide me access to file after file for well over a decade. I am particularly grateful to those both at Kew and their offsite storage facility that transported and handled the almost 300 boxes of ED 123 school meals files that threatened to crush us all. If they never wanted to see me again, I would understand. The staff of the London Metropolitan Archives, the British Library (particularly its Asian and African collections), the Wellcome Collection, and the Imperial War Museum, London, were equally helpful. The Lancashire Archives kindly sent me files the old-fashioned way. The Interlibrary Loan Department at the University of Utah's Marriott Library was prompt and efficient, and I appreciate Mary Ann James's willingness to pursue digital collections for me.

Many administrators at the University of Utah have over the years said "yes" when they could just as easily have said "no." I thank Stuart Culver, Dianne Harris, Eric Hinderaker, Jake Jensen, and Isabel Moreira for their confidence in this project.

I am fortunate to have been helped by a range of generous scholars who have read my work, listened patiently to works in progress, written me many letters of support, found me things to read, suggested topics worth pursuing, translated documents, shared their ideas and their scholarship, asked me great questions, forced me to rethink things, provided encouragement, and reminded me over and over again how important community is to the production of knowledge. I thank Julie Ault, Jordanna Bailkin, Anna Clark, Anne Clendinning, Brian Cowan, Mark Crowley, Sandra Dawson, Paul Deslandes, Jim Epstein, Aidan Forth, David Fouser, Sue Grayzel, Lisa Jacobson, Seth Koven, Lara Kriegel, Philippa Levine, Marjorie Levine-Clark, Chris Otter, Tammy Proctor, Erika Rappaport, Caitlin Rathe, Ellen Ross, Tehila Sasson, Lacey Sparks, Michelle Tusan, Deborah Valenze, James Vernon, Judith Walkowitz, Amy Woodson-Boulton, and Ina Zweiniger-Bargielowska. Sandra Midgley and Susan Farwick kindly shared their photographs and memories of welfare orange juice with me. In London, Melanie Clews and Geoff and Rita Crossick repeatedly housed me, fed me (much better food than I write about), and treated me like family.

I received important feedback from audiences at several meetings at the North American Conference on British Studies, the Pacific Coast Conference on British Studies, the Rocky Mountain European Studies Consortium, the University of Texas at Austin, the University of California, Santa Barbara, the Food History Seminar at the Institute for Historical Research (London), and the University of St. Andrews. Members of the British Studies Research Interest Group at the University of Utah have heard almost every chapter of this book, and I am deeply grateful to the stalwarts: Matt Basso, Scott Black, Vincent Cheng, Andy Franta, Disa Gambera, Anne Jamison, Richard Preiss, Tom Stillinger, Jessica Straley, and Barry Weller. My colleagues in the History Department at the University of Utah, especially those who attended my works-in-progress presentation, have also been extremely helpful, and I am fortunate to be in such good company.

At Cambridge University Press, I thank Liz Friend-Smith, who has expertly and enthusiastically shepherded this book through the publication process. Her sensitive handling of the manuscript (and its author) and her insights at each stage have been much appreciated. Atifa Jiwa provided invaluable assistance, as did the production staff, including Natasha Whelan. In addition, I thank Preethi Sekar at Lumina. Two anonymous external reviewers carefully read an unwieldy manuscript. Their extraordinarily generous feedback helped me to see both the forest and the trees. This book has greatly benefited from their input, though its shortcomings are of course my own.

I was raised in a family in which food was central. It was the way we communicated our joys and sorrows. There was little that couldn't be cured by a nice cup of tea, and no one returned home from a voyage without a *milchika* waiting for them. It is no wonder that my brother grew up to be a chef and that I should have finally got around to writing a book about food. Not only did I learn in the home that food was vital to culture, but growing up in the context of Canada's welfare state, I was also taught that the government provided nourishment for its youngest citizens. My parents explained to me that the Family Allowance check that arrived each month was meant for milk and bread, despite the fact that it became my pocket money to spend as I pleased (sometimes, I confess, on chips and chocolate). I would thus like to thank my parents, Errol and Oona, for preparing delicious food, for teaching me what it signifies, and for making clear not only their role but also the state's in providing for my well-being. My brother Andrey, who makes the best food I have ever eaten, has patiently offered up his wealth of food knowledge. My sister-in-law Sian has shared not only countless cups of tea but also her boundless good cheer with me. The fond memories of the food of my grandmothers, Ruth and Sarah, remain alive and well, even though both have long passed. When we joined our lives together, Benjamin Cohen welcomed me into a family with its own food traditions. Steve and Bobby and my brothers- and sisters-in-law – Ed, Caren, Jeff, Kim, Peter, Andrea, Tammy, Matt, Susie, and Brent – have taught me the joys of lasagna on Thanksgiving (though preferably the day after) and that sometimes it is okay just to order pizza. Ben has mulled over with me every topic explored in this book and many others that were abandoned along the way. His enthusiasm, interest, encouragement, patience, and support were crucial to this book's completion and are vital to everything that matters most. My most profound lessons about food and power have come from my children, Miles and Finn. This book is dedicated to them with love.

A version of Chapter 1 appeared as "Roast Beef, the New Poor Law, and the British Nation, 1834–1863," *Journal of British Studies* 52(4) (2013), 963–89 © The North American Conference on British Studies, 2013. A summary of Chapter 7 appeared as "One British Thing: A Bottle of Welfare Orange Juice, *c.* 1961–71," *Journal of British Studies* 57(3) (2018), 564–7 © The North American Conference on British Studies, 2018. Both are reprinted with the permission of Cambridge University Press.

Introduction
The Politics of Pickles

In 1968 Magnus Pyke argued that what "human communities choose to eat is only partly dependent on their physiological requirements, and even less on intellectual reasoning and a knowledge of what these physiological requirements are." Pyke, a nutritional scientist who had worked under the chief scientific advisor to Britain's Ministry of Food during World War II, illustrated his point by recounting that, in preparing the nation for war, military officials had demanded that land be allocated to grow gherkins. They had insisted, Pyke recalled, that the British soldier "could not fight without a proper supply of pickles to eat with his cold meat." The Ministry of War had apparently been "unmoved to learn from the nutritional experts" that pickles offered little of material value to the diet, as they had almost no calories, vitamins, or minerals. The Ministry of Food, Pyke asserted, nevertheless designated precious agricultural land for gherkin cultivation. For what the human body requires, this former government official conceded, often needs to be subordinate to what "the human being to whom the body belongs" desires.[1]

This pickle episode exemplifies why a book about government feeding must be more than merely a study of the impact of food science on state policy. The nutritional sciences, which began to emerge in the late eighteenth century and made significant advances from the 1840s,[2] established that the nutritive and energy potential of food could be measured, calibrated, and deployed. Food science might have been one of the "engine sciences" that Patrick Carroll positions as central to modern state formation, particularly in the British Isles.[3] But if science was integral to modern forms of governance, it must nevertheless be understood not as preceding and dictating state action but rather, as Christopher Hamlin has argued, as "a resource parties appeal to (or make up as they go along) for use wherever authority is needed: to authorize themselves to act, to compete for the public's interest and money, to neutralize real or potential critics."[4] That there was "a sharp division" between "theoretical knowledge" of nutrition and "its practical implementation"[5] was thus often strategic. The results of scientific studies of food were deployed as "facts" both by and against the state when it was useful to do so, exposing the ways in which this body of knowledge has been constructed not only through objective, neutral, and experimental practices but also through historically contingent social, cultural, and political processes.[6] That researchers rarely agreed among themselves as to dietary standards during the period under investigation here only made it more difficult for any individual or single body of experts to garner enough authority to control the discourses of food values and then convince state agents to prioritize this expertise over other political, economic, or social concerns. It is for these reasons that the nutritional sciences make sporadic, and always culturally and politically contextualized, appearances in this study of government food rather than acting as either its narrative thread or its chief explanatory device.

The decision to plant gherkins on agricultural land desperately needed for growing nourishing foodstuffs for the home front had nothing to do with nutrition, given that it was widely agreed that a pickle had almost no nutritive value. Pyke acknowledged that the Ministry of Food understood that this decision in fact undermined its own attempts to replace imported foods – which had provided two-thirds of the nation's calories before the war – with homegrown healthy produce.[7] That the Ministry of Food felt compelled by the Ministry of War to prioritize the morale of soldiers by catering to their food preferences, even at the expense of the health of civilians, suggests that state agencies had to negotiate feeding priorities, often pitting the presumed needs of different British populations against each other. In defending cultural tastes and traditional eating habits, even during a moment of severe food shortages, these government authorities demonstrated that they understood that food was a complex "munition of war." If the Ministry of Food repeatedly claimed that it was "vital to the nation that every scrap of food is used to the best advantage," its officials nevertheless conceded that the uses of food exceeded the material.[8] However unassuming, the soldier's pickled gherkin was thus part of a broader cultural politics of state feeding that this book analyzes from the workhouses of the 1830s to the postwar Welfare State.

Following the dictum of anthropologist Claude Lévi-Strauss, *Many Mouths* analyzes government food as something that may or may not be "good to eat" but is definitely "good to think [with]."[9] Food has symbolic power and carries cultural meaning because eating is intimate: One takes food into one's being, assimilating it into the self.

Consuming particular foods, sometimes in ritualized ways, is not, however, only an individual act as it frequently also marks the eater as a member of a group, reinforcing the centrality of food to culture.[10] If eating is part of fashioning individual and group identities, this takes place within political and economic contexts in which its "animal reality" is laid bare.[11] As the most crucial scarce resource, the essence of bare life,[12] food is a highly politicized object of exchange. Its distribution exposes the ways in which relations among the ranks, sexes, races, and generations have been established and managed, thus revealing social hierarchies.[13] This is most evident when viewed on a planetary scale. That the Global North is currently suffering a crisis of obesity at the same time that the Global South experiences chronic hunger is not, Chris Otter argues, "a gigantic paradox." Instead, it is the result, he asserts, of modern economic and geopolitical processes. These two sides of the worldwide food crisis are thus "the starkest, most basic way in which global inequality is manifest."[14] That the highest rates of obesity in the United States and Britain occur among groups who also have the highest poverty rates complicates understandings of the ways in which socioeconomic disparities affect food consumption and are thus written on the body itself.[15] Since this happens in ways that are neither self-evident nor consistent over time and space, historians have studied food fights in order to elucidate how power has operated in a range of past societies.[16] Given that food serves as "the most visceral connection between government and population,"[17] focusing on government feeding in particular allows for analysis of the nature of a state's investments in specific groups of subjects. At the same time, it reveals how a variety of publics have contested the state's authority by asserting their own needs, desires, and rights, either through making specific claims on government resources or by refusing the services offered.

Many Mouths thus follows other recent historical scholarship that in taking "the culinary turn" has brought "the mental, discursive worlds of cultural history together with the material, embodied understanding of the past."[18] It is a study of the material and the symbolic importance of feeding programs initiated by the British government for particular target populations from the 1830s through the 1960s. I use a series of case studies – paupers, prisoners, famine victims, prisoners of war, schoolchildren, wartime civilians on the home front, and pregnant women, infants, and toddlers – to think about the role that food played in debates about the appropriate relationship between these different groups of British subjects and the state. I demonstrate the ways in which government food was central to negotiations around national, class, ethnic, racial, colonial, generational, and gender identities and the cultural meanings attached to these subject positions during a period when the role of the state was consistently being reevaluated from within and without.

This is not, however, a top-down administrative history of government programs. As Patrick Joyce has argued, the state is productive: "[I]t confers on us identities, rights and values, enabling us as citizens to criticise and refashion it."[19] *Many Mouths* proposes that potential beneficiaries of state-feeding programs were not passive recipients of food aid. As we shall see, paupers demanded roast beef dinners, famine victims refused to eat food that compromised their caste practices, prisoners of war expected that culturally familiar foodstuffs be dispatched to them, and the home front population across the class spectrum utilized canteens that had been established for the working poor. If in other national contexts government food produced a national cuisine through the disciplining of consumer habits,[20] in tracking these consumers' assertions of their food rights, my case studies illustrate how much the British state was forced to concede and cater to the public's conservative tastes and traditional eating practices, though in some cases it deployed these food habits to achieve its own ends. Although these publics were differently constrained by a range of social, economic, cultural, and political factors, they were nevertheless agents that actively shaped government feeding initiatives and thus the nature of the state itself.

In order to expose the complexities, nuances, and multiple logics of these programs, I offer a close reading of several key moments in the history of state feeding that reveal the tensions that emerged around the role of government, the rights of subjects and citizens, and the place of particular populations within the British nation and its empire. Unlike other European histories of state food where a strong centralized state significantly impacted the development of policies and their deployment,[21] *Many Mouths* focuses on the introduction and operation of these schemes as negotiated processes that suggest the limits of the modern British state's ability to control its food programs in practice and thus to stabilize their meanings. Following James Vernon's argument that food and its lack can serve as a "critical locus for rethinking how forms of government and statecraft emerge and work,"[22] I argue that disputes over state feeding expose the ways in which the relationship between the governing and the governed was made and remade throughout the nineteenth and twentieth centuries. But instead of offering a generalized theory of the modern British state, this study foregrounds the inherent messiness of food fights in particular precisely because what we eat is always both materially and culturally significant.

This book is bounded by two critical moments in the history of the modern British state. It begins with the reorganization of poor relief that was predicated on a centralized bureaucracy and solidified the state's commitment to market principles. It ends with the introduction of the Welfare State that explicitly rejected both the ideology of the poor law and the mantra of limited state intervention in its refashioning of the relationship between the citizen, society, and the state. But this book does not trace a growing state interest in feeding its citizens. Analyzing the period from the 1830s through the 1960s in fact underscores the incoherence and inconsistencies of the British government's food policies and the ways in which it instigated them anew to solve the problems it had identified at each historical juncture. *Many Mouths* thus seeks to understand the social, economic, and political theories that influenced the implementation of some feeding schemes but not others; the historical contexts in which these programs were formulated, implemented, and reworked; and crucially, how both the administrators and the recipients (intended or otherwise) of government food services realized, interpreted, and made meaning out of these exchanges.

Many Mouths begins in the workhouses of the 1830s, where Charles Dickens's Oliver Twist memorably and politely asked for more gruel. In doing so, the fictional Oliver and his real-life counterparts, who frequently demanded not only more gruel but also roast beef and plum pudding, challenged the state's claim to be providing sufficient and appropriate foodstuffs to those in its care.[23] By this moment what scholars have called the nineteenth-century "revolution in government" was well underway.[24] With the end of the Napoleonic Wars in 1815, the British state (at least temporarily) levied fewer taxes and decreased public spending on the military. At the same time, however, it began to play a much greater role in the daily lives of British subjects despite prevalent discourses of laissez-faire, on the one hand, and the persistence of a culture of paternalism and voluntarism, on the other.[25] This is most evident in the reforms of the 1830s and 1840s, which saw increased government intervention (though some would have said interference) in the regulation of industries, in public health, in maintaining social order, and in the management of poverty.[26] To carry out these reforms in a uniform way that stamped out individual and local abuses, the British government evolved techniques that led to more centralized and more bureaucratic forms of administration. The first half of the nineteenth century thus witnessed the beginnings of a new form of statecraft predicated on the accumulation of empirical knowledge and the management and deployment of this information by those who claimed to use their specialized (though never actually disinterested) expertise in the service of the public good.[27] The expansion of bureaucracy in general led to a trained, salaried civil service and systems of governance that relied as much upon a range of professional administrators, who operated at varying removes from Westminster and Whitehall, as on the centralization of the structure of the state.[28] The 1834 New Poor Law, as we shall see, heralded these changes as its administrative architecture set the stage for a distinctly modern approach to statecraft.

In practice, the modern British state was shaped by the principles of classical political economy that emerged at the end of the eighteenth century. Based on the economic theories of Adam Smith and David Ricardo, the utilitarianism of Jeremy Bentham and his disciples, and Thomas Malthus's principle of population, the field of political economy started to provide the ideological foundation for many of the state's decisions about the distribution of its scarce resources beginning in the 1830s. Although unevenly applied, this philosophy continued to inform some policies through at least the end of the nineteenth century. The rules of political economy dictated that the nation's wealth could be increased through the promotion of self-interest and the protection of individual liberties. The foundation of this system was free market capitalism. This did not mean that the state had no role to play beyond the securing of private property. Proponents of laissez-faire generally agreed that the state should provide services where individuals and corporations had failed to do so, or in cases where government could do so more efficiently, with less waste, and thus more cheaply. However, political economists argued that too much government intervention in market forces would only perpetuate poverty. Because the potential for the population to increase far outstripped the ability of the food supply to meet the needs of subsistence, Malthus argued in 1798 that population growth would need to be checked if individuals, and thus the nation, were to flourish. Malthus theorized that this would happen through war, famine, and disease, as well as through the deliberate decision to limit reproduction, though he advocated delayed marriage and sexual moderation rather than technologies of birth control.[29] Later couched in terms of the Social Darwinian maxim "survival of the fittest," this justified minimal government interference in the economy, particularly in relation to food resources, so as to allow natural and moral forces to weed out the "surplus population."

Although these ideas were heavily contested, the persistence of this philosophy frequently resulted in parsimonious policies that sought to minimize public spending on those widely considered overly dependent upon the state. This included the population of Ireland, much of which was left to perish in the name of political economy when famine ravished the country between 1845 and 1852. At the same time, however, and despite this rhetoric of cheap government, the state actually grew in the 1830s and 1840s as successive Whig administrations enacted reforms that attempted to address the effects of rapid industrialization and urbanization, which had led to marked class conflict. It was in this period that the British government began to regulate factories and mines, to introduce public health measures, to inspect railways, to increasingly assume responsibility for the maintenance of social order, and to provide more central oversight of prisoners and paupers who, as institutionalized populations, were now being fed at government expense.

The period from the 1850s through the 1870s saw a further expansion of state powers, even under the administration of the Liberal Party, which had emerged out of a coalition of Whigs, free traders, and radicals in 1859. Under the leadership of William Gladstone, the Liberal Party championed personal liberties, laissez-faire capitalism, and a minimalist state. The second half of the nineteenth century nevertheless saw increased government intervention in the social life of the nation during both Liberal and Conservative administrations. This included the state provision of services such as libraries, museums, baths, and wash houses that the public could make use of at their discretion. But this period also witnessed the introduction of primary education (which became mandatory in some school districts from 1870 and across England and Wales in 1880), the state regulation of prostitution, and the tightening of the laws enforcing compulsory smallpox vaccination, all of which were widely contested in the name of personal rights.[30] Gladstonian liberalism, however, spawned no initiatives to feed the large numbers of people across the British Isles who remained desperately hungry even as others prospered during this era of relative political and social stability. But it was in this period that humanitarian rather than politico-economic theories of famine relief first began to circulate in India in response to a series of devastating food crises that imperiled the subcontinent in the wake of Britain's imposition of direct rule in 1858.

Although, as Elaine Hadley has argued, mid-Victorian political liberalism was fraught with contradictions,[31] it was not until the 1880s that new political ideologies began seriously to challenge the gospel of limited government, despite the fact that the functions of the state had been expanding over the course of the century. The term "liberalism" has a complex history within both British society and its historiography, not least of all because its definition was increasingly contested from within the Liberal Party itself.[32] Through the 1870s, this focus on the securing of a free market and personal liberties – the latter assumed largely to be the property of middle- and upper-class white men – was intimately associated with Gladstone's Liberal Party. But in the last decades of the nineteenth century, a progressive faction within its ranks began advocating for more government intervention in the social and economic life of the nation. Government should not merely safeguard the rights of individuals and their property, they argued, but seek to better society by improving the lives of the most vulnerable British subjects.[33]

This New Liberalism emerged in the 1880s, the decade when the global output of manufactured and agricultural goods began to outpace Britain's own. The resulting economic downturns in both the agricultural and industrial sectors and the growing influence of Marxism across Europe led to the flourishing of trade union activity and the emergence of a range of socialist ideas and organizations in Britain, which could no longer confidently claim to be "the workshop of the world."[34] Several industrial disputes that culminated in the 1889 London dock strike revealed the extent of working-class discontent with standards of living, despite an expansion of the franchise in 1884 to include a majority of working-class men. At the same time, a series of social investigations, such as George Sims' 1883 *How the Poor Live*, exposed the middle-class reading public to the scope of urban poverty, warning them of the social instability wrought by the ever-growing gulf between rich and poor that persisted in one of the wealthiest nations in the world. These exposés suggested that these stark economic divides were endemic to capitalism rather than resulting from an individual's moral failure to pull oneself up by one's bootstraps. The solutions, they argued, must therefore be systemic changes driven by the state, though housing tended to take precedence over food in these accounts. Sims, who was a dramatist as well as a journalist and thus favored a colorful metaphor however condescending, compared the working class to a "good, patient, long-suffering dog, chained to a filthy kennel for years, and denied even a drink of clean water." This "snarling" dog, he warned, was now "sniffing viciously in the vicinity of someone's leg." Thus, Sims called not for an increase in charitable giving but rather for "a good marrowy bone, with plenty of legislative meat upon it," as only government measures, he implied, could ameliorate economic and social conditions enough to stave off revolution.[35] New Liberals heralded this call, maintaining that the nation could no longer ignore these profoundly destabilizing problems; their answer was for the state to take direct action.

In the 1880s and 1890s, a range of socialist associations and political parties began to emerge that echoed and buttressed New Liberalism's call for increased state intervention.[36] These progressive philosophies of governance resulted first in housing reforms and in municipal experiments in the "gas and water socialism" that became identified with the London County Council around the turn of the century.[37] By the early twentieth century, these demands for a much more interventionist state also became central to the platform of the new Labour Party, which explicitly sought to ameliorate the lives of the working class not only through strengthening the trade union movement but also through social reforms that addressed economic disparities head on. There were significant disagreements between the parties, particularly around issues of industrial labor.[38] The coalescence of New Liberalism and Labour ideals about the role of the state as an agent of social reform nevertheless led to a range of parliamentary legislation in the first decades of the twentieth century that reflected this shared belief that the purpose of government was to create the conditions in which all individuals had equal opportunities to flourish. The New Liberals' introduction of old age pensions, unemployment and medical insurance, and crucially, school meals and medical inspection was a rejection of the economic liberalism that had shaped government policy during much of the nineteenth century. But it also meant that, on the eve of World War I, the state was much more present in the daily lives of the British public than ever before.

Although the British wartime state attempted to minimize government regulation of the economy, the exigencies of total war in the end required increased state control. These measures included the introduction of home front rationing during the last months of the hostilities and the regulation of food parcels dispatched to British POWs abroad. The industrial depressions of the interwar period in turn stimulated more, rather than less, state involvement in the economy despite attempts after 1918 to return to "business as usual." The Liberal Party went into decline during this period, divided by profound philosophical differences within its ranks as well as a range of political, economic, and imperial issues. But both the Labour and Conservative Parties, from 1931 working together as a coalition National Government, increasingly promoted protections and subsidies for local industries, as well as the expansion of state services. The state's assumption of administrative control over a scheme to provide free and subsidized milk in schools in 1934 embodied both of these trends. When war loomed again in 1939, the British public's daily experience of the state, both central and local, was thus even more tangibly felt, which prepared citizens for the controls that were swiftly put into place at the onset of the hostilities.[39] These included an almost complete regulation of the food supply. Not all food policies were universally welcomed or consistently embraced on the home front. The government's assurance that all would have access to adequate amounts of the basic alimentary requirements nevertheless maintained the nation's morale and rendered the Ministry of Food one of the most popular government agencies during the hostilities (though not in its aftermath, given the extent of postwar rationing).[40] Significantly, it also paved the way for a new vision of the modern British state that emerged in the wake of the war.

Many Mouths ends in the period of the Welfare State. Born out of longer trends in the government provision of social services, the 1942 Beveridge Report, and the immediate experiences of a state-controlled economy during World War II, the Welfare State attempted to actualize a new philosophy of government that stood in direct opposition to the New Poor Law. When the Labour Party won the election in 1945, it introduced a comprehensive system of social welfare programs that provided cradle-to-grave care to all citizens. Only the National Assistance program that furnished cash benefits to the necessitous was means tested. Health care, unemployment insurance, family allowances, and a range of other programs including the Welfare Foods Service, the subject of Chapter 7, were provided to all citizens, regardless of need.

Although the Welfare State did not sweep away social inequalities or firmly held beliefs about the distinction between the deserving and undeserving poor, historian Carolyn Steedman remembers its food programs as explicitly reconfiguring the relationship between the citizen and the state. Looking back on her 1950s childhood, Steedman maintained, "I think I would be a very different person now if orange juice and milk and dinners at school hadn't told me, in a covert way, that I had a right to exist, was worth something."[41] In Figure I.1, Dr. Edith Summerskill, Parliamentary Secretary to the Ministry of Food, hands a bottle of this orange juice to a small child. This 1950 photograph, likely produced by the Labour government for propaganda purposes, illustrates the state's deliberate positioning of itself as the provider of welfare benefits to its most vulnerable citizens. If welfare orange juice instilled in Steedman a sense of self-worth, a message this photograph attempted to inspire, in my story it has a more complicated history. I interrogate the ways in which the government pitted the welfare of its domestic citizens over its colonial subjects, thus questioning the ideology at the heart of the Welfare State and the way its tenets actually played out in practice.

My case studies trace these shifts in philosophies of governance as they pertained to the modern British state's strategic use of food.

Figure I.1 Dr. Edith Summerskill, Parliamentary Secretary to the Ministry of Food, presenting a bottle of welfare orange juice to a child, *c.* 1950. Courtesy of People's History Museum.

But neither political ideologies nor party politics provide adequate explanations for either the policies or the practices deployed by successive administrations. Each chapter tells a much more complicated story that explores the fraught nature of attempts to realize any abstract theory of government when providing a range of different publics a basic necessity that was always potentially rich in cultural resonance. My approach, following Patrick Joyce's model, is to interrogate how the state actually operates in practice.[42] Indeed, analysis of the execution of initiatives by officials on the ground tends to disrupt any coherent narrative about either the evolution or the integrity of politico-economic theories. This book is as much about how public feeding was implemented in local institutions and communities as about the policies that undergirded these programs (or the administrations that introduced them) precisely because their outcomes were the result of complex negotiations at all levels.

Elected officials in Westminster made policies in response to the exigencies of particular political moments and charged the civil service in Whitehall with working out their implementation. But the day-to-day administration of government food programs happened on the local level in communities that were often quite distant (both geographically and culturally) from London. To understand how they actually worked and were experienced by the intended (and sometimes unintended) beneficiaries, one must move from central to local government. As Joanna Innes has argued, the term "central government" only emerged in the early nineteenth century and, in the process, reconfigured "local government" as its "antithesis."[43] The eighteenth century was characterized by an expansion of local bodies charged with civic improvements. By the nineteenth century, local government, however unsystematic, had come to be understood as traditionally "English" as opposed to continental models of statecraft, which were often derided as "Prussian" and thus despotic.[44] The emergence of a modern centralized state was, however, a "gradual and accretive process" that Vernon has argued led to layered systems of government. This meant that as the state became more abstract and impersonal, it nevertheless generated or reinvigorated local jurisdictions, officials, and institutions. The central and the local state were thus mutually constitutive elements of modern forms of governance as "abstracted, standardized, and transferable systems of bureaucratic authority" continued to rest on "decidedly personal forms of power."[45] Since the British public primarily came in contact with government food programs at the local level, how individuals (and the groups they identified with) experienced the state was at least partly a function of geography, however much they were or were not aware of central policies.

While the local administration might not have always stood in direct opposition to the central authority, throughout the period under study here, there were significant tensions between policy makers and those obliged to oversee the operation of these food services. This was because legislation often allowed for considerable local variation. State agents who oversaw feeding initiatives in communities across the nation, and in some cases the empire, often clashed with central authorities in London as "between the higher Civil Servants of Whitehall and local councillors and officials there yawns a wide black gulf" of education, expertise, interests, and practical experience.[46] Whether out of expedience, budgetary measures, opposing political views, different knowledge bases, or accumulated experience, local officials frequently bent, broke, or rewrote the rules they had been instructed to follow or simply developed distinctly different ways of implementing statutes and directives where this diversity was permitted, if not always encouraged. This occurred both in the context of emergencies such as war and famine as well as in regard to daily services such as school meals. Historians of public health have asserted that in the middle of the nineteenth century local officials were not merely "executors of distant state policies." Instead, they often "create[d] policy in implementing it."[47] This holds true over the longer period of time studied here even as the nature of local government significantly changed.[48] For "ultimately, it was at the local level," in institutions, homes, and communities, "and in and around human bodies," where these policies had to work in practice.[49] When they did not work, either practically or ideologically, officials on the ground altered them accordingly. This meant that throughout the nineteenth and twentieth centuries, an array of stakeholders negotiated each food initiative anew. How and why they did this is the subject of this book.

Many Mouths focuses on several particularly telling moments when the modern British state attempted to enact feeding policies and the debates these initiatives generated. In each of these cases, the government provided foodstuffs (or in the last chapter a nutritious beverage), made foodstuffs available for purchase outside of market relations, or in other ways, was directly involved in supplying food items to particular populations. These cases were relatively rare, even as market principles began to be contested or were temporarily suspended due to emergencies, though there were certainly other instances that I do not explore here. The ones I have chosen were highly contentious in that they raised a range of troubling issues for several government departments and, for this reason, have left a significant trace in state archives even if they do not always occupy a substantial space in the British public's collective memory. Although most of the cases in this book involve England and Wales, as separate policies often existed or played out differently in Ireland and Scotland, three chapters deal explicitly with imperial policies and practices. This is because domestic feeding programs had imperial effects and the feeding of these populations was part of the wider strategies of colonial governance, which as Joyce has argued, was an integral part of British state formation.[50] Each of these chapters addresses a variety of political, economic, social, cultural, and sometimes imperial concerns as the attempt to feed target populations had unforeseen consequences that made it difficult to control the meanings, reach, and effects of government food.

Chapter 1 examines the tensions that erupted in the 1830s and 1840s in reaction to the Poor Law Commission's ban on serving festive meals of roast beef and plum pudding to workhouse inmates. This chapter explores the symbolic meaning of roast beef to the institutionalized poor, the local officials that superintended them, and the communities in which both paupers and overseers were imbedded. It argues that a study of when and why paupers were and were not furnished with what was often termed "old English fare" in the early years of the New Poor Law provides a way of rethinking the place of the poor within local and national communities at a moment when the transition from moral economy to political economy was far from complete.

Nineteenth- and early twentieth-century debates over prison dietaries in Britain and in its overseas colonies are the subject of Chapter 2. Although uniformity could easily have been imposed through the issue of a single dietary mandated across the nation and then converted into local ingredients for use in all the colonies, the government consistently chose not to apply any rigid rationing scheme to prisoners. Instead, differences of sex, race, and ethnicity were central considerations in the preparation of suitable diet scales. Prison authorities were animated by, and in the process reinforced, a variety of bodily imaginaries that distinguished British subjects from each other and thus had effects well beyond the walls of the prison. While in theory all might be equal before the law, after the law had passed its judgment, the bodies of criminals played an active role in performing, inhabiting, and thus reinforcing the categories of difference that structured British society.

Chapter 3 examines the provision of cooked food as famine relief in India from the 1860s through the turn of the nineteenth century. Famine relief was undertaken at the local level by officials who managed the balance between cost-saving and life-saving policies in different ways. But by the 1890s, there was widespread consensus that government "kitchens" should provide aid in the form of cooked food to children, as many local officials claimed that children were victims of parental neglect. Feeding the "field labourers of the future," rather than expecting them to be sustained out of their parents' relief wages, was a way to maximize the future utility of these "units." For by the end of the nineteenth century, imperial revenue production and saving colonial subjects from starvation were no longer seen to be in tension with each other; rather they were intimately linked projects. This chapter demonstrates that the provision of cooked food was a central element of famine relief precisely because it was part of late Victorian attempts to reconcile humanitarianism and the ongoing economic development of the British Empire.

The British government's role in feeding British POWs and civilian internees during World War I is the subject of Chapter 4. Here, I focus on the uncertainty around whether British POWs were in fact starving in the German camps and the troubling questions this raised about who was ultimately responsible for keeping these men in health. This stimulated debate about how to provision them adequately within the rules of war, how to evaluate objectively what constituted a sound diet, and what food was culturally acceptable to prisoners and their governments. This chapter argues that throughout the war the British government often made surprisingly impractical, unscientific, and costly decisions around the provisioning of their own POWs. These can only be explained by examining shared, cultural meanings around food that were far from irrelevant in the context of the war. It also reveals that even though their liberty was severely curtailed, POWs were active agents in shaping their own diets and manipulating food aid despite severe wartime shortages.

Chapter 5 explores conflicts over the provision of school meals during the interwar period. It focuses on a 1934 policy shift, whereby the Board of Education instructed local education authorities to focus their efforts and funding on school children suffering from malnutrition rather than merely feeding the children of the poor and unemployed "indiscriminately." These children were to be identified, the Board mandated, not by assessing their parents' income, which had previously been a common practice, but rather through a process of clinical examination. Proponents of "economic selection," among them many large school districts, contested the new policy of "medical selection" on its own terms, undermining its claim to be scientific. They argued that the use of an income scale was instead a more objective, practical, and humane method of identifying and serving the needs of necessitous children and was therefore in the best interests of the nation. Even in the heyday of "the newer knowledge of nutrition,"[51] how the government could best serve its most vulnerable subjects was open to serious contestation, which ultimately forced the Board of Education to backtrack on its policy.

The chapter that follows analyzes the communal feeding centers opened during World War II. These not-for-profit institutions run by local authorities initially targeted the working poor in order to ameliorate their chronically deficient diets and boost morale. That these "British Restaurants" eventually came to serve a much broader cross section of the civilian home front population was not the product of a coherent government policy. Rather, Chapter 6 demonstrates that it was the result of a proactive public who used these services for their own purposes and thus became not merely passive recipients of government food control policies but active agents in the project of mass feeding. It concludes that these institutions were politically popular because they reflected a wartime "fair shares" mentality. But, crucially, they were also part of a larger project bent on transforming the poor from beneficiaries of the British state into citizen-consumers and thus full members of an economically healthy postwar society.

The Welfare Foods Service that supplied free and subsidized concentrated orange juice, milk, and cod liver oil to expectant mothers and young children, like Carolyn Steedman, from 1942 to 1971 is the subject of Chapter 7. Unlike milk and cod liver oil, concentrated orange juice could not be domestically produced. The British government thus initiated an orange-growing industry and juice-concentrating plants as a "colonial development" project in the British West Indies. Because liquid concentrated orange juice was a highly specialized product with little export market beyond the British government that used it solely for the Welfare Foods Service, the Caribbean orange industry was almost entirely at the mercy of the consumers of welfare orange juice, which was only available within the United Kingdom. Decisions about who should be entitled to it and how much they should pay for the product ultimately pitted the needs of domestic British citizens who consumed the juice against those of colonial British subjects who produced it. The history of welfare orange juice thus suggests that the meanings invested in the term "welfare" were far from transparent in a period that witnessed decolonization, on the one hand, and cuts to the Welfare State, on the other.

In tracing the trajectory of state feeding from the real-life Oliver Twists' exclusion from the national community to Steedman's assertion that it was government-issued food itself that instilled a sense of self-worth, I am not, however, positing a narrative of progress. The organization of this book into a series of case studies presented in chronological order is intended, paradoxically, to reveal that feeding a range of publics was in no way a progressive or linear enterprise. These case studies are thus presented not as episodes in a seamless narrative but instead as evidence that the state dealt with feeding in an ad hoc and piecemeal fashion. If as Vernon has argued, Britain was in good part responsible for modern global hunger, its achievements in eradicating it were "partial and precarious."[52] This was, at least to some extent, because no single department of state was consistently responsible for Britain's food policy. The British government rarely learned from its previous experience and generally failed to transfer its knowledge effectively between agencies. But it is also because these initiatives varied quite widely. Some were meant to be short-term emergency measures, while others were intended to have more staying power. Some were part of larger practices of institutionalization and the mass feeding that accompanied this, while others expressed and involved different kinds of state investment in, and responsibility for the well-being of British subjects. Although there were continuities between some state feeding schemes, the government programs I discuss here were products of discrete cultural moments. Their implementation and outcomes are best understood not as part of a coherent, evolving state effort to feed its neediest citizens made possible by scientific research into nutrition but instead as responses to historically contingent political, economic, social, and cultural circumstances. This book is a study of these moments that stimulated the modern British state to initiate the feeding of some members of its population (but not others) and what government food meant to those who devised, those who executed, those who used, and those who refused the state's alimentary interventions.

1   Old English Fare
Festive Meals, the New Poor Law, and the Boundaries of the Nation

The Poor Law Amendment Act of 1834 was one of the first pieces of legislation passed by Britain's newly constituted parliament as part of the reforms that characterized the 1830s and 1840s. The receipt of poor relief was a legal right established by the statutes that made up the Old Poor Law. The right to state welfare remained unaltered by the introduction of the New Poor Law. Rather, what changed was the nature and location of that relief – which for the able-bodied was now only available within the workhouse – and the bureaucratization of its administration. The poor consistently understood and claimed their right to relief. However, after 1834, they experienced it not as a series of obligations enacted between fellow members of a parish community but instead as a "modern public law relationship" transacted between individuals (who were increasingly institutionalized) and the state.[1] Despite this new centralization of relief, which was intended in part to standardize its provision and render it impersonal, local authorities frequently overrode and undermined policies that interfered with their right to dispense aid in traditional ways that they felt enhanced social stability. This included providing a roast beef dinner to workhouse inmates on festive occasions. The tensions that erupted among local and central government officials, paupers, and communities in reaction to the Poor Law Commission's attempt to ban these meals suggests that debates over food were part of much broader negotiations about both the role of the modern state and the place of the poor within local and national communities.

Scholarship on the New Poor Law consistently notes the parsimonious and often putrid nature of workhouse food, highlighting the disciplinary role that food played within the political economy of this Victorian institution.[2] Historians who have attempted to reevaluate the relative "cruelty" of this legislation and its enactment, have similarly raised the issue of the workhouse diet, arguing that, though uninteresting, it was sustaining and no worse than what was being eaten by the independent laborer.[3] The scholarly debate over workhouse food has

18

thus focused on its quantity and nutritive value, frequently relying on standards and tools to calculate the food's ability to nourish that were unavailable at the time and thus played no role in early nineteenth-century deliberations. The symbolic meanings of food to workhouse inmates and those that governed them, however, has not been fully analyzed. In the early years of the New Poor Law, its Commissioners explicitly prohibited workhouses from serving roast beef and plum pudding – that most English of celebratory meals. Unpacking the contentious disputes between local and central poor law authorities over the provision of roast beef to paupers reorients the discussion of the workhouse diet to address not the amount or quality of food provided but rather the cultural politics of what the state's dependents were allowed to eat. This conflict illuminates the extent to which a new breed of centralized government bureaucrats attempted to exclude from the nation those who had patently failed in the market by deploying food as a potent signifier and the reason why many local officials resisted this strategy. A study of when and why paupers were and were not furnished with a festive meal – of what was often termed "old English fare" – thus provides a way of rethinking how the poor's relationship to the nation was being reconstructed and how a nascent modern state actually operated at a critical moment in Britain's "revolution in government."

Classical Political Economy and the Administration of Relief

The 1830s mark the beginning of significant shifts in the nature of the British state. As Christopher Hamlin has argued, early nineteenth-century Britain was "more an agglomeration of counties parishes, and common law courts than a state." A modern state did emerge over the course of the century, Hamlin demonstrates, not as a precondition for dealing with social issues, such as public health and poverty, but as a product of attempts to address them in new ways.[4] This decade and the one that followed ushered in a range of reforms under successive Whig administrations that led to increased centralized regulation of political, economic, and social life despite a persistent rhetoric of limited government intervention in the name of personal liberty. This began with the Reform Act of 1832, which extended the vote to a significant number of middle-class men by introducing a £10 householder franchise. The Reform Act perpetuated the principle of governance by the propertied class but expanded this population to include those whose wealth was not tied to landed estates. By redistributing seats in parliament, this

Act also gave political representation to growing cities, whose economies were increasingly rooted in industrial production, thus allowing
the interests of this new middling class of property owners to be represented in parliament.

At the same time, the 1832 Reform Act prevented those who had
received government poor relief at any time during the previous year
from voting. This firmly established the distinction between full members of the nation who were allowed to exercise their political rights and
those whose dependency on the state had rendered them unfit to participate in the polity even as they exercised their legal right to relief. It also
signaled that the existing policies and practices of government relief,
which being parish-based had allowed for considerable local variation,
would now be receiving increased scrutiny. Indeed, one of the first legislative acts of the newly reformed parliament was to address what many
saw as twin evils: the escalating cost of poor relief and the increasing
transfer of responsibility for ensuring that workers earned subsistence
wages from the market to the state.

Local rates, which funded (among other things) government relief to
the poor, had grown considerably over the course of the late eighteenth
and early nineteenth centuries. These costs had skyrocketed in part
because of the widespread unemployment and underemployment that
characterized the period that followed the end of the Napoleonic Wars
in 1815. Advocates of reform, however, largely blamed the schemes of
relief adopted by some parishes that guaranteed all subsistence-level
benefits, by topping up wages of underemployed or low-wage workers
or issuing allowances based on family size.[5] Critics of these practices
argued that these types of schemes interfered with the natural laws of
the economic market. On the one hand, they provided no incentive
for workers to seek additional paid labor. On the other, they allowed
employers to pay extremely low wages, knowing that the parish coffers
would make up the difference. In addition, many argued that any system of child allowances merely promoted population growth that was
not sustainable and actively contributed to the vicious cycle of poverty.[6]

Statesmen, theorists, and others bent on reforming the poor law system across a particularly diverse political spectrum proposed a range
of solutions in the late 1820s and early 1830s. When rioting, the burning of harvested crops, and a spate of attacks on threshing machinery
gripped the countryside in 1830–1 in response to declining living standards among agricultural laborers, pressure mounted for the government to take action. Parliament's answer to these intensifying problems
and widespread unrest was to convene a Royal Commission, which sat
between 1832 and 1834, to investigate the operation of the poor laws.

Its 1834 report led directly to the passage of the Poor Law Amendment Act later that year. The New Poor Law, as it was commonly known, stipulated that the "able-bodied" could no longer receive "outdoor" relief: support in kind (such as food, medicine, or the payment of rents) and/or cash payments that topped up or substituted for wages. Instead, the government would only issue poor relief to the able-bodied within workhouses that were to be constructed in every poor law union, the newly configured administrative districts that provided relief at the local level.[7] The New Poor Law required that "indoor" paupers bring their dependents with them, though segregated wards for men, women, and children broke up family units. These institutions furnished inmates with only the most basic amenities, did not permit personal belongings (including clothing), and required most residents to engage in relatively onerous and often meaningless labor.

The New Poor Law extended the Tudor policy of providing government aid to the destitute, upholding the poor's legal right to relief.[8] But its philosophy of relief and the changes it introduced in relation to the administration of this relief were based on deterring all but the most destitute from becoming reliant on the state. The New Poor Law thus rested on what the political economists who had sat on the Royal Commission had termed the principle of "less eligibility." This meant that the workhouse could not be more "eligible," in other words desirable, than earning one's own keep. In order to discourage reliance upon government relief, the conditions within these institutions were intended to deter all but those with no other means of support. The parsimony of the workhouse was integral to the larger strategy of curtailing public spending on poor relief and disciplining the poor to be more frugal, responsible, and productive.

Although not all Whigs subscribed to it, the New Poor Law's "science of dispauperization" epitomized the classical political economy that frequently influenced government policy until the middle of the nineteenth century and continued to rear its head until the 1800s drew to a close.[9] Many of the parliamentarians who voted for the New Poor Law and certainly the bureaucrats who administered it derived their philosophy regarding how the government should apportion its scarce resources out of a potent, if selective, mixture of the doctrines of economic liberalism, Malthusianism, and utilitarianism. They believed that the economic market was self-regulating and that government intervention interfered with its natural laws including David Ricardo's theory of the "iron law of wages," which stipulated that real wages naturally tended toward the minimum required for subsistence. While this implied that efforts to raise wages were futile, it also suggested that the market, without the need for state regulation, could support all those who chose to work. Thus, adherents to laissez-faire theorized that if work were rendered more appealing than state aid, then destitution would automatically be curtailed, since able-bodied men would become more industrious in their own self-interest.

If laissez-faire capitalism was central to Victorian political economy, the doctrines of Malthusianism haunted many state policies. That the market was self-regulating, Thomas Malthus had argued at the tail end of the eighteenth century, was because it operated according to broader natural laws. In *An Essay on the Principle of Population*, Malthus explained that population growth would inevitably outstrip the food supply. Since population must always be kept at a level that allowed for the means of subsistence, "positive checks" to the population were unavoidable and even necessary. These included famine, war, disease, and extreme poverty, which he claimed would wipe out those unable to survive and naturally reduce the "surplus population." But he also argued that "preventative checks," such as the control of reproduction through the practices of moral restraint, were necessary to curtail overpopulation.

Diehard Malthusians, and indeed Malthus himself, disparaged all forms of government poor relief as this increased the population without increasing the food supply. They advocated for the abolition of the poor laws in their entirety, forcing all to compete in the market.[10] However, Edwin Chadwick, secretary to the Poor Law Commission (PLC), which between 1834 and 1847 was the central authority that oversaw state relief, and one of the architects of the New Poor Law itself, maintained that to provide no relief at all was "repugnant to the common sentiments of mankind."[11] Lord Althorp, the Whigs' Chancellor of the Exchequer who introduced the Poor Law Amendment Bill in the House of Commons, agreed that the support of the "really helpless" was "not only justifiable but a sacred duty imposed on those who had the ability to assist the distressed," underscoring his own and his party's continued commitment to paternalism.[12] In providing only minimal support to the poor, however, the New Poor Law underscored that deaths from starvation, privation, and their concomitant diseases would continue to be positive checks to population growth. By separating families within its institutions, it further sought to limit the reproduction of those unable to compete in the market as a preventative check. The Malthusian ideology that excessive investments in the destitute were a waste of public funds was thus implicit within the new parsimonious relief policies.

The idea that public funding for the relief of the poor was a waste, owed much to utilitarian conceptions of efficiency and economy. Utilitarianism contributed to the assumption that if left alone the market would self-regulate and that the state's primary role was to increase the public good by reducing unnecessary government spending and regulations. But the utilitarians that had sat on the Royal Commission, such as Chadwick (who was mentored by Jeremy Bentham himself) and Nassau Senior (first holder of the Drummond Professorship of Political Economy at Oxford), conceded that state intervention was sometimes necessary to promote efficiency and productivity as economic liberalism was connected to efficient industrial management.[13] The principle of "less eligibility" that lay at the heart of the New Poor Law was the realization of attempts to curb wasteful government spending on those who could and should be working by making the labor market more appealing than the workhouse. The strict rules and regulations so central to the New Poor Law system were a deterrent to malingerers and the embodiment of a philosophy that intended to make the provision of state welfare independent of the arbitrary or capricious decisions of local authorities and render it uniform, efficient, and impersonal.[14] The New Poor Law was decidedly ideological even if the Whig Party was not. According to Raymond Cowherd, those who formulated it paid little attention to the copious data they had collected on poverty and its relief, preferring their "axioms" to their "arithmetic."[15]

It was not just that the New Poor Law put the philosophy of political economy into action; its operation was also predicated on new administrative techniques that attempted to create efficiencies through centralization and the promotion of uniformity. Despite their reformist agenda, the Whigs had not embarked on a mission to centralize government and as themselves owners of landed estates often championed the value of paternalistic communities governed by traditional hierarchies of local elites. But significantly, they were also open to the expansion of the state if this facilitated the type of "disinterested" governance they sought to cultivate.[16] The bureaucratic reforms so central to Chadwick's vision of efficient administration of state relief (along with those he would later introduce as part of his public health initiatives[17]) set in motion substantial changes to how government was henceforth expected to work. The architects of the Poor Law Amendment Act had invested control in a three man Poor Law Commission that was not answerable to parliament. The Commissioners' oversight of local operations depended on twenty-one Assistant Poor Law Commissioners, who were appointed piecemeal over the course of the Act's first two years. Once dispersed into the field, the Assistant Commissioners inspected the administration of poor relief carried out in the poor law unions by local Boards of Guardians (who a range of underlings reported to), then reported directly back to the PLC.[18] Although this marked a major innovation in governance in that it brought increased central control to a system that had previously been parish-based, standardization of practice was difficult to achieve. This was in good part because the PLC and its Assistant Commissioners often faced considerable resistance from those who actually dispensed poor relief in their local communities, as the Whig administration should have anticipated. In practice, then, the directives of the central authorities were constantly contested, undermined, and reworked all along the chain of command, setting the stage for tensions between local and central government officials that were to characterize the modern British state throughout the rest of the nineteenth century and well into the twentieth.

The Poor Law Amendment Act amalgamated the parishes that had served as the units of administrative oversight under the Old Poor Law to create poor law unions, each of which was overseen by a Board of Guardians. The configuration of the Board in any given union varied in relation to the population: a small union might have only a handful of Guardians, while a larger one could have closer to 100, though not all members actively and consistently performed their duties. Local ratepayers elected Guardians annually, and the number of votes they were each allowed was determined by the value of their rateable property. This system of plural voting, in which large landowners might have up to nine votes each, thus invested a significant amount of power in the gentry to determine the composition of the Board. Members of the Board were unpaid, but they were required to be local ratepayers. Unions could also stipulate that to be eligible to stand for election, potential Guardians must also occupy property of a particular value (though the law set an upward limit of £40 per annum). This meant that Guardians were often members of a propertied elite rather than the small farmers and tradesmen who had rotated through the role of overseer under the Old Poor Law. In addition to the elected Board, Justices of the Peace were by default *ex officio* Guardians empowered to carry out all the rules and regulations of the New Poor Law by virtue of their legal authority within the community.[19] Those who served as Guardians of the poor (as well as those who elected them) were members of what the Poor Law Commissioners identified as "the upper and middles classes."[20] Their wealth and social status were the main qualifications necessary to govern those who had patently failed to make ends meet in the new industrial economy. But as we shall see, they were more likely than the central authorities to treat the destitute they oversaw with compassion, precisely because doing so reaffirmed their own social capital.

Anthony Brundage has argued that the New Poor Law shored up the power of these local elites who were instrumental in drawing the boundaries of the new poor law unions to preserve their long-standing spheres of influence.[21] Although the utilitarians who formulated the new policies intended a rigid centralization of relief, in practice, the Boards of Guardians had wide discretionary powers and exercised them, even in the face of directives from the PLC, as a means of enhancing the solidarity of "local regime[s] of property." Thus, despite the assertion that the New Poor Law had superseded the Old, in many places, it continued to operate under the community's traditional leadership who tolerated practices such as the perpetuation of outdoor relief that had been denounced and even forbidden by the new central authorities.[22] The provision of festive meals to workhouse inmates in the early years of the New Poor Law's operation emerged as a particularly contentious issue that pitted some Boards of Guardians against the PLC. In providing roast beef and plum pudding to the indoor poor, these local authorities upheld what they saw as their duty to perpetuate practices that simultaneously respected the customary rights of the poor and shored up paternalistic relationships, even as government relief became more centralized and bureaucratic.

The Gift of Roast Beef

The festive meals that some Guardians attempted to provide on special occasions stood in stark contrast to the fare provided regularly to indoor paupers. The dietary was a central component of the workhouse regime and was calculated based on the principle of "less eligibility." Workhouses provided poor quality and unvaried food in amounts calculated to sustain the inmates without exceeding in either quantity or quality the diet of the laboring classes in the immediate vicinity.[23] However, as Valerie Johnston has noted, the PLC had no standard working-class diet against which to evaluate potential workhouse rations.[24] As an Assistant Commissioner to the Royal Commission, Chadwick had studied the diets of workhouse inmates and prisoners and had been startled to discover that these were often superior to those of ordinary laborers. He argued that this "unnecessary" expenditure on paupers "operates as a bounty on imposition" and as a "discouragement to industry, forethought, and frugality."[25] Chadwick was heavily influenced by officials already deploying utilitarian methods to keep the costs of feeding paupers as low as possible, calculating the food in half-ounce increments to prevent waste and unnecessary spending.[26] Food was thus a central component of the attempt to standardize the system of relief and ensure that the workhouse deterred all but the destitute.

Paupers were fed based on a dietary table approved by the Poor Law Commissioners and later the Poor Law Board (PLB), which took over the administration of relief in December of 1847. In 1835, Chadwick circulated six sample dietaries for unions to choose from. If there was broad consensus in the early nineteenth century that food was one of the only true "necessaries of life," how much and which types of food any individual required was heavily contested in this period.[27] These sample diets had not, however, been vetted by anyone with expertise in the nourishing and sustaining properties of food nor compared with other institutional models that explicitly used these sites of mass feeding to assess appropriate dietary regimens.[28] Rather, they were chosen only because they had been found acceptable under the Old Poor Law,[29] suggesting that accumulated experience was in this instance a more significant factor in the state's decision-making than current scientific knowledge. Chadwick deemed all of these diets "sufficient in quantity," noting that they varied only in relation to the local availability of ingredients and regional eating habits. He thus instructed Boards of Guardians to assess "the usual mode of living of the Independent Labourers of the District" before choosing which dietary to adopt. This would ensure that inmates of the workhouse were not fed more, or superior, food than those who subsisted by their own "honest industry"; to do otherwise, Chadwick maintained, would lessen the "stimulus to exertion" and only encourage "idle and improvident habits."[30] These dietaries clearly stipulated the specific meal to be provided on each day of the week and the amount of food allotted to each inmate. That inmates could request that their portions be weighed in front of them indicates that for all parties quantity was the most critical factor in assessing the adequacy of the daily dietary. Any changes to the dietary table once formally adopted, no matter how seemingly insignificant or expedient, needed to be approved by the central poor law authority.

The meals prescribed by these dietaries consisted largely of bread, cheese, broth, gruel, porridge, suet or meat pudding, potatoes, root vegetables, bacon or salt pork, as well as boiled or baked meat. Indeed, with the exception of coastal fishing communities, the Commissioners did not generally sanction dietaries that included no meat at all, as meat was second only to bread in terms of its centrality to the nineteenth-century British diet.[31] But in order to keep the cost of poor relief low and to discourage the working poor from seeing the workhouse as preferable to competing in the labor market, inmates were generally fed bacon and salt pork more often than fresh butcher's meat.[32] None of the dietaries allowed more than 15 ounces of cooked fresh meat per week, and most provided considerably less.[33]

What was expressly forbidden in the workhouses were food and drink considered "luxuries" or "indulgences" such as fresh or dried fruit, alcohol, sweets, and prime cuts of roasted meat.[34] The Poor Law Commissioners explicitly directed Boards of Guardians and workhouse masters that they should not provide any special meals to paupers even when paid for through charitable donations, since this would render the conditions within these institutions, at least for a few hours, superior to those outside. However benevolent the impulse behind the desire to furnish paupers with a treat, to do so, the Commissioners repeatedly maintained, contravened the deterrent policy at the very heart of the New Poor Law.[35] In refusing to provide the type of "luxuries" exemplified by Christmas dinner, the PLC attempted to control ratepayers' relationships to both paupers and the working poor. It asserted that the state would no longer use the public's taxes to finance workhouse inmates above the level of subsistence. At the same time, the PLC orchestrated that private donors' philanthropic funds could only be directed at those who had managed to maintain themselves independent of state aid.

In the 1830s and 1840s, most Boards of Guardians and workhouse masters probably stuck closely to the letter of the law and provided no special meals. In fact, at times, the PLC had to police excessively parsimonious practices such as in the notorious Andover Union where the workhouse master was accused of starving the inmates.[36] But in a significant number of cases, the principles of the New Poor Law, even in the early years when the regulations were most stringent, were balanced by the generosity of local overseers who broke the rules and regaled their paupers with a Christmas dinner of roast beef and plum pudding.

Historians and anthropologists have focused increased attention on the cultural meanings invested in specific food products.[37] Beef had long held both a material and symbolic significance in Britain. In preindustrial agrarian communities, Britain's laboring classes consumed beef in large quantities as it was widely seen as the necessary food for the industrious body, especially when accompanied by a boiled pudding.[38] Henry Fielding's popular 1730s song "The Roast Beef of Old England" promoted beef as central to the superior stature of the English body. He contrasted "the Englishman's food" that "ennobled our hearts, and enriched our blood," with the "nice dainties" and "ragouts" of "effeminate Italy, France, and Spain." The song

Figure 1.1 James Gillray, "French Liberty. British Slavery," December 21, 1792. Library of Congress, Prints and Photographs Division.

thus championed the "mighty roast beef" as the food that forged the national character. The opening stanza asserted that its consumption had in days of yore made England's soldiers "good" and its courtiers "brave." Although it critiqued contemporary British habits and fashions that drew heavily on Continental trends, its rousing chorus assured that it remained popular well into the nineteenth century and was frequently sung on patriotic occasions.[39]

These associations between roast beef and Englishness (sometimes expressed as Britishness) were commonplace in the vibrant print culture that characterized the middle to late eighteenth century and were further cemented during the next 100 years. William Hogarth's best-selling prints frequently drew on the imagery of plentiful beef as evidence of Britain's superior status among European nations. John Gillray's 1792 satirical illustration "French Liberty-British Slavery" affirmed this connection by portraying John Bull, the corpulent personification of the nation, gorging himself on roast beef, while his scrawny French counterpart gnawed on raw onions (Figure 1.1).[40] By the early decades of the nineteenth century, the idea that beef was linked to liberty, particularly its English form, was firmly established. In this period of reforms and revolutions that spanned the late eighteenth and early nineteenth centuries, meat was widely touted as the food of freemen rather than slaves, and the right to beef was popularly regarded as "the very basis of English liberties."[41] In the 1830s and 1840s, radicals seeking the extension of the franchise to the working classes deployed roast beef as a potent symbol of the rights of the freeborn Englishman. They frequently invoked the days of "Merrie Olde England" where jobs were plentiful, all men were equals under the Magna Carta, and "John Bull enjoyed roast beef, beer, and plum pudding every night."[42] By the time the New Poor Law was passed in 1834, roast beef had become fraught with meaning for members of all social classes, and its worth was valued more than its price per pound. As a food gift, it was a particularly significant object of exchange.[43]

The impulse to furnish a Christmas dinner of roast beef and plum pudding to the inmates of workhouses stemmed from a belief that this was an old English practice and that adherence to ancient Anglo-Saxon customs was an important expression of national character.[44] Christmas had not consistently been celebrated in the British Isles and had been suppressed under the Puritans.[45] Victorians, however, embraced Christmas and reestablished its importance as one of the few holidays that was universally celebrated across the nation, drawing all English people together through shared rituals that explicitly evoked continuities between past and present. Christmas was thus a time to practice what were widely viewed as the quintessentially English values of domesticity, benevolence, and hospitality through extending the comforts of the home to those less fortunate.[46] Charles Dickens's 1843 *A Christmas Carol* blatantly attacked the utilitarian and Malthusian ideologies that underlaid the New Poor Law's isolation of the poor from these rituals. Here, the miserly Ebenezer Scrooge maintains that the "Union workhouses" are the solution to poverty and overpopulation: those who'd "rather die" than enter them, he insists, "had better do it, and decrease the surplus population."[47] Scrooge's stinginess, Dickens implies, is magnified at Christmastime precisely because the Yuletide season was widely acknowledged to be "a kind, forgiving, charitable time; the only time I know of, in the long calendar of the year, when men and women seem by one consent to open their shut-up hearts freely, and to think of people below them as if they really were fellow passengers to the grave, and not another race of creatures bound on other journeys."[48] Early Victorians valued the universal participation of all members of the national community in festivities that drew on old charitable customs because these rituals of mutual obligation, which were often publically performed, promoted a sense of social harmony during a period when class conflict was marked and provided an anchor at a time of rapid change.[49] Thomas K. Hervey's 1836 *Book of Christmas* claimed that old Christmas customs promoted "a reciprocal kindness of feeling" and forged the "bond of good will" between "those remote classes, whose differences of privilege, of education, are perpetually operating to loosen it, and threatening to dissolve it altogether."[50]

One of the most important components of the celebration of Christmas in the 1830s and 1840s was the demonstration of benevolence to the poor through attention to their material needs.[51] If gift giving was central to the Christmas spirit, aid to the destitute at Christmas often came in the form of gifts of food, particularly those specific food products that were identified with a mythic English identity. "Food-wealth," Tara Moore argues, was relatively unproblematic because it could be redistributed "without undermining class relationships."[52] Roast beef and plum pudding were foods that early Victorians most associated with Christmas and were often furnished to the poor. Despite the fact that this specific festive meal was a relatively recent invention and its consumption was by no means universal, Victorians invested roast beef with the authority of tradition. Exotic birds, game, and wild boar had taken pride of place at medieval and renaissance feasts, and by the eighteenth century, turkey had become the centerpiece of the middle- and upper-class Christmas table and remained so into the twentieth century.[53] But, beef – and high-status blood-rich roasted beef in particular – was almost universally acknowledged to be the food of the English people.[54] Partaking of what was often referred to as "old English fare," or merely "Christmas Fare," was synonymous with keeping Christmas Day in "the good old English fashion."[55] In his 1823 *Letters on England*, the French commentator Victoire, Counte de Soligny observed that the "English custom" of eating roast beef and plum pudding on Christmas "is perhaps without exception the most universal of any that prevails in this country."[56] When the Ghost of Christmas Past returns Scrooge to the Christmas feasting and dancing of his days as a young apprentice, Scrooge takes note that his employer served copious amounts of beef. Dickens suggested that these festivities that united master and man through the sharing of particular foodstuffs stretched back not only into Scrooge's recent past but into the deep historical past. The ritual consumption of roast beef and plum pudding was thus an invented tradition that linked the English people across space to each other and across time to their ancestors as members of an "imagined community."[57]

Anthropologists and sociologists have studied celebratory feasting as particularly significant cultural rituals that involve the articulation and reproduction of social relations and allow for negotiations around identity in a public context. As such, they have played an important role in the "creation and maintenance of networks of social power."[58] But relationships of mutual obligation in paternalistic societies are dynamic and can be redefined as much from below as by those with greater social authority. Historians have not identified the existence of a working-class culture of Christmas celebrations that stood outside this paternalistic gift relationship. But that does not mean that the poor were merely passive recipients of these middle- and upper-class expressions of goodwill. Gifts from those in power can over time be appropriated as a right, especially when construed as a ritual practice.[59] By 1834, the provision of roast beef at Christmas and other festive occasions had become an established prerogative of the poor, an entitlement that the poor claimed for themselves from the propertied classes with whom local Boards of Guardians identified. The working-class "demand" that their right to charity at Christmas be upheld by the social elite in fact extended well into the twentieth century.[60]

For those on both sides of this gift relationship, a roast beef dinner served as a stabilizing force that blunted tensions at a moment when the industrialization of the economy (including the agricultural sector) meant that the divide between rich and poor was keenly felt. For many Guardians, paupers, and ratepayers alike, the provision of roast beef to the poor was thus not merely an ancient rite (and right) but performed a critical social function. As the Guardians at Thirsk argued in 1837, these types of traditions had a "beneficial effect" not only on the poor but on the "public" drawing all members of the nation together.[61] When the PLC attempted to enact its principles by prohibiting the provision of festive meals, many local state authorities ignored, attacked, contested, or otherwise undermined this directive, precisely because it threatened cultural practices that were central both to their own identities and their vision of the role of the state.

"Less Eligibility" in Action

In the decades leading up to the passage of the New Poor Law, the tradition of providing roast beef to the poor at Christmas was alive and well. Large landowners frequently furnished a Christmas dinner of "old English fare" to their tenants and laborers.[62] But it was not just private monies being used for this purpose. The inmates of workhouses operational under the Old Poor Law were also regularly and "liberally regaled with the true old English fare of roast-beef and plum-pudding" in the 1820s.[63] Even prisoners and debtors were sometimes afforded a proper Christmas dinner in this period.[64] In the first years of the New Poor Law's operation, there was considerable confusion and concern over the provision of Christmas dinner. Given that roast beef and plum pudding had been provided not only to the outdoor poor but also in workhouses and other institutions in the recent past, the Commissioners' policy seemed at variance both with age-old charitable traditions and with the ways in which government funds had been expended up until this point. Boards of Guardians, ratepayers, the press, and even paupers themselves contested what appeared to be a draconian policy that seemed to establish that workhouse inmates were not in fact Dickens's "fellow passengers." Instead, the New Poor Law configured them, in the words of one critic, as an "unfriended race of paupers," highlighting their double otherness as a separate tribe cut off from a caring community.[65]

In 1836, the first year that some workhouses were fully operational under the new welfare regime, the Guardians at Ringwood wrote to the PLC to ask whether a Christmas dinner of roast beef and plum pudding could be provided to the paupers if paid for by subscription. The PLC responded that they could not justify such a departure from the dietary, as "all indulgences of this nature have the tendency to lessen the objections which should be entertained by the independent poor to parochial relief."[66] The Poor Law Commissioners maintained that this was a question of utility and deterrence, stressing the importance of holding firm to the principle of "less eligibility." They informed Guardians who wrote with similar requests that the provision of special meals was at "variance with the principles" upon which the "efficiency" of the "workhouse system" depended. The condition of the workhouse inmates, the Commissioners argued, should not be "desired or envied" by the independent laborers. Paupers could not, therefore, be supplied with "indulgences" that the working poor were obliged to forgo.[67] The PLC further stressed that in the winter months and during holidays the independent laborer, "pressed by difficulties from which the inmate of the workhouse is free, begins to despair of being able to maintain himself and his family." Thus, it was even more, rather than less, important at Christmas time, the PLC implied, that "the prospect of luxuries which are probably far beyond his means to provide for himself and his family" should be withheld from the pauper, lest the workhouse become more appealing than the labor market.[68] As a political cartoon from December 1836 illustrated, it was the refusal to provide a roast beef dinner at Christmas that most clearly distinguished the parsimony of the New Poor Law from the generosity, some would have said lavishness, of the Old Poor Law (Figure 1.2).

Even though the PLC forbid expenditures on holiday meals, regardless of who was footing the bill, many Boards of Guardians ignored

Figure 1.2 Thomas McLean, "Poor Laws: As They Were, As They Are," December 1, 1836. Hulton Archive/Stringer via Getty Images.

these directives and provided special treats to workhouse inmates without asking permission. Because much of the Old Poor Law was not statutory, a variety of different practices had "flourished in luxuriant profusion" around the country.[69] Although the "workhouse test" was supposed to be self-regulating and impersonal in distinguishing the proper objects of relief, when the Poor Law Amendment Act was introduced in 1834, many Boards of Guardians found it difficult to break from these deep-rooted local customs that stressed reciprocal rights and responsibilities and personal connections.[70] Paternalism, and the philanthropy it generated, remained alive and well in the early Victorian period and was expressed even within the local provision of government relief despite the about-face in state policies that the New Poor Law was supposed to represent.[71] In part, this was because exercising their discretionary powers shored up the Guardians' own local corporate authority that relied on their ability, as members of a respectable social elite, to define and identify those deserving of relief and enhance social cohesion through traditions of popular patronage.

For, as Douglas Hay and Peter Dunkley have argued, benevolence is imbued with social significance by virtue of its contingency.[72] The decision whether or not to provide roast beef and plum pudding at Christmas was thus part of local state agents' attempts to maintain longstanding paternalistic relationships between rich and poor that provided many across the social spectrum with a sense of social stability. That it was the taxpayers' money being used to this end did not strike these Guardians as inappropriate as the provision of Christmas dinner, they reasoned, was a component of the state's maintenance of social order.

In 1839, thirty-six adult male paupers in the Eastry Union petitioned the local Board of Guardians to provide a proper Christmas dinner. Although the Guardians were reluctant to accede to this request, their clerk was not. He argued "that it is notorious, that in almost every other union in this county, as well as in London, the Old English Fare of Roast Beef and plum pudding" was provided at Christmas. He claimed that it was perfectly reasonable for the paupers in his workhouse to "request the same indulgence." The Guardians disagreed but nevertheless wrote to the PLC for guidance. This suggests that they were not unconvinced by the paupers' and the clerk's attempts to draw connections between the Eastry inmates and, at the very least, their fellow subjects in other workhouses through the ritual consumption of "old English fare." Unsurprisingly, the PLC reaffirmed its position that the Guardians should not capitulate to the paupers' request.[73]

While the Eastry Guardians did not consent to this request, many of their counterparts in other unions used the language of the customary rights of the poor to defend what they saw as a well-established tradition of providing roast beef at Christmas.[74] The Gloucester Guardians claimed that they had "invariably" provided "roast beef, plum pudding, and ale" on Christmas because they felt that the paupers were "entitled to it." They were not inclined to be the ones to withdraw a privilege and "comfort" that the paupers had become accustomed to receiving and was likely, they maintained, provided for in other districts.[75] In the central London workhouses, many of which had been incorporated before the New Poor Law was passed and operated independent from the PLC's oversight, the "good and wholesome custom" of providing "the old English cheer" of roast beef and plum pudding on Christmas Day "prevailed."[76] Given that the poor themselves were unlikely to have understood the difference between the incorporated and unincorporated unions, some Boards of Guardians felt that it was unfair that London paupers should receive these treats, while those in the rest of the country were denied them.

One of the reasons the PLC's policy on Christmas dinner rankled so many is that it seemed to deny the most deserving, rather than the least deserving, members of society participation in a collective celebration. The New Poor Law had been introduced precisely to solve the problem of government expenditure on poverty relief for the able-bodied, particularly able-bodied men.[77] Because outdoor relief – in the form of money, food, medicine, or clothing – was still possible under the New Poor Law for the elderly, disabled, and infirm, the rhetoric of the "workhouse test" assumed that inmates would all be able-bodied adult men (and their families). In fact, this was not the case, or at the very least, not perceived to be true by those with local knowledge.[78] For some Boards of Guardians, paupers existed not as an abstract group to be treated according to a general philosophy of poverty but as real individuals who were members of their community and directly under their care. In making the case for festive roast beef dinners, Guardians often stressed that their workhouses were free from able-bodied paupers. The poor they housed were instead the elderly, the infirm, widows, and children, groups that for most Victorians, including the PLC, existed firmly within the category of the "deserving poor."[79] These Guardians argued that their inmates were not the type of paupers that the PLC was referring to in its orders when it forbade the provision of special meals.

The press often articulated a similar position. In January of 1837, the ultra-Tory periodical *John Bull* reported on the "Whig-Radical Poor Laws." It noted that for the "first time in the memory of the oldest inhabitant" of Bridgwater, the tradition of providing a roast beef dinner on Christmas Day to the inmates of the workhouse had been "discontinued" by order of the PLC. Similarly, it reported that in Bath from "time out of mind" the "deserving aged, sick, and poor" were furnished with roast beef and plum pudding on Christmas Day. The PLC, it complained, had now restricted "'paupers'" from receiving this "extra and unnecessary beneficence," forcing the "aged and crippled poor" to be "deprived of their Christmas allowance" and fed instead upon "the scanty fare of bread and cheese."[80] Here, the journal's use of quotation marks around the word "paupers" suggested that this was new terminology with specific and negative connotations. This journalist clearly contested the understanding of poverty that the word "pauper" embodied, maintaining instead that the workhouse inmates were in fact merely the elderly and the disabled (and thus the deserving poor), not the malingerers the PLC assumed were sponging off the generosity of the state.

The muckraking journal *The Satirist* took this critique even further and, in January of 1837, argued that Christmas had now became a "day of mortification and disappointment" rather than gladness for the pauper class. While hitherto they had been "treated like human beings, regaled with a scanty portion of roast beef and plum-pudding," there was "no beef and pudding now for them." When men become "paupers," it argued, they clearly "cease to be Christians; losing their all in this world, they may properly forfeit their inheritance in the next; having no money they have no souls." Rather than uniting the people in this Christian and humane ritual of Englishness, the PLC had, this journalist charged, rendered Christmas a time to exclude some people from the national and spiritual community merely because they had failed in the commercial market. Facetiously deploying Malthusian theory, he argued that the PLC implied that it would be "an act of patriotism" for paupers to commit suicide in order to "relieve their country of a mass of wretchedness," thus promoting the greater good by reducing the surplus population.[81]

The provision of festive meals to inmates of workhouses raised thorny issues around ancient customs and the rights of the poor that were magnified by the symbolic power of roast beef itself. The problems raised by the outlawing of Christmas dinner became more acute and more difficult for the PLC to navigate when, in 1838, many unions requested that paupers be allowed to participate in the festivities planned for the coronation of Queen Victoria.

Coronation Beef

Before the introduction of the New Poor Law, roast beef and plum pudding had been provided in some workhouses on the coronation of both George IV and William IV.[82] When Victoria's ascension to the throne was celebrated in 1838, several unions continued this tradition.[83] In Southwell, the Guardians hosted a "Workhouse Festival" and provided not only roast beef and plum pudding but also plum cake, tea, and ale.[84] The PLC's response to the provision of these meals was inconsistent. It allowed these dinners on this day of "festive celebration," provided they were financed through subscription and not out of the rates.[85] It was improper, the PLC asserted in response to several different unions, even on so "joyful" an occasion, to increase the "burthens" of ratepayers, many of whom by "the most strenuous exertion and rigid economy can only just keep themselves above parish relief," and thus by implication would not also be enjoying a roast beef dinner.[86] However, in unions that did not request prior sanction and merely charged the expense to the workhouse accounts, the PLC ultimately did not require the auditor to disallow the charges and, in effect, passed on the cost to taxpayers, despite having asserted that it could not do so.[87] The unevenness of the PLC's reaction suggests the newness of the New Poor Law's administration. But it also exposes the Commissioners' difficulty in balancing their resistance to providing "luxuries" to those they considered the undeserving poor and their recognition that the celebration of this event among all members of society was part of a national expression of loyalty to the Crown.

When the Guardians at Gateshead fed their workhouse inmates roast beef and plum pudding on the coronation of Queen Victoria, the paupers were waited on by members of the town council, the Board of Guardians, the town clerk, and the local churchwardens.[88] This inversion of relationships of deference evoked the spirit of the early modern carnival, underscoring the ways in which these local officials deployed the provision of roast beef dinner to the poor as a safety valve that helped to regulate a society where differences of rank and status constantly threatened social harmony.[89] But in the context of the coronation, this roast beef dinner served another explicitly patriotic purpose as well.

Much of the debate around the provision of a coronation dinner in workhouses rested on whether paupers could and should be understood as British subjects, making the position that was often implicit in discussions of Christmas dinner much more explicit. Although some Welsh unions also protested these regulations, the unions that positioned these festive meals as central to patriotic rituals overwhelmingly appealed not only to their local and regional traditions but also to the trope of Englishness. Linda Colley has argued that, by 1815, a distinctly British identity had emerged that drew members of the four kingdoms together in a newly configured sense of nationhood.[90] This did not mean that the rhetoric of, and meanings attached to, Englishness had disappeared. Indeed, for the English, these identities were often, and easily, conflated. When lobbying for festive meals, the language of Englishness was paramount as it embodied ideas of popular constitutional rights as well as traditional customs that stretched back to time immemorial. It was thus to the language of the freeborn Englishman that many turned as this invoked long-standing practices that, although national in nature, continued to be enacted through local and personal relationships.

In a critique of the "uncontrolled dictatorial powers" of the PLC, George Palmer, Member of Parliament (MP) for Essex Southern and a senior partner in the Huntley and Palmer Biscuit firm, defended "the constitutional rights and liberties" of all members of the national community, which seemed to include the right to a coronation dinner.

In a speech in the House of Commons, Palmer argued that the "poor of England" should have a "protector" as did "the unfortunate negroes, whose case had excited so much sympathy in this country." He argued that it was unjust that, as he had read in the papers, a workhouse master should be condemned to one month's imprisonment for ordering roast beef and plum pudding on Coronation Day for the inmates of his workhouse.[91] By comparing paupers with recently liberated African slaves, emancipated by an act of parliament in 1833 (though subject to an "apprenticeship" program until 1838), Palmer implied that the rights of the latter had, to date, taken precedence over those of the freeborn Englishman. "A Humane Observer" had made this same point the year earlier in a letter to the *Hampshire Advertiser*. This correspondent condemned the policy of banning "old English fare" in workhouses as similarly infringing on English liberties. The "Negro" might now be free, but the New Poor Law, the letter intimated, had turned Englishmen into slaves.[92] This was a common rhetorical move in the 1830s, deployed by factory reformers, Chartists, and other reformers and radicals who sought to position the working classes as full citizens precisely because of their national and, by implication, racial affiliation.[93] Both of these critics were drawing on the language of popular constitutionalism in order to extend the rights of the freeborn Englishman to the pauper class.[94] They asserted that no distinction should be made in practice between the destitute and other more fortunate subjects of the Crown who should all be entitled to partake of a coronation dinner.

Requests from Guardians were also framed using a rhetoric that either explicitly or implicitly included the pauper class in the nation through participation in the coronation festivities. When the Guardians at Shepton Mallet and at Ashby de la Zouch wrote to ask for beef and plum pudding for workhouse inmates, they stressed that this meal was to be given to the outdoor poor as well. This indicated that they did not draw a distinction between the working poor and the pauper who, they suggested, were equally eligible to participate in the festivities.[95] The Guardians of the Northampton Union argued that they wished "to see everyone from the highest to the lowest enjoy themselves on the day of the coronation of our Gracious Queen." They resolved that the inmates of the workhouse be "regaled with the old English fare of roast beef, plum pudding, and beer."[96] In the Bridgwater Union, the Guardians felt that the paupers "should celebrate the glorious event in common with all her majesty's loyal subjects" by being provided with a "substantial dinner...without stint" accompanied by beer or cider so that they could "drink the health of her majesty and prosperity to her reign."[97] These Guardians attempted to establish that the inmates were also loyal subjects of the Crown and that this loyalty, because it was a shared feeling, was best expressed "in common" with their compatriots. At Bridgnorth, a similar inclusive spirit reigned for not only were the paupers to receive a special dinner on Coronation Day but also to take part in a procession (provided they were not the parents of illegitimate children).[98] Those paupers deemed morally upright, and thus eligible for inclusion in the national community, were to be visible in the streets taking part in the local expression of national belonging. Their relationship to other devoted subjects was not merely imagined but tangibly felt as all classes of people celebrated the day in each other's company.

Even those who were not directly responsible for the welfare of the paupers proposed including them in the coronation celebrations. In June of 1838, several inhabitants of Haverhill wrote to the PLC asking for permission to provide a "good dinner" to the poor and tea and buns to workhouse inmates on the occasion of Victoria's coronation. They had undertaken to collect these monies and host these meals as a "testimonial of our Loyalty," stating that they desired the inmates of the workhouse to participate in "the enjoyment of a festival" marking the occasion.[99] This community's own loyalty to the Crown was thus expressed through a bond with its least fortunate members who, it was argued, should be included in, not barred from, the national rejoicing.

Sanctioning Subscriptions and Enforcing Audits

In March of 1840, in the wake of numerous requests to provide Christmas dinners as well as meals on the coronation of Victoria and on her wedding day,[100] the PLC issued a circular to its Assistant Commissioners that explicitly articulated its new policy on festive meals in workhouses. The circular announced the PLC's "respect for the motives which have given rise" to the provision of festive meals to paupers but reiterated that it could not sanction payment for these meals out of the public rates. It was an "injustice," the Commissioners maintained, to apply "the proceeds of a compulsory tax, raised only to relieve destitution, to provide for the inmates of a Workhouse luxuries which are beyond the reach of those by whom the tax is paid." Henceforth, they instructed all auditors to disallow these expenses. If these special meals were limited to "extraordinary occasions" and paid for by private individuals, the Commissioners maintained that they would no longer object.[101]

The PLC's shift in policy from outlawing special meals entirely to allowing those funded by public subscription or by the Guardians themselves was in fact a remarkable move as it explicitly contravened the principle of "less eligibility" upon which the New Poor Law rested.

By refusing to use state funds for these meals, the Commissioners continued to uphold the rights of the "deserving poor," who paid their taxes and, as the Commissioners insisted, should not be called upon to furnish the "undeserving poor" with luxuries that they themselves could not afford. However, the 1840 circular also represented a concession to the demands and desires of local Boards of Guardians. The Commissioners acknowledged that "many persons" wished "to extend to others the enjoyments which have been immemorially connected" to Christmas and have been "unwilling to cut off from the inmates of the workhouse all such manifestations of sympathy."[102] In conceding to the desire of the Guardians to provide these meals, the PLC ultimately loosened the state's commitment to the principle of "less eligibility" and to uniformity. It recognized the rights of communities to adhere to long-standing local traditions, especially when these customs promoted national feeling and sympathetic bonds that ultimately served the larger purpose of maintaining social order.

In 1840, the London workhouses governed under the New Poor Law provided "upwards of 30,000 of our fellow-creatures" with "the staple fare of Old England" on Christmas or New Year's as they had in the past, but the costs were born by Guardians and the "benevolent ratepayers" in order to be in compliance with the regulations.[103] After 1840, several other unions also paid for roast beef dinners, either themselves or through private subscription.[104] In 1841, the Bishop of Norfolk used these new rules in order to provide a "good dinner of old English fare of roast beef and plum pudding" to the inmates of the local workhouse on the occasion of the birth of the Prince of Wales, heir to the throne. The *Norfolk Chronicle* reported that it was a "pleasing sight" to see so many unfortunate people "sitting down before fine joints of beef" of the "primest kind." The Bishop toasted Queen Victoria and proclaimed that as an "English-woman" with an "English heart," "the beloved Sovereign of a loyal, free, and grateful people," nothing could give her "more real pleasure" than seeing "400 poor persons regaling themselves on the occasion of her son's birth." It was gratifying, he declared, to see so many poor people enjoying themselves "on an occasion joyful to England itself."[105] The Guardians at Norwich similarly decided to furnish a roast beef dinner to the workhouse inmates on the day of the prince's christening. They believed "that giving the poor a good dinner on an occasion which cannot but be peculiarly interesting to their gracious Queen is by no means adverse to the inculcation of loyal and right sentiments in their minds."[106]

Although it is much more difficult to assess how paupers interpreted their role in these rites, some seem to have willingly expressed their gratitude and their patriotism. In 1843, the inmates of the St. Pancras workhouse in London celebrated Christmas with a roast beef dinner during which they toasted the Queen, Prince Albert, the Army, and the Navy and sang the patriotic naval song "Arise, Arise, Britannia's Sons Arise."[107] Both those who provided roast beef and those who consumed it demonstrated the role that state food could play in the cultivation of loyal citizens, if it was used to signify the poor's inclusion within rather than mark their exclusion from, the nation. In doing so, they underscored the politics of social control embodied in this gift exchange. At the same time, however, they challenged the New Poor Law's attempts to render the pauper a second-class citizen.[108]

This new policy was not universally embraced, however. Many Boards of Guardians continued to maintain that these meals should not only appear to emanate from the state but be paid for with state funds. They continued to charge the costs of providing roast beef to the workhouse accounts.[109] Some Guardians went further and openly challenged the PLC's decision. In 1845, the Dudley Union provided a traditional Christmas dinner to the inmates of their workhouses. When the auditor disallowed the expense (for the first time ever), the Guardians wrote to the PLC to complain. They argued that Christmas dinner was an "ancient privilege" that they were extending to their "unfortunate fellow-creatures": the "impotent or aged and infirm adults, or destitute children," who were residents in their workhouses. The provision of this Christmas treat was "in conformity with a custom which has been invariably adhered to not only since the formation of the union, but from time immemorial."[110] The Guardians at Trowbridge were equally upset by the refusal to sanction a Christmas dinner paid for out of the poor rates. They declared that the paupers should be able to "rejoice at this season with the rest of the Christian world."[111] The Bourn Guardians similarly defended the long tradition of providing a "Christmas treat," arguing that in their union this had not only been provided to the "*unfortunate* inmates of the workhouse, but even to the *criminal* inmates of the prisons," extending even further the boundaries of the national community to include even the patently undeserving poor.[112]

These Guardians argued that the ratepayers in their communities supported financing Christmas dinner out of state funds precisely because it was the outward expression of the "feeling of benevolence and 'goodwill,' (so characteristic of the season)."[113] The Dudley Guardians maintained that it was "cruel" to "deprive the poor in future of an enjoyment which by them is received with gratitude, and which the ratepayers feel a pleasure in providing for them."[114] This policy was cruel, these Guardians implied, not merely because the paupers were deprived of their dinner but also because it prevented the more fortunate members of society from themselves rejoicing in these acts of benevolence, thus underscoring the reciprocal nature of the exchange. The Trowbridge Guardians made this complaint patent, arguing that, "it was the established custom" for workhouse inmates to "partake of the usual Christmas fare with their richer neighbours." They declared that, "at least nine tenths of the rate payers would hold up their hands in favour of such an indulgence being allowed."[115] This sentiment was echoed in other unions.[116] The townspeople of Sheppey proved this point in 1840, when they immediately donated the funds required "to give a cheerful and substantial repast to the sons and daughters of distress" in order to counter the parsimony of the PLC's order.[117]

The Guardians at Bourn and Dudley warned the PLC that the withdrawal of these customs that linked the nation across socioeconomic lines could lead to widespread discontent with the New Poor Law itself. The Bourn Guardians maintained that they were "anxious for the success and continuance of the new [poor] law" but strongly felt that this order was "inexpedient" and "impolitic."[118] The Dudley Guardians went further, arguing that withholding this "privilege will have a tendency to exasperate the feeling of the community against the New Poor-law system."[119] These were not idle threats as the decade between 1834 and 1844 had witnessed widespread rioting, attacks on the construction of new workhouses, and other acts of civil disobedience in opposition to the Poor Law Amendment Act.[120] That this discontent might extend into the middle and upper classes was decidedly unsettling. These Guardians preyed on these anxieties by emphasizing that it was not only the customary rights of the poor that were threatened but also the rights of the propertied classes to participate in these customs of benevolence through the dispersal of their poor rates for this purpose.

What was equally at stake for local officials was their power to dispense relief as they saw fit within their own communities. Guardians sought to preserve not only the rights of ratepayers to have their monies used for these ends but their own reputations as benevolent overseers of the poor and not merely lackeys of the Poor Law Commissioners. Despite the fact that the PLC did not have absolute control over the administration of poor relief, its independence from parliamentary oversight rankled those who chafed against any centralization of authority that undermined the system of checks and balances that many saw as the very basis of the English constitution. In 1839, the Commissioners declared that they sought to "exercise their powers" to avoid all "unnecessary interference" with local authorities.[121] To many opponents of the New Poor Law, however, the PLC appeared despotic. Often called the "three Bashaws," "the Tyrants of Somerset House," or the "Triumvirate," local authorities complained that the PLC's meddling and its unchecked power ran contrary to "the spirit of local independence and self-government," which the Commissioners themselves had proclaimed was key to the "characteristic excellence of the English people."[122]

The Guardians of the Bourn Union attempted to negotiate their delicate relationship to the PLC while asserting their own authority. They maintained that they had always had a "cordial" relationship with the central officials, "cheerfully acknowledged and respected" their "authority and opinions," and frequently sought their advice. However, they argued, it was "beneath the authority and official importance of the Poor Law Commissioners to interfere in such a matter" given the trifling cost to the ratepayer of the "excess" expense of providing roast beef. They also resented the idea that they themselves were expected to foot the bill for such meals. Given that their jobs were unpaid, they saw the performance of their duties as itself a charitable act. To pay for this extra meal out of their own pockets seemed an unreasonable expectation, as it rendered their "onerous duties...still *more* onerous" and undermined the philanthropy inherent within their position as Guardians.[123] The Dudley Guardians were less diplomatic, arguing that this regulation was "arbitrary, oppressive, and cruel" and contrasting the Commissioners' tyranny with their own benevolence. They announced to the PLC that they considered it their duty "to take every step to relieve their own character from the odium of having ever given their assistance or sanction to this cruel" policy. These Guardians distanced themselves from the PLC's decision and argued that it interfered with their own authority, underscoring the local-central tensions at the heart of this dispute. The Dudley Guardians strenuously objected to being "placed in the degrading situation of not having the power to order a small addition to a dinner on Christmas-day to the inmates of the workhouse." It was not only that this had "been customary from time immemorial," they asserted, but also that they were now "subject to the interference and caprice of the auditor" who clearly represented the interests of the PLC rather than their own.[124]

As the case of the Dudley Union makes clear, local authorities had been providing a Christmas dinner and paying for it out of government funds in some unions without any "interference" from the auditor. If the 1840 directive on festive meals attempted to make these practices more uniform, it was the changes to auditing practices that were passed four years later that had the greatest impact on rationalizing expenditures across the over 600 poor law unions. As the Dudley Guardians pointed out, although the policy of funding special meals through subscription had been in place for five years before they lodged their complaint in 1845, this was the first time the auditor had disallowed the expense. Until 1844, local Boards of Guardians appointed their own auditors.[125] They were often lawyers who took these appointments precisely in order to drum up more business for their private practices.[126] It was in their best interest to turn a blind eye to these illegal expenses. In retrospect, Poor Law Commissioner George Nicholls conceded that this mode of appointing auditors was "obviously open to much objection" given that the auditor's job was to oversee the accounts of "the parties by whom he was appointed."[127] It was not until 1844, with the consolidation of auditing districts and the employment of full-time auditors responsible for many unions to which they had no tie, that incompetence, corruption, and embezzlement on the part of auditors was curtailed.[128] It was the combination of a clearly articulated written policy on festive meals and the increased scrutiny now brought to bear on all workhouse expenditures that irritated many Boards of Guardians who had been enacting their own local interpretations of poverty relief even a decade into what was supposed to be a revolutionary centralization of the nation's welfare system.[129]

The Right to Roast Beef

The 1840 directive was in the end short-lived. In the mid-1840s, the PLC came under increased scrutiny largely due to the Andover scandal, which exposed the excessive cruelty of this workhouse's regime. During the course of the 1845–6 inquiry, an inmate was asked whether roast beef had ever been provided at Christmas. This suggests that the provision of a festive meal was in fact considered to be the norm in most unions despite the fact that the state refused to pay for it. When the pauper answered, "No," the Radical MP Thomas Wakley, an outspoken opponent of the New Poor Law, further inquired whether the Guardians had not themselves taken up a subscription to furnish such a meal. The witness answered: "We never had it."[130] That no Christmas dinner of roast beef had been provided, even though this was entirely optional and not financially supported by the central state, spoke volumes to reformers such as Wakley and became fodder for attacking the New Poor Law itself. Indeed, the notorious and inflammatory *Book of the Bastiles*, published in 1841 as an open attack on the New Poor Law, had listed the denial of festive dinners to paupers as one among

many outrages the PLC practiced upon the destitute within these
institutions.[131]

As the Bourn and Dudley Guardians had intimated, the debate over
the financing of festive meals in workhouses was beginning to reflect
badly on the PLC. In 1847, in the wake of the Andover scandal that had
exposed the extremes to which some poor law officials had taken the
parsimonious dietary policies of the New Poor Law, the PLC reformed
its statutes again. Article 107 of the new General Order that spelled
out relief regulations allowed for unions to alter their dietaries so that
a special meal could be provided, and paid for out of the rates, only
on Christmas Day.[132] Providing the meal was optional and exactly
what this meal might consist of was left to individual unions. This was
the PLC's last directive as it was dissolved in December of 1847 and
replaced with the PLB, which was headed by a member of Parliament
who was in turn responsible to Parliament.

Given that under Article 107 of the new order Christmas dinner
was entirely optional, some Boards of Guardians continued to treat
Christmas as any other day or provided merely cake and tea. Others
such as Bridgwater sanctioned a double allowance of dinner rather than
specifying a special meal.[133] However, many seem to have consistently
furnished roast beef and plum pudding.[134] At Ruthin, not only was a
"liberal" supply of beef provided on Christmas but, on this one day of
the year, the inmates were allowed to eat "to their hearts content," as
opposed to having their rations carefully portioned and weighed out.[135]
In the metropolitan unions of London, roast beef and plum pudding
appeared in the official dietary for Christmas Day, making the provision of the meal binding upon workhouse staff and not left to the discretion of an elected and thus shifting Board of Guardians.[136]

In the 1850s and 1860s, under the leadership of several presidents
who were members of the Liberal Party, the PLB permitted roast beef
to be furnished not only on Christmas but also on other celebratory
national occasions. By the middle of the nineteenth century able-bodied
men had become a small minority within the workhouse system. As Ian
Miller has argued, the PLB began to adjust its food policies, moving
away from alimentary regimes that were explicitly disciplinary to cater
to the specialized needs of the sick, infirm, aged, and young, groups
that Guardians had long defended as the deserving poor.[137] With these
changes came a shift in attitude toward festive meals.

In several workhouses, all the paupers were treated to special meals
in conjunction with the military successes of the Crimean War.[138] The
South Molton Guardians justified these festive meals by arguing that
it was "rather a hard and severe infliction upon the inmates of the

workhouse" to know that "great rejoicing and festivity" were taking place "outside their walls whilst not kindred feeling or consideration was manifested toward themselves to enable them also to participate in the general enjoyment."[139] In Barnsley, the Guardians unanimously decided to treat the paupers to a special dinner of Christmas fare in celebration of the peace. When the clerk and the master of the workhouse both informed them that this was illegal, the Guardians retorted that "as all the work people in the town were being entertained by their employers, the inmates should also have a dinner, and they desired the master to provide a dinner accordingly." As well as the meal, all the children of the workhouse and approved adults were to be allowed to "go into the town," asserting their membership in the community.[140] In each of these cases, the auditor disallowed the charges as Article 107 allowed a special meal only on Christmas. While the PLB upheld this decision as right and proper, it consistently remitted the charge based on the special circumstances of the occasion. By the 1850s, the PLB, which unlike the PLC was responsible to Parliament and to the propertied class that had elected its MPs, was conceding that paupers could take part in patriotic celebrations that promoted social cohesion. This was clearly evident in the PLB's attitude toward the celebration of the Prince of Wales's marriage in 1863.

When the Princess Royal was married in 1858, a correspondent to the *Times* argued that those who were to attend the Royal balls in conjunction with the marriage should also donate money so that the poor could be fêted with a celebratory roast beef dinner. The fact that the poor are not forgotten on these occasions, he maintained, "endears the English gentleman to his less affluent fellow-subjects." This "loyal subject" announced that he had been surprised to hear respectable members of the working classes disparage the royal marriage. If the rich were to donate dinner for the poor, then the less-fortunate members of society could also enjoy the day and "remember with gladness the marriage of England's eldest daughter."[141] This correspondent explicitly underscored the two important uses of the roast beef dinner that had been central, though often implicit, in the earlier debates over these meals. It united society across divisions of class and promoted national feeling among the lower orders, those most likely, it was widely felt, to cause social upheaval. Identifying himself as a "loyal subject," this writer underscored the importance of cultivating a sense of allegiance among the working classes to the Crown. But he also championed the need for the upper classes to form affective bonds with their poorer "fellow-subjects," suggesting that these paternalistic feelings were waning by the mid-Victorian period. Roast beef dinner, this "loyal subject" implied, was the fine print in the social contract and central to national harmony and security.

If only a few unions sought to acknowledge the marriage of the Princess Royal with an improvement to the dietary,[142] more than 100 of the over 600 poor law unions provided a special meal, generally roast beef, for their paupers on the wedding day of the Prince of Wales, the future King of England. In all cases, the PLB allowed the meal and ultimately footed the bill, suggesting that the tide had turned in relation to the provision of roast beef in workhouses. The requests for these meals, and the justifications for providing them after the fact, returned repeatedly to the rhetoric of solidifying the national bonds that cut across lines of class and, by extension, the promotion and expression of loyalty to the Crown. At Newport, a roast beef dinner was provided on the Prince's wedding day for a "loyal purpose": "So that the poorest as well as the highest may take pleasurable part in the national rejoicing."[143] The master of the Thorne workhouse also furnished a roast beef dinner to the paupers because, he argued, the "rejoicings" were "universal."[144] When the auditor for Keynsham initially disallowed this expense, the aptly named workhouse master, Humphry England, proclaimed that he was surprised that the government would not cover the costs "connected with the universal, and loyal, celebration of that event."[145] In Kingston upon Hull, the Guardians proposed a roast beef dinner for "the unfortunate people under their care" because they too were "wishful that all proper and loyal respect may be shewn to the Prince."[146] When the Guardians at Stamford sought to substitute a nuptial dinner for the allowable Christmas dinner, even the auditor petitioned the PLB on their behalf. He expressed his "hope that the spirit of loyal attachment to the throne, evinced by this proposal, may well and wisely be encouraged not only at Stamford but in every union in the kingdom."[147]

These pleas to provide roast beef on the marriage of the Prince of Wales clearly articulated that paupers were also the Queen's loyal subjects. To deny them the right to participate in the national rejoicing ultimately removed their ability to express a patriotism that should be cultivated. Conversely, providing paupers with a special festive meal out of the poor rates allowed the more fortunate to express their own sense of themselves as compassionate and model English subjects, whose elite status required them to engage with, rather than distance themselves from, the poor. In practice, the draconian principle of "less eligibility" did not always trump the claims of the poor precisely because the gift of roast beef served an important social function. The ritual provision of "old English fare" to the poor on festive occasions was a practice that many felt was worthy of upholding precisely because it promoted a sense of unity, loyalty, and national belonging among all members of society at a time when the transition to an industrial economy had led class distinctions, and thus tensions, to become more firmly entrenched.

Debates over roast beef were, therefore, not trivial negotiations. In fact, they illuminate how the boundaries that demarcated the national community were being constructed and contested at a crucial moment in the making of modern Britain. The desire of some Guardians, clerks, workhouse masters, and even auditors to provide a roast beef dinner to the inmates of their workhouses, and their ultimate success in upholding their right to do so, suggests that the transition from moral economy to political economy was a much more protracted and uneven process and one that was perhaps never entirely complete.[148] For, as this chapter has demonstrated, local poor law officials frequently sustained a set of cultural practices that reflected and attempted to uphold an older vision of authority over, and thus responsibility for, the poor despite a growing impulse toward the rationalization of the problem of poverty, in particular, and the centralization of government services in general.[149]

2 Gendered Portions and Racialized Rations
The Classification of Difference in British and Colonial Prisons

If festive foods spoke volumes to inmates of workhouses, it was the daily fare of the Victorian state's other total institution that reinforced the criminal prisoner's cultural location. When journalist and amateur sociologist Henry Mayhew visited London's Pentonville prison in the early 1860s, he observed an intricate system being used to track the multiple dietaries provided that day to a range of convicts. These "hieroglyphics," which had been chalked up on a slate in the serving room, were, Mayhew explained, "interpret[able]" only by the cook.[1] This code of letters and numbers, erased daily and rewritten in a new equation the next, suggests that the feeding of incarcerated populations was a complex affair. Uniformity could easily have been imposed through the issue of a single dietary mandated across the nation and then converted into local ingredients for use in all the colonies. From the 1830s to World War I, however, the British government consistently rejected this option both in the British Isles and in its empire. Instead, local and central authorities considered a range of factors, particularly those of sex, race, and ethnicity, when determining how to classify prisoners and which dietaries they would subsequently be placed on.

Historians have tended to privilege reformist narratives of prison feeding that emphasize a drive toward uniformity.[2] But in doing so, they have missed the ways in which the diversity of prison diets reflected and helped to construct the categories of difference that formed the foundation of Victorian and Edwardian culture. Far from adhering to a type of mass feeding rooted in the principle of uniformity and shaped by objective scientific research into the body's nutritional needs, prison authorities were animated by and, in the process, reinforced bodily imaginaries that were predicated on essentialist views of sexual, racial, and ethnic difference. The prison diets issued in the nineteenth and early twentieth centuries did not merely attempt to punish those who had failed to act as liberal subjects. But precisely because they were based on sex and race, they reinforced these hierarchies of difference as the fundamental organizing principles of imperial British society.

The Discourse of Uniformity and Revisions
to the Prison Dietary

In 1921, Evelyn Ruggles-Brise, having just retired from the Prison Commission (which he had overseen since 1895), reflected on the difficulties inherent in framing the prison dietary given that it needed to be "sufficient and not more than sufficient, for the varying needs of many thousands of human beings of different ages and physique."[3] Local and central authorities revisited prison dietaries throughout the nineteenth century precisely because of this seemingly irresolvable tension between an administrative requirement for simplicity and concerns that a just system needed to account for the readily apparent differences among prisoners. A workable scheme required limiting the number and types of meals provided, but a fair system acknowledged that different bodies had different food requirements. The compromise solution was to organize the prison population into a series of classes. Although in the late nineteenth century, reformers lobbied for special privileges for those inmates whose position in the social hierarchy had accustomed them to a more "luxurious life" and, it was argued, were suffering disproportionate hardship due to their change in circumstances, these were not based on social class.[4] Instead, prison classes were based on sex, age, length of sentence, the labor the inmate was expected to perform, and, in the colonial context, race and/or ethnicity. While this brought a measure of standardization to the regimen, the state's provisioning practices maintained these distinctions even when it may have been more efficient to introduce a single diet scale.

Throughout the Victorian and Edwardian periods, prison officials repeatedly argued for greater efficiency in the provisioning of prisoners. These discourses of uniformity and efficiency emerged first in the 1830s as part of a utilitarian attempt to reform the penal regime. Their ideology was informed by the same principles that governed the workhouse: that prisoners were to be maintained at a basic level of subsistence, which was not superior to the poor but honest classes, that the regimen must act as a deterrent to crime, and that expenditures must be kept in check to ensure that no state resources were being wasted on the least deserving subjects of the Crown.[5] In this spirit, the 1835 Prison Act, which as part of the Whigs' reform agenda subjected local prisons to greater oversight by the Home Office, boldly claimed to effect "greater Uniformity of Practice."[6] It did nothing, however, to standardize prison rations. It was not until 1843 that the Home Secretary Sir James Graham, a Tory who had begun his political career as a Whig, decided to apply the principles of "consistency and the utmost practicable uniformity" to the prison diet itself.[7] This resulted in the development of dietaries for each class of prisoner that consisted of fixed amounts of specific foods: bread, potatoes, meat, meat-based soup, oatmeal gruel, and cocoa. However, since these were suggested but not mandated, only a minority of prisons (63 out of 140) adopted them. Even those that did adhere to Graham's scales nevertheless gave their prison medical officers wide latitude as to the prescribing of extra diet and special items.[8] In practice, even after pledging increased uniformity, prison food regimes varied considerably.

It was this patent lack of uniformity that led various individuals and official committees investigating prison regimes in the early 1860s to call for reform of the diet scales.[9] A series of inquiries (1863–4), launched by a Liberal government increasingly concerned with a lack of standards, advocated for the rationalization of feeding practices in both convict establishments, which were managed by the central state, and jails, which were funded and administered by local authorities but, after 1835, subject to the regulation and inspection of the home secretary. Convict establishments housed felons sentenced to penal servitude or awaiting transportation overseas; jails held those guilty of lesser crimes, short-sentenced prisoners, debtors, and those awaiting trial. But this flurry of investigations did little to mitigate the fact that "great differences" persisted, particularly within local prisons.[10] Even after some of the recommendations were actualized, local prisons containing both men and women, adults and juveniles, with various sentences and labor regimes, might have "14, 16, or 18 different diets" in use the same day. Rather than making the provisioning of prisoners more efficient, the recommendations forwarded by the 1863–4 committees remained a source of "confusion," its critics argued, and led to "much diversity of practice," especially in the local jails.[11]

In 1877, during the second administration of Conservative Prime Minister Benjamin Disraeli, prisons were nationalized. This brought the management of local jails and convict prisons under the same centralized Prison Commission and stemmed in part from a renewed attempt to "establish a system of equal and uniform punishment under the direct authority of the State." This included the introduction of a "uniform and scientific dietary."[12] With the passage of the Prison Act of 1877, the responsibility of framing dietary scales for all institutions was conferred upon the home secretary who sought to provide "uniformity of diet in all prisons" and to introduce a much-needed measure of "simplicity" in its administration.[13] The committee formed for this purpose in 1878 recognized the necessity of establishing dietary scales "wherever bodies of persons must be dealt with in the mass." But the difficulty inherent in all scales, its members noted, was that a "uniform diet is given to persons of various age, weight, height, idiosyncrasy, and physical conformation." Those in charge of framing dietaries, its report concluded, must therefore be guided by "averages" and exceptional cases provided for by special means.[14] The 1878 committee streamlined provisioning by reducing the number of classes and the different dietaries in use, rendering it simpler to oversee. It also diversified the components of the diet, introducing suet pudding, beans and bacon, tinned meat, and varieties of porridge. This dietary remained in place, at least on paper, until the 1890s when, for the first time, the Prison Commission began to consider new scientific studies of food when revising their feeding policies.

Prisons had been sites of nutritional experiments since the first decades of the nineteenth century. Most of these, however, were not undertaken in the name of science. Rather they were cost saving and disciplinary measures that, following the utilitarian imperative, reduced prisoners' diets to the bare minimum both to minimize waste and to deploy food as a form of punishment. When underfeeding led to epidemics of diseases and, in some cases, deaths that were too numerous to explain away, these regimes were ameliorated.[15] Prisoners were always already unwitting experimental subjects for those who tested the limits of "bare life."[16]

In the 1850s and 1860s, Edward Smith, assistant physician to the Hospital for Consumption, Brompton, assisted by W. R. Milner, surgeon to the Wakefield convict prison, undertook a series of studies on prisoners that were animated not by a desire to curtail costs but rather by scientific questions. These were primarily concerned with the relationship between the consumption of food and the ability to labor. Appointed as head of the British Association for the Advancement of Science's committee formed to investigate the effects of diet and discipline on the health of prisoners, Smith extended the work of the pioneering food chemist Justus von Liebig who had argued that protein was the only necessary nutrient as it was the source of the body's energy. Assisted by Milner, Smith calculated the amount of nitrogen and carbon excreted by prisoners in urine and feces to determine the energy being expended through physical work. In addition, they collected data on the weights of prisoners and their rates of pulsation and respiration to assess how well their bodies tolerated the prison regime. Smith concluded that those engaged in particularly hard labor required additional food to compensate for physical exertion. This led him to advise that the use of strenuous labor as a form of punishment was counterproductive as it necessitated additional feeding.[17] These prison experiments were part of Smith's wider research agenda that included the collection of data about the diets of agricultural and industrial workers and generated questions about metabolism and the "minimum subsistence level" required for survival. Although this body of scientific work as a whole significantly contributed to the emergence of the nutritional sciences, which was still in its infancy in the 1860s,[18] Smith's prison studies had only modest effects on the British government's practices of feeding incarcerated populations. This was because local prison officials tended to favor their own accumulated experience over novel scientific theories, particularly those that required overhauling the entire prison regimen. But it was also because the government stacked its committees of inquiry with "experts" that continued to view the dietary as an integral part of the disciplinary regime. These authorities saw the meager provisions coupled with onerous labor as a deterrent that made imprisonment, like reliance on the workhouse, "less eligible" than pursuing an honest day's work. As we shall see in later chapters, the sciences of nutrition played only a relatively minor role in the state's decisions about feeding those in its care. Throughout much of the nineteenth century, science took a back seat to ideologies that focused on the principles of deterrence and economy.[19]

It was not until the turn of the century that scientific studies of food began to shape prison diets. The 1898 Departmental Committee on Prison Dietaries, which had been convened in response to concerns that some of the prison diet scales were "conspicuously insufficient," drew attention for the first time to the importance of considering the "nutritive value" of the foods furnished to each class of prisoner.[20] However, before World War I, only Scottish prisons utilized the novel tool of the calorie.[21] The calorie as a unit of heat had been theorized by late eighteenth- and early nineteenth-century French scientists. Its emergence as key to the nutritional sciences owed much to the English chemist Edward Frankland's attempts to use a calorimeter to quantify the energy value of foods. After a visit to Frankland's laboratory in 1860, German physiologist Carl von Voit experimented with the relationship between food intake and energy output, work further developed by the German Max Rubner and the American Wilbur O. Atwater.[22] Although British scientists such as Smith and Frankland were among the first to study foods for their quantitative energy values, the 1898 committee explicitly based their recommendations as to the appropriate diets for "individuals of both sexes, and various ages, performing an average day's work" on the biochemical calculations of the German scientist Joseph König, who the committee identified as a "recognised authority" on the nutritive components of food.[23]

This decision was controversial, but not because the committee had privileged the nutritional qualities of food in general while paying little attention to the quantifiable energy output that research into calories had made available. Rather, it was that some officials thought it "rash" to apply a standard that had been developed by a German and based on the study of German bodies to those of the English "race." "Is it not a matter of common knowledge," queried a member of the Home Office's staff, "that the minimum food-stuff required for daily subsistence varies greatly for different races – even for different European races?"[24] While prisons began to make use of scientific studies of food values, there was not yet widespread agreement that bodily needs could in practice be either quantified or standardized.

The idea that state policies on institutional feeding should be guided by nutritional research only began to emerge at the turn of the century. However, the questions about race and labor that these studies generated were not new. They were merely the latest iteration of long-standing debates about how to address physical differences among prisoners. As we shall see, the feeding of prisoners of different racial and ethnic populations was of primary concern in the colonies. In Britain, it was the issue of labor that was paramount. But even attempts to objectively calculate the food requirements of a laboring body were shaped by cultural, and thus deeply gendered, understandings of the physical and psychological differences among bodies.

The Average Man and the Question of Labor

These scientific calculations made explicit what had been implicit in much of the nineteenth-century discussions about the prison dietary: that those who oversaw the penal system conceived of the "average" prisoner as male. Herbert Smalley, a member of the prison medical inspectorate that since 1865 had been responsible for paying weekly visits to oversee the health of prisoners, justified this at the turn of the century. He argued that the male dietary had always been "the crucial question" as all other dietaries followed from this norm, presumably because men represented the bulk of the prison population[25] (Figure 2.1). Thus, the prison dietary was based on assumptions about the food requirements of the average man and did not take into account age, height, weight, or other physical factors. "A man of six feet high" was allotted the same amount of food as "a man of smaller stature, and a man of 40 the same amount as a young man of 18."[26] It was only in Scotland, and only after 1900, that the prison dietaries explicitly catered to men of larger build: those over 12 stone (168 pounds) without

Figure 2.1 Wormwood Scrubs Prison, feeding prisoners, 1895. Mary Evans/The National Archives, London, England.

boots or over six feet tall were allowed 4 ounces of bread and 1 ounce of cheese added to their daily rations.[27] As we shall see, women's rations were also adapted from these norms.

If body type and age were not factors, considerations of labor were central to the dieting of male prisoners. Most prisoners performed some type of labor because it was widely believed that a harsh regime deterred crime and that the devil would find work for idle hands. Throughout the nineteenth century, however, there were significant tensions around whether labor should function within local prisons as a form of punishment (and could therefore be unproductive exertion) or whether productive work was to play a reformative role (and have the added benefit of defraying the institution's expenses and/or training inmates for a life outside the prison). This meant that different forms of labor existed side-by-side in local prisons and varied considerably over time and space. Labor was absolutely central to penal servitude, thus always part of a convict's sentence. This included quarrying, brickmaking, stone breaking, dockyard work, and other forms of physically demanding industrial employment that were categorized as "hard labor."[28]

But since this term was also applied to the penal use of the treadmill, the crank, and the shot drill, which were often deployed in local prisons where some inmates were similarly sentenced to "hard labor," these definitions were imprecise and interfered, many argued, with the ability to rationalize rationing.

Long before Smith's experiments, prison administrators acknowledged that the body required food as fuel, the need for which increased in relation to the energy expended through labor.[29] When the City of London jails adopted the Graham recommendations, for example, they adhered to the principle that those performing hard labor would be permitted extra meat-based soup.[30] The trouble with using labor to determine appropriate amounts and types of foods, however, was that, as the inquiries of the 1860s had noted, the term was imprecise. That officials had different understandings of what was and was not hard labor led to marked inconsistencies in relation to rationing.[31] Smith was profoundly disturbed by the fact that the government inquiries of the 1860s had identified this problem but had made no attempt either to define the term "hard labor" or to correlate this labor with food requirements more precisely. They do not, he fumed, "make any experimental inquiries as to the effect of the various kinds of hard labour upon the body, with a view to estimate accurately the food which is required to meet the waste thus caused." "How then is it possible," he demanded, "for them to apportion food to a condition of the body which had not been ascertained?"[32] As Smith noted, the government's lack of interest in conducting scientific experiments (or using the ones that he himself had already undertaken) meant that the dietaries in use in the 1860s and 1870s continued to provide more food for men on hard labor, but how much and what constituted hard labor remained local decisions. Until the dietaries were nationalized in 1878, there remained significant variation in how prison authorities assessed the amount and types of food required to compensate for this type of physical exertion.[33]

When the new dietary was introduced in 1878, it was much more explicit about using the hard-laboring male as the standard prisoner to be provisioned. The 1878 diet scale devised four classes of prisoners that correlated with length of sentence. In Class 1 – set aside for prisoners serving terms of seven days or less – no prisoners were subjected to hard labor and all were fed on an identical diet. But Classes 2, 3, and 4 all distinguished between men with hard labor, on the one hand, and the rest of the prison population, on the other. This latter population included men not undergoing sentences of hard labor, women of all ages, and boys under sixteen. These prisoners received the same articles of diet as hard laboring men just less of them. This suggests that women and juveniles were not envisioned as performing hard labor in any form, a subject I will return to later. But it also clarified that the nonlaboring male body need not be differentiated from that of either the female or the juvenile.[34] This implied that male and female bodies were not inherently different in their need for nourishment. Rather, what distinguished the adult male (and in this context largely white) body was the labor it performed; thus, only male physical activity was to be compensated with additional foodstuffs. The 1878 dietaries introduced a two-body system whereby the male body undertaking hard labor became the norm and all other bodies dieted alike on a scale adapted downward from this norm. This dietary did not privilege the male body as male, since (at least on paper) nonlaboring men received the same amounts and kinds of foods as women.

The food requirements of male laborers were not formally revisited again until the 1890s when more careful distinctions were made between the types of labor men were expected to perform and the diets to be associated with these particular forms of bodily activity. The convict dietaries introduced in the wake of the 1898 reassessment more rigidly distinguished types of labor and provided diets more appropriate to the work these men actually performed. They classified male convicts according to whether they were engaged in "industrial employment" (Class D) or "employed at certain prescribed forms of Hard Labour" (Class E). A Standing Order of 1901 specified exactly which forms of labor entitled a prisoner to Diet E: bricklaying, carpentering, excavating, farm work, foundry work, gasmaking, outdoor laboring, painting and glazing, plastering, platelaying, plumbing, quarrying, rigging, sawing timber, slating, smithing and fitting, stoking, stone cutting and sawing, and stone dressing. Since this was the most generous of all diets, the list was specific in order to prevent local authorities from using their discretion.[35]

The local prison diet, however, moved away from using labor as the critical tool for classifying prisoners. The 1898 committee investigating prison dietaries recommended that in local prisons no distinction should be made between hard labor diets and others. This was because, its members reasoned, those in local prisons were rarely performing the types of demanding physical labor undertaken by convicts. Instead, its report argued, they were engaged in lighter work, which prisoners who had not explicitly been sentenced to hard labor were also performing. In addition, the report claimed, in local jails, three out of every five men sentenced to hard labor were apparently exempted from performing it due to "physical defect, age, or infirmity," and yet they still received the hard labor diet.[36] This meant that dietaries formulated to replenish the body with energy lost through vigorous physical activity were in the end being given to those who were largely, or in some cases entirely, sedentary as a privilege associated with longer sentences.

Thus, the 1898 committee recommended that in local prisons all "males over 16 years of age" be designated in the dietary table as "men" and, "speaking generally, the diet for men will be larger in quantity than that for women" and for juveniles.[37] The 1898 committee also recommended replacing the two-body system with one in which men, women, and juveniles of both sexes were treated as separate categories of prisoners to be dieted accordingly but not in relation to the physical activity they actually performed. The new dietary introduced in local jails in 1901 created two categories of prisoner predicated on sex and age, making no mention of prison labor: "Men," meaning all males over sixteen years old and "Women and Juveniles." In practice, however, the two populations that made up this latter group were dieted differently from one another as juveniles had extras such as milk automatically added to their rations in recognition that they were "growing boys" (and girls, though this fact was rarely officially acknowledged).[38] This returned to the principle that had earlier in the century been taken for granted: that adult men, as men without regard to labor, required more food than juvenile males and all females.

This decision to provide an increased diet to men at the turn of the century may reflect the hardening of ideologies about inherent sexual difference at a moment when women were demanding increased rights. But the state's provision of more food for adult male prisoners was also bound up in other discourses of male labor. The ordinary diet furnished in prisons was expected to maintain the body in health. For a man, this meant a body fit for his regular occupation upon discharge. This was crucial lest he be unemployable and become a "burden on the parishes of the Kingdom," thus moving from one state institution (the prison) to another (the workhouse).[39] The politician John Burns, a socialist who aligned himself with the progressive wing of the Liberal Party, argued to the 1898 committee that an inadequate diet "renders a man unfit for work when he goes out, and to that extent makes him a worse citizen," as good citizens remained independent of either the state or charity, supporting themselves and their families through honest labor.[40] One of the tests of the adequacy of the prison diet, many argued, was therefore not merely whether the food provided could support the needs of the body while incarcerated but also whether prisoners could return to their previous occupations upon release. Since 1883, the Prison Commission had urged that a prisoner be inspected twenty-one days before discharge and placed on a superior diet if he should be found to

be "so weak as to be unfit for a good day's work."[41] The 1898 committee upheld this principle that it was the state's responsibility to ensure
that every prisoner, here presumed to be male, should receive food that
would maintain his general health and "bodily condition." This was not
only because inmates were wards of the state but also, on release, they
must be capable of taking up "any honest means of livelihood."[42]

The new turn-of-the-century dietaries that privileged men as men
thus reflected the state's view that adequate prison feeding was imperative as recidivism and pauperism were ultimately more of a drain on
government coffers than furnishing food that maintained the potential
productivity of male prisoners. The state's decisions around the average man's rations, however, also supported a range of gendered cultural
assumptions about men's inherent need for more food, their bodies'
ability to undertake hard labor, and their social roles as family bread-
winners. All of these were to affect not only the treatment of male prisoners but, significantly, female prisoners' access to an adequate diet.

A Fraction of a Man

If prison dietaries were formulated with the needs of the male body in
mind, prison officials could not ignore the presence of female inmates
who were often incarcerated either alongside men or in separate wom-
en's prisons, which began to be established in the second half of the
nineteenth century. This opened up questions about the nutritional
requirements of female versus male bodies. Although authorities grap-
pled with the implications of this, no scientific reasoning underpinned
their decisions about how to translate a widespread belief in sexual difference into appropriate feeding practices.

The 1843 Graham dietaries had differentiated prisoners by sex:
women occupied the same prison classes as men, but the rations allotted to them in each class were reduced from the male norm. These
reductions were inconsistent; no clear logic underpinned the relationship between male and female rations in the period before the nationalization of prisons.[43] This was equally true in prisons that did not
adopt the Graham dietaries. Most of these institutions also operated
on the principle that women required less food than men, but they
used a range of different formulas to calculate what precise fraction
of the male diet the female inmates were entitled to receive. At the
Surrey House of Correction in 1843 (which became a female convict
prison ten years later), women undergoing hard labor or solitary confinement received two-thirds of the men's bread allowance although
they received the same portion of oatmeal gruel, soup, and potatoes.

Those not sentenced to hard labor or solitary confinement received the same portion of oatmeal gruel, beef, and soup as the men, but four-fifths the bread.[44] At Millbank in 1844, female convicts received half the potatoes as their male counterparts but four-fifths of their cooked meat ration.[45] These variations continued into the 1850s and 1860s at both the local and convict establishments, revealing great inconsistencies as to how female bodies were maintained in prison.[46] This suggests that while differences of sex were taken for granted, there was no generally accepted or theorized relationship between male and female bodies in relation to their need for nourishment in wide circulation at this time.

The committees convened in the 1860s were well aware of the plethora of practices and of the Graham dietaries' inconsistencies. It is "impossible to detect any distinct rule or principle which can have presided over the construction of the dietaries of the two sexes," one of the committees argued.[47] Their reports recommended that, when diet scales were next altered, the "respective dietaries of male and female prisoners should be adjusted by a fixed rule and proportion." This should be based, it was argued, on the "principle" that women should receive one-fourth of male prisoners' solid rations, leaving the liquids unaltered in both quantity and strength. This had been calculated based on the assumption that women weighed one-sixth less than men. This must be considered alongside the fact, maintained one report, of the "less active habits and employments of women," leading to a conclusion that one-fourth, rather than one-sixth, would be the appropriate deduction to account for both smaller frames and less energetic bodies.[48] These proposals were not uncontroversial as Smith called out the fuzzy logic of what he considered patently unscientific calculations. He nevertheless perpetuated the assumption that scientific studies of the prison diet should focus on the "average man": of the nineteen questions regarding prison feeding that Smith maintained the committees had failed to answer, none addressed the nutritional needs of the female body.[49] In the end, despite these recommendations, the 1860s inquiries had little practical impact on the state's policies of provisioning incarcerated women. But the idea that women should be fed less food than men had traction well into the twentieth century. In fact, even when the government introduced a dietary that at least on the surface appeared not to distinguish male from female bodies, the practices of reducing women's rations persisted.

The two-body system introduced in 1878 de-emphasized any essential difference between the female and male body as women and nonlaboring men were to be given an identical diet. The recommendations of the inquiries of the 1860s were not therefore followed at this juncture either. Indeed, there was no suggestion that because women were on average shorter or weighed less than men that they required less food. Nor was there any assumption that because their "habits" were "less active" this warranted a reduction in their diet. On paper, the 1878 dietary thus represented a radical break both with the gendered ideology of the late Victorian period – that saw the female body as inherently distinct from the male – and with the traditional practice of dieting female prisoners on a reduced scale.

The desire for greater uniformity and simplicity that underlay the 1878 dietary did not trump either the gender norms of the period or long-standing institutional practices. Thus, even after 1878, women continued to be dieted differently than men. Prison authorities contended through the end of the nineteenth century that "the diets of Female Prisoners would naturally follow that for Males, at a slightly lower rate, and with such slight modifications as has been found in the past to be suited to their constitutional requirements."[50] This revealed both an enduring belief that women required less food but also that the practices of giving women different foods had persistent in harmony with what was clearly a widespread belief, requiring little explanation, that women's bodies had different physiological needs wholly apart from the issue of labor. This was even though the official 1878 dietary had undermined these assumptions and mandated the same dietary as for nonlaboring men. Prison dietaries thus perpetuated what Dunlop asserted in 1900 was a "generally accepted fact": that women required less food than men, "both absolutely less and less relative to their body weight; the average woman having a smaller average weight and a smaller proportion of active tissue than a man"[51] (Figure 2.2).

This "generally accepted fact" was complicated, however, by a fact not always so readily apparent outside the walls of the prison: that female inmates were often required to perform hard labor whether they had been sentenced to it or not. In 1844, several female convicts working in the laundry at Millbank had requested more food precisely because they were engaged in hard labor. They received the support of the medical superintendent who acknowledged the "laborious nature of their occupation" and recommended supplementing their diet with a pint of porter daily (except on Sundays).[52] Throughout the 1840s, 1850s, and early 1860s, it was common practice in both local and convict prisons to supplement the diet of women engaged in laundry work with extra rations of bread, cheese, meat, soup, and/or cocoa.[53] The 1864 report on convict dietaries recommended institutionalizing

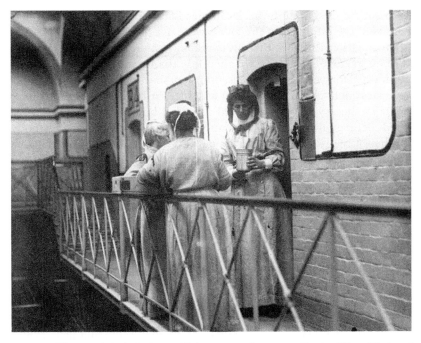

Figure 2.2 Aylesbury Prison, serving out food. The National Archives, London, England.

this widespread practice of allowing additional foodstuffs to women at "hard work in the laundry," though as we shall see, only "partly in consideration of the extra exertion" required for this form of labor.[54] The home secretary reiterated this policy in 1896 but only in relation to convict prisons.[55]

In local prisons, as opposed to convict establishments, the nature of women's labor and its relationship to the diet was more complex. When the 1878 committee revisited the issue of the local prison diet, it had concluded that it was labor rather than sex that should be the determining factor in setting scales. Men with hard labor were to receive the most rations, while nonlaboring men, women, and juveniles would be rationed according to the same scale. The 1878 report argued that the demands made upon the "physical energies" of female prisoners were practically the same whether the sentence was with or without hard labor. This was because their "employments" within the prison system did not "admit of that sharply drawn distinction between hard labor and light labor which is possible among the males." There is not among female prisoners, it maintained, the same "inequality as to expenditure of energy."[56] Thus, the 1878 dietary for local prisons denied the fact that women engaged in strenuous labor of any sort. Because women apparently did not expend more energy than any other within the local prison system, no additional food needed to be stipulated for women working either in laundries or anywhere else. This type of female labor persisted, however, and some local authorities chose to acknowledge and compensate female prisoners for it by allowing extra foodstuffs, as was the practice in convict prisons.[57] By not mandating the provision of extra food, the central government allowed other local prison authorities to naturalize this type of women's work as a gendered practice rather than recognizing it as a form of physical exertion that took its toll on the body. When the 1898 committee decided to do away entirely with all diets for local prisons that distinguished between those on hard labor and those not, regardless of sex, it failed to acknowledge the need to continue to nourish women's bodies in order to make them capable of physically onerous work. While prisons scaled back on forms of hard labor that were merely forms of punishment – such as the treadmill and the crank, which were often not being used to power anything at all – someone still had to do the laundry. That job continued to fall largely to female inmates who were not always afforded the extra food that they claimed their laboring bodies required.[58]

When it came to approving the new dietaries based on the 1898 recommendations, women's hard labor was not considered. The dietary approved for local prisons by the home secretary in 1901 was silent on the issue of an extra diet for female laundry workers.[59] Although the long-standing practice of providing additional rations to hard laboring female convicts had been reinstated in 1896, and put into policy when the rules were still in draft form,[60] when the new convict dietaries were finally approved in 1901, there was no mention of this extra allowance. Only in the 1900 rules for Scotland was the practice of providing an extra allowance to women at work in the laundry, the baths, or in the reception rooms officially sanctioned. In the end, however, this amounted to no more than a quarter of a pint of tea between breakfast and dinner and again in the afternoon, a comfort and privilege rather than a nutritional supplement.[61] This meant that in practice extra food could continue to be prescribed by the medical officer to those women he felt required it, but no local or convict prison was obliged to compensate women nutritionally for their labor. The turn-of-the-century prison dietaries thus diverted attention away from the female body's physical requirements, casting women's work within the prison as merely an extension of their domestic, and gendered, duties.

Pacifying Volatile Women

Prison officials tended to construct any additional foodstuffs provided to laboring female prisoners (such as the tea in Scotland) as catering to their psychological, rather than physical, needs. This was part of the discourse that it was not so much productive female bodies that demanded extra nourishment but female emotions that needed to be controlled through perquisites in the form of food. As historians have repeatedly demonstrated, Victorian prison officials often "psychiatriz[ed]" female prisoners who they understood to be "temperamentally unstable" and more "intractable, violent and difficult" than male prisoners, which in turn led to specialized interventions.[62] The 1864 committee had downplayed the physical requirements of the female laboring body for extra food, focusing largely on the depressing conditions within the prison and the widespread understanding that an improved dietary had beneficial effects on the mental stability of prisoners undergoing long sentences. When its members argued for an increased diet for women engaged in laundry work, their recommendation was made "chiefly in consideration that female prisoners are obliged to undergo the whole of their sentence within the prison walls, the majority of them being under sentence for four years and upwards." Its report argued that this could take a toll upon the prisoner's mental rather than physical health.[63]

The 1878 committee felt justified in doing away with any differences of diet for female local prisoners founded upon distinctions as to labor. This was because they charged that these differentiations were "for the most part hypothetical" and apt to be considered "a source of injustice and to give rise to bickering and jealousy."[64] This was not entirely a problem of female prisoners: the 1864 report on convict dietaries had also recommended that men on the hard labor diet should be kept separate from men on the light labor diet, since "jealousies" tended to arise out of men "associated together having different dietaries."[65] Unlike the debates surrounding the diet of male prisoners, however, this focus on the need to manage the emotionally volatile bodies of female inmates was widespread. While female prisoners on different dietaries could just as easily be separated from each other, making all women's diets identical, the 1878 report implied, would make the female prison population more docile, thus easier to manage.

During the 1898 inquiry, the few who ventured an opinion on increasing the diet for women performing laundry work reinforced the notion that the extra food served more of a psychological than a physiological purpose. Reverend A. W. Baldwin, the chaplain at Wormwood Scrubs, a local prison where women were not supposed to be undergoing sentences of hard labor, undermined women's physical need for an additional diet. Although his expertise was clearly with the spirit rather than the body, this did not stop him from confidently asserting that women could work on less food than men. If women working in the laundry were to receive more or special food, he argued that this should only be after eight or nine months and should be understood as a privilege.[66] Using this language of privilege and allowing additional diet only after a very lengthy period, suggested that, rather than fulfilling the needs of the female laboring body for additional nourishment, the food was a reward for a particular kind of behavior. The governor of the female convict prison at Aylesbury provided the extra bread and cheese for women in the laundry and maintained that he would continue to do so, but not because he considered it necessary to keep up with the physical demands this type of work placed on the body. Instead, he furnished the extra allowance because it would cause a "great disturbance" were it to be discontinued, and because it was a great incentive to go into the laundry. This again gestured to this food as a perquisite, an incentive to labor, and a way to maintain control over volatile women rather than a dietary supplement necessary for energy replacement.[67]

Other alterations were made to the female dietary in the 1890s for similar reasons. The only recommendation put forward by the 1894 Departmental Committee on Prisons regarding the prison diet scales was to discontinue the stirabout (a porridge made from a mixture of cornmeal and oatmeal) for female inmates. Female prisoners, particularly those in London, apparently disliked stirabout and routinely returned it uneaten (though some witnesses claimed that in the northern counties this was well tolerated and even liked). At some prisons, such as Holloway, women routinely knocked their window glass out when served stirabout, which even the medical officer admitted was "very unpalatable," compelling the kitchen to substitute oatmeal porridge to keep order. When the home secretary approved the discontinuance of stirabout in 1895, it was clearly as a means to curb unruly female behavior.[68] The 1898 committee similarly proposed providing tea to long-sentenced women in local prisons as a concession to their need for familiar, comforting food, lest their emotional lives become unbearable. The provision of tea, the committee had concluded, would "tend to make the lives of the women in prison more contented," again focusing on their emotional and mental well-being rather than on their bodies' physical needs.[69]

The female dietary did not become an issue again until the second decade of the twentieth century when suffragettes began to pose difficulties for prison administrators. Militant campaigners for the female franchise, with their slogan of "Deeds Not Words," increasingly found themselves imprisoned for crimes against persons and property in the early twentieth century. Since 1865, the British justice system had recognized political and conscience offenders as special cases entitled to First Division status within the prison system. This classification entitled prisoners such as anti-vaccinators, religious opponents of compulsory education, and others whose causes were politically motivated to special privileges, which included working at their own trades, receiving extra visitors, and having food and spirits sent in for their own consumption.[70] At the same time, it implicitly validated these causes as legitimate political struggles even while punishing those who broke the law. Whether or not one was sentenced to the First Division, however, was entirely in the hands of the justices who tried these cases, many of whom were unsympathetic to these causes and denied the claims of all or some of the individuals who sought this status. When suffragettes found themselves routinely denied recognition as political prisoners and instead classed as common criminals, they launched a series of hunger strikes that placed food and the starving body at the very center of heated debates over political rights.

Much has been written about suffragettes' use of the hunger strike and the government's deployment of forcible feeding in response.[71] But these tactics were only one way in which food became a weapon in the battle between feminists and the state. In 1910, Winston Churchill, who as home secretary was himself a target of suffragette violence, introduced Rule 243A to deal with the significant numbers of middle- and upper-class female inmates who had turned to the hunger strike to protest the state's refusal to grant them political prisoner status. Rule 243A allowed special privileges to be bestowed upon Second and Third Division prisoners "of good previous character who have not been committed for offences involving dishonesty, cruelty, indecency or serious violence."[72] One of these privileges was that of receiving outside food. Rule 243A was conceived before Herbert Gladstone, Churchill's predecessor, left office and was intended, he had argued, to divest imprisonment of the features, "which strike people as degrading and harmful to the class of prisoners we have to consider" and to "remove conditions which are particularly galling to some nervous temperaments, and trying to weak physiques" without allowing "political hooligans" to achieve First Division status.[73] Thus, Gladstone suggested acquiescing in the provision of special foods to these women precisely because their twin disorders – emotional volatility and feeble bodies – made them difficult to manage within the context of the prison regime.

Ruggles-Brise was, however, opposed to allowing suffragettes access to outside food, regardless of what other privileges were granted to them. This was the most "valuable" of all the First Division privileges, he argued, and to concede it was for all intents and purposes to grant them First Division status. No public end could be served, he claimed, by "allowing a fastidious prisoner to spurn the food provided and to assume an invidious superiority by ordering luxuries from the neighbouring tavern."[74] Churchill was, however, adamant that prisoners of "a certain class" should be permitted to purchase food from outside the prison. This was a means, he stated, to prevent a renewal of suffragettes' hunger strikes and the concomitant "advantages of martyrdom" they afforded. "I am anxious to deprive them of the slightest excuse for contumacy, or of any ground on which the public sympathy could be excited," Churchill explained. By providing them with the "indulgence" of eating their own food and thereby according them "the fullest measure of creature comforts compatible with imprisonment," he reasoned, the state will not only avoid "unpleasant developments" but will also wield "a powerful weapon of ridicule against various forms of suffragette lawlessness."[75] Although in the end, Rule 243A did not spell out the dietary privileges afforded to suffragettes, an accompanying memorandum made clear that these inmates should be dieted as First Division prisoners.[76] At the same time, those who refused either the prison diet or the food that they had procured for themselves would be subjected to forcible feeding with "no delay."[77] If forcible feeding was the stick, privileged access to superior food was the carrot. Both were part of the state's arsenal of weapons used to shame, humiliate, and assert the state's ultimate authority over the lawless female body, which unlike the male, Churchill asserted, required indulgences and creature comforts.

If Rule 243A was a political tool, it was nevertheless clearly a source of discomfort to the Prison Commission and, like most other policies introduced to deal with suffragettes, it was soon altered. Once Churchill had left his post as home secretary in October 1911, Ruggles-Brise reopened the issue. In 1912, he urged the Home Office to modify Rule 243A, which he claimed had caused "embarrassment" to the prison administration in having to admit for suffragette prisoners "numberless articles of diet, many of them fanciful, and none of them essential to health." Instead, he argued, medical officers should be given discretion as to the dietary given to these prisoners, "having regard to their age, condition, and state of health." The privilege of obtaining outside food, he argued, was widely felt by the Prison Commissioners to be an unreasonable one to concede to lawbreakers "whatever class they may belong, or whatever opinions they may profess."[78] In March 1913, this alteration was made, leaving it to prison medical staff to prescribe the appropriate diet for suffragettes. The new orders permitted these prisoners only one parcel of outside food (of 11 pounds or less) once a week, though the medical officer was permitted to disallow any of its contents.[79] This policy was introduced a month before the passage of the Cat and Mouse Act, which temporarily released suffragettes undergoing hunger strike from prison should their health be endangered. Both policy shifts suggest the ways that food continued to be a problematic, but central, concern in the management of female prisoners.

If suffragettes laid bare the very physicality of their bodies through the practices of the hunger strike, the government continually reframed this behavior as another aspect of the hysteria that it claimed characterized all their activities. While the government's rejoinder to suffragette hunger strikes was forcible feeding, it also attempted to deploy food as a perquisite to pacify women seen to have "nervous temperaments" and unruly dispositions. Although the Prison Commission refused to grant them First Division status, providing privileged access to food was itself a political maneuver aimed at curtailing unreasonable objections to the penal regime by allowing these women to partake of what Ruggles-Brise noted were "fanciful," and emotionally pleasing, rather than nourishing provisions. The government's techniques of feeding suffragette prisoners, both forcibly and through granting access to special foods, were connected to longer standing state practices that used the prison dietary to draw attention to women's psychological and emotional difference while simultaneously denying their material needs.

Food and Climate in the Colonial Caribbean

If prison diets within Britain shored up understandings of bodily difference in which sex was central, those in use across Britain's empire performed a similar function in relation to a range of differently racialized bodies that included "whites" and mixed-race populations. Colonial authorities were ultimately responsible for feeding their prisoners based on their own expertise and experience, which was shaped not only by local eating habits but also by local ideologies of racial and ethnic difference. Prison diets varied among colonies and within colonial jails because the officials on the ground often formulated dietaries for distinct populations of prisoners. The legacies of slavery and indentured servitude, as well as colonial settlement itself, meant that in some British colonies the local population, and by extension that of the prison, was far from homogenous. In other territories, a range of indigenous but culturally distinct peoples found themselves incarcerated alongside each other. The colonial administrations' decisions to feed groups of inmates based on a racial or ethnic classification system suggests that they recognized that food consumption was a cultural practice. At the same time, it reinforced the idea that differences between the "races of mankind" were more than merely skin deep. If there were doubts that the research König undertook in Germany could apply to British bodies, the myriad colonial prison dietaries in force suggest a widespread belief, circulating throughout the empire, that the food appropriate for the "different races" varied "greatly" both in relationship to and "independently of climate."[80] It was not merely that uniformity in rationing was challenging to achieve across a far-flung empire; it was detrimental to the imperial project. The practice of rationing prisoners according to imperial racial taxonomies that differed from place to place performed a valuable ideological service within colonial societies: it essentialized physical, in this case physiological, difference – a principle that underlay imperial rule.

In 1829, Tory Secretary of State for War and the Colonies Sir George Murray issued a circular to governors in the West Indian and South American colonies that specified "no distinction of colour should be made in the allotment of provisions to prisoners," a policy that continued into the post-emancipation era.[81] In many of the Caribbean colonies, dietaries that were race neutral remained in existence throughout the nineteenth century even as racial ideologies became more rooted in theories of bodily difference.[82] But the debates that repeatedly erupted over suggestions that white prisoners needed more and different foods precisely because their bodies were not well-adjusted to colonial climates, reveal the ways in which the prison became an important site of race making in the West Indies.

In the second half of the nineteenth century, concerns about the treatment of British soldiers and sailors in West Indian jails increasingly took up questions of acclimatization and thus the vulnerability of the white body. In 1868, the medical director general of the Navy objected to the diet provided at the Kingston Penitentiary because, he claimed, it was not "suitable or sufficient for European Seamen and Marines in the climate of Jamaica."[83] When Surgeon-Major James Jameson visited the Nassau Prison in 1874, he too was incensed by the dietary being provided to British soldiers in the Bahamas. Speaking from recent experience, having overseen an outbreak of yellow fever in Trinidad in 1870, Jameson warned that a "young English soldier unacclimated [sic] is placed under circumstances very disadvantageous to himself," which, he argued, "in all probability will tend to the development of disease."[84] In 1882, dissatisfied with the ways in which their previous complaints had been dismissed by the colonial government, naval authorities repeatedly condemned the Jamaican prison diet as "improper and insufficient for white men."[85] The local ingredients and meager portions provided in Caribbean jails, these authorities insisted, could not preserve the white body in health as it had not yet become accustomed to the tropical environment. It was inappropriate, they insisted, to diet the white man on a scale that had "been framed specially for the black man."[86] Attempting to stoke colonial anxieties about potential unrest in the Caribbean colonies – a very real concern in the wake of the October 1865 Morant Bay rebellion in Jamaica – Jameson made explicit what the other authorities had implied: that this was a question of national security. For if white military prisoners "were suddenly called on for active service, they would probably break down" and be unable to defend the colonies either against external forces or the enemies within.[87]

Concerns about acclimatization, often referred to as "seasoning," had emerged in the West Indies in the eighteenth century as much in relation to the bodies of enslaved peoples as whites. As Suman Seth and Rana A. Hogarth have demonstrated, many eighteenth-century medical practitioners claimed that enslaved peoples, forcibly relocated from their homes in Africa, often took a full year to become acclimated to the Caribbean environment. Thus, their bodies had to be treated gingerly upon arrival if they were to become productive and remain profitable to their owners. The idea that black bodies, wherever their natal homes, were, unlike white bodies, inherently adaptable to tropical climes was deployed in the nineteenth century to shore up proslavery arguments that rested on the inability of whites to undertake plantation labor. This effaced these earlier scientific theories of race and environment that focused on bodies out of place in general rather than specifically on the phenotype of the displaced.[88] The idea that white European bodies were particularly vulnerable to tropical climates was part of a long-standing, but dynamic, imperial and scientific discourse[89] that took on a specific racially charged significance in the Victorian period.

Despite these claims that rested on scientific theories of acclimatization, until the end of the 1880s the colonial officials who oversaw prison dietaries largely rejected assertions that there needed to be a wholly different diet for white prisoners, as did the Colonial Office.[90] Some West Indian prisons did accommodate European tastes by making slight adjustments, such as providing wheat bread in lieu of hominy or furnishing some extra meat to military men used to a protein-heavy diet.[91] But in general, officials on the ground rejected any notion that the prison regime had been formulated, as Jameson had charged, "specially for the black man." John D. A. Dumaresq, the colonial secretary at Nassau, argued that the rules and regulations of the prison had been instituted "with the full knowledge of the fact that there are always some white prisoners in the Gaol." Moreover, Her Majesty's Government, he insisted, drawing in the Colonial Office, had always been kept informed of the number of white prisoners and the diet assigned to incarcerated seamen and soldiers. Dumaresq maintained that not only was the governor unprepared to increase the diet of these white prisoners, but that he had in fact threatened to render it "somewhat more penal."[92] Anthony Musgrave, governor of Jamaica, also found it "objectionable to make any difference between the diet for white prisoners and that for black unless there is a clear reason on the score of health which does not appear to exist."[93] The Colonial Office had concurred with these conclusions through the 1880s, arguing that although white prisoners might prefer the foodstuffs they were accustomed to eating, there was little evidence that their health was suffering disproportionately due to the prison diet.[94]

If throughout much of the nineteenth century it had seemed "most unjust to extend to one prisoner a diet not extended to others," the same did not hold true as the century drew to a close.[95] By 1890, the Colonial Office's opinion had apparently shifted under the leadership of the Conservative Lord Knutsford who did not hesitate to recommend race-based dietaries in the West Indies. Upon visiting the Glendairy Prison in Barbados, A. H. Luck, the commanding officer of the Second Battalion of the York and Lancaster regiment, observed the afternoon meal, which consisted "of a large sweet potato and a small piece of dried salt fish." This did not appear to be "suitable food for Europeans," Luck argued. Since the white prisoners in Glendairy were at the time almost exclusively military, the assistant military secretary inquired of Governor Walter Sendall as to whether a "special diet could be provided for European soldiers." However, as much as he may have concurred with this assessment, Sendall feared, as had previous colonial officials in the West Indies, that providing European soldiers with a different diet might in fact be objectionable. He wrote to Knutsford to inquire whether questions of this nature had been raised by other colonies where troops (in this statement implicitly white, though this was not always the case) were "quartered amongst a coloured population." The staff of the Colonial Office maintained that it was not uncommon for "a more generous scale of diet" to be provided for "European" prisoners. If the medical staff at Glendairy found the diet unsuitable for Europeans, the Colonial Office maintained, a separate diet scale could be created as had been done in the "Eastern Colonies.[96]" If race-based dietaries were in fact already in place in other imperial locations, the race neutral practices in the West Indies were anomalous, suggesting how much they were shaped by local imperial politics. At the same time, the debates that arose around this issue in the West Indies help to expose what was taken for granted in other colonies: that racial differences penetrated deep into the body's internal structures, ultimately shaping its alimentary needs.

Europeans, Natives, and Mixed-Race Populations

The provision of different kinds and amounts of foodstuffs to various types of colonial prisoners was clearly the norm outside of the West Indies even before Knutsford took office. Diets for "European" and other "white" prisoners in Britain's colonial jails tended to be based on meat and bread instead of on the local foodstuffs furnished to what were often termed "Native" prisoners. In Ceylon in 1867, "European" prisoners had bread-based diets, while all other prisoners were fed largely on rice.[97] In the Bombay Presidency in the 1860s, "Europeans" had mutton, beef, bread, and *soojee* (semolina), while "Natives" ate mainly rice and *dhal* (lentils). Here, the "Europeans" not only received different foods than "Natives" but more of them: 35 ounces per day versus 29.[98] The diet at Lagos, a Crown Colony in present-day Nigeria, also distinguished "European" prisoners from "Natives." The former were given a daily allowance of 1 pound of meat, 3 pounds of vegetables or 1 pound of rice, while the latter received 1.5 pounds of farina flavored with a half pint of fish soup.[99] The "European" diet in the southern African colony of Natal in 1875 consisted of mealie meal (cornmeal), sugar, potatoes, bread, meat, vegetables, gruel, soup with oatmeal, and for those serving sentences longer than six months, milk. At its most generous, this "European" diet included more than four times the meat given to non-Europeans.[100] By 1898, the penal facilities in Cape Town also had a segregated diet for whites only.[101] The Gold Coast added a diet for "white persons" in 1876 that provided bread, meat, fish, eggs, rice, tea, and sugar, while "Native" prisoners were dieted only on fish and *kenkey*, a fermented cornmeal dough.[102] The dietaries approved by the British government for use in Hong Kong in 1874 similarly used only two categories, collapsing racial, ethnic, and national diversity into a binary: "European or White Prisoners" and "Chinese or Coloured Prisoners." "Europeans or Whites" received meat each day, while

"Chinese or Coloureds," the latter largely Indians, had fish twice a week. The staple food product for "Europeans or Whites" was bread, while the "Chinese or Coloured" rations were rice-based.[103]

The logic behind these divergent diets may well have stemmed from a recognition of culturally distinct eating habits. Meat and bread were central to the British and European diet in the nineteenth century and had been imported to the colonies by settlers who had not radically altered their eating habits.[104] But these foods were also thought to be particularly energizing and invigorating for white bodies vulnerable to the stresses of colonial climates. Concerns about acclimatization, explicit in West Indian debates over prison feeding, were prevalent in other colonial locations as well. In 1870, the diet scale in the Cape Coast was "greatly reduced," but not for the rare cases of "white" prisoners as it was thought too "dangerous" to lower their scale given that they were bodies out of place.[105] When the dietary was improved for "Europeans" in Natal in 1869, no attempt was made to ameliorate the dietary for the other prisoners: the assumption being that indigenous Africans required no buffer against the environment because their bodies were already adapted to it.[106] The authorities of the Gold Coast went even further as the Colonial Office itself conceded that, "imprisonment, in this climate, is to the European certain death." After 1884, British subjects sentenced in the Gold Coast were allowed to undergo their term of imprisonment in England. For those who stayed, a special diet was permitted.[107]

Theories of acclimatization and adherence to cultural aspects of food do not, however, properly account for the range of diets in use throughout the empire's prisons, which betray a complex imaginary about the presumed physiological needs of a variety of racialized bodies. These race-based diet scales explicitly challenged any assumption that, despite external differences, human bodies were like machines and as such had the same alimentary needs for fuel. But at the same time, the sheer diversity of these dietaries exposes the ways in which race was being differently constructed across an array of colonial spaces. In underscoring the flexibility of the Colonial Office's policies on prison feeding, the Earl of Kimberley, secretary of state for the colonies 1870–4 in Gladstone's first Liberal administration, had noted that there were divergent opinions about the relationship between race and diet. The inspector of Antigua, Kimberley noted, considered the "negro" prisoners of that island overfed on a diet equivalent to 176 ounces of white bread per week, while the authorities of Mauritius did not consider a diet scale equivalent to 250 ounces excessive. "The difference of constitution between negroes and coolies cannot account for this divergence, and indeed might have been expected to bear the other way," he insisted, implying that it was commonly understood that the bodies of Asians needed less food than those of African descent.[108] Although the colonial secretary here exposed the contested nature of both the racial and the nutritional sciences in this period, he nevertheless underscored the ways in which prison dietaries participated in the construction of racial thinking and, in the process, shored up the basis of imperial rule. This is particularly evident in locations with mixed-race populations.

In places where "whites" and "Europeans" were to receive additional and extra foodstuffs, care was taken to determine who was entitled to be categorized in these ways as this diet reflected colonial racial taxonomies in which whites were privileged. Because the racial and social orders were intertwined, prisons with mixed-race populations had to decide what provisioning policies were to be upheld for those that straddled these divides. In 1874, the Straits Settlement's prison dietary distinguished between "Europeans and Burghers," on the one hand, and "Natives," on the other. In the 1870s, the term "burgher" designated Eurasians who had migrated from Ceylon, most the descendants of the Dutch East India Company's employees.[109] In the context of the prison, the term clearly conveyed privileged social status, on the one hand, and a type of whiteness, on the other, as it provided access to more food than allowed to "Natives" and the kind of food believed to be most suited for the white body – bread and meat. In contrast, the diet for the ethnically varied population of the other prisoners, many of whom may not have been indigenous to the region, included rice products and salt fish.[110] Similarly, some of the South Asian jails dieted mixed-race prisoners according to the scale set aside for Europeans. The Akyab jail located in a port city in British Burma with a relatively large European population of sailors provided a single dietary to "Europeans and Eurasians," the latter presumably the offspring of the sailor class.[111] The Madras Presidency also provided two dietaries: one for "European and East Indian" prisoners and another for "Natives." The former consisted largely of bread, meat, soup, potatoes, suet pudding, gruel, and rice, closely resembling the British prison dietary. "Native" prisoners, however, received *ragi* (millet), *dhal*, rice, and only small amounts of salted or fresh fish and meat.[112] The term "East Indian" here denoted Eurasians primarily of Indo-Portuguese descent, sometimes with some British blood, who were often Christians and who adopted the norms, values, and lifestyles of European society.[113] That "East Indian" prisoners were fed on the same diet as "Europeans" supported the racial distinctions apparent within the colonial society of Madras that permitted those of mixed race who comported themselves as Europeans, like the burghers of the Straits, to be classified as such. This reified not only their social distance but also their bodily divergence from the "Native" community.

In other colonial locations, those of mixed race or whose Europeanness was suspect were barred from receiving the diet set apart for whites. This suggests that a different colonial logic was at play that explicitly discouraged interracial relationships. At the Tanna jail in the Bombay Presidency, "Half-Europeans" were entitled only to the same diet as that issued to the Chinese and Malay prisoners. This was a hybrid diet that included rice, wheat, local grains, pulses, and some mutton. Placing "Half-Europeans" on this diet had little to do with their regular eating habits. Rather it suggested that mixed-race peoples were seen to require some of the meat and wheat products provided to Europeans, but as "half-castes" were not entitled to fully embody whiteness with its concomitant special diet.[114]

The distinctions made in Gibraltar in 1865 also illustrate that these categories of "white" or "European" had to be carefully parsed in a colonial context. Here, the comptroller general argued that rather than the meat, soup, and potatoes issued to Englishmen, "Spaniards and natives of Gibraltar" should receive a different dietary that alternated between *potage* (thick soup usually made of legumes) and *bacallao* (salt cod) accompanied by rice and a pound of bread. This, he argued, would be more suitable for "such men."[115] This suggested not only different food preferences but also that, as southern Europeans, the Spanish did not automatically inhabit the same category of "white" or "European" as Englishmen. Instead, their body type and physical needs were configured as closer to the "natives" of Gibraltar, a category that would have included a range of people of different and mixed ethnic, religious, and national origin, including British, Spanish, Portuguese, Italian, North African, Maltese, and French, as well as Jews and Muslims from around the Mediterranean.

The fraught nature of racial categorization evident in these prison diets lay at the very heart of colonial societies. Although policies differed from place to place, that colonial prison authorities often distinguished between different racial, ethnic, or national groups in their rationing policies suggests the ways in which colonial prison diets were part and parcel of broader imperial techniques of governance. This is evident not only in the decisions made about the dieting of "white" and mixed-race prisoners but also in those that governed feeding in prisons where inmates were categorized according to a more complex taxonomy.

Ethnic Diets and Strategies of Rule

The diets in use in the South African colonies expose the diversity of these communities. In 1874, Natal's dietary appeared to be twofold: one for "Europeans" and the other for "Hottentots, Coolies, and Kafirs." The diet for this latter group, however, was subdivided so that each of these populations was separately provisioned. The diet for "Hottentots" (those of *San* or *Khoi* descent often classified by having a lighter skin tone) was framed for those on hard labor. This suggests that all "Hottentot" prisoners were by virtue of their ethnic affiliation expected to carry out hard labor, regardless of their crime or length of sentence. Their diet consisted of meal (usually from maize), sugar, potatoes, meat (three times a week), bread, gruel, vegetables, and soup. Indeed, only the "Hottentots," whose various ethnic groups had traditionally been cattle farmers, were given meat regularly but no more than 12 ounces per week. The diet for "Coolies" (laborers of Asian origin, particularly those from India) at hard labor was meatless and consisted of meal, rice, bread, sugar, and gruel. For those sentenced to one month or less, this diet was reduced as presumably no labor was expected. "Coolies" with sentences of three months or over were to be dieted as "Hottentots," suggesting that Asian bodies required meat only if their labor was expected to be productive over a long period of time.

The diet of "Kafirs" (which in the nineteenth century referenced dark-skinned southern Africans) consisted of meal, mealies (corn cobs), potatoes, and for sentences longer than twelve months, 16 ounces of meat divided between two days of the week. Thus, "Kafirs" received more meat than "Hottentots" but only after a full year's sentence had passed. This implied either that meat was a privilege, rather than a necessity, or that their bodies could be pushed to greater limits than either "Hottentots" or "Coolies" before their need for nourishment asserted itself. Yet another dietary existed for "Coloured" women, a racial category that could include those of mixed race, of Malaysian descent, as well as Africans who were neither "Kafirs" nor "Hottentots." This population, here used to refer only to women, and the only category of non-European women identified within this prison system was to be placed on the diet of "Kafirs" serving less than one month. Regardless of length of sentence, these prisoners thus received no meat at all, only starches. European women, however, were provided with the same foodstuffs as European men, receiving a three-quarters ration of the solids.[116]

Unlike British dietaries that at least for men tied food directly to labor, this scale of rations suggested that the body's need to replenish the energy it expended was based largely on its ethnic affiliation. That these different populations were distinguished from each other for the purposes of provisioning also suggests the ways in which the feeding of prisoners was part of much broader colonial discourses that rested on a strategy of divide and rule. This was to have long-lasting effects in South Africa whose system of racial classification only became more intricate and institutionalized over time.[117]

The dietaries in use in Indian prisons also reveal the multiethnic nature of the population, the richness of the bodily imaginaries this occasioned, and ultimately, as in South Africa, the political utility of maintaining a policy of separate diet scales. In the late 1830s and 1840s, many Indian prisons had introduced a system whereby prisoners ate rations prepared by prison cooks alongside fellow inmates. This ended the practice of providing an allowance to purchase food that prisoners then cooked for themselves. This innovation sparked protests, hunger strikes, and rioting as common messing threatened to contravene religious and caste observances in which food consumption and preparation were central.[118] Although the uprisings against the messing system were crushed by the "overwhelming coercive power of the colonial state," rationing in Indian prisons continued to be shaped by issues of caste that could not entirely be ignored by colonial administrators.[119] In the Bihar jail in 1856, 53 cooks were employed to prepare meals for the 504 prisoners in order that the customs of all the different groups could be upheld. Similarly, at the Maldah jail in West Bengal, while there was only one "Mahommedan cook," there were as many Hindu cooks as there were castes.[120] While most of the meals provided in Indian jails were vegetarian, Muslims, and at times other ethnic and caste groups that were accustomed to eating meat, were frequently permitted mutton.[121] In most of the jails, Brahmins were allowed rice-based diets even when this was not the local grain. In the Sawunt Warree jail, even the type of rice furnished was dependent on caste. Other grains were also furnished to prisoners dependent on their caste group or regional identity. In the Poona jail in the 1860s, the "Banyan, Chambar, and Khombar" prisoners were given wheat, while the "Coonbees, Bhamtahs," and other "low castes" were provided with *bajree* (pearl millet). In the Rutnagherry jail, "Hindoostanees" had wheat, "Deccannee and Goojarattee" had *bajree*, while "Konkunnee" had half rice and half *naglee* (finger millet).[122] By catering to caste and cultural practices in fairly intricate detail, colonial authorities shored up differences among the indigenous population that Britain had long exploited in its rule over the subcontinent.[123]

The prison dietaries introduced in India also participated in other regimes of bodily difference that were central to strategies of imperial rule. Although the nutritional sciences had failed to make much of an impact on prison feeding in the United Kingdom, from the 1870s, officials began to deploy them for this purpose in South Asia. As David Arnold has argued, "Food and diet formed part of a colonial acquisition of knowledge about (and presumably power over) India." Nutritional studies, he argues, were "part of the colonial reconnaissance and categorisation of India, its people and its resources."[124] From the 1860s, some colonial officials were using new biochemical studies of food components to convert the ingredients widely used in British institutions into local foodstuffs in order to furnish an equivalent diet to Indian populations.[125] However, several newly proclaimed experts in the food sciences were engaged in nutritional research that focused on the differences among racialized bodies and, in the process, questioned whether approximating the British prison diet was even an appropriate goal. They theorized that Indian bodies converted food into energy differently than Europeans and reached two convenient conclusions: that Indians needed much less food than their British counterparts and that there was no correlation between reduced diets and jail mortality rates.[126] For Surgeon-Major T. R. Lewis, special assistant to the Sanitary Commissioners with the Government of India, the question of race was of primary importance in formulating an appropriate dietary. "A small-built but a highly energetic people require, proportionally to their weight," he insisted, "considerably more food than an apathetic or indolent race."[127] This was not merely about the tendency of Indians to be less active by choice, he suggested, but also that their bodies were inherently less capable of labor. When comparing the "capacity of physical exertion between English and Hindu workmen," Lewis argued, it became evident that the former can perform more work in relation to their weight than the latter.[128]

David McCay, professor of physiology at the Medical College, Calcutta, supported this assertion in his 1911 study of the prison dietary of the United Provinces. Commissioned by the sanitary commissioner of the Government of India, McCay carried out a series of experiments that mimicked those of Smith and Milner and similar tests that Smith had performed on himself.[129] McCay's studies led him to conclude that in Indians "the amount of energy worked off in muscular contraction is very much less than in Europeans, and that the climate being tropical, the heat requisite for the maintenance of body temperature should be considerably less than in Europeans."[130] Thus, he concurred with Lewis that the dietaries in use in Indian prisons were excessive, since the inmates were excreting nutrients their bodies did not require and literally wasting state resources.[131] In the process of making these recommendations that purported to be derived from objective empirical data, these experts reinforced an image of Indians as wasteful, apathetic, indolent, and inefficient workers who by implication required the structure of imperial rule in order to function productively.

McCay's studies not only offered up a series of practical suggestions for prison dieting but also justified British colonial rule and the deployment of particular South Asian peoples in the maintenance of empire by positing diet as the key to racial development. McCay attributed the physical differences among, and character of, the "races of mankind" to the amount of protein consumed. He argued for the superiority of a protein-based diet by citing Sir James Crichton-Browne, the eminent British physiologist. Crichton-Browne had theorized that the practices of the "more successful races and the more affluent classes of a nation" were more likely to yield "good dietetic models" than those of the "more backward races and poorer classes." There is a "definite relation," Crichton-Browne argued, between "protein consumption and racial success" likely based on a "biological law."[132] McCay used this theory not merely to make recommendations as to appropriate prison rations but to argue that the "miserable standard of the Bengali's physical development" in general was due to a lack of protein in the diet. Contrasting the Bengali and Behari with the "great fighting races of the Punjab," he argued that while all of these peoples shared religious beliefs, climatic conditions, and marriage customs, the "rightful position of these races in the category of men" differed dramatically. Their respective claims to "manly qualities," he argued, forced him to conclude that, "diet or absorbable protein is the all-important element in the development and character-formation of a people." He attributed the fact that the Bengalis had never been recruited by the British colonial state for the fighting lines – in contrast to the Sikhs, Dogras, Jats, and Rajputs – to the former's vegetarianism and lack of wheat consumption, which he argued was superior to other grains. A high level of protein interchange in the body, he reasoned, was accompanied by a high development of physique and "manly qualities," as opposed to the Bengalis' "poor physique" and "cringing, feminine disposition." McCay concluded that "manliness in a race is a function of its diet," specifically the amount of protein consumed and processed efficiently by the body.[133]

This argument performed two functions in relation to the reinforcement of imperial ideology. It shored up the justification for British rule based on a gendered imperative: the feminized subcontinent, unlike the manly United Kingdom, was inherently weak, poorly developed, cowardly, and unfit both to rule itself or lead the world by example.[134]

It also extended the techniques of divide and rule by positing some Indians as fit to participate in the colonial project because their bodies were more physically developed and by extension their manly, thus civilized, qualities more highly cultivated.[135] This, McCay argued, was entirely a product of a meat and bread-based diet that resembled that of Europeans. McCay's investigations into Indian prison dietaries participated in much broader discourses not only of the logistics of colonial rule but of its racial logics. In formulating prison dietaries then, colonial officials were not merely ensuring that sufficient and appropriate foodstuffs were being issued to incarcerated populations. They were also maintaining and contributing to the system of racial and ethnic classification that undergirded the British empire.

Even as some nutritional experts studied the body's input and output in relation to the laws of nature, they nevertheless shored up assumptions about differences of sex and race that in fact undermined any stated goal of standardizing the prison dietary. Throughout the nineteenth and early twentieth centuries, prison authorities clung to ideas about innate bodily differences and fed inmates accordingly. Because prison diets were based primarily on sex and on gendered views of labor in Britain, and on racial and ethnic taxonomies in the colonies, they reinforced sex and race as two of the fundamental organizing principles of imperial British society. It was not, therefore, that prisons struggled to achieve uniformity in rationing and failed. Nor was it that the feeding of prisoners became progressively more standardized based on advancements in scientific knowledge of nutrition. Rather, uniformity and standardization in this context was of little political value either at home or abroad. Thus, differences among prisoners were consistently amplified within British and colonial prisons through the policies and practices of rationing. Prison dietaries not only reflected but also buttressed hierarchies predicated on essentialist theories of biological difference. The precise portioning out of bread, meat, oatmeal, rice, *dhal*, salt fish, *kenkey*, hominy, and a range of other foods within Victorian and Edwardian prisons significantly contributed to maintaining the social and colonial order of things.

3 Famine, Cooked Food, and the Starving Child
Rethinking Political Economy in Colonial India

Local colonial administrations implemented their own policies of prison rationing, but the nineteenth-century imperial state faced its greatest feeding challenge, both philosophically and practically, in relation to famine relief. Victoria's reign was marked by famine in India. On her ascent to the throne in June 1837, the monsoon rains were failing across India's North-Western Provinces – an early warning sign of the famine that was imminent. Within two years of instituting direct rule over the subcontinent in 1858, famine struck northern India again; four years later it hit the Madras Presidency and then Bengal and Orissa. When Benjamin Disraeli crowned Victoria Empress of India in January 1877, a famine was intensifying in Mysore and the Bombay and Madras Presidencies. According to the journalist William Digby, while preparations were being made for the ceremonies and the celebrations underway "65,000 subjects of the Queen-Empress" died of starvation and its concomitant diseases in the Madras Presidency alone.[1] During 1897, the year of Victoria's Diamond Jubilee, India was again devastated by the first of two back-to-back famines that began to subside only in 1901, the year of her death. The colonial state's response to these famines was largely to provide relief in the form of paid labor on public works projects. But from the 1860s, local officials increasingly dispersed cooked food at government-run institutions. Although these relief practices were pervasive, they did not prevent widespread starvation. These measures should not, therefore, be deployed to defend either the Government of India or local administrations against charges of mismanagement. Their prevalence nevertheless exposes the unevenness of the discourses and practices of famine relief in the late nineteenth century, some of which explicitly challenged the doctrines of classical political economy.

The historiography of these Indian famines has focused on the catastrophic effects of the colonial state's response to food shortages, exposing the ways in which laissez-faire and limited interference in the market were not symptoms of a lack of policy but themselves "politico-economic interventions" that allowed for the deaths of many in order to preserve the entitlements of others.[2] The tens of millions of people who starved to death in the famines that struck the subcontinent over the course of the nineteenth and early twentieth centuries are a testament to the veracity of this analysis. But this scholarship has not adequately accounted for the fact that from the 1860s the discourses of classical political economy were increasingly challenged by humanitarianism, which while unevenly deployed, nevertheless maintained that the goal of the state should be the saving of life at whatever cost. This new focus on saving all life, regardless of the financial cost to the Crown, during what was conceived of as an emergency characterized by temporary food shortages, opened up space for colonial officials, especially those on the front lines, to question and then to challenge the rules of economic liberalism that had governed famine management. The widespread consensus reached by local administrators in the 1890s was that they should take responsibility for the feeding of dependent children in particular. This reveals that, by the turn of the century, imperial revenue production and saving colonial subjects from starvation were no longer seen to be in tension with each other. Rather, they were intimately linked projects requiring increased state intervention.[3]

Political Economy and the Emergence of Humanitarianism

As scholars and activists have consistently demonstrated, famine is not the result of a "natural disaster." If the failure of the monsoons precipitated the droughts that plagued India for hundreds if not thousands of years, it was the political decisions made by the Raj about land tenure, taxation, the circulation of capital, infrastructure, deindustrialization, and the value of their subject populations that turned crop failure into food shortages for a wide swathe of the population during much of the nineteenth century. Amartya Sen and Jean Drèze have foregrounded the political, social, legal, and economic structures that explain why and how some people (but not others) starve when the rains fail.[4] Indian nationalists such as Romesh Chunder Dutt and Dadabhai Naoroji, however, had already articulated this political critique of Britain's administration of India a century earlier. They had argued, publicly and pointedly, that the loss of life during the late nineteenth-century famines had been the direct result of Britain's "perpetual economic drain from India," which had robbed the people of their own natural resources, disrupted social networks, and left the population chronically poor and susceptible to starvation.[5] The argument that follows thus takes as its starting point the assumption that while famines may be "triggered by a discrete *natural* event, they are the tragic consequences of human *activities*."[6] In the context of late nineteenth-century India, as had been the case in the Irish famine of 1845–52, these human activities were part of colonial political processes.[7] But it also argues that even if the colonial government did not acknowledge its own complicity in precipitating famines, these crises changed the nature of the imperial state as local officials on the ground increasingly abandoned economic liberalism and instead implemented schemes to feed a range of suffering bodies that included dependent children. This was a strategic biopolitical approach to famine administration that suggests an important relationship between colonial development policies and the discourses of humanitarianism.

Victoria's reign over the subcontinent was haunted by recurrent and severe food shortages triggered by periodic droughts, thus providing multiple opportunities for the colonial state to experiment with relief practices. This period witnessed substantial changes as to how famines were handled administratively. The famine of 1837–8 was the first to see the application of "modern" techniques of famine management and relief brought to bear in India. It was during this emergency that the principle of public works emerged as the major form of government relief, as the colonial state acknowledged for the first time that it bore some responsibility to provide for its starving subjects.[8] The East India Company provided task work for subsistence wages, preferably in cash, but alternatively in uncooked food, and substituted famine victims for convict labor on a range of infrastructure building projects. It also furnished a very limited amount of food rations to those unable to work, expecting that all other forms of aid were to devolve to private individuals and agencies.[9] The model for this was Ireland, for in the first decades of the nineteenth century public works had been used in this part of the empire to alleviate distress. An Irish Board of Works had been established in 1831 to oversee this form of relief.[10] It was premised on the idea that engineering projects that materially improved the landscape and infrastructure at the same time morally improved those who contributed their labor to these ventures.[11] When famine struck Ireland again in 1845, labor on public works became the primary form of government aid. This strategy stemmed from the utilitarianism that also informed the New Poor Law, which had been extended to Ireland in 1838. These policies accorded with the philosophy that "indiscriminate" state relief was "demoralizing," led to permanent dependency, and discouraged hard work and self-help.[12]

The principles of classical political economy put into play in India were heavily shaped by the work of Thomas Malthus who had argued that famine was a natural "positive check" to population growth (and a necessary evil) as too much state intervention would only artificially prop up a population that could never sustain itself. Malthus was professor of political economy at Haileybury, the East India Company's college, from 1805 to his death in 1834. He trained generations of the Indian civil service. Many of these imperial administrators remained committed to these and other principles of economic liberalism that, by the mid-Victorian period, were given new life by Social Darwinism with its maxim "the survival of the fittest." Throughout the nineteenth century these bureaucrats argued for limited state intervention in the market and favored public works projects as the most responsible form of famine relief. They claimed that this allowed people to labor for wages, preserving their independence and their self-respect without blunting their habits of industriousness or disrupting the invisible hand of capitalism, and crucially, without merely delaying the inevitable deaths of the unfit who "were 'designed by nature' to perish."[13] In turn, the profitability of the empire was enhanced as relief workers built, repaired, or improved water tanks, roads, canals, and other aspects of the infrastructure that supported agriculture and other forms of revenue production. As Sanjay Sharma has contended, famine relief in the form of public works was thus part of a larger process of consolidating the colonial state.[14] Low-paid wage labor on public works formed the basis of famine relief throughout the nineteenth and early twentieth centuries with disastrous results. As Mike Davis has argued, millions died of starvation and famine-related diseases not outside the "modern world system" but rather "in the very process of being forcibly incorporated into its economic and political structures."[15]

Michael Barnett has suggested that the colonial state (in the guise of the East India Company) constructed the public works projects of 1837–8 as humanitarian acts of government charity.[16] But the discourses of humanitarianism, and the challenge to political economy that this represented, emerged only in the 1860s after the imposition of direct rule in 1858 and after another series of devastating famines. Although this new approach stemmed in part from shifts in public opinion,[17] it was the experiences of local administrators – who witnessed death and distress on a daily basis – that were instrumental in forcing the Government of India to rethink and retool its relief policies.

In the wake of the 1857 mutiny, the administration of India was reorganized. The East India Company was dismantled, and a secretary of state for India was introduced as a cabinet-level post in the

London-based imperial government. The secretary of state provided oversight of the Government of India. This was based in Calcutta and headed by the governor-general who after 1858 was more commonly referred to as the viceroy to indicate his additional function as the Crown's liaison with the indirectly ruled Princely States. The provinces and presidencies that made up British India were led by representatives who reported to the viceroy. During the second half of the nineteenth century, these officials held one of various titles: governor, lieutenant-governor, commissioner, or chief commissioner. Their territories were organized into divisions each of which was administered by a commissioner. These divisions were subdivided into districts, which became the basic administrative units of the Raj. The chief administrative officers for these districts were responsible for maintaining law and order and collecting revenue and held the title of collector, district magistrate, or deputy commissioner.

It was these divisional and district authorities that were on the front lines of famine relief. In 1866, as famine ravaged Orissa (a division of the Bengal Presidency), some of these officials began to raise serious concerns about the rules of political economy given the extent of the "calamity," which they argued necessitated increased "Government action."[18] Gordon Forbes, the collector of Ganjam, argued that "if there is a point at which it becomes allowable to depart from those general principles or polito economic laws, which seems to forbid direct State assistance, in order to prevent starvation ... such a crisis is certainly approaching."[19] George Barlow, Forbes's counterpart at Puri, also queried "what, in a political economical point of view, are the exact duties and responsibilities of Government," during times of severe famine? This suggests that Barlow believed that merely providing labor on public works was insufficient.[20] T. E. Ravenshaw, commissioner of Orissa, maintained that it was "necessary for Government to step in to save these helpless objects from a lingering and miserable death." Ravenshaw acknowledged that providing waged labor on public works projects had stemmed from a "sound and proper principle." But to "save a large class of people from actual starvation," he insisted, would require more gratuitous relief. This commissioner appealed "to the liberality and sympathy of Government" to make more funds available for this purpose.[21] Many of the officials on the ground who witnessed widespread starvation first hand in the mid-1860s thus began to chafe against the philosophy, entertained by those distant from the actual distress, that the provision of paid employment marked the limit of appropriate state intervention in the market.

The high death toll during the famine of 1866 awakened a widespread sentiment, even among hard-line proponents of market principles such as Sir John Strachey (who went on to become Lord Lytton's finance minister), that it was no longer possible "to look upon human suffering from an economical point of view alone." Although it was essential to reduce the "evils" that necessarily accompanied charitable relief, presumably the potential permanent pauperization of the population, "if we can save people from present starvation," Strachey asserted, "we must do so."[22] When the 1866 famine had subsided, H. M. Durand, a British Army officer and colonial civil servant who was to be appointed lieutenant-governor of the Punjab in 1870, insisted that it must henceforward be understood that "the first duty of a Government is the preservation of the lives of its people." A "visitation of this awful character," he asserted, could only be met by the "free and timely application of the revenues of the Empire." The relief measures must be proportionate to the magnitude of the catastrophe, Durand insisted, "which in this case demanded imperial, not petty exertions."[23] Since the commissioners who investigated the famine concurred that a more "humane policy" needed to be introduced, after 1866, it became a more mainstream philosophy that the state was responsible for alleviating the suffering of Britain's imperial subjects.[24]

The Limits of Humanitarianism in Action

This marked ideological shift became evident in the official response to the 1868–70 famine in the North-Western Provinces where, "for the first time," the very "object of Government" became "to save every life."[25] Having had only a few short years to digest the extent of the mortality that he had presided over in the Madras Presidency, Bengal, and Orissa during the famine of 1865–6, Sir John Lawrence, in his final days as viceroy, perhaps ashamed that he had not done more earlier, declared that, "the State should distinctly announce its full responsibility for the really helpless, irrespective of charitable contributions." District officers, he directed, should be empowered to "make such advances for food as might be necessary to save life." If "public charity should fail from any cause," he mandated, "the Government must step in to save life."[26] The lieutenant-governor of the North-Western Provinces demurred but eventually followed suit, issuing orders that he would hold every district administrator "personally responsible that no death occurs from starvation which could have been avoided by any exertion or arrangement on the part of the District Officer, or of his staff."[27] Although statistics on famine deaths were only imperfectly kept,

Frederick Henvey, officiating junior secretary to the Government of the North-Western Provinces, assessed that while the mortality in the 1860–1 famine in the region was "believed to have been great," the 1868–70 famine was, with the exception of Ajmere, "believed to have been small" as a direct result of this policy shift.[28]

This moderate success in mitigating starvation deaths in 1868–70 raised questions about past practices not only in India but also in Ireland during the recent potato blight. By the 1860s, colonial administrators had begun not only to urge more state intervention but also to draw more concrete comparisons between famine management on the subcontinent and in Ireland.[29] Although Charles Trevelyan, who had overseen the government's disastrous response to the Irish famine that had begun in 1845, became first the governor of Madras and then finance minister for the Government of India in the 1850s and 1860s, with a few decades of hindsight, other colonial officials now began to question Trevelyan's slavish devotion to the rules of political economy. The members of the commission inquiring into the management of the 1866 famine had explicitly asked that all relevant information about famines in both India and Ireland be collated so that they might "acquire that knowledge which will enable them to work out in practice results far more satisfactory than could be obtained from any rules or models of conduct."[30] This suggested that the practical experience in Ireland, during which approximately one-eighth of the population had perished, was more valuable to Indian administrators than any abstract political theory. When famine threatened again in 1874, Sir Bartle Frere – seasoned veteran of the Indian civil service and president of the Royal Geographical Society – warned that "the calamity which threatens us is at least five times as great as that which occurred in Ireland" and would necessitate increased action.[31] Arthur Howell, a deputy secretary to the Government of India, pointed out that if anything was to be learned from the Irish case it was that public works alone could not mitigate distress on this scale. He argued that the famine had only been brought under control in Ireland when the labor test – that required work in exchange for relief – was abandoned and cooked food provided gratuitously. Given that the circumstances in India are not entirely dissimilar, Howell maintained, the experience in Ireland argued for an "extension of the system of gratuitous distribution of food" as a central strategy of government famine relief.[32]

Thus, the official policy during the 1873–4 famine was to use all means, not merely task work, to save life at all costs. Frere, who had been trained at Haileybury during Malthus's tenure there, believed that the laws of "political economy" were "equally applicable" to India as to Britain.

He nevertheless publicly proclaimed in December 1873 that "there is not a government official from one end of Bengal to the other who is not at this moment fully aware that he will be required, by rulers the most intelligent and most exacting, to strain every nerve and every faculty of his being, to prevent the death from starvation of the Queen's subjects."[33] In March 1874, Sir George Campbell, the lieutenant-governor of Bengal, acted on this promise by issuing an order to all local relief officers that they would be "held responsible that no deaths from starvation occur which could have been avoided by any exertion or arrangements within their power and the means placed at their command."[34] Sir Richard Temple recalled later in life that when he assumed Campbell's position a few weeks later, he had similarly assured the viceroy of his commitment that there would be "no loss of life in this famine," importing rice from Burma to stave off starvation. There were a limited number of deaths during 1873–4, which Temple attributed to the principle, "acknowledged and acted upon," that "saving life from famine – at any cost, at almost any sacrifice" was the government's primary goal.[35] Unsurprisingly, he said little about the major role he had played in the famine of 1876–8, during which the mounting costs of aid became central to the Government of India's justification for its limited famine relief and thus its about-face on the importance of a humanitarian approach.

This commitment to humanitarian relief practices was thus short-lived. The 1873–4 famine had demonstrated that saving the lives of the "Queen's subjects" was possible. But this had come at a price that threatened to transform the empire from a revenue source into a drain on the state's resources. Lord Northbrook, a Liberal statesman who served as viceroy 1872–6, though committed to Gladstonian laissez-faire economics, had also been a "humanitarian liberal" intent on remaking the Raj to reflect his social values.[36] His successor, the Conservative Earl of Lytton, who was sympathetic to Social Darwinism and Malthusianism, had little patience for what he saw as excessive government funding for famine relief, preferring to divert funds to what would prove to be his disastrous Afghanistan campaign. In 1877, his government asserted that while "every effort should be made, so far as the resources of the State admit, for the prevention of deaths from famine," it was also essential "in the present state of the finances that the most severe economy should be practised." If the state was resolved to "spare no efforts which may be necessary and practicable, with reference to the means at its disposal, to save the population of the distressed districts from starvation," it also warned that, "the task of saving life, irrespective of the cost, is one which it is beyond our power to undertake."[37] Thus, Lytton's Raj reasserted the older utilitarian principles of efficiency and waste and condemned his critics' "humanitarian hysterics."[38] His attempt to suppress the collection of philanthropic funds from private donors in Britain (which included Queen Victoria, newly crowned Empress of India) prompted his critics to decry these "Anti-Humanitarian" acts of Parliament as a new legislative low.[39]

However, once gratuitous relief had been used successfully, it was difficult for local officials to reverse course when famine struck again. Indeed, not all colonial officials subscribed to Lytton's "gospel of inhumanity."[40] Some local administrators found the new viceroy's directives obscure, inconsistent, difficult to translate into action, and morally objectionable. This led them to bend, if not entirely break, the rules of relief.[41] The secretary to the Government of Bombay's Public Works Department interpreted the language of "necessary" and "practicable" relief more liberally than Lytton had intended. He asserted early in 1877 that, "no one shall die of starvation if it be in the power of the Government to prevent it."[42] Two of the members of the 1880 Commission charged with inquiring into the 1876–8 famine – James Caird, an agriculture expert, and Henry Sullivan, commissioner of Madras – openly critiqued what they viewed as the parsimonious dispensation of state relief that had resulted in a shameful number of famine deaths especially in comparison to those of 1873–4. Although Caird was an advocate of free trade, he was also intimately acquainted with the effects of famine on Ireland and drew analogies between the two colonial sites.[43] He was horrified that five million (other contemporaries doubled this estimate[44]) had been "allowed to perish," which he and Sullivan attributed entirely to the "failure" of proper administration. Famine relief had in the end not been "ruled by the principle that, before all other considerations, the saving of life should be the first object of a British Government," they argued. Instead the imperial budget had been at the forefront of administrators' minds. Drawing on an older discourse of benevolent imperial rule and the new humanitarian imperative, Caird and Sullivan argued that it was precisely because the Raj was "armed with absolute power" that it was all the more "responsible for the lives of its helpless subjects."[45]

Most of the members of this Famine Commission, however, followed their chairman, Sir Richard Strachey (brother of Sir John), who returned to a familiar narrative that it was the individual rather than the state who was ultimately responsible for preserving his or her own life even during acute distress. It was the "paramount duty" of the state to provide "practical assistance" in times of famine, the 1880 Famine Commission's white-washed report asserted, and to devote all its "available resources to this end."[46] The use of the words "practical" and "available" signaled that limits were inevitable and expedient solutions might in the end trump humanitarian actions.[47] The politics of the report was most fully embodied in its reaffirmation that famine relief should enable the people to "provide for their own support by their own labour" and encourage them to "cultivate habits of thrift," saving their "surplus" from "years of plenty to meet the wants of years of scarcity."[48] For, the Government of India was haunted by the specter of a population of millions, whose tendency many argued was to shirk work whenever possible, becoming permanently dependent upon the state.[49]

One of the tangible results of the 1880 Famine Commission was the formulation of the Famine Codes, the rules and principles that would govern the administration of relief during future crises and could be put into action at the first sign of distress, making relief more efficient and presumably keeping costs in check.[50] The 1883 Famine Code for Madras, developed from a template that was intended to serve as a model, explicitly stipulated that, as a "first principle," the "object of State intervention" in times of famine was "to save life, and to this end all other considerations must be subordinated." The success or failure of relief efforts, its Introduction asserted, "cannot be subjected to a financial test" as the "bills of mortality will furnish the only true criterion."[51] This had not in fact been the practice in the previous famine, however, and by the time a series of major back-to-back famines hit the subcontinent again starting in 1896, this philosophy had once again been abandoned.

The stated policy in 1896 – "to prevent the loss of human life from starvation at the smallest expense to the tax-paying community" – embodied both a humanitarian imperative and a utilitarian focus on the promotion of efficiency and the reduction of waste.[52] When the Conservative Lord Curzon became viceroy in 1899, he perpetuated the discourse of humanitarianism during the famine that erupted that year. In October 1900, he insisted upon the state's "whole-hearted devotion to the saving of life and the service of the people." He claimed that, "every man, woman, and child who has perished in India in the present famine has been a burden upon my heart and upon that of Government."[53] These were at best crocodile tears, for Curzon had also insisted that it must be understood that "prodigal philanthropy" "imperiled the financial position of India." Any Government, he argued, "which by indiscriminate alms-giving weakened the fibre and demoralised the self-reliance of the population, would be guilty of a public crime."[54] Curzon thus authorized a reduction in wages to those on the public works, a renewed emphasis on "tests" for all forms of government relief, and diverted funds and attention to the war underway in South Africa. These dramatic battles were a much more exciting imperial display than the emaciated bodies of the nineteen million Indian famine victims who perished between 1896 and 1902 and were no longer a novel sight for an imperial public that likely suffered from famine fatigue.[55]

The discourses of humanitarianism were decidedly uneven in the second half of the nineteenth century, largely because Lytton and Curzon were more concerned with the ways in which "indiscriminate" relief starved the exchequer than with their starving subjects. But if the empathetic engagement that had initiated the humanitarian turn in the first place had come most strongly from local rather than central authorities, it was these state agents who also had most control over the practices of relief. Some local officials such as Charles Blair, executive engineer to the Indian Public Works Department, had recognized the Indian subject as "a man and a brother," transferring the humanitarian imperative of the abolitionist movement to a different colonial setting. Having done so, he explicitly attacked the "laws" of "political economy," questioning in 1874 whether colonial officials should "obey these laws in India until they prove themselves true, while we look on numbers of human beings dying of starvation?" Or, he argued rhetorically, "are we to prove these laws wrong by stepping in and supplementing them?"[56] It was these state actors who when presented with suffering on a massive scale challenged the rules of classical political economy. Throughout the second half of the nineteenth century, they supplemented the public works programs with aid in the form of cooked food. Although this was always too little and too late, it nevertheless rendered gratuitous relief a standard practice of colonial famine management that was not in fact forbidden by the Government of India.

Gratuitous Relief and Institutions for "the Helpless"

From 1860 the state supplemented public works with what was called both "gratuitous" and "charitable" relief: state aid that came largely in the form of cooked food and that did not require recipients to labor on public works in return. While cooked food had been furnished by the East India Company during eighteenth-century famines, providing continuity with the practices of the Mughals who had fed the population during food shortages with doles of both cooked and uncooked grain, its provision was "limited in extent and had mainly symbolic value."[57] In contrast, gratuitous relief, fully funded by the government, was in the second half of the nineteenth century conceived and configured by the state as a modern approach to famine management, despite the fact that it conflicted with the principles of political economy. In the 1860s, the Government of India and the provincial governments released "liberal" grants to be used only for the purposes of gratuitous relief.[58] The imperial state also agreed to supplement charitable donations with matching funds. Thus, for every rupee collected in India or pound sterling in the United Kingdom, the Government of India, or in some cases the provincial governments, would contribute an equal amount.[59] Thus so-called "charitable" relief funds were in fact made up of at least 50 percent government monies. During the famine of 1868–70, the viceroy announced that "the equivalent of private contributions" was not to be understood as the "limit of the Government gift," and that the state would take "full responsibility" for the "helpless" "irrespective of charitable contributions," though private subscriptions to famine relief funds continued to be encouraged and formed a significant part of famine relief into the twentieth century.[60] Thus, from the 1870s through the turn of the century, gratuitous relief was largely funded by the state.[61] The 1880 Famine Commission Report reiterated this policy. It declared that an appeal to private subscriptions was unnecessary, a "relic surviving from a past state of things" that was not "suitable" to this new age where an "efficient" system of relief was to be "carried out on a uniform plan" that had been "designed to give security to the whole population." This could only be done, it asserted, "at the public cost, and on the responsibility of the Government."[62] Although this justified Lytton's suppression of private donations in 1877, which he feared as "indiscriminate alms-giving" perpetuated dependency, it also placed the onus for providing gratuitous relief firmly on the colonial state.

The state allowed cooked food to be provided as gratuitous relief to those who were "not fit for out-door labor" starting in 1860.[63] Some officials, such as the collector of Sarun in Bengal, interpreted these regulations strictly in accordance with the market principle that, "total and utter incapacity for work is an absolute condition for gratuitous relief."[64] The Report of the Indian Famine Commission of 1898 also stated that gratuitous relief was intended for all those classes that are "other than able-bodied," reasserting the rules that also governed Britain's poor laws.[65] These rules were not consistently followed, however, as officials on the ground either did not fully understand these principles or simply disregarded them. The sections of the population that might be deemed "helpless" varied from place to place, including the elderly, small children, the infirm, the disabled, the diseased, women with infant children, widows, abandoned wives and children, orphans, professional beggars, "idiots and lunatics," and pregnant women.[66] In some places, all women and children were eligible.[67] In others, more than half of those in receipt of gratuitous relief were adult men.[68] At some times and in some places, even the able-bodied were allowed access to gratuitous relief when no work was available.[69]

The screening of applicants was left to local relief officers, government appointees generally drawn from other parts of the Indian civil service who were to supervise district famine measures. These decisions were very local in nature and flexible in practice. Many chose to follow the lead of the Famine Commission of 1867, which had asserted that, "to the starving," a broad and imprecise category, "food must of course be given gratuitously."[70] By 1874, the Government of Bengal was asserting that it may indeed be necessary to provide cooked food to "all the needy," the only test being whether they would accept it or not.[71] In Mysore (a "Native State" under British regency), cooked food was apparently given "liberally" to "all-comers" in 1877, intimating that the capacity for labor was not assessed.[72] An official report of the famine of 1896–7 maintained that the distribution of gratuitous relief "expanded" throughout the famine.[73] Although more Indians were consistently employed on the public works projects, millions of people had at least a single meal furnished by the state, and tens of thousands were kept alive by accepting this relief for months on end during the late-Victorian famines.[74] By the summer of 1900, gratuitous relief in fact represented 70 percent of all government aid provided in this last of the Victorian-era famines, demonstrating that cooked food played "an increasingly important part" in state strategies of famine management.[75]

The decision to provide gratuitous relief in the form of cooked food (whose consumption was supervised), rather than doles of raw grain, was strategic. During the Irish famine, soup kitchens had briefly been provided under government auspices on the grounds that cooked food could not become a tradable or resalable commodity if required to be consumed on the spot.[76] Policy makers also reasoned that if grain was made freely available, too many people, and not merely the destitute, would find this "attractive," leading the whole population to become dependent upon the state.[77] Accepting cooked food, on the other hand, was more fraught. It involved a disruption to home life as it required taking meals elsewhere, it was "degrading" as it marked one publicly as a dependent of the state, and, as we shall see, it compromised caste observances. Given this, the Government of India saw the willingness to accept gratuitous relief in the form of cooked food as an adequate test of true need.[78]

The institutions developed to distribute cooked food and the rules that governed their operation were locally established and decidedly elastic. No state institutions dispensed aid to the poor in India outside of the context of emergency famine relief as the Government of India accepted no responsibility for widespread, and what it understood to be endemic, poverty. At the outbreak of the 1860 famine, John Strachey, who was then the district magistrate of Moradabad in the North-Western Provinces, and Sayyid Ahmad Khan, a Muslim reformer who had been employed by the East India Company and had become the district's "Chief Native Judge," opened the first "poorhouse." This was intended to provide relief to those who could not take advantage of the public works projects.[79] Like the workhouse in the United Kingdom, the poorhouse dispensed cooked food on a continuous basis to those who were prepared to take up permanent residence within its confines. Those who were only "partially helpless" were expected to undertake light work once admitted given a widespread belief in the "cheering influence" of labor as opposed to the "extreme depression" experienced by those that accepted relief without making any contribution to their own upkeep.[80] These residence rules were, however, more lenient in practice. Cooked food could also be obtained from the poorhouse without a residency requirement by those whom "competent sub-committees" (made up of local elites) had personally selected for relief. In addition, no conditions were applied to those seeking casual relief on a temporary basis, except evidence of "suffering from hunger." Nor were "female paupers of respectable position" observing *purdah* required to be admitted as residents as their appearance in public would be "felt as an intolerable degradation."[81]

These poorhouses were reopened or established anew in each subsequent famine, becoming a feature of state relief throughout the rest of the nineteenth century. Their administration, however, continued to vary greatly. In the North-Western Provinces in 1868–70, residence in the poorhouses was generally enforced.[82] But in other places and at other times, this was not the case. In Tirhoot during the famine that struck Bihar in 1874, officials preferred those receiving food aid return to their homes after being fed. Only if they were unable to do so would they be permitted to remain on the premises.[83] During this famine, poorhouses generally gave cooked food "at once to all starving people who desire to have it" without "waiting for inquiries" to be made about their ability to labor.[84] Over the course of the late nineteenth century, however, as famines reappeared at regular intervals, some administrators mandated that these institutions provide only temporary forms of relief for those able to support themselves. Once individuals had regained strength by being fed, they were to be "turned out" with the expectation that employment could now be sought at the public works.[85] For those who refused to labor despite their capacity to do so, such as professional beggars, the poorhouse remained a source of continuous relief as the Famine Codes stipulated that "once received into a poor-house," the "inmates shall be kept there" "compulsorily" even if able-bodied.[86] In some districts, these poorhouses also provided overnight accommodation for those traveling to relief works. Those who presented an order from a relief officer were entitled to food and shelter for the night.[87] The poorhouses thus reflected the ideals of political economy that deterred all but the truly destitute from becoming a charge on the state. But in practice, they also opened the door to the widespread distribution of cooked food at a variety of newly developed state institutions that served a range of people in need who were not necessarily "helpless."

From 1866, poorhouses existed alongside other new institutions that were not always easily distinguishable from each other. In 1866, local administrators also opened what were variously called relief or feeding "centres," "depots," or "stations" to distribute cooked food gratuitously to those in need. The term "kitchen" was also introduced in 1876, becoming the most common name for a government-run feeding site after 1896. Unlike poorhouses, these were not residential. Although some people slept on their grounds having nowhere else to go, the key feature of these institutions was in fact that all applicants could "get their food and go home," which was less work and less responsibility for the relief officers in charge, and it was hoped more attractive to the needy than the residential poorhouses.[88] Here, officials inspected all applicants, registered the needy, and issued them tickets (worn like a military dog tag around the neck) that entitled them to be fed regularly.[89] While the "able-bodied" tended to be rejected and expected to find employment with the public works projects, the only "general test" applied was "that of extreme emaciation." The body itself testified to the need for gratuitous relief, and in most places, "no starving object was turned away."[90]

Local officials also encouraged a range of populations to make use of the "relief camps" that emerged during the famine of 1876–8. These were complex institutions that served multiple purposes. One of their stated functions was to house laborers on the public works projects who had been forced to relocate due to the imposition of a "distance test." This distance test attempted to establish true need by furnishing paid employment only to those so desperate for aid that they were willing to travel at least 10 miles from their homes. In some places, residence in the camps was compulsory.[91] Camps also served work gangs en route to the public works projects as well as beggars and other wanderers with no permanent abode who could apply for shelter and cooked food. The colonial government increasingly used these camps to control the movement of migrants. In the name of maintaining social order, famine officials and the police were permitted to remove starving wanderers to a camp even against their will.[92] These institutions thus became holding pens for large numbers of disparate peoples who were differently impacted by famine.

Initially, the administration of the camps was uneven, and some insisted that their provisions were too generous.[93] As one administrator argued, so little has been asked of camp inmates until recently that many seemed to think that, "the *raison d'être* of the place was to provide for all comers one or two meals a day in the manner most agreeable to the applicants and least laborious to the distributors."[94] Relief camps became more regulated spaces over the course of the 1877 famine, despite the fact that the government maintained that it sought to attract famine victims to these institutions. As the famine dragged on and the population of camps soared (some holding up to 8,000 people[95]), the conditions of relief became more stringent. The Mysore Famine Code of 1877 specified that camps must be "enclosed" and admission or exit only possible by a gate that was to be constantly guarded. Inmates were obliged to submit to residence within its confines and to some form of labor, "however slight," except those "who are actually sick."[96] This was not necessarily meant to discourage Indians from seeking state relief. Temple was concerned that the camps did not in fact "fill so rapidly as might be expected under existing circumstances," urging that they needed to be made "more attractive or rather less repulsive to the poorer classes than they now seem to be."[97] This directive was totally at odds with the philosophy behind the workhouse system in the United Kingdom and the orthodox views on government famine relief, which discouraged state dependency. It was nevertheless consistent with a widespread official view that blamed the poor themselves for not taking advantage of government services and served to justify the policy of rounding up itinerants and forcibly incarcerating them within these camps.[98] These contradictions reveal the complexity of these and other relief institutions both in theory and in practice. The actual administration of crisis feeding ultimately forced those on the ground to rethink the rules of economic liberalism as they actively sought to attract famine victims to accept cooked food as part of modern strategies of famine management.

Dietary Calculations

If gratuitous relief came primarily in the form of cooked food to be eaten at relief centers, this was not only for economic but also for medical reasons as famine administrators attempted to calculate how to sustain those on the verge of starvation. Experience had shown relief officers that when given uncooked grain, the famished (either out of desperate hunger or because they lacked cooking facilities) often ate it raw. This had serious effects on the digestive system and sometimes led to death. Dr. N. Jackson, the civil surgeon at Balasore in Bengal, asserted that "some of the paupers used to eat the rice raw then and there, and died immediately afterwards at the side of the road; many whom I dissected had their stomachs full of raw rice."[99] Why one would dissect a famine victim, given that the cause of death was evident and emaciated bodies made for poor anatomical specimens, remains an open question. But Jackson's actions point to the medical community's use of those who suffered the ravages of famine as an experimental population that, like prisoners (and later prisoners of war), could help to determine the body's nutritional requirements – a highly contentious subject of scientific and political debate.

Initially, it was availability, expedience, and local eating habits that governed the decisions officials made about what kind of cooked food was to be served. The meals provided generally consisted of rice and other local grains, wheat breads, *dhal* (lentils), and sometimes vegetables.[100] Medical officers were also authorized to provide special foods to those in need. Milk or *kanji* (a rice porridge) was often given to children and to invalids, and proprietary baby food, such as Mellin's (which had been donated by the company), to emaciated infants.[101] In the 1860s, some medical officers began to urge the introduction of protein, or what they called "nitrogenous" foods, such as meat, fish, or pulses as well as fat such as *ghee* (clarified butter) or oil, alongside grain and vegetables.[102] After Campbell visited one of the most distressed regions of Bihar in 1874, he issued instructions that cooked food "should not be rice only; a fair proportion of *dhal* or similar nitrogenous food should be given, and salt of course," suggesting that in many places only rice was being issued. To those dependent solely on public charity, he asserted, "a proportion of nitrogenous grain, pulses, &c., should as much as possible be given with three parts of rice."[103] Campbell and Temple (who succeeded him) had both learned from Surgeon-Major E. J. Gayer that those fed on rice alone "will starve just as surely though not as quickly as if not fed at all." Gayer, a surgeon in the Indian Army, had recommended giving at least one part protein to five parts rice.[104] This reveals that scientific knowledge of food values, which from the 1860s increasingly emphasized the importance of protein, could now be used to standardize the provision of food aid. Although practices varied, some local authorities followed suit, issuing guidelines, sometimes for the first time, which specified that rice, *dhal*, and salt (and sometimes also fish and vegetables) be given in fixed proportion in order to provide adequate nourishment.[105]

These guidelines developed during the Bihar famine were not adhered to during the famine of 1876–8, despite the fact that Temple was the key administrator overseeing both crises. In many places, only cooked grains were served with very small amounts of legumes or vegetables.[106] As Figure 3.1 illustrates, at Monegar Choultry, a relief camp in Madras, in 1877, relief rations consisted only of boiled rice (Figure 3.1). Thus, despite the Government of India's assertion that

Figure 3.1 The relief camp at Monegar Choultry: serving out boiled rice, *The Graphic*, May 26, 1877. Chronicle/Alamy Stock Photo.

relief was being provided according to a "scientifically arranged diet," explicit consideration of protein requirements were often conspicuously absent until the 1890s.[107] It was only from the famine of 1896 onward that the use of protein-rich legumes became a standard practice. That this shift happened only at the turn of the century suggests the government's imperative to save money during times of crisis even at the expense of the population's health. However, it also exposes the highly contested nature of the nutritional sciences, and the persistence of local eating habits that could not be so easily changed even in the face of both an emergency and new expertise.[108]

The amount of food to be dispensed during famine was a much more contentious issue than its nutritional makeup. In the famines of the later 1860s, no scale of rations was laid down, leading to great divergences between the relief centers.[109] F. R. Cockerell, superintendent and remembrancer of Legal Affairs, argued that the rations provided in Bihar in 1866 were inadequate. He drew on the only established knowledge available: the jail dietaries. Cockerell noted that the dietaries in use in the Bengal jails during 1860–2 suggested that the minimum daily allowance of food necessary for the preservation of the physical condition of the prisoners was 30 ounces for each nonlaboring adult. It was thus "clear on the authority of the general testimony of medical men, that even the greatest quantity of food given to each person at any of the relief centres was insufficient," given that famine victims were generally allotted half this amount or less.[110] The report of the commission investigating the famine in Bengal and Orissa in 1866 similarly appealed to the jail dietaries as a convenient comparison. But rather than assuming that they should set the standard for famine relief, these Famine Commissioners dismissed them as "excessively liberal."[111] When the severity of famine is doubtful, it is incumbent upon authorities, the report argued, "to guard against too free a resort to the feeding places." In these situations, it would be appropriate to give "only so much as may support life when eked out by anything that the people can pick up."[112] This parsimonious attitude to relief underscored the state's commitment to sustaining merely "bare life" and calculating this to the minimum.[113] As Aidan Forth has argued, the optimal diet for famine victims was one that would preserve human life but was nevertheless so low that people could not live on it "without some suffering."[114] The Famine Commissioners thus settled on 16 ounces of grain as sufficient with an additional allowance where substantial labor was required, the understanding being that the rice or grain was to be supplemented by pulses and fat.[115] This served merely as a recommendation, and their own unwillingness to mandate these rations, or even to pretend to expertise in this matter, meant that little standardization was achieved in the famines of the later 1860s and 1870s.[116]

This flexibility was itself political. As lieutenant-governor of Bengal during the second half of the 1873–4 famine, Temple had presided over a policy of relatively generous relief predicated on the state importation of grain that had led to very little mortality and enabled the agricultural population to return to their fields with the coming of the rains. He had, however, also faced strong criticism for what many considered "excessive expenditure." When the Government of India appointed him to oversee the famine in Mysore and the Madras and Bombay Presidencies in 1877, Temple's tactics shifted to reflect the central state's "priorities of economy, efficiency, and control."[117] This included the reduction of relief wages on the public works to the equivalent of a pound of grain daily per adult man. This so-called "Temple wage" marked a reduction of one-third from the scale that had been used on the relief works in 1873–4. It was explicitly a cost-saving measure; it nevertheless required a justification that was not entirely economic, particularly for those who had been more closely involved in institutional feeding and made claims on this basis to nutritional expertise.

The "Temple wage" provoked outrage from a variety of corners. Digby, whose journalism consistently critiqued Lytton and Temple's famine policies, argued that a man recently convicted of "knocking out the brains of a near relative" received a larger and more varied diet in jail than a laborer on the relief works.[118] This fact was corroborated by Surgeon-Major W. R. Cornish, sanitary commissioner for Madras, who had considerable experience in relation to the diet of both prisoners and agricultural workers in India, and who similarly argued that a pound of grain was inadequate for an able-bodied laborer. Cornish insisted that the prison dietaries had been framed only after "practical food experiments on many thousands of persons" had been carried out over a "long series of years under very strict tests as to supervision and observation." Cornish contrasted his own careful scientific process with Temple's mere "opinion" that a single pound of grain would be adequate. This opinion, argued Cornish, when embodied in policy amounted to a cruel "'experiment' on the starving poor of this country," the results of which could never be scientifically "tested and recorded."[119] Temple's directives suggested that the knowledge generated through state-feeding initiatives was not necessarily cumulative and that no single group of experts had been able to monopolize decisions around the feeding of dependent populations.[120]

While the vociferous debate that erupted between Cornish and Temple was specifically about relief wages paid in cash and pegged to the current price of grain, at its heart, this controversy centered on the amount of food that should be considered adequate to support "bare life" and thus had implications for the provision of gratuitous relief. These heated debates impacted the formulation of the Famine Codes, only some of which stipulated the amount of cooked food to be distributed gratuitously.[121] The Famine Codes differed from each other and were rarely adhered to by local officials. This meant that there was significant variation in practice as some rations were comparatively generous, while others were meager.[122] As Pandit Rama Shankar Misr, collector of Basti, testified to the 1898 Famine Commission, the ration in poorhouses may have been calculated to be "sufficient to support life," but "the distinction is a delicate one between supporting life and living."[123] Although a wealth of experience had been accumulated over the second half of the nineteenth century, the colonial state in the end made little effort to assess scientifically what an appropriate famine relief portion should be, leaving this decision to various experts and even those with no expertise at all. This significantly undermined the value of providing cooked food as famine relief by allowing political and economic expedience to take precedence over the physiological needs of the human body.

Complications of Caste and Corporeal Anxieties

The bodies to be relieved during famine were not, however, merely biological organisms whose minimum needs could be objectively calculated. Those who suffered the ravages of famine were embedded within social and spiritual communities in which food played a significant role. As David Arnold has noted, "food did not lose its sacred or sacrilegious connotations just because there was a famine."[124] Gratuitous relief was necessary for many high-caste Hindus because their caste observances debarred them from laboring for wages, thus preventing them from making use of the public works projects. The state had, since the 1860s, acknowledged this refusal to labor for wages as a religious observance associated with caste.[125] The use of cooked food was equally problematic. Because the Hindu laws of caste strictly regulated the preparation and consumption of food in complex ways that were not always clear to colonial administrators, much of the population was wary of accepting prepared food.

Some British officials felt that in a time of famine caste scruples should be irrelevant and that the willingness to accept cooked food was an appropriate test of distress precisely because it challenged deeply held beliefs.[126] Most were both more accepting of Indian cultural norms and practices and more realistic about the likelihood of Hindus abandoning their caste system even during an emergency. Nevertheless, several administrators argued that while cooked food certainly undermined caste, this was not insurmountable as this did not affect Muslims, Sikhs, or low-caste Hindus, and there were ritual practices that could restore any loss of status to orthodox high-caste Hindus.[127] According to Blair, at the end of the Orissa famine of 1866, "It became a matter of great anxiety…to know what the result of receiving cooked food would be; whether the recipients would again be admitted into their castes." "Happily," he recounted, "the matter was settled in a clear and decisive manner by the high priests of the community."[128] The Famine Commission of 1898 similarly heard evidence that those of the "respectable castes" could perform some "penance" that would guarantee "re-admission into their society," suggesting that even if some were cast out for accepting cooked food, restoration was assured.[129]

The idea that readmission to caste was a simple process was contested by other administrators and observers. Lala Baldeo Narayan Singh, who testified in front of the 1898 Famine Commission, maintained that being cast out was not reparable. Only "low caste people," he argued, would agree to use these kitchens "whatsoever the degree of their distress may be." The "respectable classes" would never go, he insisted, for if they did, "they will not be admitted to their castes."[130] Even among "the low class of people," some argued, the state kitchen was anathema as they have "to pay a penalty to the caste which is higher than their own caste if they went to the Government kitchen," which would be nearly impossible for those with minimal income, or "be put out of caste altogether.[131] Rai Sitla Bakhsh Singh Bahadur, a revenue collector in the Allahabad District of the North-Western Provinces, refocused the state's attention on the fact that these caste practices were not merely social customs that could be relaxed when inconvenient. They were a religious matter of great importance. He argued that, although people "even of higher castes" might eventually resort to taking cooked food from state kitchens, this would "cause a great discomfort and leave a caste stigma for a durable time." Insisting that this would be the only form of gratuitous relief, he suggested, will foment belief that this is "an intrigue for change of religion, as these sentiments constitute one of the bases of religion."[132] To force an individual to abandon his religion in order to receive state aid, Bahadur implied, would only undermine the legitimacy of the colonial state that, since the beginning of direct rule in 1858, had guaranteed religious freedom for all Indian subjects of the Crown.[133]

In fact, the Government of India had long been aware of these issues. When cooked food was first introduced as a form of gratuitous relief during the 1860–1 famine, the details of its provision had been left to "Native Committees" organized by local Indian elites in order that the population should feel confident that all measures had been taken to uphold caste laws.[134] As the infrastructure for gratuitous relief developed and expanded in subsequent famines, relief officers aimed to "provide cooks who [would] not interfere with caste prejudices" and wherever possible furnished segregated spaces for different caste groups to consume their meals.[135] But even with these accommodations, some distrusted all food disbursed "under Government auspices." While a relief kitchen overseen by "a wealthy Hindu" might be able to attract those in need, some argued that this could "never be the case with a Government kitchen."[136]

This was because caste observances were extremely complex, and local populations did not always trust that colonial overseers properly understood the norms even when they explicitly attempted to cater to them.[137] Digby reported that in relief camps, although procedures had been put in place to guard against the violation of caste scruples, "whispered" rumors were easily spread that the food had been mishandled, causing even the "sudras and mussulmans" – the former one of the lowest caste groups and the latter outside the caste system – to vacate the premises *en masse*.[138] A state kitchen was thus an extremely fraught enterprise. While one official optimistically claimed in 1900 that "the fashion of resorting to kitchens has now become universal; and caste scruples in this connection appear to be altogether a thing of the past," in many districts, even the truly needy absolutely refused to make use of these services.[139]

If caste was one reason that prevented Indians from partaking of government food, it was not the only one as wider anxieties about bodily safety also shaped willingness to accept this form of relief. The collector of Anantapur in the Madras Presidency maintained that during the 1896–7 famine people "gave all sorts of reasons" for not using the relief centers. They not only declared that it was against their caste scruples but "said they would die if they partook of the food in the kitchen."[140] Some state officials suggested that refusal to make use of the poorhouse or other centers of relief stemmed merely from the same sentiment that makes "the work-house detestable to the poor in England," who also preferred to remain independent of the state.[141] Others, however, acknowledged that many Indians feared that there was a "sinister motive" behind the government's provision of cooked food.[142] During the 1873–4 famine, Campbell maintained that the "lower orders" were "afraid" that if they took advantage of government feeding centers, "we may ship them off beyond seas and what not."[143] Officials became more cognizant of these fears, or at least reported them more frequently, in the famines of 1896–1901. Rumors circulated during 1897 "that everyone who accepted relief was to be subjected to demoniacal influences; or sent across the sea to labour islands or to people new countries which the *Sarkar* [government] had conquered; or made to apostatize; or marked down for future sacrifices to the deities who are supposed to watch over the stability of great railway bridges."[144] In some places, parents feared that the state kitchens, which as we shall see were opened on the work sites to feed the dependents of relief workers, were "poisoning the children." At one camp, parents evacuated all their children when a hospital assistant showed up. With the plague raging alongside the famine, hospitals had come to be understood as places not of healing but of certain death.[145] An American missionary stationed at Ahmednagar in the Bombay Presidency reported in 1898 that children taken to a relief kitchen had believed "the Government wanted to take them to South Africa." They were so frightened, he claimed, that they "jumped over the boundaries and ran away." One child reportedly cried out "that people were going to kill them."[146]

These rumors were part of a range of fears around the security of the body that had emerged after the tumultuous events of 1857 and grew in the last decades of the nineteenth century in reaction to colonial public health measures.[147] The introduction of smallpox vaccination, which became compulsory in many parts of India from the 1860s, and later experimental immunizations against cholera, plague, and typhoid provoked a range of fears around the state control of the colonial body in ways that were intimate and thus insidious. These intensified in response to the plague measures introduced in 1896, which included a campaign of urban cleansing, house-to-house inspections, quarantine, the policing of public gatherings, the removal of sufferers to hospitals and camps, the postmortem dissection of victims, and the disposal of their bodies in ways that contravened religious rites. In 1897, at the height of the famine and the plague that accompanied it, these measures sparked rioting and the spread of rumors that overlapped with fears that the government's distribution of cooked food was part of its wider plan to utilize the bodies of the helpless for its own "sinister" purposes.[148]

Local officials attempted to deal with these anxieties and encourage the use of their relief facilities by framing them not as institutions of the colonial state but rather in terms that would be culturally assimilable. The provision of cooked food as a form of relief during times of distress was not a British innovation. It was a form of charity that the precolonial rulers of India had often dispensed and that landowners furnished their tenants during food shortages as an expression of paternalistic responsibility.[149] During the nineteenth-century famines, landowners and the governments of the Princely States continued to provide this form of relief, often adopting quite "liberal measures."[150] Thus, when resistance to government establishments mounted, some administrators attempted to make their relief centers appear to be indigenous institutions. In Orissa during the 1866 famine, in Bihar during the 1873–4 famine, and in Madras during the 1876–8 famine, food was distributed at *dharamsalas* and at depots that the officials called *annachatras, choultries,* or *serais*.[151] *Dharamsalas* were rest houses or sanctuaries for pilgrims. The term *annachatra* meant "food canopy" in Sanskrit and denoted a place either linked to temples and monasteries, or furnished by a wealthy donor, where free meals were provided to pilgrims, mendicants, and ascetics. *Choultry* or *serai* had similar connotations (see Figure 3.1).[152] The government made use of these existing sites of charity and styled their own centers on these indigenous institutions that had little stigma in order to combat local resistance. E. A. Lugard, executive engineer of the Bhandara Division in the Central Provinces, found that concerns about using these services were not "maintained to the same extent where we styled the kitchens as *serais* (*dharamsala*) instead of poor-houses (*kangal khana*)."[153] Officials hoped that the use of these labels would domesticate these spaces by constructing them as Indian institutions associated with travel, pilgrimage, or spiritual care rather than colonial innovations linked to state relief, since the latter clearly provoked a range of anxieties. Unlike the United Kingdom's Poor Law Commissioners, whose parsimonious policies discouraged the destitute from applying for relief, India's famine officials actively attempted to encourage the needy to partake of gratuitous cooked food. Many local administrators clearly understood that the relief of a diverse and distrustful population required a degree of flexibility. The solutions they offered to these problems sometimes openly challenged the rules of political economy, even as public works remained the face of government famine relief.

Biopolitics and Children's Kitchens

By the last decades of the Victorian period, the colonial state increasingly focused its relief efforts on children. Feeding truly helpless subjects allowed the government to skirt some of the more vexing issues of political economy. But this was also a strategy of colonial development.

David Nally, Benjamin Siegel, Tehila Sasson, and James Vernon have argued that the policies and practices of famine relief must be located within the context of "colonial biopolitics." Following Michel Foucault's argument that the modern state derives its power and authority from its calculated management of the life, death, and health of its populations, they argue, the feeding of distant starving subjects should be understood as a political and economic strategy of the imperial state.[154] Anna Clark has positioned the 1890s as a key moment for the deployment of "humanitarian imperialism" as a technique of the "biopolitical control of populations."[155] If by the 1890s the object of gratuitous government relief was first and foremost the starving child, this was largely because the colonial government was harnessing this population's productivity for future exploitation. This was particularly true in a context in which famine itself became a justification for the intensification of economic, specifically agrarian, development of the subcontinent.[156] The feeding of children at kitchens established on the public works allowed the colonial state both to marshal a humanitarian discourse and to construct this form of gratuitous relief as an investment in empire rather than as a drain on its coffers or a disruption to the principle that able-bodied men were solely responsible for the upkeep of their dependents. To achieve this, the state cast Indians as inherently bad parents whose children needed to be saved by a benevolent paternalistic state.[157]

Until the famines of the 1890s, relief workers were given extra subsistence allowances to support their dependent children. Since many officials had reported that cash doles led to "great abuses," this system was eventually stopped, and instead, children's kitchens were established on many of the works to feed dependents.[158] Local officers were instructed to open kitchens so that these children could be fed "on the spot" instead of receiving cash payments to take home to their parents.[159] This ensured that the relief was "wholly expended on its professed object." Cash relief was "always liable to be abused and diverted to other objects," officials claimed. But when cooked food was issued, under the proviso that it must be eaten at the kitchen under the watchful gaze of state employees, the government could be certain that its relief reached its intended recipient: the helpless child of those who had availed themselves of the state's preferred method of relief, having signed on to labor on public works projects[160] (Figure 3.2).

Although the provision of children's kitchens was generally more costly than the cash dole, famine administrators claimed that relief workers were neglecting their children and diverting their allowances for other purposes or to supplement their own diets. There was no central directive to eliminate cash doles, but administrators across

Figure 3.2 The "Nursery" at the famine camp at Shetphal Tank, 1897. © The British Library Board, Photo 940/1(9).

India seemed to concur that, "there was no alternative but to either acquiesce in [the] maltreatment [of children] or to provide them with a daily meal."[161] Many public works projects in the 1896–7 famine thus undertook "special measures to secure that the children are properly fed," replacing the cash dole with kitchens providing cooked food.[162] Since the 1870s, officials had been concerned that "parents sometimes neglect [children] or deprive them of the food" because they were "starving" themselves and could not in this condition be "entrusted with the means of relieving their children." Some of the Famine Codes explicitly argued that this was justification for providing cooked food to children "eaten in the presence of the relief officer."[163] The discourse of negligent or cruel parents, however, only became widespread in the middle of the 1890s. If some have argued that "no particular attention" was given to child famine victims in 1896–7, a range of state records suggest that in fact quite the opposite was true.[164] As future revenue producers of the Raj, children received special consideration from the colonial state during the last famines of the nineteenth century precisely because their relief was tied to the policies of colonial development.

In covering the 1900 famine for the *Manchester Guardian*, Vaughan Nash reported that, "famine often breaks up family affection, and that under its stress children are sold or abandoned or robbed of their food by their parents. When the stomach presses against the spine, the heart may sometimes get displaced." Although he had also seen "half-savage parents with the death-pangs at their heart comforting their dying children," it was the former situation that government officials took to be the norm in the famines of the late 1890s.[165] As Andy Croll has argued, not all hungry bodies garnered the same amount of public sympathy in the 1890s. In the case of strike-induced hunger in England and Wales, it was only the "innocent" wives and children of striking miners and other industrial workers, not the equally hungry male strikers themselves, who became objects of compassion and received food aid. The former were starving and blameless, according to public opinion, while the latter had brought their hunger upon themselves.[166]

The ideological position that women and children were innocent victims and deserving of humanitarian intervention was enhanced at the turn of the century by the discourses of maternalism and child welfare. As Ellen Ross, Deborah Dwork, and Anna Davin have demonstrated, from the 1880s, increased state and voluntary attention was drawn to the practices of mothering among Britain's working poor. The desire to rear generations of healthy and fit imperial citizens to populate the empire resulted in legislation aimed at educating, protecting, nurturing, and preserving the health of British children. Acts to prevent cruelty to children, to extend compulsory education, and to provide school meals and medical inspection were all passed in the period from 1889 through 1907. At the same time, clinics geared at maternal and child health and schools to teach domestic and childcare skills to working-class mothers began to emerge as part of new concerns about the mothering practices of those responsible for rearing Britain's future imperial citizens.[167]

Just as the children of Britain's poor and working classes were being harnessed by the state as essential to the defense and population of the empire, so too were the children of colonial subjects imagined as resources of the Raj whose value was being compromised by "negligent" parenting and "savage" domestic practices. Since the eighteenth century, the colonial state had attempted to discipline the Indian family by outlawing domestic and sexual practices that did not accord with its civilizing mission. Infanticide, *sati* (widow-burning), child marriage, polygyny, prostitution, and miscegenation all came under fire from the state, which attempted to remake the Indian family to conform to British norms.[168] In the context of famine relief, in the 1890s, the colonial state attempted to act *in loco parentis*, deciding that the only way to save "the lives of the field labourers of the future" was to provide them cooked food and supervise their meals. Under the banner of rendering "a service" to "humanity," administrators thus assumed responsibility themselves for the feeding of their child "units," a term frequently used when calculating the relief accounts.[169] This was a means to shore up the next generation of agricultural laborers who would be responsible for producing revenue for the Government of India.

The Colonial Logics of *In Loco Parentis*

By the 1890s, the collective wisdom that Indian parents could not be trusted to care for their offspring gained momentum through constant repetition by British and Indian officials and observers alike to such an extent that this statement became enshrined in the Famine Codes of each province. They declared that, "experience having shown that starving parents very often cannot safely be entrusted with the means of relieving their children in time of famine, it is essential, where this is apprehended, that a daily supply of cooked food be issued to them under proper supervision."[170] Only two witnesses before the 1898 Famine Commission testified that parents fed their children well and would rather "starve themselves" than see their offspring suffer.[171] Many others parroted what had by this time become a well-known "fact" that rarely needed to be elaborated or supported precisely because it was consistent with well-established colonial narratives of the Indian family: that Indian parents were inherently selfish, negligent, and cruel, preferring to feed themselves even at the expense of their emaciated children.[172]

Many proponents of kitchens accused parents of grossly neglecting or deliberately starving their children so that they themselves could consume this portion of the family meal or save the child allowance for future use. Reports came from all over India during the 1896–7 famine that Indians "would allow their children to starve before they would starve themselves" and would even buy tobacco before provisioning their offspring.[173] The acting collector of Ganjam asserted that the Famine Code did not adequately cover the case of these children who were "deliberately starved by their parents in order that they may receive doles, which the parents (themselves fairly well nourished and able to work) consume."[174] Official accounts of the 1896–7 famine reiterated this point. T. W. Holderness, deputy secretary to the Government of India, argued that kitchens were frequently substituted for cash doles because of the "neglect of parents to feed their children, though receiving money for their food." It was found that they "either spent the extra allowance on themselves," he remarked, "or saved it against the day when the works would be closed."[175] This was an ironic statement given how much value those who favored market solutions placed on saving for a rainy (or in this case nonrainy) day. A report of this famine in the North-Western Provinces and Oudh similarly maintained that "it was sometimes found necessary to provide relief in the shape of cooked food for children neglected and starved by parents who appropriated the cash doles for their own uses."[176] In the 1896 Mysore Famine Code, cash allowances were permitted in some cases, but officers were alerted that the "danger" of this practice must "be constantly borne in mind." They were warned to "specially inspect the children and dependents so relieved; and, if the health and strength of many of them appear to be deteriorating," to replace the payments with cooked food from kitchens.[177] Relief officers quickly built consensus during the 1896–7 famine around the substitution of cooked food for cash doles.

It was not merely that cooked food be substituted for cash but that it should be issued to children "under proper supervision." When children were being fed at various institutions, "especial watchfulness" was required, argued an official report, for children "are liable to have the food snatched from them by other children, or by adults," or may be "induced by fear to save a part of it to give to their parents."[178] For this reason, the children had to be constantly supervised by the authorities and by specially selected female "nursery" supervisors, who ensured the children ate their food themselves and did not remove any from the kitchens.[179] The state thus deliberately removed the children from their parents for the purposes of feeding, treating them as individual "units" of future manpower that needed to be sustained rather than as part of a mutually dependent family.

Colonial officials used the bodies of Indian children as evidence of parental negligence or cruelty. As Thomas Laqueur and Karen Halttunen have argued, humanitarianism emerged in the late eighteenth century as a narrative form of evoking empathy for others that placed the suffering body at the very heart of these emotional and sentimental relationships.[180] According to the executive engineer of the Meerut Provincial Division of the North-Western Provinces and Oudh, it was "a noticeable feature throughout the famine that, whilst the adults improved in condition" once employed, their children "showed little or no signs of improvement" until cooked food was substituted for the cash dole.[181] As might be expected, noted another official, "the condition of the children is much better" where food rather than cash was dispensed, a statement often repeated during the 1899–1900 distress as well.[182] Other local administrators also testified that it was the "appearance" of the children that suggested neglect, claiming that the bodies of children showed "signs of privation" sooner than those of adults.[183] The superintending engineer for the Central Division of Bombay reported that when cash doles were given, the children "got thin and could not have been given the value of the payments made to their parents." "They got thin," he repeated, implying that their bodies were themselves proof of their parents' neglect.[184] The meaning of these children's bodies was even clearer when contrasted with those of their parents, officials often reported, claiming that many parents were in good physical condition "while their children were absolutely starving and emaciated."[185]

If the emaciated bodies of child famine victims served as indisputable evidence of parental neglect, some observers blamed the context in which the struggle for survival was so acute that both the social and natural orders were upended, hence Nash's maxim "when the stomach presses against the spine, the heart may sometimes get displaced." However, this too posited a presumed inherent Indian weakness not only of body but also of spirit and stamina that impacted the ability to form affective bonds in the same way as Europeans. During the famine of 1876–8, Digby maintained that, "it was found" that though Indian mothers had an "animal affection" for their children, they "loved tobacco and betel nut more."[186] Indians' affection for children, he suggested, was merely "animal" and instinctual rather than a deeply human bond; thus, it was quickly abandoned at moments of stress when other survival instincts kicked in. Many officials similarly argued that, "under the stress of want the natural affection of parents seemed to fail."[187] Parents' "callous neglect" of their children was consistently explained as resulting from the fact that their "natural instincts were weakened by continued scarcity." This implied that Indians were baser creatures driven by "animal affection" and not by higher sensibilities such as the sacred mother-child bond that was so central to ideals of the middle-class Victorian family.[188]

This interpretation of parental behavior, although it emphasized the material context, denigrated Indian familial bonds. In doing so, however, it also allowed some to refocus attention on the suffering of India's adult population. The president of the 1898 Famine Commission, former lieutenant-governor of the Punjab Sir J. B. Lyall, repeatedly cross-examined witnesses about their assumptions that parents could not be trusted to feed their children properly precisely in order to undermine this assertion. When asked by Lyall whether he thought that "in every country there are certain mothers who cannot be trusted to feed their children under similar conditions," the deputy commissioner of Bilaspur in the Central Provinces responded, "Perhaps; but I think generally mothers starve themselves to feed their children," implying that Indian mothers were inherently different.[189] In almost every other case, Lyall was able to manipulate witnesses into admitting that this neglect of children was not a deliberate act of calculated cruelty but stemmed instead from the parents' own suffering. When P. Gray, the deputy commissioner of the Lucknow district of Oudh, testified that kitchens were opened on the work sites "as soon as it was seen that mothers were neglecting their children," Lyall probed further. Mothers in India are "generally fond of their, children, are they not?" he asked, forcing the witness to acquiesce to this statement. He followed up by suggesting that any neglect could be explained by the parents' own privation. "If mothers on works stinted their children, is that not a sign that the mothers were much underfed?" Lyall suggested, implying that wages had perhaps been too low and thus casting blame back onto the state itself. "It might be argued so," replied Gray.[190] Lyall engaged in similar exchanges with a range of other witnesses, leading them to concur with his own opinion that any perceived neglect or abuse stemmed from the fact that parents were also "in a state of acute privation."[191]

The final report of the 1898 Famine Commission clearly reflected Lyall's desire not to blame parents in each and every case for neglecting their children without considering the context in which they too suffered. Lyall was one of very few to cast Indian parents as themselves victims of famine rather than as perpetrators of atrocities during famine. But even his empathetic engagement was not enough to overturn what had, by the end of the nineteenth century, become an established state prerogative: the right of the colonial government to act *in loco parentis* for the purpose of feeding children even when the parents were alive, had not abandoned their children, and were capable of making decisions on their behalf. The 1898 report acknowledged that the neglect of children during famine "may or may not be for reasons beyond the control of the parents." It nevertheless determined that state-run kitchens were necessary to meet the "requirements of young children who in times of acute famine run the risk of being neglected by their parents," reinforcing the widespread view that poor parenting was the norm.[192]

At the turn of the century, both local officials and the Government of India took credit for having undertaken a humanitarian mission to sustain the next generation of colonial subjects. The official narrative of the 1896–7 famine in the North-Western Provinces and Oudh stressed that "thousands of little children owe their lives" to the switch from cash doles to cooked food "eaten by the children in [the] presence" of state employees.[193] According to one official, the relief kitchen "may, without exaggeration, be said to have saved the lives of thousands of children."[194] An array of state agents thus cast their gratuitous provision of cooked food to child famine victims as part of a range of interventionist practices aimed at the welfare of imperial children. The same imperative that had stimulated the state to introduce services targeted primarily at working-class children in the metropole also justified the nourishment of Indian children at the government's expense. Children's kitchens, which became central to government famine relief during the late nineteenth century, were part of a wider state platform that Anna Davin has demonstrated linked "imperialism and motherhood" in a variety of ways.[195]

The 1898 Famine Commission Report asserted that "the saving of human life" must take precedence over "economy."[196] Yet by the turn of the century, humanitarianism had ceased to stand in opposition to imperial economic planning. Rather, it had become integral to it. The state saved these children from starvation largely because they were the key to future imperial revenue production. The concern of the modern colonial state to maintain life was thus intimately tied to anxieties about productivity.[197] The executive engineer to the Chhattisgarh States Roads Division in the Central Provinces declared that "a considerable saving of life is undoubtedly effected by feeding these units at the kitchen" under strict supervision.[198] Indian children were always already "units," resources of the Raj to be accumulated for potential use as "the field labourers of the future."[199] If as Nally has argued in relation to Ireland, famines "can serve a strategic function" for colonial states,[200] the children's kitchens that formed a significant part of state famine relief at the turn of the century are best understood in this light. They allow us to see how and why recurrent famines challenged the state to rethink the rules of classical political economy. In addition, this form of state feeding compels us to reassess humanitarian aid to famine victims not only in terms of its failure to save millions from starvation but as a tool of Britain's larger imperial project.

4   Tommy's Tummy
Provisioning POWs during World War I

The famine camps of the late-Victorian period, which played a role in the state's modern famine relief efforts, also provided an important model for the concentration camps and prisoner of war (POW) camps that became central technologies of twentieth-century warfare.[1] During World War I, the British government supplemented the rations of British POWs held in German camps, a population that included both combatants and civilians. This raised troubling questions, however, about who was ultimately responsible for keeping these men in health. The British state's multiple attempts to provision their own POWs, even when they were not obliged to do so under the extant international agreements, were made in a context in which food itself had heightened significance as its control had become central to Britain's military strategy. This involved the blockade of German ports, which led to widespread hunger among the continent's civilian population. But the feeding of POWs also threw into stark relief the tension between providing what nutritional scientists purported to be a sufficient and nutritious diet and furnishing food that was culturally familiar and could sustain British prisoners not merely as physical organisms but as whole persons whose national identities were a particularly salient aspect of the self during wartime. The feeding of POWs thus posed a special problem for Britain's wartime state.

As scholarship on World War I has turned its focus from the trenches to the camps – where millions of combatants and civilians were held as POWs during the hostilities[2] – historians have reaffirmed narratives that foreground the centrality of hunger and starvation to the experience of captivity. Reproducing these familiar accounts of privation, which seem to resist interpretation, however, risks closing down more complicated analyses of state food policies and practices. Unlike paupers, criminals, and some famine victims, POWs were not positioned by the state as having failed to thrive in the economic marketplace. In fact, many were hailed as model productive citizens. As loyal subjects who were sacrificing their bodies for the safety of the nation, British

POWs' claims on their state's food resources thus raised a series of complex issues in a climate in which all belligerent nations understood that food was a critical weapon of war. The decisions made by the British government in relation to the rationing of its subjects held as POWs were in the end shaped both by science and by culture and were always already political even when uneconomical.

A Frightful Starving Match

At the turn of the century, Polish banker Jean de Bloch predicted that "the future of war" was "not fighting but famine, not the slaying of men but the bankruptcy of nations and the break up of the whole social organisation."[3] Bloch was prescient: the first "total war" was won and lost as much on the home fronts as in the trenches. While it was a distinctly modern war fought with industrial armaments, one of the most critical weapons was the oldest of resources – food.[4] The industrialization and globalization of food supply networks in the late nineteenth century meant that the belligerent nations were no longer self-sufficient and fed their populations through the importation of widely traded food commodities.[5] The disruption of the shipment of food supplies during the war made it increasingly difficult for European governments to ensure that an adequate food supply was available for either their militaries or their civilian populations. For Germany, this was compounded by the fact that it had gone to war against its major food suppliers.[6] This widespread shortage of provisions led to domestic unrest, causing several of the warring states to question whether either military or civilian morale could be sustained long enough to achieve victory. Russia withdrew its fighting forces in 1917 after a revolution caused at least in part by widespread hunger on the home front. In 1918, the German population revolted against their wartime government, having suffered severe deprivations throughout the hostilities. While this revolution had begun as a naval mutiny, civilians were soon rioting in the streets primarily because the military had been consuming a disproportionate amount of the country's limited foodstuffs and leaving the home front population quite literally starving.[7] That the United Kingdom could draw on the output of its colonies and was supplied by its ally, the United States, was a decisive factor in its ability to quell home front food fights.[8] Indeed, some historians contend that the diet and health of the British population actually improved during the war.[9] Britain's eventual victory over Germany owed much to the fact that the latter had been brought to its knees in good part by political fallout from chronic and severe food shortages. World War I, assessed George Bernard Shaw, was above all else "a frightful starving match."[10]

It was not just that Germany did not have the extensive colonial and diplomatic relationships that would have allowed it to continue to import much-needed meats, grains, and fats. Its population's chronic hunger was largely a product of Britain's primary military strategy – the blockade. Before the outbreak of hostilities, Germany was importing at least one-third of the calories its human population consumed (most of which arrived via shipping). Britain had thus hoped to avoid a large-scale land war by using its naval power to blockade the Continental ports and prevent the importation of staple food items. This was not intended as a siege that would literally starve out the German people. Rather, it was an attempt to disrupt the economy. Britain calculated that its blockade would compel the enemy to produce all of its own foodstuffs, thus diverting labor and capital from war industries to agriculture and other aspects of food manufacture.[11] The war would not be fought at the front, British officials theorized, but in the kitchen and in the wider economy. Although ultimately Britain was forced to raise a massive land army, the blockade proved to be a decisive factor in the Allied victory, since Germany's increasingly serious food crises eventually led to economic collapse and political defeat.[12]

If the blockade was a strategic military success, it created logistical and moral dilemmas for Britain in relation to its subjects taken as POWs as it compromised Germany's ability to feed them adequately. World War I marked a significant shift in the ways in which POWs were managed. During the hostilities, prisoners were taken on an unprecedented scale and distributed among camps established for this purpose across the European nations and their colonial possessions. By 1918, more than 185,000 British servicemen were being held prisoner alongside other Allied troops in over 100 German camps.[13] In addition, over the course of the war, approximately 5,000 British civilians had been interned at Ruhleben, a camp for enemy aliens on the outskirts of Berlin.[14] The treatment of these POWs – both combatants and civilians – was governed by the 1907 Hague Convention on Land Warfare that had sought to curtail abuses and standardize how belligerent governments handled captives. When the war broke out in 1914, for the first time, there existed a shared international legal framework for the humane treatment of military captives and civilian internees.[15] The Hague Convention stipulated that, "the Government into whose hands POWs have fallen is charged with their maintenance," including board, lodging, and clothing. This meant that POWs – both captured combatants and interned civilians – were to be fed by their captor state rations equivalent to its peacetime army, although officers were housed separately and allowed to organize their own messing. These agreements assumed, however, that food for these purposes would be readily available.

Despite the international agreements, there had been no prewar planning for the maintenance of prisoners and little evidence of an integrated uniform "camp system." This meant that there was "considerable variation in the conditions" across time and space. According to Lord Grenfell, a veteran military leader, the "real fact" of the matter was there was no "settled system" of rationing in use throughout Germany; thus, camp commandants were left "to treat these unfortunate British soldiers in whatever way they please."[16] James W. Gerard, American Ambassador to Germany from 1913 until the United States entered the war in 1917, also emphasized this point. He noted that district military commanders were largely independent, neither reporting to the war department nor answerable to local civilian officials. This had led to a situation, he claimed, in which the "treatment of prisoners varied greatly."[17] These differences among the camp regimes, including how their staffs managed the food parcels that families and friends regularly sent to prisoners, made it difficult to assess whether British POWs were being adequately fed.

Under Article 16 of the Hague Convention, POWs were allowed to receive parcels free of any customs duties. This included foodstuffs. Parcels leaving Britain that weighed 11 pounds or less could be sent through the regular postal service; heavier ones could be conveyed by the American Express Company.[18] Until January of 1918, when the British government put an end to the practice, individuals could also contract with businesses or charities located in neutral countries (such as Switzerland) to send food supplies directly to prisoners held in German camps[19] (Figure 4.1). Germany and the United Kingdom also had a reciprocal agreement allowing food parcels to be sent for general distribution among POWs not already receiving them from family, friends, or voluntary associations.[20] Thus, over the course of the war, a considerable amount of food entered POW camps by post. Although parcels leaving the United Kingdom went first by ship before being transported across the European continent via the railways, even perishable food such as cheese and bacon often arrived in "splendid condition."[21] As hunger became more acute in Germany due to the effects of the blockade; however, these parcels were increasingly liable to be pilfered either by railway workers or by camp staff. American Express numbered all its packages, recorded their weights on the packaging, and (sometimes successfully) sought compensation from German authorities when

Figure 4.1 Crossen Prisoner of War Camp, Germany. Handing out the post. ICRC Archives (ARR), World War I. Crossen. Prisoners of war camp. Distributing parcels, V-P-HIST-E-05262.

items had been removed en route to their destination.[22] Britain's public postal service does not seem to have employed similar safeguards; thus, prisoners and their families frequently complained to the government about the theft of precious foodstuffs. The Foreign Office was well aware of the issue but was wary of doing anything to jeopardize the reciprocal agreements that allowed Britain to send food into the camps for their nationals.[23] When the German government "emphatically denied" claims that pilfering had become routine, Britain did not openly contest this, preferring to focus on what it could control, such as the total amount of food permitted to leave the United Kingdom bound for the camps.[24]

There has been wide consensus among historians that these food parcels played an essential role in sustaining British POWs during the Great War and that without them many would have starved.[25] Indeed, veterans frequently framed their reminiscences with accounts of "the agony of hunger."[26] But during the war, the Foreign Office and the War Office were bombarded by contradictory reports, some emanating from prisoners themselves, as to whether or not the German rations were adequate and whether they ate their food parcels out of need or preference.[27] Furthermore, there were those who stated that they ate

only the food that arrived in parcels from United Kingdom "on principle," evading the question entirely of whether the rations were in fact
sufficient.[28] Others used the reverse ethical reasoning and took only
German rations, confusing the moral issues at stake in these choices
and making it more difficult to assess who was eating what and why.[29]

That there appeared to be no centralized oversight of the German
camps, and that narratives about the need for parcels were divergent, raised
questions for the British government about how much it could trust that
its subjects across this "carceral archipelago" were being sufficiently
provisioned.[30] That its own blockade had substantially limited the
amount of food available in Germany exacerbated concerns that British
POWs were suffering alongside German civilians. When Dr. Alonzo E.
Taylor, a neutral American inspector and scientific advisor to the US
Food Administration, reported on the deteriorating food conditions at
Ruhleben in 1916, the implications of his findings generated heated
debate among British officials. "It is preposterous," asserted Lord
Newton, assistant under-secretary of state for foreign affairs, paymaster-
general, and soon to be appointed controller of the Foreign Office's
Prisoners of War Department (POWD), "that we should be expected
to feed these men" when that duty, by international law, fell to the captor state.[31] Lord Robert Cecil, the under-secretary of state for Foreign
Affairs, similarly considered it "very undesirable to relieve the German
Government of their obligation to feed the prisoners."[32] Foreign Office
staffer Sir Horace Rumbold argued that the German authorities had
deliberately reduced the official food rations at Ruhleben and by doing
so had "accumulated a large sum of money – estimated at anything
between 60,000 and 2,000,000 marks – which should have been spent
on those rations."[33] Sir Edward Grey, who served as foreign secretary
from 1905 until the end of 1916, was insistent that whatever the British
response was to the food situation at Ruhleben, he was in no way admitting the "liability [of the British government] to feed their prisoners in
Germany, which is the recognised duty of the captor Government," and
had significant implications regarding the financing of the war.[34]

The German government countered these accusations by arguing
that if the food at Ruhleben was less abundant and less varied than
prisoners themselves might desire, "the blame for this must be imputed
solely to the British Government, who by every means in their power,
and without respect to their admissibility in international law, strive to
restrict the import of foodstuffs" to the detriment of Germany's own
civilian population. "It is no more than just," the German authorities concluded, that "British civilian prisoners [should] also be made
to suffer hereby." The British government, "who aim at the starvation

of the German nation," Berlin argued, could not therefore demand increased rations for its POWs.[35] This argument was quite difficult for the British government to undermine. As early as December of 1915, B. W. Young, honorary secretary of the Prisoners of War Help Committee (POWHC), a philanthropic organization that had been formed by the War Office (and was partially funded by the Treasury) to dispatch parcels to British POWs, claimed that the Germans "could not give what they had not got." He implied that the moral questions surrounding wartime feeding were much more complex than some might have it.[36] Sir Herbert Belfield, head of the War Office's Directorate of Prisoners of War, similarly reminded those keen to retaliate for underfeeding that "a large portion of the civil population of Germany is but little, if any, better off than our own people at Ruhleben." We are doing all we can, he claimed, to prevent food from entering Germany; thus, we are "making it as hard as possible for Germany to feed either our men or her own population." "Can, in fact, Germany afford to feed our men better?" Belfield queried.[37] His colleague Sir Bertram Blakiston Cubitt, assistant under-secretary of state for the War Office, agreed that the Germans could "reasonably say, and with truth, that the bad feeding of their prisoners is mainly caused by our blockade."[38]

If they were among the first to feel the effects of the blockade, POWs were also best placed to see what was happening on the ground in relation to Germany's food supplies.[39] According to repatriated Ruhlebenites, when the camp administration reduced the bread ration in 1915, it declared, "Your Government wants to starve us out. Very well, then, you shall be the first to be starved out!"[40] Norman Cowan, a POW at Quedlinburg, similarly recalled that all questions lobbed at his German guards about the dwindling camp rations were met with the same response: "Tell your navy not to squeeze us, tell them to release their stranglehold and we will feed you."[41] Alec Waugh, older brother of the novelist Evelyn Waugh, was held prisoner during the war at Mainz. He wrote in 1919 that while the "starvation of prisoners has become almost an axiom, and indeed they were miserably underfed," so was the "entire German people"; given there was only enough food in the country "for a bare existence," Waugh argued, the Germans had chosen "that the diet of the enemy should come last."[42] Waugh's tone was sympathetic rather than belligerent and suggests that even POWs understood that their provisioning raised larger moral and tactical questions that were not so easily answered in the midst of a seemingly endless war. But some British POWs also took advantage of the food situation in Germany. Although it was against the camp regulations to do so, prisoners who found themselves "overstocked" with perishable items frequently sold the contents of the parcels they received from home to their guards or German civilians who loitered at the camp gates for this purpose.[43] This was precisely what the British government feared: that if too much food entered the camps for British POWs, some of it would eventually wind up in the enemy's hands and undermine the blockade.

Government Food Control in Wartime

The British government's decision to intervene in the provisioning of its own nationals held as POWs thus required extremely delicate political maneuvers and must be understood within the broader context of wartime food control. As early as 1915, Grey declared that "if there is a danger that British prisoners in Germany will be exposed to starvation, it will be the duty of His Majesty's Government to provide them with food" at its own expense.[44] Britain in fact encouraged its allies also to supply food to their POWs so that Germany could not refuse to let in British supplies on the grounds of favoritism.[45] If the German government emphatically repudiated the suggestion that they were not adhering to their obligations under the Hague Convention, it nevertheless granted permission for bulk parcels to be dispatched from the United Kingdom. As Heather Jones has argued, the German authorities had long encouraged the Allies to send food parcels into their camps in order to justify reducing the rations they provided.[46] Rumbold's 1916 declaration that, "the food sent to Ruhleben from this country is, of course, sent privately and government have nothing to do with it," was thus disingenuous.[47] Indeed, J. Davidson Ketchum, who had been interned at Ruhleben, reported quite the opposite. He maintained that the British government had "largely fed and supplied" these civilian prisoners.[48] Though neither statement is entirely accurate, the British government had everything to do with the food that reached its civilian and combatant POWs from the United Kingdom and neutral countries, and it grew more interventionist as the war dragged on.

The scale of World War I had necessitated government intervention into private and economic life across Europe, particularly in relation to food.[49] Initially, the British state had been wary of introducing government controls, preferring as much as possible to continue with "business as usual." But Secretary of State for War Herbert Kitchener's decision to raise a large land army, and the introduction of conscription in 1916 (which considerably expanded its forces), stimulated a variety of experiments in state control as private interests had to become subordinate to the successful prosecution of the war. These were not part of a coherent policy. Rather, they were introduced piecemeal and effected civilians on the home front in varying degrees, perhaps none more so than food control.[50] The Ministry of Food, established in 1916, was one such experiment. It was staffed partly by temporary administrators – businessman largely drawn from the catering, brewing, and retail food trades – who initially resisted rationing and other attempts to interfere in the market.[51] It was not ideological commitments, therefore, but rather the need to provision such a large land army, a strategy that deviated from Britain's initial planning for naval warfare, that led to increased state intervention in the economy in general and centralized control of foodstuffs in particular.[52]

It was not merely the state that no longer found laissez-faire a tenable policy during wartime. As Frank Trentmann has argued, inflation, shortages, market failures, skyrocketing prices, and profiteering during the war led to a widespread loss of confidence in free trade, the hallmark of the liberal agenda.[53] In this context "choice, cheapness, and competition" had lost their attraction for the public to be replaced with "stability and coordination," particularly in relation to the food supply. Mounting anxieties and protests on the home front about dwindling food supplies as the war entered its fourth year, particularly in the context of German U-boat attacks on British ships and the Russian Revolution, raised the specter of widespread industrial and civil unrest. Public opinion and its impact on national security also contributed to the government control over food as the war dragged on, the introduction of rationing in 1918 marking the end of any attempt to preserve a market economy.[54] Thus, World War I reshaped attitudes toward government and its responsibility for the well-being of the British people in good part because of its role in imposing controls over the nation's food supply.[55]

If the provisioning of combatant POWs can be seen as an extension of military rationing in general, which was necessarily under centralized control, the decision to provide some maintenance to interned civilians had a more complex logic. As Nicoletta Gullace has argued, World War I redefined British citizenship not as a series of rights and privileges that accrued to the individual but in terms of one's service and sacrifice to the nation.[56] As noncombatants who had been denied the opportunity to demonstrate their patriotism either by enlisting or by heeding the call of conscription, interned men were forced to construct their sacrifice in other ways. British civilian POWs thus positioned their internment as "a service to their country because their liberation cannot be secured without the simultaneous release into Germany of a considerably larger number of trained fighting men."[57] Internment, they claimed, was patriotic work that demonstrated their good citizenship and entitled them to treatment that was similar to combatant POWs. The government's call for voluntary food economization on the home front, and the introduction of rationing, also underscored the bodily sacrifices being made by British civilians at home. The state thus felt obliged to ensure that its subjects held as enemy aliens overseas were fed neither considerably better nor notably worse than British nationals on the home front, which required constant government oversight and intervention.

Like all of the state's efforts to tighten its control over foods supplies, the schemes to provision British combatant and noncombatant POWs were varied and emerged gradually over the course of the war as several government departments attempted to ensure POWs were sustained without that food falling into the hands of the enemy. Even before the food situation in Germany became acute, the state dispatched supplemental food supplies to the camps with the aid of the US Embassy at Berlin, the American Express Company, and the American International Commission at Rotterdam in the neutral Netherlands.[58] In addition to this food, the state provided civilian POWs who had no private means "relief" payments of 5 German marks per week so that they could purchase extra food at camp canteens (though these stocked fewer and fewer items over the course of the hostilities). These payments had initially been structured as loans, but as the war dragged on, this appeared increasingly untenable and parsimonious especially given that many internees had lost all means of financial support.[59] In addition to these relief payments, Britain established a fund administered by the US Embassy in Berlin for the care of British POWs and asked Gerard to purchase extra food supplies locally for the Ruhlebenites.[60] Most significantly, the Foreign Office and War Office formed and subsidized the Central Prisoners of War Committee (CPOWC), having disbanded the POWHC. The government charged the CPOWC with regulating the number and weight of food parcels leaving the United Kingdom for German camps. This was to ensure that POWs were adequately fed but neither received more food than civilians on the home front nor became overstocked with items that could then be sold to Germans.[61] Given these and other government schemes, Conrad Hoffman, secretary of the International Committee of Young Men's Christian Associations in Charge of Prisoner-of-War Work in Germany, claimed that British POWs fared much better than their Eastern Europeans allies "for their respective governments sent in food in large quantities to care for them."[62]

In a variety of different but interrelated ways, the state was intimately involved in both the policies developed to provision British POWs and the practices of feeding associated with them. Despite the seeming clarity of international law, which placed the onus for maintenance entirely on the captor state, the question of responsibility for the maintenance of POWs was much more complicated in practice. That a baffling variety of government departments – including but not limited to the Foreign Office, the War Office, the Home Office, the Colonial Office, the India Office, the Admiralty, the Board of Trade, and the Treasury[63] – were involved in feeding POWs, even when they were not compelled to do so, reveals the state's investment in the health of POWs, their anxiety that the enemy would not uphold its duties under international law, and their recognition that Britain itself had made it almost impossible for Germany to fulfill these obligations. The decisions made in regards to the POW diet, however, also reveal a tension at play throughout the war between the idea that food was fuel for the body whose physiological needs could be disinterestedly calculated, and the fact that food also carried cultural meaning and was central to national identity, particularly in the context of a patriotic war.

The Deployment of Nutritional Expertise

World War I was a major experiment in dietetics. While large numbers of people were being killed by the new technologies of modern warfare, many others were deliberately being kept alive and in basic health in POW camps with the goal of repatriation. According to J. C. Drummond, who would become the chief scientific advisor to the Ministry of Food during World War II, World War I provided "the first occasion in history" when scientists were able to study nutritional problems "by precise methods and to offer advice on their solution."[64] The state agencies responsible for overseeing POW camps purported to deploy this nutritional expertise in the construction of the dietaries in order to address concerns about both underfeeding and malnutrition. How they did so, however, was highly contested.[65] As Dana Simmons has argued, world war "transformed nutrition into a medical population science, with human experiment at its core."[66]

For food scientists working in this period, the components of a healthy diet consisted of a correct balance between protein, fat, and carbohydrates, on the one hand, and the total calories provided, on the other. While there were numerous complaints regarding the quantity, quality, and taste of the provisions within the camps, these diets were often defended or challenged based on whether they were sufficient to maintain physical strength and bodily and mental health by appealing to what scientists and government officials claimed were an increasingly universal set of standards.[67] This was despite the fact that neither the British nor the German government seemed to hold their nutritional experts in high regard, reducing them to subordinate positions in relation to the oversight of the state's wartime food policies.[68] Discussions of feeding within the camps could nevertheless be undertaken from what was now cast as an objective scientific standpoint and framed by the discourse of food values, which, though available in the nineteenth century, had gained little traction in relation to either prison or famine feeding. This did not make these debates any less political. In fact quite the opposite was true, not merely because statistics could be manipulated to serve a variety of different ends. Rather, as James Vernon has argued, it was because hunger "hurt all the more when it was understood to be the result of misgovernment, rather than the unavoidable consequence of natural or providential laws."[69] If one knew what made a diet sufficient, and were bound by international legal agreements to furnish it, providing anything less had political ramifications. This was complicated by a fact, evident to all, that the feeding of POWs occurred in a context in which the resources necessary to meet these legal and moral requirements were unavailable precisely because of strategic wartime food policies.

Although the rations provided in its own POW camps diminished in quantity, quality, and variety over the course of the war, the British government defended them in relation to the latest nutritional sciences. Those assessing the POW dietary relied on James Lane Notter and Sir Robert Hammill Firth's *The Theory and Practice of Hygiene,* first published in 1896 and revised in 1900 and 1908. The British government was, however, equally content to draw on Continental sources. This was intended to dispel any notion that there were national biases in food science and implied that standards generated by this research were in fact objective and could be applied to German and English bodies equally. This was by no means self-evident. As Chapter 2 demonstrated, prison authorities had as recently as 1900 questioned whether the "different European races" required the same amount of foodstuffs for daily subsistence and had been wary of applying German calculations to British bodies.[70] When challenged by the Austro-Hungarian authorities about the diet provided in the United Kingdom's camps, the Foreign Office turned to Austria's own nutritional experts.[71] More often the British government appealed to the evidence provided by neutral inspectors from the Swiss and Swedish Legations to defend its POW dietaries, claiming that these inspectors were well versed in the nutritional sciences.[72]

British officials repeatedly argued that their POW dietaries had been constructed in consultation with "medical authorities" that had "prescribed" the "minimum" level of particular foodstuffs needed to keep prisoners in health, thus acknowledging that food provision was now to be understood as requiring specialized medical knowledge.[73] The state maintained that the dietaries in force at Knockaloe and Douglas – its civilian internment camps on the Isle of Man – had been carefully compiled "on the highest medical advice in consultation with the Ministry of Food."[74] At these and other camps on the mainland, Dr. O. F. N. Treadwell, a "medical authority" from the Prison Commission, served as the liaison officer between the local administration and the Ministry of Food on issues relating to diet.[75] This suggests that the government's accumulated knowledge about mass feeding garnered from other institutional contexts could be transferred to this new setting. At both of the Isle of Man camps, a medical officer was responsible for inspecting the uncooked and cooked food, presumably to ensure not only quantity and quality but also nutritional content.[76] Before changing the ration scale, the government departments overseeing the camps often sought medical advice. At a 1917 British interdepartmental conference on the rationing of POW camps, milk was removed from the dietary but not before establishing that it was unnecessary from a medical point of view.[77] When the government replaced 4 ounces of the bread ration with broken biscuits, it defended the alteration on the basis that, so far as "food value" was concerned, the biscuits were equivalent to the bread.[78] In 1918, when POWs complained about the addition of beans to the dietary, the War Office retorted that this food item had "been made the subject of special investigation" and that its "nutritive quality" had "been fully established."[79]

The British government thus justified the decisions it made about the provisioning of enemy POWs by appealing to a seemingly apolitical objective standard. Having this universal standard and an international obligation to meet it, allowed the British government to defend its feeding practices to the German authorities, to the POWs themselves, and also to its own people, some of whom argued that the "Huns" were being scandalously "pampered" within the United Kingdom's internment camps, while British citizens suffered from increasing food shortages and restrictions.[80] At every turn, the British government argued that it had made scientific inquiries into the feeding of POWs using a range of international experts as a guide and had "established beyond doubt" that the rations supplied at its own camps were "sufficient both in quality and quantity." British officials continued to insist throughout the war that "medical expert evidence" supported their claims even as they gradually reduced their rations, introduced inferior substitutes for items in short supply, and buried reports that exposed their rations as only slightly more nutritious than those supplied in the German camps.[81]

Using its own camp dietaries as a model and as a bargaining chip, the British government demanded that the "continuous and careful supervision of the food under co-operation of medical officers" also be carried out in the Continental camps.[82] Concerned about feeding in the camps for combatant prisoners a year into the war, Cecil asked Gerard if he could dispatch "a responsible American medical man" to investigate the provisions issued to the military POWs in two or three camps. Cecil asked for a "definitive and authoritative statement" as to whether the food provided was "sufficient for the maintenance of the prisoners in good health under the conditions of their internment."[83] Gerard called on Dr. B. W. Caldwell, director of the American Red Cross Sanitary Commission, who subsequently visited the camps at Klein Wittenberg and Altdamm to inspect.[84] The following year, Taylor was tasked with reporting on the dietaries at Ruhleben. Rumbold suggested that Dr. A. W. J. MacFadden, a food inspector with the Local Government Board (the government agency that oversaw many of the state's public health initiatives), should confer with Taylor as, according to Rumbold, MacFadden had "so much special experience on health and diet questions."[85] The British government thus ensured that its own experts, neutral American medical men, and later neutral Dutch authorities were supervising the dietaries of British men held as POWs to ensure that proper feeding along scientific lines was taking place.

The Testing Ground for the New Sciences of Nutrition

The new science of food values became an important tool for assessing camp dietaries. German regulations stated that the daily fare provided in their camps "must be sufficient for the proper nourishment" of the men.[86] The word "nourishing" and its variants, which were used frequently in official communications, had a variety of meanings. Sometimes nourishing was synonymous with merely being fed and at others it connoted the feeling of being well fed, particularly with either comforting or "body-building" foods. These ambiguities were complicated by the fact that an international team of inspectors – Swiss, Swedish, Dutch, American – deployed the term in their communiqués, drawing on their own cultural assumptions. Increasingly, however, the word nourishment was associated with an objective standard that could be measured. Foodstuffs could be evaluated based on their "nourishing value,"[87] a term increasingly synonymous with "nutritive value,"[88] and not just on their quantity or the comfort they provided. Thus, a meal might not be large, but might still be classed as nourishing if it consisted of the right kinds of foods. During World War I, nourishment more often than not suggested a scientific understanding of proper nutrition that could be objectively evaluated.

This idea that one could be suffering not necessarily from want of food but malnutrition had emerged in the 1890s from biochemical and physiological laboratory studies and social surveys of diets undertaken by researchers working in the United States, the United Kingdom, Germany, and elsewhere in Europe.[89] The major innovation of this turn-of-the-century food science was the ability to assess a diet based on its calories and its balance of essential nutrients: calculations that had only begun to be used in the planning of prison dietaries at the very end of the nineteenth century and appear to have made almost no impact on famine management. This allowed meals containing significantly different foods to be "objectively" evaluated in relation to each other.[90] It was also convenient at a time when food was limited as it meant that appropriate substitutes could be furnished when particular staples were in short supply. Sprats could be exchanged for smelts, swedes for turnips, split peas for dried beans, rice for oatmeal, not to mention the range of *ersatz* products that German scientists developed during the war to serve as inferior, but adequate, substitutes for essential foods and beverages.[91]

The belligerent governments understood that it was not merely the amount of food that mattered but its constituent components as malnutrition posed as much of a danger to health as underfeeding. In the interwar period, as we shall see in Chapter 5, malnutrition was intimately linked to vitamin deficiency diseases. Knowledge of vitamins was, however, still in its infancy during World War I. Historians have argued that it was the war itself (which provided nutritional statistics on large populations) that helped to advance research into the role of vitamins within the diet.[92] But very little medical attention was in fact paid to the lack of fresh fruit and vegetables within the POW diet. While prisoners often complained about the lack of fresh vegetables,[93] and some camps had or were encouraged to plant vegetable gardens,[94] only once, in all the voluminous correspondence on POW feeding that crossed the desk of British officials, did anyone raise concerns about scurvy.[95] This may have been because the abundance of potatoes in the POW diet provided sufficient vitamin C, a fact later confirmed by studies undertaken in World War II.[96] Food scientists like Taylor argued that the diet should contain "certain substances of unknown chemical nature that are at present grouped under the term vitamins" found in vegetables and the coverings of grains, but he gave these foods short shrift in his dietary analyses.[97] Indeed, even what counted as a vegetable was not self-evident. In the dietary for the Cologne prison, rice and other grains were classified as vegetables. In fact, rice was typically used as a substitute for fresh vegetables or legumes in the rations provided in British POW camps, suggesting that the significance of the vitamins found in fresh fruit and vegetables was not yet widely theorized.[98] Medical practitioners taken as POWs did, however, identify occurrences within the camps of beriberi, a vitamin deficiency disease associated with rice-based diets. Members of the Royal Army Medical Corps drew the attention of their German overseers to the prevalence of beriberi in camps where polished white rice, which unlike brown rice lacked thiamine, was central to the diet.[99] The British had encountered beriberi in India; however, Germans had little experience with rice-based diets, and thus this knowledge was newly acquired during the war.[100]

If vitamins did not occupy a significant place within debates over the POW dietary, protein, fat, and carbohydrates were central to the food analysis performed on POW dietaries. Proteins, Notter and Firth had maintained, contained the elements of which the essential tissues and organs of the body were made, while fats and carbohydrates provided energy and heat.[101] Although there were noticeable disagreements between experts as to the necessary daily intake of these types of foods, the data generated by scientists studying nutrition provided guidelines for calculating "the proportionate supply of Proteids, Carbo-hydrates, and fats, being physiologically sufficient to maintain health."[102] When Caldwell had been tasked with investigating the diets of British POWs in 1915, he had found the food at the German camps of good quality and sufficient in quantity but lacking in the essential elements of a well-balanced and satisfactory diet. He noted that the rations lacked protein and fat and had a superabundance of vegetables and carbohydrates. He thus recommended that extra fat and protein be provided during winter.[103] When Taylor reported on the diet at Ruhleben the following year he found it deficient in both "protein-carrying foods" and in fats, as Germany was deploying almost all of its available vegetable fats to manufacture glycerine for use in propellants and explosives.[104] In April of 1918, six random German camp dietaries analyzed by Dutch inspectors revealed enormous disparities in nutrients.[105] According to Cubitt, despite differences among camps, the protein provided was consistently "far too low," the fat so limited as to "actually endanger life," and the carbohydrates, "totally inadequate."[106] By most standards then, British officials concluded, these dietaries were nutritionally insufficient.[107]

Although POWs seemed to be at risk of malnutrition at least in some of the camps, in the end, the belligerent governments tended to focus most of their attention on calories, which largely signified the amount of food provided not necessarily how it broke down into key components of a healthy diet. Despite a significant amount of research that had been undertaken before the war on the body's daily energy requirements, expert opinion varied as to the number of calories required to maintain health. Notter and Firth provided tables of the caloric intake of those engaged in a variety of types of work that they had culled from British social surveys. These suggested that those doing light work relied on a diet of about 2,500 calories, those doing ordinary "muscular work" required 3,300, and those engaged in heavy manual labor needed a daily intake of as much as 4,400.[108] British officials also drew on the work of German physiologists Max Rubner and Carl von Voit who prescribed 2,800–3,000 calories for a man in ordinary work and an additional 500 calories for those doing heavy labor.[109] These were significantly lower than the standards set by the American Wilbur Atwater (3,100) and the German Joseph König (3,055), the latter having been used by authorities to determine appropriate prison dietaries in Scotland at the turn of the century.[110] When recommending an appropriate diet for the British public under a rationing scheme, Dr. D. Noel Paton, regius professor of physiology at the University of Glasgow, told the War Cabinet that 2,660 calories would be necessary for men on heavy industrial work, severely undercutting his Continental colleagues.[111]

Food scientists differed not only because research could produce different results but because the calorie was never merely an "innocuous" measurement. According to Nick Cullather, its main purpose was to "render food, and the eating habits of populations, politically legible."[112] For this reason, British officials placed the caloric content of camp dietaries into a cultural context. Arthur W. May, medical director-general of the Royal Navy, argued that British POWs at Ruhleben were being issued a diet that fell short in total food value of that of a Lancashire weaver during the "cotton famine." When a new reduced scale was introduced, he warned that it was even below that of the "starving weaver," "London charwoman," and a "London seamstress in 1865." May marshaled the cultural meanings attached to these social categories – all of which signaled lives of privation – in order to provide a more concrete understanding of the effects of what he suggested must be understood as a poverty diet.[113] The science of calories, he suggested, could only be properly interpreted if given cultural meaning.

Counting Calories in the Camps

A concerted effort to establish whether or not camp dietaries were meeting the bare minimum of calories required to sustain the human organism came surprisingly late in the war, given that the weaponization of food had been central to Britain's military strategy. It was not until April 1916, when Taylor first investigated the food at Ruhleben, that anyone had attempted a systematic scientific study of camp nutrition. Taylor's report was the result of ten days spent inspecting the preparation of the food, calculating the number of men who took the German rations, and partaking in the midday meal alongside the interned civilians as a form of participant observation. Taylor's analysis of the Ruhleben diet was meant to be a scientific investigation, but its methodology exposed practical and ideological problems with calculating food values precisely because there was considerable variability as to who actually consumed the German rations on any given day. Of the 3,700 interned men, the number who took the food varied over the course of the seven-day study: 2,258; 1,940; 2,019; 2,480; 2,235; 1,676; and 2,380.[114] This meant that there were three different data sets in play when calculating whether the rations were sufficient: those represented in the official diet scale drawn up according to "dietetic standards" set by Professor Backhaus, head of the Nutrition Department of Germany's Ministry of War; those measurable in the food that was actually provided to the limited number of men who consumed the meals on any given day, which as in many other camps differed from the stated menu; and those measured based on the ration that should have been divided between all 3,700 internees. It was this latter figure that was of the most concern to Taylor and the British government as it represented not what was actually consumed by those who took the food but rather the legal and moral responsibility of the German authorities to provide a nutritious diet to all POWs. The question of which caloric measurement to use when evaluating the dietary was thus inherently political.

During the period of observation, the Ruhleben diet consisted of coffee, chicory, tea, cocoa, sugar, fresh and dried milk, potatoes, fresh fish, salt, Quaker® oats, bread, sardines, lentil meal, dried peas, swedes, bacon, rice, macaroni, beef, margarine, string beans, corned beef, blood sausage, cheese, kippers, and tinned herring. Taylor noted that this diet had clearly "shifted from the basis established by the authorities," which according to Gerard was also of concern to Backhaus who, he recalled, seemed truly to have the POW's welfare at heart.[115] The official ration – what the German authorities claimed to be providing and that appeared in the written dietary for the week – averaged around 2,746 calories. This official figure held up well against that of the dietary of the men who actually took the ration. The calories varied from a low of 2,030 to a high of 3,335 for an average daily intake of 2,740. But if this food had needed to nourish all 3,700 interned men, it would only have averaged 1,590 calories and, on some days, fallen well below this.[116] Arriving at reliable figures was further complicated, Taylor intimated, by the place of bread within the dietary. Taylor noted that the "Englishmen dislike" the "black bread" served at the camp and "practically speaking, eat none of it," a point I will return to below.[117] Although most British POWs collected their bread ration, they often discretely disposed of it by scattering its crumbs around the camp, fearing that refusing the rations outright might have negative consequences.[118] That this bread was not actually consumed thus lowered the caloric intake considerably, Taylor noted.

Historians have argued that Germany failed to deliver sufficient food to those it had taken prisoner largely because it could not.[119] This does not mean, however, that studies such as Taylor's presented data on camp dietaries in an objective fashion. Using the standards set by Germany's own food experts, Taylor, a theoretically neutral representative, focused the British government's attention not on the calories provided to those who actually ate the meals. Rather, he highlighted the shortfall if all internees were suddenly to demand their rations, an unlikely situation given their professed preference for the parcels from home. In raising the question of the uneaten bread ration, Taylor also underscored the loss of calories from this critical food source, suggesting that the onus was not necessarily on the POWs themselves to eat the food that was made available to them. Calculating the dietary in this manner allowed Taylor to argue that the Ruhleben rations fell short even of the "consensus of the German scientific opinion."[120] This conclusion emphasized not Britain's expectations as to what their POWs should be fed, which Germany could construct as unrealistic given the blockade, but the hypocritical nature of Germany's claim to provide sufficient food to those it had confined based on their own scientific calculations. This allowed British officials such as Lord Devonport, minister of food, to skirt the whole issue of the blockade and condemn the Ruhleben dietary as "scientific cruelty."[121]

The Army Council deployed the same strategy near the end of the war. In March 1918, it used six diet sheets from separate camps selected at random by the Netherlands Legation in Berlin, which had taken over as neutral representatives once the United States had entered the war, in order to conduct a "scientific analysis" of the nutritional situation in the camps. Relying on the calculations of Rubner and von Voit, rather than on British scientists perhaps to avoid any intimation of bias, Cubitt informed the POWD that British POWs were not receiving even close to this allotment. At Münster, the dietary was yielding only 752 calories, the lowest tabulated; the highest was at Arys, but this was still only 1,830 calories. Taking the average of all of the six camps analyzed, the total calories hovered around 1,105, which was less than 50 percent of the calories considered by German authorities necessary to maintain health. This situation was made even worse by the fact, he reported, that much of the food provided is "uneatable" because of the bad quality of the raw ingredients and the "distasteful" preparation. The dietaries were recalculated to include only edible calories, a highly subjective determination. This decreased Münster's to approximately 567 and those of Arys to 1,644. Like Taylor, Cubitt used the number of calories that Germany itself had determined were necessary and similarly positioned some of the food provided as inherently inedible in order to conclude that "neutral medical men" had confirmed that the British combatant POWs were "being systematically starved." Cubitt suggested therefore that Britain pressure Germany to provide a dietary that was at least comparable to the United Kingdom's camps.[122]

That these "scientific" reports produced by "neutral" inspectors were not objective is evident. How many calories a body needed was always open to negotiation in the context of a war in which food was a central weapon. As Cullather has argued, the calorie was always already a "technology for classifying food within the inventory of resources (the 'standing reserve') at the disposal of the state."[123] For these reasons, Britain's Treasury made clear that the fixing of the POW diet scale within its own camps involved "elaborate calculations of supplies, prices, and calories," thus requiring "unavoidable discussion," and likely heated negotiations among a variety of government departments with particular but disparate stakes in these decisions, most of which had little to do with nutrition.[124] This was even more evident when the discussions were between belligerent governments.

It was not until June 1918 that Britain and Germany negotiated a concrete standard of maintenance for POWs. Under this agreement, the dietaries of both civilian and combatant POWs were not to be based on the captor nation's military rations, which had been stipulated by the Hague Convention and "virtually ignored" by all of the belligerents.[125] Instead the new index was to be the diet of the home front civilian population now that the United Kingdom had also introduced rationing. Significantly, these new standards included a minimum number of calories (something not specified in the Hague Convention): 2,000 for nonworkers, 2,500 for ordinary workers, and 2,850 for heavy workers.[126] These thresholds were well below the German army ration of 3,200 calories for those at the front, the official German camp ration that had been set at 2,700, and the ration claimed to be provided in United Kingdom camps, which was approximately 3,000 calories.[127] They were, however, well above that of the German civilian population, which by this time was subsisting on 1,000 calories per day.[128] (In contrast, the British civilian population, even after the introduction of rationing, ate on average more than 3,300 calories per day.[129]) The 1918 standardization of the POW ration was established when food shortages in Germany were acute. This seemingly objective scientific safe minimum must be interpreted in this context. It represented not necessarily the lowest amount of calories that scientists had calculated a body might need to maintain health but the maximum that a nation already hard pressed to feed its own civilians could afford to supply at a moment when it was clearly not yet apparent how long the war would last. Although the British government was decidedly concerned about the health of its subjects held in the German camps, it must also have understood that to meet this agreement would require Germany to funnel resources away from its military expenditure. The provisioning of POWs was clearly a part of Britain's wider strategy of using food as a critical weapon of war.

The POW camps of World War I provided an opportunity to see how the nutritional sciences could be applied to large populations of real bodies in real time through controlling and monitoring their diet. But the war was never a neutral testing ground for scientific principles. This was not merely because of the "the paucity of the scientists' own knowledge" or the "lack of appreciation by government officials of how the information that was available" could be applied to policy.[130] It was also because the provisioning of POWs could never be disentangled from the political context in which this took place. Given the scarcity of food throughout the war, and the dwindling supplies in Germany in particular, what a POW ration would (rather than should) contain was always a matter of negotiation and always resulted in compromise even when couched in the discourses of science. This was compounded by the question of morale and the British government's willingness to cater to POWs' tastes and their cultural attitudes toward eating even when it was inexpedient, expensive, and unscientific to do so.

Catering to the National Palate

Although a champion of the statistical analysis of diets, Taylor had also cautioned that dietary criteria should take into account "the habits, customs, tastes, and idiosyncrasies" of the subjects being fed. A "prison ration applied to foreigners would be less well tolerated from every point of view than the same diet applied to domestic prisoners," he asserted, precisely because of its strangeness.[131] Camp food, he argued, should be "prepared according to the men's taste," for an adequate diet was "a matter of satisfaction as well as of nutrition," intimately linking the two.[132] Even for medical experts then, calculations regarding an acceptable diet transcended the scientific study of calories and food values. British POWs were never seen to be eating merely to survive. They and their government expected their food to be familiar, tasty, and prepared in ways that they were accustomed to eating it rather than merely being nutritious and ample. This was good for morale, the state inferred, even if it was expensive and impractical.

The Foreign Office, particularly in the first years of the war, attempted to reassure the public that British POWs were not actually "starving."[133] Christopher Hamlin has argued that, in the early Victorian period, the word "starvation" had cultural meanings that transcended any literal definition based merely on a lack of food. To be starving was a social as well as a biological condition that gestured to a broader emotional and not merely physical experience of privation that took place within a political and cultural context.[134] This connotation survived into the twentieth century and helps to explain the divergent accounts emanating from POW camps. When neutral observers visited the German camps to investigate widespread claims that British POWs were "starving," they sometimes found a discrepancy between what the POWs said they ate and what they witnessed actually being consumed. American diplomats who visited a range of camps in 1915 and 1916 reported that the food was frequently "palatable" and "nutritious" and that a considerable number of British prisoners ate it regularly, despite claims that they were being systematically starved.[135] It seems clear from these reports, argued G. R. Warner, secretary of the Prisoners of War Interdepartmental Committee, that the men "get a good deal of food from the Germans" and were not therefore completely reliant on parcels from home.[136] If it were "literally impossible to exist on the food supplied by the German Government," argued Lord Newton, the million Russian prisoners in Germany who received no parcels at all "would have literally died like flies."[137] The discourses of starvation thus reflected wider anxieties about the food supply in general but were also a psychological manifestation of the ways in which food not only nourished but also comforted prisoners. Indeed, as a range of historians have argued, the desire for packages was primarily an expression of a prisoner's need to remain emotionally linked to the home front through tangible reminders that he had not been abandoned or forgotten.[138]

In 1915, Gerard made this distinction between having to rely on parcels and choosing to do so clearer. He stated that no POW would starve were he compelled to live entirely on German rations. The food, he asserted, is just "not such as appeals to the taste of British soldiers."[139] His officials reported in 1916 that POWs did not eat the camp food because the food their families dispatched was practically enough to cover all their needs; thus, they could choose to reject the German rations as a matter of preference.[140] When the American Lithgow Osborne visited the British POWs at Stendal (of which there were only 150 out of the 5,500 men held in the camp), the prisoners "admitted that they could live on the camp rations, if necessary, and still retain good health, as is the case with the Russians." Their objection to the food, he stated, was "on account of its sameness, and because it was not cooked in an English way."[141] That many camps provided cooking facilities for POWs or allowed them to own and use portable field stoves, facilitated prisoners' ability to prepare meals for themselves out of the contents of their packages. This made it even easier to be "choosy" in relation to the rations they took from the Germans and to demonstrate that they were not in fact totally reliant on their captors.[142]

The German military authorities had allowed their camp commandants to alter the dietary so as to accommodate "the food to the modes of life of the different nationalities" held within the camps and the "habits of living of the various nations."[143] Having visited several camps, Gerard noted that since in many of them British POWs were in the minority, the manner of preparing food "must be determined by considerations having to do with majorities of different races." Consequently, he explained, "less attention can be paid to English habits of life and wishes than is possible where only one race is concerned."[144] British POWs' primary complaint was that the camp food was "un-English." When the American diplomat John B. Jackson visited Döberitz in 1915, he reported that the British POWs made no general complaints, except with regard to the "German character of the food." It is German material, he noted, prepared principally by Russian cooks and "does not suit the English taste."[145] These grievances echoed throughout the German camps as POWs decried the unpalatable nature of a range of unfamiliar foods.[146] One British lieutenant argued that while the "Russians could manage" to eat the raw fish and gherkins, the British could not, suggesting that the food was not inherently inedible, as Cubitt had insisted, but merely unpalatable to those unaccustomed to the ingredients and modes of preparation.[147] Taylor, who had eaten many meals at Ruhleben alongside the internees, concurred that it was not that the food was "unfitted for human consumption." Rather, it was just "so different from the food to which they are accustomed that they cannot learn to regard it with anything else than distaste."[148]

As food psychologist, Paul Rozin has demonstrated, one's "native culture" or "ethnic group" is the prime predictor of an individual's food preferences.[149] That there was such a thing as national taste was a commonly held idea in the early twentieth century and recognized as an issue that had to be addressed within the camp system. An article published in the *British Medical Journal* in January 1915 on the treatment of POWs declared that "national differences of taste" accounted for most of the critiques emanating from POWs on all sides of the war about their dietaries.[150] The British government did attempt to accommodate German tastes within the United Kingdom's camps. Overseers replaced contractors in many camp kitchens with prisoners themselves so that they could have their food *"as they liked it."*[151] In addition, they often supplied the "black bread [and] the sausage for which the Teutonic stomach craves."[152] Rye flour was provided at the bakehouse at the Dorchester internment camp so that German-style bread could be provided for inmates (though this would have served British interests, leaving more of the desirable wheat flour for its own citizens).[153] At the Cornwallis Road internment camp in London, overseers had installed a mincing machine so that the German cooks could prepare the "Hamburg steaks, of which the prisoners are so fond."[154] The canteens operating in almost every camp on the British mainland and on the Isle of Man also made available for purchase articles that appealed to Central Europeans such as a range of "sausages made according to German tastes."[155] The British government could argue that it was attending not only to the nutritional needs of those it had interned but also their cultural foodways.

Debates over the most contentious item in Britain's POW ration scale – horseflesh, which was introduced into the official dietary in 1918 – suggests that state officials were well aware of the cultural significance of food. Lord Milner, secretary of state for war in its last months, had recommended the introduction of horseflesh on the grounds that it was "a common article of diet in Germany," suggesting he was catering to the tastes of the prisoners. What he failed to acknowledge, however, was that while still commonly eaten in France, horseflesh had only recently and reluctantly become part of the German diet because of extreme meat shortages.[156] When Central European POWs rejected the horseflesh outright, the British government reversed its language of national tastes. Its officials refused to alter the dietary "merely to meet the wishes or tastes of these prisoners," given that horseflesh fulfilled the same nutritive role in the diet as any other meat.[157] They declared it "unfortunate that the fact that horseflesh was being issued to these prisoners was ever disclosed to them and that if this commodity had been prescribed, and sent into the camps, as 'meat' or in the form of 'sausage' it is probable that no complaints would have been made."[158] This suggested that they fully recognized that the aversion to horseflesh was cultural but nevertheless justified their decision by foregrounding its nutritive value, though they did not here note that, according to Notter and Firth, horseflesh has more calories per pound than beef.[159]

If as Rachel Duffett has argued, in British military provisioning, calories were furnished "without regard to their form, as taste was always secondary to food values,"[160] in the case of their own POWs, government authorities did prioritize taste. When British POWs complained that they "were not accustomed to [the] diet" served in the German camps and "did not like it," officials often responded by affirming these men's right to reject unfamiliar items and sometimes acquiesced to the sending of alternative foodstuffs.[161] State officials were in fact surprisingly sympathetic to the widespread "aversion to the German styles of cooking" and made concessions to British taste even when it was inexpedient and expensive to do so.[162] They did not routinely claim, as they had with enemy prisoners, that it was not their responsibility to "meet the wishes or tastes" of prisoners of war.

As in the British camps, the protein ration featured among the most contentious complaints emanating from German POW camps. Meat formed a significant part of the British diet and was desired as the primary form of protein by those across the class spectrum. Before the war, how much animal protein one consumed, and whether it was the more expensive fresh butcher's meat or cheaper preserved meat, such as bacon, was largely dependent on gender, age, income, and status within the family.[163] As Chapter 1 has argued, beef in particular was central to British national identity, though pork products, mutton, and fish were also widely consumed in the British Isles. When a group of captured Grimsby fisherman arrived at Ruhleben, the chief representative of the British internees gave each of them "a beef steak" to welcome them into the community, a symbolic act that underscored the bonds of Englishness.[164] The shortage of beef and pork in Germany (the latter having been slaughtered by government order[165]), however, meant that British POWs were often furnished with unfamiliar meats such as horse, dog, seal, shark, and whale, all of which generated feelings of disgust.[166] British seamen interned in Norway refused to eat either salt fish or salt meat as they claimed that it was "unpalatable to British tastes."[167] Their camp leader insisted that "the men absolutely refused to touch [salt meat] and said that they would go on hunger strike" if fresh meat were not provided instead.[168] Despite the fact that Norwegian salt-cured herrings and salted cod were part of the official dietary of the British internment camps and equally loathed by the internees, the British government was sympathetic to the complaints of its own countrymen and authorized the shipment of supplies to substitute for these rations. The state here acknowledged that the taste for these foodstuffs was acquired and did not mandate that British subjects make do with this available protein source, eaten by the local Scandinavians and historically part of the seaman's diet, even when others were in short supply and even when also furnished in the United Kingdom's own camps.[169]

When the British government sent food supplies to supplement the diet of its POWS, officials considered whether the available products would be acceptable to British tastes even when their nutritional value was beyond dispute. When supplies of Norwegian pickled herring became available to send to British POWs, the POWD consulted the Army Council as to whether its members considered this to be "suitable food for the British prisoners."[170] The Ministry of Food thought it "unlikely" that this "would be suitable to be supplied to British prisoners of War," given that the British tended to eat kippered (smoked) herrings and disliked the pickled variety.[171] Jackson had noted during his 1915 inspection of Altdamm that there had been "some trouble" in relation to the "raw pickled herrings" that formed a major part of the camp diet. The Germans and Russians "relish[ed]" pickled herrings, but the English did not. Against orders, the latter had cooked theirs over fires made at their barracks and had been punished for this until Jackson negotiated the provision of camp-sanctioned fires for this purpose.[172] When Norwegian fish balls and fish puddings were made available for purchase, the War Office's purchasing agent opined that it was "very debatable whether English soldiers would like this form of fish food," given that he thought them "quite a cultivated taste."[173] He expressed "considerable doubt as to the suitability of" sending this foodstuff, which must have been a good source of protein, "as regards its acceptability by British prisoners."[174] The British government thus did not always assess food purely in relation to its calories and nutritional components. It sometimes acknowledged cultural attachments to food and did not always expect its subjects, even in these extreme circumstances, to eat what had been provided to them despite the consensus that these foodstuffs were nutritious and filling.

White Bread and English Tastes

When it came to provisioning its own subjects, the British government acknowledged that food provided not merely calories but comfort and that its consumption reified one's identity even when its nutritional value was limited. Perhaps no food provided to POWs during World War I exemplified this complexity more than bread. Bread was a staple of the British diet. Since the development of roller milling in the late nineteenth century, bread had grown whiter, purer, and cheaper, making white bread the norm for all classes.[175] Ella Scarlett-Synge, a member of the Women's Volunteer Reserve Corps of Canada who toured the German POW camps in December 1915, astutely remarked, "one must remember that German and English food differ vastly, the German dislikes our white bread and the Englishman dislikes the black bread." These, she sanguinely cautioned, "are things that must be put up with."[176] But British POWs refused merely to put up with the German bread and wrote volumes about it. They often complained that it was highly adulterated with straw, sawdust, or unknown articles, and that it produced indigestion.[177] One Ruhlebenite proclaimed it a "fearful compound – quite uneatable."[178] But even when it was fresh and pure and consistent with that served "in the ordinary beer restaurant in Berlin," they dismissed it as inedible because it was brown or black and not the white bread they were accustomed to eating.[179] Although the British POWs at Dyrotz maintained in 1916 that the bread they were given was "very good for black bread," they relied almost entirely on wheat bread sent from home.[180] The British government frequently acquiesced that the *Kriegsbrot*, or "War Bread," in use throughout Germany – a combination of rye, whole wheat, and potato flours, and as the war dragged on adulterated with admixtures of turnips, barley, oats, beans, peas, and sometimes acorns, chestnuts, beech nuts or even straw and wood shavings – was "not particularly palatable to Englishmen."[181] A report on the Friedrichsfeld camp underscored that this was a matter of taste rather than nutrition. It proclaimed that the "black bread when fresh [was] quite eatable and good," but the POWs "would have preferred white."[182]

Because British POWs found the black bread served up in the camps so distasteful, the main food item they asked to be sent to them was white bread. According to escaped POWs, "what British prisoners most want in parcels is tinned food and *bread*."[183] Many British government and charitable resources were expended on meeting this preference for "good substantial white English bread."[184] This was despite the fact that brown and black bread were widely known to be more nutritious and that the war bread, often baked on site, was considerably fresher.[185] Even when the British home front population was asked to consume their own war bread – made from wheat flour milled at an extraction rate of 76 percent in November 1916, rising to 81 percent in February 1917, and

92 percent in March 1918 (and even then combined with other cereal flours)[186] – British POWs ate white bread. When some men attempted to escape from Ruhleben, they were caught because they were seen eating white bread, which was not available in Germany at that time and was clearly a marker of Allied status.[187] Although the bread sent into the German camps did alleviate periodic shortages, as an American official noted, "enormous overhead expenses" were disbursed in order to ship bread to British POWs, thus catering to their tastes but certainly not their health.[188]

Two funds were established to send supplies of white bread to British POWs. One of these was at Berne, Switzerland, and was run by the Bureau de Secours aux Prisonniers de Guerre. This was an organization formed primarily to aid French POWs but which in April 1915 inaugurated a "Section Anglaise," generally translated as "British Section." Switzerland, a neutral country, was geographically well placed for this endeavor as it bordered Germany. The "Section Anglaise" baked and packed ventilated boxes of white bread and then addressed them to individual POWs. These were then placed in a special van or railway wagon routed to Frankfurt and from there distributed to the camps (Figure 4.2). The Swiss Government facilitated negotiations with the German authorities, ensuring that the parcels had free passage and were not subject to transshipment fees. They generally arrived within two to six days at minimal expense.[189] By the end of 1915, the Berne bread bureau was employing thirty-five administrative and financial staff and sixty packers and dispatchers. It could also claim that 98 percent of its dispatches arrived in good condition based on the return postcards included with each box.[190] By the summer of 1916, 21,000 POWs were being supplied with bread from Berne. This amounted to nearly 1.5 million loaves per week being consumed by two-thirds of all British POWs.[191] In the spring of 1917, the Berne bureau boasted that it had sent enough bread to "make a pathway from London to Algiers or from Berne to Constantinople."[192]

The "Section Anglaise," like other voluntary agencies providing humanitarian relief to British POWs, worked in "close co-operation" with the Foreign Office's POWD and initially the POWHC. When the British government disbanded the POWHC in 1916 and formed the CPOWC to oversee a centralized system of relief to British subjects confined abroad, the POWD granted the CPOWC jurisdiction over the "Section Anglaise," although both were theoretically nongovernmental organizations.[193] The British government used these organizations, partially funded them, and largely oversaw their operations to avoid any appearance that the state itself was directly provisioning its

Figure 4.2 White bread being loaded onto the truck at the "Section Anglaise" bread bureau, Berne, Switzerland, for dispatch to British POWs in Germany, September, 1916. Courtesy of Australian War Memorial, A01669.

POWs on a regular basis. For the British government to have undertaken a bread scheme under its own auspices would have implied that enemy governments were failing to discharge their duties under the Hague Convention, a charge that could have led, it was widely feared, to serious repercussions for British prisoners such as a reduction in their official rations. Although the British state did not wish to be seen to be directly forwarding white bread to its POWs, its fingerprints were all over the operation. Had it disapproved of the endeavor, the Berne bureau would have been mothballed, a fate that befell (at least temporarily) the other bread fund.

At the same time that the Berne bureau was developed, Camilla Picton-Warlow (whose husband was imprisoned at Döberitz) founded the Bread Fund for Prisoners of War in Germany from her home base in Bedford. She sent "Dujon" bread – white bread baked by and named after the local firm of Dudeney and Johnston – "AT ONCE to any prisoner who writes asking for bread, feeling sure that no man asks for it unless he is hungry." This amounted to almost five tons weekly.[194] Families of the interned, and the POWs themselves, could pay for bread to be sent. But the fund was also supported, Picton-Warlow claimed, "through the generosity of the public – including many children – who have always a very great desire to see that the men who have fought for them are supplied with their Daily Bread" direct from "Blighty."[195] "A great deal of Englishmen," requested this bread, and the POWHC, the CPOWC, and the Foreign Office all promoted and facilitated ordering of supplies as they did with Berne bread.[196] For, according to Picton-Warlow, this "good substantial white English bread is eagerly looked for in most of the German prison camps."[197]

A much smaller operation than the Berne bureau, the Bedford Bread Fund was nevertheless supplying approximately 5,000 POWs by June of 1916.[198] In October, Picton-Warlow moved her bread bureau to Copenhagen in neutral Denmark to expand the operation, to ensure that high quality bread would reach the camps more quickly, and to facilitate accurate communication regarding changes of address for POWs by working through the Danish Red Cross, which had good working relations with its German counterpart.[199] But the move to Copenhagen was fraught with new difficulties. The quality of the bread was often questionable, especially in warmer weather, and it did not always reach the camps in good time due to German railway delays. Interruptions to shipping because of the German submarine campaign also made it difficult to ensure that a steady supply of flour (165 tons each month), as well as lard, oil, string, stitching wire, coal, and other necessary supplies could be sent from the United Kingdom so that Danish stocks were not themselves depleted. This latter problem put increased pressure not only on the CPOWC but also on the Foreign Office that was compelled to intercede. These problems were compounded by staffing difficulties and personality conflicts, leading the British government to close the Copenhagen bureau on July 15, 1917, as it could no longer function efficiently.[200]

That a charitable organization could be compelled to close by the government, a fate that also befell the POWHC, reveals the complexity of this mixed economy of POW welfare and the interventionist role the state played while appearing to leave the work of supplying nonessential items to nongovernmental organizations. Indeed, the CPOWC maintained that it would not seek to expand the Berne bureau in the wake of the Copenhagen closure unless experts from the War Office sent to investigate the situation approved this measure. Given that it was widely understood that what our POWs "want and appreciate more than anything else in their life of captivity is Bread," and did not always care for the biscuits sent as a substitute, in the end, the CPOWC, Lord Newton, and the Army Council all authorized the reopening of the Copenhagen bureau at the end of the summer.[201] They hoped that a combination of better quality flour imported from Canada and the United States and cooler weather would give the loaves a longer shelf life.[202] The flour was eventually obtained through the Royal Commission on Wheat Supplies, a government organization formed during the war to ensure the nation had adequate wheat.[203] By 1918, the Wheat Commission was also supplying flour to replace the stocks used by the Dutch for British POWs who had been moved to the neutral Netherlands.[204] That these requests for flour had to come to the Wheat Commission through a government department, and that the Foreign Office and the War Office were central to these negotiations, reveals the extent of government, not merely charitable, investment in supplying British subjects with white bread. Although white bread was nutritionally inferior to the black bread that was served as part of the German camp ration, it was a culturally significant food product and nourishing in this older sense of the term.

World War I effectively weaponized food. During the conflict, food policies were central to political strategies predicated on disrupting the enemy's home front food supplies. In this environment, where food was limited and choice of foodstuffs even more so, the sciences of nutrition flourished. Captive populations were ideal experimental subjects for testing the body's basic minimum needs at a time when scientists broadly agreed that protein, fat, and carbohydrates were essential components of a human diet and that calories could be used to measure whether a diet provided enough energy to maintain health. But these standards were not deployed consistently by any of the belligerents during the war and not merely because they were contested. Nutritional experts advising the belligerent governments did not dispute that all forms of animal protein were equivalent and that brown bread was nutritionally better than white. Yet the British did not use POW camps to support these relatively uncontroversial claims and did not privilege this knowledge in making decisions governing how their subjects held captive would be rationed. Although British officials had obliged the combatants and civilians they had interned in the United Kingdom to eat unfamiliar food based on scientific standards, they did not compel British men confined by the enemy similarly to eat the food furnished to them even when it met widely agreed upon nutritional standards. Instead the Foreign Office, the War Office, and the Admiralty repeatedly and consistently made decisions regarding the feeding of British POWs that undermined the latest scientific knowledge of food values, even when it was inexpedient and expensive to do so.

The discourses of hunger and starvation will and should continue to shape our understanding of the experiences of POWs. But if probed more deeply, the narrative of the starving POW opens up a more nuanced understanding of the strategic use of food within a larger wartime strategy. While the war underscored that food was a resource to be strategically deployed and could be scientifically engineered to keep bodies alive, it also revealed that particularly in extreme situations food nourishes in ways that are deeply cultural. Black bread, pickled herring, salted meat, fish balls, and all manner of substitutes could sustain the human organism in basic health, but the state conceded that this did not necessarily mean that they could keep a British body from starvation.

5   The Science of Selection
Malnutrition and School Meals in the Interwar Years

The end of World War I did not bring an end to the problem of either undernourishment or malnutrition despite significant advances in the nutritional sciences. In the interwar period, as a series of economic crises heavily impacted several British industries leading to widespread unemployment, malnutrition again became a significant topic of medical research, social policy, and public debate. In this climate, the Board of Education began to identify malnutrition among schoolchildren as a central concern, fearing that a sizeable number of children were not able to take advantage of the state education system because their physical condition interfered with their ability to learn. In 1934, the Board thus instructed Local Education Authorities (LEAs) to focus their feeding efforts on those who were suffering from malnutrition rather than merely feeding poor children "indiscriminately." These children were to be identified, the Board mandated, not by assessing their parents' income, which had previously been a common practice, but rather through a process of clinical examination.

This policy shift has generally been understood as a plank in the government's "techno-political" solution to the problem of poverty diets; an attempt to render malnutrition "amenable to precise measurement" and to treat it in a politically neutral manner.[1] The Board, however, consistently rejected the "newer knowledge of nutrition" that by this period was widely and readily available. Its officials rarely translated recent scientific studies of the nutritive properties of foodstuffs into meals that actually nourished British children, clinging to ideas about malnutrition informed as much by cultural assumptions as by relevant medical research. In addition, it deployed scientific techniques known to be faulty to identify which children were to be fed, ignoring other approaches and a range of data that pointed to a different population set in need of school meals. Rather than marshaling what James Vernon identifies as the "seemingly apolitical set of technical knowledges and forms of expertise" already in existence in the 1920s and 1930s,[2] the Board of Education consistently used the discourses of medicine and science only when it suited their political and economic purposes: to ensure their services reached only a targeted, and limited, population. A study of school feeding in the interwar period reveals the extent to which the state failed to follow through with one of the original intentions of the school meals service, which was to use government intervention to improve the well-being of suffering children who were blameless for their condition. Despite the existence of a vehicle to provide good food to children, an expansion of research into food values, and a nationalistic rationale for the feeding of future citizens, school meals remained substandard in the interwar years. This was due not primarily to government budget cuts but to the Board of Education's own ideologies and practices that often undermined attempts to address the problem of childhood malnutrition head-on and rewarded precisely the parents that the state itself had identified as "undeserving."

The Stigma of School Feeding

The 1906 Education (Provision of Meals) Act was part of a range of social legislation, which also included school medical services, old age pensions, and National Insurance, passed by a "progressive alliance" between New Liberals and the Labour Party (or Lib-Labs) between 1906 and 1914.[3] These new social services, which for the first time made forms of state welfare available outside of the poor law system, ensured a minimum standard of living by providing a safety net to those most vulnerable within the capitalist economy. The 1906 Act was among the first of these reforms because children epitomized those least able to help themselves. It had increasingly become clear that if the state was to compel children to attend school, and public monies were to be spent on educating them, then the state should also make certain that these students were not prevented from benefiting from their schooling because they were distracted by chronic hunger. This legislation gave LEAs the statutory power to provide free meals to schoolchildren who were "unable by reason of lack of food to take full advantage of the education provided for them." It did not, however, require them to do so. Significantly, the Lib-Lab government distinguished free school meals, which were originally financed out of local taxes, from other forms of state welfare by stipulating that parents whose children were fed at school would not be deprived of any "franchise, right, or privilege" or subjected to "any disability."[4] Bentley Gilbert has asserted that this was the first time the British state "offered to support its citizens without reciprocal deprivation of right for those who applied for relief."[5]

However much this "progressive" administration may have wished to "prevent any danger of the stigma of pauperism attaching to the child" in receipt of school meals, it was not entirely successful in this endeavor. For many, the legacy of the poor law continued to taint these services well into the 1930s.[6]

The 1906 Act was a recognition that the chronic poverty endemic in many urban centers and industrial regions had left the children of the poor famished. Many children were equally hungry in the inter-war period as a series of industrial slumps and the worldwide economic depression took their toll on communities across the British Isles. But school meals were not always popular among the classes that needed them the most, even during this period of widespread financial distress, precisely because some continued to associate them with stigmatizing forms of government relief. In districts that offered meals, and where these were provided both for paying and nonpaying students, education authorities generally maintained "canteens" for paying students and separate "Feeding Centres" for those partaking of free meals. Most LEAs offered only the latter facilities or alternatively contracted with local cafés to feed their students. Given that in the interwar period children generally ate their midday meal at home (except in rural areas where packed lunches were the norm because of the often considerable distance between home and school), those who ate at the Feeding Centres were conspicuous as these facilities tended to be located in the center of town. A child's "attendance at a free meal centre," the Board of Education admitted, was "known to all his neighbours."[7] Some of these institutions were located within sites that continued to smack of charity such as Salvation Army headquarters, the mission halls of other Christian groups, or institutions that primarily served the unemployed.[8] According to J. Alison Glover, one of the Board's senior medical officers, some of these centers exuded a "soup-kitchen atmosphere."[9] Although the school medical officer (SMO) for Stoke-on-Trent maintained in 1934 that there was no "'Oliver Twist' atmosphere" in his district's Feeding Centres, in doing so, he drew attention to the Dickensian potential of school feeding. So too did the director of education for Wigan. He touted the success of his centers on national radio in 1937, maintaining that any "Oliver Twist" who asked for more could have it, thereby continuing to associate the children in receipt of free meals with paupers in the Victorian workhouse.[10]

In the interwar period, the Board's officials sometimes perpetuated the idea that only "low grade children" used these services.[11] In Farnworth in 1935, an inspector reported that the children all had "filthy dirty hands" and ate their meals like "wild animals," "stuffing" their mouths.[12] This accentuated not the children's hunger but rather what other officials also identified as their lack of "civilised table manners."[13] These attitudes were widespread and self-perpetuating. Those that ran the Feeding Centres generally did not supply knives and forks as they assumed that "these implements might be dangerous in the hands of some of the low grade children who are fed." Supervisors feared that a child might "stick a fork into his next door neighbour out of mischief or in a quarrel."[14] This meant that the children either had to eat their entire meal with a small spoon or use their hands, which did little to mitigate stereotypes that those who took free meals were "low grade" or "uncivilized." For these reasons, parents that considered themselves of a "higher social grade," the Board observed, did not "like their children to associate with the 'regular beggars' in the feeding centre."[15] As a matter of self-respect and because they preferred not to "advertise their poverty by accepting meals" for their children, many parents refused school meals even when they qualified for them.[16] Some children may also have imbibed the stigma of the school meal and rejected them on these grounds. In 1938, one of the Board's officials identified a decline in the uptake of school meals in Stockton-on-Tees, which she attributed to the "disinclination on the part of the children to accept the meal provided" for "social reasons."[17] In Oldham in the following year, the inspector noted that "this is not a cheerful centre" and "many of the children look sad and one feels that they are having a free meal, and are conscious of it."[18]

If some parents and their children rejected the meals services in order to maintain their respectability, others found that there were financial implications to the receipt of free school dinners that they had not anticipated. Families in receipt of public assistance or allowances from the Unemployment Assistance Board (established in 1934) often had their weekly stipends reduced if their children took free school meals. These government departments argued that to do otherwise meant that the state was paying twice for the feeding of dependent children. In these situations, parents often withdrew their children from school meals or refused to sign them up, preferring instead to have the full allowance, which they felt was more economically beneficial to the family as a whole.[19] This exacerbated the already "chaotic" and inefficient nature of government relief, which came from multiple agencies, during the Great Depression.[20] In extreme cases, parents who refused the meals could be prosecuted for cruelty or neglect under the child protection statutes. Sometimes the education authorities did pass these cases on to the National Society for the Prevention of Cruelty to Children, which pursued prosecutions of this nature, but this was a rare occurrence.[21]

LEAs kept few records on these refusals, since they were not required to report them to the Board. The extant statistics revealed that in Middlesbrough in 1933, 36 percent of eligible families refused the meals; in Norwich in 1935, 22 percent; and in Wigan in 1937, approximately 30 percent.[22] Although most who qualified for meals took them, the precise reasons why a significant minority rejected these services were often hard for local authorities to disentangle. But it is clear that the ways in which the meals were delivered to students and the administration of the service itself shaped the public's reaction to school dinners and led some to reject this form of state feeding outright. While local officials sometimes followed up these cases and urged parents to allow their children to be fed, the central education authorities did little to mitigate the "'poor law' taint" that many felt continued to adhere to this form of state feeding in the interwar period.[23]

The Introduction of Medical Selection in 1934

Rather than attempting to encourage more of those who qualified for school meals to make use of the services, in 1934, the Board of Education, under the presidency of the Conservative Earl of Halifax, former viceroy of India, introduced a new policy that in practice led to a further reduction in the number of those fed gratis. Since the introduction of school feeding in 1906, LEAs that chose to provide meals were required to use some method to identify which children were to be fed. Before 1934, the Board permitted local officials to apply either "the poverty test" or "the physical test," both of which involved a type of means testing. The "poverty test" was exclusively a financial qualification. Parents applied for meals either on their own initiative or because school attendance officers or teachers had encouraged them to do so. Children were approved for feeding if their household income fell below a minimum established locally by the LEA, regardless of the physical condition of the child. The "physical test" required that, in addition to qualifying financially, the child was to undergo a medical examination to determine if he or she exhibited signs of undernourishment or malnutrition.

In 1934, the Board introduced a policy shift that mandated that LEAs practice what it referred to as "medical selection." This did not mean that the state committed to feed all children identified as suffering from malnutrition gratis. Rather, the new policy required that all schoolchildren be subject to the "physical test" first, thus privileging the body's ability to speak for itself. Only those diagnosed by a medical professional as suffering from subnormal nutrition would then be subject to an income assessment to determine whether or not they qualified for free meals. Children found to be malnourished whose parents did not meet the income qualifications could still opt to receive meals at cost and pay out of pocket, but the Board of Education took no responsibility for ensuring that this population received school dinners. In fact, its officials tended to discourage parents who could afford to pay from using the meals services and instead offered them advice on the proper home feeding of children.[24] As a result, only a very small number of parents whose children were found to be malnourished but did not qualify for free meals made use of school feeding. In practice, the 1934 policy reduced the number of children being fed solid meals by the state as the family's income on its own no longer qualified a child for free meals.

The 1934 policy shift occurred in a context in which malnutrition, rather than underfeeding, had taken center stage in debates over the relationship between food and health. The interwar period witnessed a growth in the nutritional sciences as further research into the components of food began to focus increasingly on newly discovered vitamins and minerals as essential to growth and health.[25] Historians have often characterized this period as a watershed in the "discovery of malnutrition," noting that much of the research was performed in a colonial context.[26] Unlike the term undernourishment that tended to mean a lack of food and made quantity the defining factor, malnutrition denoted a condition wrought by consumption of the wrong kinds of foods, particularly those lacking in vitamins. Malnutrition centered on quality and the prevention of vitamin deficiency diseases such as rickets, xerophthalmia, and scurvy.[27] If the 1906 Act had been passed to address the problem of undernourished children, by the 1930s, a school dinner could also theoretically treat malnutrition. As a captive population, schoolchildren could be provided an ample and well-balanced main meal that would alleviate their hunger and nourish their bodies with the right kinds of protective and bodybuilding substances. Hence, the SMO for Cumberland could claim that in his district "they had got far past calories" and were "now on vitamins!"[28] By the interwar period, therefore, the school meal had become not merely a means to provide additional food to undernourished children. The many social surveys conducted throughout the 1920s and 1930s had revealed that Britain's poorer classes lived largely on tea, bread, potatoes, sugar, jam, margarine, tinned milk, cheap meat pies, and chips from the shops.[29] The school meal promised a way to compensate for deficiencies in the home diet of working-class children in particular, which were assumed to be high in carbohydrates and lacking in fresh fruit, vegetables, and animal proteins.

The ability to address malnutrition was made possible by this "newer knowledge of nutrition," a phrase coined by American biochemist E. V. McCollum after World War I.[30] But the desire to do so was part and parcel of long-standing and widespread anxieties about national efficiency. In her 1938 tract, "School Feeding in England and Wales," the children's rights advocate Marjorie E. Green argued that the state had only become motivated to bring school meals within the scope of its educational services at the end of the South African War of 1899–1902 because of widespread "anxiety about the quality of recruiting" and the need for "race regeneration."[31] Historians have tended to agree with Green, frequently noting that the passage of the 1906 Act, and the sudden concern that students were not in fact profiting from their education decades into a state-run school system, was part and parcel of the Lib-Lab agenda that positioned state intervention as the route to the amelioration of social conditions for the least fortunate members of society. It was also the product of a cultural moment in which the body of the child citizen became a focus of state investment in reaction to larger military and imperial concerns.[32] The poor physique and physical fitness of the working-class men who had volunteered to fight in South Africa had raised alarming questions about Britain's ability to defend its empire. When the war was over, the British government launched an investigation into the causes of this perceived "physical deterioration" and actively sought solutions to the problem, one of which was the state provision of meals to schoolchildren.[33]

If the aftermath of the South African War created an ideal climate for state investment in the physical bodies of its future citizens, the 1930s saw similarly near perfect conditions for the consolidation of an efficient, targeted, and beneficial national school meals program as economic depression threatened national efficiency and war loomed again. The state continued to justify school meals in this period by arguing that it needed to secure the "physical powers" of the "children of the nation" so that they should be "equipped in body and in mind for the duties which will fall to them as the men and women of the future."[34] By the 1930s, some could posit that school meals were serving "a great eugenic function."[35] In the words of the SMO for Torquay, it was the responsibility of those involved in school medical inspection and school meals to play their part in bringing "the growing boy or girl up to a full measure of health and physique along the trusted paths of physiological righteousness."[36] This was critical for Britain as other countries, particularly Nazi Germany, were pursuing explicitly eugenic solutions to perceived problems of national efficiency, on the one hand, and heavily investing in the training of its youth, on the other. If Britain did not follow suit and channel its resources into the physical education and proper feeding of its children, many feared, "the younger generation will be unfit to carry on the traditions of vigour, strength and independence which formerly characterised the nation."[37] In her introduction to the 1936 tract, "Nutrition: A Policy of National Health," family allowance advocate Eleanor Rathbone made this clear. She contended that it was not mainly "humanitarian, nor social, nor even business or economic considerations," which had finally placed the problem of malnutrition in the foreground of public affairs in Britain and other countries. Rather, it was "considerations which are fundamentally military."[38]

The president of the Board of Education was, however, less persuaded by these arguments that investing in the health of all children was vital to the security of the nation. When he was transferred to the post of foreign secretary in 1938, the Earl of Halifax became the chief architect of the catastrophic policy of appeasement toward Adolf Hitler. Had he taken the threat of Nazi Germany more seriously, Halifax might not have insisted that the chief purpose of the state school system was "to train [these children] up as servants and butlers"[39] rather than as "the men and women of the future." The Board nevertheless repeatedly downplayed any suggestion that the mandating of medical selection was "solely or even primarily" a way to economize on the services it provided to this population.[40] Instead, Cecil Maudslay, one of its principal assistant secretaries and the civil servant most intimately involved in the administration of school meals, positioned medical selection as the best means of ensuring that the *right* children were being fed, which he defined as those not able to benefit from the state's educational services because of a lack of food or improper feeding.[41]

But in the 1910s and 1920s, school feeding had become more widespread and more costly. In 1914, the Board of Education had assumed significant financial responsibility for school meals by providing grants in aid to LEAs that covered 50 percent of the total cost of the service.[42] When a coal strike was launched in 1921, it resulted in an "unprecedented scale" of school feeding: over six million meals were provided that year at the cost of £943,353. The Board charged that much of this had been "indiscriminate" as nearly all the schoolchildren in certain regions affected by the strike had been fed without any consideration of their physical condition.[43] These anxieties about overspending were compounded by the findings of a government-appointed committee of inquiry that in 1922 recommended a reduction of 27 percent in the education budget for "Special Services," of which school meals were a part.[44] This climate led the Board to cap its grants for school meals at £300,000.[45] Although this cap lasted only a year, the Board warned LEAs that they did not have "carte blanche to spend as much as they like and very much in any way they like."[46] Sir George Newman, chief medical officer of the Board of Education 1907–35, reiterated in 1924 that the "machinery of the School Medical Service" should be used "to administer this Act in a sensible and scientific way" on an "educational-medical" rather "on a pauper relief basis."[47] The following year, the Board issued new regulations for the administration of school meals intended to curb "indiscriminate" feeding in times of crisis and emphasized that children be "proper[ly]" selected for meals though it did not yet mandate a preferred method.[48] Consequently, during the coal strike of 1926, LEAs provided only half the number of free meals as had been furnished during the 1921 strike, leading the Board to argue that it had discharged its duty "effectively and economically."[49]

As the Depression took root after the stock market crash of 1929 and many families were plunged into unemployment, it became clear to the Board that a very large number of children would now qualify for free meals under the income scales that most LEAs continued to use exclusively to determine who would be fed at the state's expense. When the administration of Labour Prime Minister Ramsay MacDonald collapsed in 1931 over pressure to reduce public expenditure, it was replaced with the first in a series of coalition National Governments. Two national committees convened in this climate of belt-tightening were charged with investigating how to make cuts in public expenditure at a time when the budgetary deficit was growing. The 1931 report of the first of these committees resulted in immediate cuts to the education budget. In 1932, the report of the second committee urged review of expenditure on Special Services, particularly because of the gross disparities among the LEAs.[50] By 1934, the time was ripe for the Board to exercise more stringent and centralized control over the administration of the provision of meals with a view to reducing expenditure without being seen to compromise the health of schoolchildren. Although the Board insisted that its 1934 policy shift was not intended as a cost-saving measure, it occurred in the midst of a budget crisis that required the Board to make cuts, particularly to the services it provided that were not explicitly educational. Indeed, the Board's officials frequently claimed that if all districts fed solely based on the income of the child's parents, the "expenditure would be enormous," indicating quite clearly that cost was a factor in these decisions.[51]

If this was the general context for the Board's policy shift, an opportunity to introduce medical selection as an official selection process emerged in relation to changes in the distribution of milk within the school system. In the fall of 1934, the government took over a commercial initiative that had been started by the National Milk Publicity Council in the late 1920s to promote milk consumption among schoolchildren. The newly launched Milk in Schools Scheme (MISS) was voluntary and allowed parents to purchase reduced-price milk for their children to be drunk at school. Milk was also to be provided free to necessitous children in need of supplementary nutrition either in lieu of or in addition to meals (Figure 5.1). Research in the 1920s and 1930s had demonstrated the nutritional value of milk as a "complete food" for developing bodies.[52] But the MISS was initiated primarily to help farmers find new markets for their surplus milk. This was deemed necessary because milk consumption across the nation was low, there had been a steady increase in the importation of cheap foreign butters, margarines, and cheeses since the late nineteenth century, and there were fewer protections for British milk products after the introduction of the Ottawa trade agreements in 1932. By the 1930s, Britain's dairy industry was experiencing

Figure 5.1 Coopers Lane School: morning milk, Lewisham, London, 1936. © City of London, London Metropolitan Archives, COLLAGE: The London Picture Archive, ref: 205430.

diminishing profits. While administered by the Board of Education, the MISS was an initiative of the Ministry of Agriculture and Fisheries.[53] Like the United States' school lunch program, it had been introduced primarily to benefit farmers rather than schoolchildren.[54]

The Board of Education used the inauguration of the MISS to mandate how children should be selected not only for subsidized milk but also for solid feeding. Since LEAs were to provide the milk free to necessitous, malnourished children, it became clear that some would need milk only while others would continue to require meals. Medical selection was even more important in this context, the Board implied, because the distinction between those that needed milk, those that needed meals, and those that would require both became finer and harder to determine. Many LEAs solved this problem themselves by taking advantage of the chance to offer milk only, dropping the meals service (which was considerably more costly) entirely, a move that the Board did not always discourage.[55] In 1932–3, 22,116,042 dinners and 32,255,262 milk meals were provided across England and Wales to 399,377 individual children in 174 LEAs.[56] In 1935–6, 19,903,006 dinners and 63,710,297 milk meals were provided to 479,343 children in 235 LEAs.[57] While the number of LEAs that provided meals increased, and the number of milk meals more than doubled, the number of solid meals declined. This suggests that new cases were primarily being given milk only and that some students had been shifted from solid meals to milk. Indeed in 1934, the Board declared that when an LEA provided milk only they did not "like to see a changeover to solid meals unless there is a good case for such a change," presumably as this was more expensive.[58]

The "Science" of Medical Selection

In September 1934, the Board of Education formally introduced its policy of medical selection. It released Circular 1437, which explained the MISS and the process that LEAs should adhere to in selecting children for milk and for solid meals. It stated that the Board "regard it as proper that children should be selected [for supplemental feeding] who show any symptoms however slight of subnormal nutrition." This was the first time that the Board had officially spelled out the method of selection for school meals that it considered "proper." It proclaimed that the LEAs were "no doubt aware" that the Board considered that the selection of children for free meals should be made "by a system of medical selection." It noted that a "considerable number of authorities select the children who are to receive free meals solely by means of a family income test." The Board was now investigating these cases, the circular continued, "with a view to securing a change to a medical basis of selection."[59] The new directives broadened the scope of the bodily conditions that were to be remedied by state feeding – both a lack of food and improper feeding – and provided milk as a new way to address symptoms of malnutrition. At the same time, however, this policy appeared to limit the population to be fed for free only to those who exhibited clinical symptoms of subnormal nutrition *and* whose families met the income test.

The Board of Education justified its decision to mandate medical selection by claiming that being unable to profit from education because of lack of food or improper nourishment was a "question of fact which needs to be determined independently of family income" and the conclusions must be drawn from "evidence" so that school meals were not merely a form of indiscriminate relief.[60] The Board thus instructed the LEAs to conduct surveys once or twice a year and then to classify the schoolchildren according to a "precise, uniform, and comparable" classification system that categorized children as A (excellent), B (normal), C (slightly subnormal), or D (bad).[61] All the D cases and many of the C cases, depending on circumstances, the Board suggested, would be eligible for meals and/or milk.[62]

However, in introducing medical selection and the ABCD scale, the Board of Education downplayed the fact that no body of experts had previously felt confident developing standards, guidelines, or definitive tests to measure nutrition. The British Medical Association (BMA) contested the idea that identifying malnutrition was a neutral or simple process, arguing in its 1933 report on the subject that there "exists no satisfactory and accepted routine method by which the nutritional condition or state of individuals can be assessed, and by which the findings of different observers can be compared."[63] Critics noted that the Ministry of Health's Advisory Committee on Nutrition (ACN) had similarly reported that it was unable to recommend any known method of assessing nutrition that was reliable.[64] Even while defending the ABCD system, Arthur MacNalty (who took over from Newman in 1935 and inherited the policy shift) was forced to admit that there was no test that could usefully and consistently be applied to assess nutrition. Since there was no single sign that could be relied upon, these categories, he conceded, "have to be determined by mental concept – by the 'impressions' of the medical officers rather than by measurable objective standards."[65] The Board nevertheless stuck to its policy and, throughout the second half of the 1930s, continued to promote medical selection as a scientific, and proper, process of selection, despite a steady stream of criticism launched by furious and vocal proponents of economic selection.

Many of the LEAs that wished to continue to feed on the basis of financial need alone – which included major metropolitan areas such as Manchester and London as well as smaller provincial cities such as Derby and Smethwick – vociferously attacked the new policy. The Association of Education Committees (AEC) (which feared among other things that this would demand an increase in staff) also resisted the change. It was joined by pressure groups such as the Children's Minimum Council (CMC), formed in 1934 to ensure that no child was deprived of an adequate supply of food or other basic necessities merely because his or her parents were poor.[66] This unexpected pushback from key constituencies, including many SMOs, forced the Board to alter how medical selection would work in practice without withdrawing the policy itself. The CMC and the AEC worked with the Board, now under the leadership of Conservative Oliver Stanley, to develop new guidelines that were more flexible as to what counted as a symptom of subnormal nutrition and that allowed a range of non-medical personnel to recommend children be evaluated for feeding.[67] These negotiations led to the inclusion of "educational symptoms," such as "lassitude" or "overstrain," as grounds to initiate feeding on a temporary basis. However, the Board continued to insist that only medical practitioners had the "experience, tact and commonsense," in short the necessary expertise, to make the proper final selection of children eligible for free meals.[68] Although this was clearly intended as a compromise, these new guidelines did little to quell criticism that in practice the system was no more scientific than any other mode of selection.

One of the major problems with the ABCD scale, its critics maintained, was that while D children might be readily apparent to the naked eye, C children were harder to classify, since C required distinguishing from B and no definition of the "normal" child existed. There was clearly no consensus as to what constituted "normality" and great confusion about whether "normal," "average," and "mean" were equivalents.[69] The "definition [of normal] is too difficult, at present, for me," Glover concluded in 1936, "and has been, I believe, for six nutrition committees."[70] Critics of medical selection attacked the whole premise of the ABCD system as decidedly unscientific as the Board could provide no way to standardize what a B, and thus by implication C or D, child should look like or how to test for either normal or subnormal nutrition in any objective and consistent way.[71]

The Board attempted to deal with this criticism that in assessing nutrition even well-trained medical personnel "have to deal with opinions and impressions rather than with scientific data capable of accurate determination."[72] Its medical staff tried to educate local officials – their most important allies in this venture – by paying site visits to train school medical personnel how to "calibrat[e]" their methods and results.[73] During these visits, they shared lantern slides and then jointly examined a range of students so that SMOs and their assistants (ASMOs) could be taught how to identify signs of malnutrition and how to use these signs to classify students based on the ABCD model.[74]

Despite these efforts, in practice, the SMOs and ASMOs who conducted the medical inspections often applied different standards from each other; thus, statistics on malnutrition and the number of children being fed varied widely among and within districts. A change of SMO in a district might mean that cases of malnutrition could increase enormously or plummet within a brief period of time due to the subjective nature of classification.[75] At Ebbw Vale, during routine inspections in 1937, the SMO claimed to have found (out of a population of 1,930 children) no D cases and only seven C cases, which in this chronically depressed area of South Wales, even Maudslay asserted, was "obviously absurd!"[76] The SMO for Manchester argued that even his conscientious ASMOs found it "impossible to formulate a definite standard which might enable an accurate differentiation [among A, B, C, and D cases] to be made."[77] The statistician Robin Huws Jones – who had written his Master's thesis on the unreliability of the classification of the nutritional health of schoolchildren – argued in 1937 that this was an insurmountable problem. The distribution of As, Bs, Cs, and Ds in any community, he concluded, was "largely dependent upon the particular doctor" who made the assessments.[78] Another study in Cheshire found that the same doctors examining the same children in a short interval failed to put them in the same category twice.[79] This and similar studies were a "sad commentary on the instability of human judgment," commented the SMO for the Isle of Ely. He underscored the "futility of endeavouring to measure in terms of figures a state of being for which there is no known or agreed standards." It is like "trying to express beauty by the pound and music by the square foot," he lamented.[80] In the end, which category a child was placed into, critics charged, was entirely a subjective decision shaped by the experience, opinions, unconscious influences, and sometimes political or social views of the examiner.[81]

Prioritizing Prevention

Opponents of medical selection also objected to the idea that the state's goal should be to identify and then treat those already suffering from malnutrition. Economic selection, its supporters argued, was aimed at prevention. The LEAs and pressure groups that defended the exclusive use of income scales insisted that preventative feeding ensured the long-term health of the child, was more economical than treating conditions that could arise in the future due to malnourishment, and was more humane than allowing poor children to endure a period of deprivation before being provided with school meals. Many medical researchers and practitioners had come to understand malnutrition as a process that slowly developed and stressed the body long before its signs could be detected.[82] According to Somerville Hastings, president of the Socialist Medical Association, by the time signs of malnutrition had become evident, "irreparable damage" had already been done as malnutrition, he maintained, left a "permanent scar" on the child's constitution.[83] The BMA supported this contention, arguing that since the detection of early signs of subnormal nutrition by way of clinical examination was "extraordinarily difficult," by the time physical signs were apparent, they likely indicated a "well-established condition of malnutrition" that might have been prevented.[84]

Other officials argued that it was more than merely an "impractical" or an unscientific way to address malnutrition, but actually inhumane. Economic selection prevented malnutrition, argued the Manchester authorities, because even if the children of necessitous families were not currently underfed or malnourished, eventually poverty would take its toll and the children would suffer.[85] To force children to undergo a "trial period of starvation" before the state would feed them, many argued, was a "retrograde" policy, "brutal, inhuman, and a relic of barbarism."[86] The LEAs that opposed the new policy, many of which were home to large numbers of poor children, pointed out that it would require them to remove children who appeared well nourished from the feeding lists only to put them back on later once their home diets had depleted their health enough for the signs to be visible. In effect, argued the director of education for Edmonton, this amounted to a cruel experiment on the bodies of the nation's children, evoking a language reminiscent of Cornish's critiques of famine relief discussed in Chapter 3. It would be "a foolish, if not a callous policy," he chided, "to deprive such children of their regular school meals and then wait to see what the effect would be," especially given that the results of these trials were a foregone conclusion.[87]

The argument that malnutrition "produces a slow, silent rot of verility [sic], vitality, and fibre from which recovery soon becomes impossible," was extremely persuasive, and the Board did feel compelled to respond to this critique.[88] Maudslay initially attempted to use the wording of the Education Act itself to justify the policy shift. He initially argued that the text of the Education Act referred to children who "*are* unable" to take advantage of their education. The meals were, therefore, designed to treat a current condition and not meant to prevent future problems. For this reason, he insisted, the child needed to manifest some sign of subnormal nutrition before feeding could commence.[89] But many of the Board's medical officers, including Glover, were forced to agree that since malnutrition was a process, its deleterious effects would likely take their toll before any symptom became apparent.[90] Although the Board did everything it could to counter the accusation that its policy was "deliberately" to wait until children are "diseased or under-nourished" before free school meals could be supplied, its officials had to concede that this was in fact the implication of the new regulations.[91] Fearing criticism that it was "taking the bread (or milk) out of the children's mouths," the Board thus attempted to compromise with the LEAs that were resistant to introducing medical selection, allowing them to use this method for new cases only without removing any children who were currently on the lists.[92] It was only the "fat as butter" children, the Board explained to its critics, who should definitely be removed from the free meals lists.[93]

Even as it attempted these compromises, the Board nevertheless insisted that the most salient question was "does the child need feeding?" not "are the child's parents poor?" when determining which children should be placed on the feeding lists.[94] Beginning to emerge in the 1930s, proponents of "social medicine," such as Somerville Hastings, insisted that poverty both compromised the ability to maintain an adequate diet and necessarily meant that access to health care was limited. Because these both had significant long-term effects on health and well-being, advocates of social medicine lobbied for free preventative and curative medicine for all and for wider access to free school meals. If the Board's officials acknowledged that poverty and malnutrition were often linked, they claimed that this was not necessarily the case. The Board insisted, therefore, that the meals services should not be used as a backdoor to supplement the income of poor or unemployed families, drawing monies out of the Education budget that should properly be charged to the Public Assistance Authorities or the Unemployment Assistance Board.

Disentangling poverty from malnutrition was key to the Board's promotion of medical selection over economic selection. It justified the 1934 policy shift by demonstrating that not all children of the poor and unemployed were malnourished, on the one hand, and that not all malnourished children were being identified in a system that required parents or nonmedical officials to initiate the process, on the other. When Swansea introduced school meals for the first time following the policy shift, its SMOs (who had been instructed to abide by the new regulations around medical selection) found that 50 percent of children of unemployed parents had normal levels of nutrition. The Board frequently quoted this statistic when confronted by lobbyists for economic selection who claimed that all poor children must be suffering from malnutrition.[95] Conversely, the Board deployed evidence that "the areas showing the largest number of malnourished children are not necessarily those suffering from the severest economic stress."[96] If the statistics on Swansea had established the former point, they were also used to make the latter. The same surveys that had found surprisingly good nutrition among those with unemployed parents also disclosed that 35 percent of the Swansea schoolchildren overall were suffering from some form of subnormal nutrition, despite the fact that this was not, comparatively, a particularly depressed area. This was alarmingly high given that the average for England and Wales hovered around 10 percent. Rather than question these figures, as Swansea had only started their meal service in 1934 and fully adopted the medical selection process, the Board used this district to demonstrate that malnutrition might be found in any community. While many of these malnourished children did qualify for free meals based on income, the Board suggested that they did not necessarily come from chronically unemployed or low-wage families. Its officials stressed that these children's parents may not have applied for free meals if the LEA had only used economic selection to identify which children to feed. The Swansea statistics became key evidence in the Board's defense against charges that medical selection was intended to limit the numbers of children fed. "From the point of view of defending our policy against the charge that it is merely one of economy," argued Maudslay in late 1934, "the figures in this case should prove very useful."[97]

Assimilation, "Inefficient" Parenting, and Ethnic Communities

The Board explained away any perceived correlation between income and malnutrition not only by marshaling these statistics but by arguing that the ability to identify which children would benefit from school meals was a complex process. Rather than seizing upon malnutrition as a condition that could easily be remedied through a scientific identification of the precise components that a diet was lacking, the medical professionals involved in the school meals and medical services often used the term to refer to the body's failure to assimilate and use the food ingested properly, regardless of the components of the child's diet. In 1906, experts had repeatedly identified the broader context for a child's malnourishment that might be due to social and environmental factors.[98] In 1914, Newman had reiterated this position, explaining that malnourishment arises from a variety of conditions, which could be "quite remote from the actual provision of food for the child's consumption." These might include lack of sleep or sleeping in a bad atmosphere, employment out of school hours, "eating unsuitable food, at unsuitable times, unsuitably prepared," the "irregular habits of family life," or an underlying disease or pathological condition. Any of these might be the root cause of malnutrition, Newman explained, "the remedy of which will not be found only in the provision of meals."[99] This understanding of the multitude of causes of malnutrition remained dominant among the central education authorities even after the discovery of vitamins and the explosion of research into deficiency diseases in the 1920s and 1930s. As late as 1938, Marjorie Green rightly argued that the Board of Education had "minimised the importance of dietary deficiencies as a cause of malnutrition and have stressed the factors which may impede proper assimilation."[100]

Far from being a modern scientific approach to malnutrition derived from the growth of research into food values that historians have repeatedly argued characterized the interwar period, this interpretation of the causes of malnutrition harkened back to the ancient Greek and Roman focus on bodily regimen. This medical cosmology understood health as dependent upon the "six non-naturals." These were defined as food and drink; air; exercise and rest; sleep and wakefulness; excretions and retentions; and the impact of emotional and mental states. In a 1928 lecture entitled "The Foundations of National Health," Newman had posited that, "the elements of nutrition for the body are six in number": food; warmth; fresh air and sunlight; cleanliness; exercise; and rest.[101] Adhering to this ancient model of health in relation to the correct processing of food – which circulated among the medical officers of the Board as well as those of some local LEAs – meant that many involved in school feeding continued to see malnutrition as a complex individualized problem that could not in each and every case be remedied merely by the regular provision of balanced abundant meals. Newman had argued in 1910 that "two children, each alike suffering from malnutrition, may have had the condition caused in the one case mainly by insufficient food and general neglect; in the other by unsuitable feeding and pampering."[102] He had not abandoned this position in the interwar period, despite the "newer knowledge of nutrition." Newman's long tenure at the Board that began with the inception of the medical services in 1907 and ended only in 1935 meant that this view helped to shape its approach to malnutrition well into the 1930s.[103]

The Board's officers also frequently maintained that the root cause of malnutrition was not the lack of good food itself but rather "inefficient" mothering, a position shared by many at the Ministry of Health through the 1930s.[104] Dr. D. Noel Paton and Leonard Findlay's influential 1926 report to the Medical Research Council on poverty, nutrition, and growth in rural Scotland had concluded that "of all the factors studied the character of the mother is the most directly associated with the nutrition of the child."[105] Paton, as discussed in Chapter 4, had advised the British government during World War I that fewer calories were actually required to keep a laboring body in health than figures suggested by other scientific experts. He and his colleagues in the "Glasgow School" were also actively opposed to "this present craze for vitamins" and to biochemical explanations for subnormal nutrition in general.[106] Instead, Paton and Findlay's study had identified "maternal inefficiency" closely correlated with the physical condition of the child, suggesting that the root of the problem was individual lifestyle and behavior, a theme discernable in their work and that of their colleagues for over a decade.[107] Newman had long been sympathetic to this position. While subnormal nutrition among schoolchildren might be caused by poverty, he conjectured in 1926 that "more often it is careless mothering, ignorance of upbringing and lack of nurture than actual shortage of food which results in a malnourished child." The fact that malnutrition can be seen and starts in infancy and becomes a habit of the body before school age, he asserted, suggests that, "maternal insufficiency is concerned."[108] This implied that the education of mothers, rather than the feeding of their children, was the most appropriate solution to the problem. In defending themselves against the charge that widespread malnutrition was due to poverty, Newman and others harkened back to early Victorian attempts to normalize poverty by disassociating it from the root causes of morbidity and mortality. Hence, Edwin Chadwick's assertion in the 1830s that death could not be caused by "starvation" and should not therefore be registered in this way.[109] These governmental slights of hand persisted even a century later. As David Smith and Malcolm Nicolson have demonstrated, the "conservative thought" of the "Glasgow School" continued through the end of the 1930s to lend "scientific authority to successive governments' policy of minimal intervention in the health problems associated with poverty," which included the Board's half-hearted investment in school meals.[110]

This focus on individual behavior – in this case "bad management on the part of the housewife" or the intemperate habits of her husband – circulated widely in discussions of the root cause of malnutrition.[111] Many SMOs maintained that the children they identified as having subnormal nutrition came from homes where the mother knew nothing about food values or preparation or the father was lazy, profligate, or a drunkard.[112] These types of parents, argued a female SMO in Yorkshire's West Riding, "more or less allow the children to go their own way and do not take much care as to what time they get to bed and whether they have anything before going to school in a morning."[113] Inquiries into the distressed mining areas of Glamorgan and Monmouthshire in the early 1930s similarly concluded that "the reaction of women to the same economic circumstances varies greatly" and their "capacity for domestic management" impacted the health of their children.[114] Similar investigations in Tyneside had led health visitors and others providing social services in the community to conclude that "the extreme variations of household management" had a "decisive influence" on the malnutrition of children.[115] In 1936, the SMO for the Isle of Wight quantified these contentions. Of the 16.3 percent of the school population he found suffering from subnormal nutrition, "home management" was at fault, he declared, in 52 percent of the cases.[116] In a minority of cases, it was found that overindulging children could have similarly detrimental results. Overly "fussy" mothers, suggested the SMO for Smethwick, might introduce "a neurosis in the child."[117] This helped to explain why subnormal nutrition could also be found among children from middle-class homes. A 1938 report on the nutritional condition of schoolchildren in Northumberland had determined that malnutrition was not confined to the children of the poor and working classes. One often finds that the children of "better-class" parents, it claimed, are "not permitted to play in the streets" and are "overclothed, over-fed, un-exercised, pampered, spoilt and indulged." These children are "absolute directors of their own feeding and destiny" and, as a result, are not eating properly.[118] The Board of Education thus counseled LEAs as late as 1939 to institute cookery classes for mothers, a solution to malnutrition proffered by other public health officials.[119]

If the discourses of "inefficient" mothering placed the onus on the individual to learn how to care for her child appropriately, downplaying the need for state intervention, the marked variations in nutrition among schoolchildren within the same locality and whose families had experienced similar economic distress were also explained away by focusing on the differences between populations inhabiting the same area. Local and national officials sometimes spoke not only of individual "inefficient" mothers but also of entire populations "of indifferent social type" unable or unwilling to nurture their children.[120] These populations tended to be cast as members of the "lowest class" of the community.[121] But the discourses of "race" and "stock" were also deployed to explain why only some portions of the population had malnourished children, a connection between race and parenting that evoked the colonial government's position on providing famine relief to Indian children decades earlier. When Dr. Robert Weaver, one of the Board's medical officers, visited Cumberland in 1929, he found that despite the effects of long-term industrial depression in the region, malnutrition was rife only in the Cleator Moor district. He attributed this entirely to the large numbers of Irish who had settled there. "I gathered that the population of the Western coastal area of Cumberland is made up of two races," he reported, "the Cumbrians who are hard-working and thrifty and the Irish who settled here during the famine period of the middle of last century." He characterized this latter group as "thriftless and lacking in initiative, making no effort to find work elsewhere in times of stress," and more likely to have malnourished children.[122]

That children suffering from malnutrition were most often found "among the rather shiftless immigrant" was an often repeated maxim of the South Wales community.[123] The inquiry into Glamorgan and Monmouthshire in the 1930s had confidently claimed that "parental care appears to be higher in the older established communities where the old Welsh stock predominates, and lower in places where, in times of great prosperity and mining development, much immigration has occurred." In Abertillery, where 22.3 percent of schoolchildren had been found to have unsatisfactory nutrition, the population was said to be "largely Irish, with large families." "Racial differences may be a factor," the report asserted, "and there has probably been more immigration than in Country Durham, a similar mining district in England, and more admixture of the original stock."[124] Much was made of the "old Welsh stock" as an explanation for the absence of malnutrition in areas that had been hard hit by industrial depression.[125] This term suggested a hereditary type of hearty and resilient body but also gestured to a culture of independence from the state maintained through hard work and thrift. The Board's Dr. J. E. Underwood reported in 1930 on the nutrition of children in the Welsh mining districts, underscoring both of these points.

In the South Wales Colliery districts, as in other large industrial areas are found colonies of an "alien" population, who in the past have been attracted by high wages and prosperity, and have eventually settled down in the places of their adoption. This migratory type is not up to the same standard of social and moral qualities as that of the indigenous population. They are less provident, less hard working, less self-reliant and have less pride in the social qualities which distinguish the typical Welsh miner. The settlement of a few members of an undesirable type appears to act as a nucleus of attraction for other undesirables. Hence are formed in the midst of a community consisting for the most part of old established Welsh stock, provident, hardworking and courageous, isolated "pockets" of an inferior type of population.

It was in these "socially inefficient communities," argued Underwood, that one finds the greatest incidence of malnutrition. If the "social" factor could be "eliminated," he argued, the "economic" factor could be overcome.[126] Newman repeated Underwood's assertions in his 1930 annual report, underscoring this approach to malnutrition, which seemed to place as much emphasis on heredity and social and moral factors as on access to nutritious food.[127]

These claims that gender, race, class, and ethnicity all shaped the nutritional state of children were sustained by some of the Board's officials, as well as several SMOs and other public health officials, throughout the 1930s.[128] This discourse deflected responsibility for the feeding of schoolchildren away from the state by emphasizing that some economically stressed populations had been able to nourish their children while others had allowed them to deteriorate. It was the domestic practices of unassimilated ethnic groups, the Board of Education concluded, that led to their children's inability to assimilate food properly. This suggested that the issue was primarily parenting rather than finances or the availability of state services.

Deploying Different Data

Those who critiqued medical selection and strongly preferred economic selection were not, however, convinced by either the Swansea statistics or the Board's "social" explanations for malnutrition. Indeed, they continued to insist that it was poor parents and not poor parenting that had led to widespread malnutrition. Proponents of economic selection thus turned to other data to argue that their method of identifying which children should be fed by the state was in fact more scientific than medical selection.

In the early 1930s, decades of research into food values, calories, and the components of a healthy diet, and very recent studies stimulated by widespread hunger during the Depression, allowed different groups of experts to produce standards as to what constituted sufficient and appropriate food for persons of all ages. These experts did not always agree: the BMA's Committee on Nutrition and the ACN (which was itself made up of members who had long-standing intellectual differences) were very publicly at odds about the numbers of calories and protein a healthy body required, much to the government's dismay and embarrassment.[129] Nevertheless, statistics on the cost of living in different regions across the United Kingdom allowed for the use of these studies to calculate the cost of either the "minimum" or "optimum" diet (the difference between the two itself a politicized issue) required to keep a body properly nourished.[130] In 1933, *The Week-end Review* commissioned an inquiry into the state of nutrition in response to public outcry over sensational news stories of death by starvation. This "Hungry England" report had concluded that it was impossible to achieve a diet that met the ACN's minimum standard with the allowances provided by the Public Assistance Committees, which had replaced the Poor Law after a 1929 reorganization of relief.[131] The BMA's subsequent report recommended a higher minimum standard in terms of calories and protein but similarly calculated the minimum weekly expenditure on foodstuffs that must be incurred by families of different sizes if the BMA's standards were to be met. It concluded that the unemployed and the low-wage worker would not be able to afford the necessary foodstuffs.[132] G. C. M. M'Gonigle and J. Kirby's 1936 *Poverty and Public Health* also maintained that whether one used the standards set by the BMA or the ACN, many families simply could not afford the minimum recommended diet.[133] In his even more influential 1936 *Food, Health and Income*, John Boyd Orr, one of the nation's leading nutritional researchers, calculated that an adequate diet for "optimum" health could almost be reached by families earning 20–30 shillings per head per week, if 10 shillings per head per week was spent on food. Only approximately half of British families, however, achieved this level of appropriate nutrition, Orr argued, a figure that other researchers suggested was in fact an overestimate.[134]

Proponents of economic selection did not see the disagreements between these inquiries as to what constituted an appropriate diet as an intractable problem, despite the fact that they exposed, as David Smith has argued, the subjective nature of dietary standards.[135] Although this lack of consensus and its manifestation in heated public debates contributed to what M'Gonigle and Kirby identified as widespread "confusion," "political feeling," and "bitterness" around the subject of malnutrition, the LEAs and pressure groups that resisted medical selection argued that local authorities could use these and other findings alongside the Ministry of Labour's monthly cost of living statistics to determine objectively whether or not the "expenditure available for food" in the family of any given child was "insufficient for full health."[136] Income scales could be calculated and revised by each LEA based on local cost of living standards. School meals could then be provided where these straightforward mathematical calculations revealed a deficit in the family budget.

In 1934, the Walsall Education Committee used the BMA report in this manner to determine its income scale.[137] This argument allowed LEAs that practiced economic selection to defend their method as equally scientific as those who argued for medical selection. Given that it was possible, argued the CMC, to produce "scientific estimates of minimum needs," an income test was therefore the "simplest and most scientific method" of selecting children for school meals.[138] The SMO for Hendon similarly insisted that it was "unquestionably more accurate to determine the need for assistance by an arithmetical examination of the family income than by a physical examination of the child," a sentiment widely shared even among SMOs.[139]

Those who lobbied for economic selection contested the Board's new policy on its own terms by undermining its claims to objectivity and scientific rigor, deploying their own statistics and mathematical calculations in response. But others preferred "the poverty test" precisely because it was not impersonal. Since it was so difficult to identify the clinical evidence of malnutrition, having a complete view of the child's circumstances was to many SMOs preferable as it allowed for a better determination of the child's need. Many school doctors welcomed having the knowledge of the financial means of the child's family made available at the time of the medical inspection (as opposed to only after a clinical diagnosis had already been made) in order to put any physical signs that might become apparent into their proper social context. The SMO for Torquay considered the "intimate" knowledge he had built up over years serving the medical needs of this relatively small community a distinct advantage. He claimed that it had allowed him to see the child as "a whole against the background of its home" and to consider "all factors" in making a recommendation.[140] Similarly, the director of education for Preston argued that many officials besides the SMO had important information about the "whole circumstances of each child" that was crucial to establishing who should be fed.[141]

The combination of an objective calculation of a child's household income with an intimate knowledge of its home life was preferable to a brief and impersonal clinical examination, proponents of economic selection argued, precisely because a child was not an individual medical case but rather part of a family unit. If one of the innovations of school meals, as Susan Pedersen has argued, was to treat children as citizens with rights independent of their families,[142] rights affirmed by the CMC and others organizations, this became a complicated position to sustain once it became clear that this actually allowed the government to deny that it had responsibilities to others within the home who may also be suffering. Those who favored economic selection frequently argued that if the children of the unemployed and low-wage workers were not malnourished, this was only because someone else within the family was sacrificing his or her health to keep the children fed. Those familiar with the families of the poor frequently noted that mothers stinted themselves in order that their children not go short of food. It was only because mothers were themselves badly malnourished, many argued, that the children appeared healthy and fit.[143] To move to a system of medical inspection, its opponents claimed, would mean that mothers would have to make difficult decisions. Should they deny themselves even more in order to nourish their children in the absence of the school meal that had previously been provided on the basis of the income scale? Or should they allow their children to become malnourished in order to qualify for school meals based on clinical symptoms?

Many LEAs feared that in practice medical inspection actually encouraged the "inefficient" parenting that the Board itself had identified as one of the primary causes of malnutrition. A Manchester official suggested that in his district "some poor parents might deliberately let their children become under-nourished again so that they could be fed by the Authority," if they had been removed from the feeding list.[144] Given this, medical selection, it was charged, favored parents "of the feckless type" who were irresponsible and had allowed their children to suffer. Two children, living side by side, whose families had the same income, would be treated differently. The responsible parents who kept their children well-nourished at the expense of their own well-being would be overlooked, while the irresponsible parents who fed themselves first or gambled and drank away the family income would have their children fed at the expense of the state.[145] According to a member of the Ipswich Education Committee, "very often the best mothers were penalised because they had managed by superhuman self-sacrifice to feed their children so well that malnutrition did not appear."[146] Those who favored economic selection thus manipulated the Board's discourses of "maternal inefficiency" and "socially inefficient communities" to challenge the state on the grounds that it was precisely these families that would be benefitting from medical selection while the responsible parents would suffer as a result.

The Board's officials acknowledged that some mothers stinted themselves; thus, by implication, medical selection favored the feckless.[147] They continued to feed the children of "socially inefficient communities" according to a similar logic that had governed child famine relief on the subcontinent: that these parents could not be trusted. But because not all British children were victims of poor parenting, the Board reasoned that their limited funds needed to be directed only at the children who were not benefitting from their education due to improper feeding. Since school meals were an educational service and not intended as a means of subsistence, the Board's staff consistently maintained that these funds were not therefore to be expended on these children's families. Their relief needed to come from other government agencies whose budgets were separate from the Education monies. For this reason, the Board cautioned against authorities allowing children to take home any part of their school meal, fearing (as had famine officials) that the milk or bread might wind up in the stomachs of their parents or other children within the household.[148] While the Board acknowledged that its policy of medical selection was in some respects discouraging good parenting, it maintained that this was not its primary concern and ultimately could not be helped.

Although critics of medical selection may have failed to change the Board's attitudes toward the communities that it served, they were ultimately successful in advocating for the continuance of economic selection. In the end, the Board was forced to concede that it could not in fact enforce its own policy, given that the LEAs in many major metropolitan areas refused to comply. It grudgingly allowed the LEAs that forcefully resisted medical selection to retain their old systems as long as they were effectively serving the needs of their local communities.[149] Economic selection – with its ideology that all children of the poor should be fed by the state lest they become malnourished – thus continued in some regions unabated throughout the 1930s, despite the stated policy shift. The Board, even under National Labour leadership from 1938, nevertheless continued to uphold medical selection as the best means of determining who were the "proper" beneficiaries of free school meals.

The Deficiencies of the School Dietaries

The heated debate over medical selection exposed the range of attitudes toward malnutrition and poverty in circulation during the Depression and the Board's limited commitment to scientific solutions to the problem once the policy had been put into practice. However, neither the shift to medical selection nor the opposition marshaled against it had any significant impact on what schoolchildren were actually fed in the second half of the 1930s. In the midst of what might be called "the malnutrition moment," the Board nevertheless, as John Welshman has argued, increasingly avoided the issue of nutrition itself.[150] This was a symptom of what Derek Oddy identifies as the "lack of political will to implement any solution to the problem of poor growth and health" during the 1930s in general.[151] Although after 1934 the Board began to urge LEAs that offered no meals or milk to provide these services, ultimately local authorities could choose whether or not to offer meals, which meals to cater, and what foods were in these meals.[152] This meant that there was no consistency as to what schoolchildren were being fed across the United Kingdom and in fact limited oversight of the meals themselves. Thus, if the Board claimed to be using science to diagnose malnutrition, it paid scant attention to how current research might be deployed to treat the problem.

Some LEAs provided healthy and well-balanced meals that reflected the recent advances in knowledge of food values, however contested these might have been. The London County Council (LCC) periodically sent samples of school meals to their own chemists to ascertain their protein content and caloric value.[153] In Bedfordshire in 1938, the dinners included a variety of meats, wholemeal bread, cooked greens, salad, and fruit-based puddings.[154] Leyton was similarly proactive about using local expertise to formulate menus according to "modern physiological and medical knowledge." This involved furnishing a variety of fresh fruits and vegetables and serving only small amounts of potatoes, which many feared accounted for too many of the calories in the working-class diet.[155] Despite the scientific advances of the interwar period and the Board's attempt to bring the school meals services into closer collaboration with the School Medical Service, most LEAs did not appear to have planned their menus or recipes "in a sensible and scientific way" and took little account of the nutritional composition of the meals.[156] In 1935, Dr. Muriel Bywaters, a member of the Board's medical staff, found that even in areas of the country that had not been hit hard by the economic depression, the school meal often had little nutritional value. It frequently consisted of milk, bread and jam, and a main dish of potato pie, potato hash, or a soup made from bones (the same used all week) and dried peas or beans.[157] The menu for May 1939 in Rochdale was particularly grim: it included "brown vegetable stew with green peas" followed by a "steamed fig pudding with shite [sic] sauce," which one can only hope was really white sauce.[158]

Ironically, it was the Board's strong preference for a hot dinner that led many LEAs to offer these substandard meals. These required fuel and cooking and storage equipment, leading some contractors or the schools themselves to economize on quality. It was experiments with cold foods in the 1930s that revealed the Board's bias was misplaced. In places where cooking a hot dinner was impractical, some LEAs introduced cold meals that required limited preparation. Glossop, Cambridge, and Ipswich provided sandwiches made from wholemeal bread, butter, brewer's yeast (a living organism high in B vitamins), and a variety of fillings chosen for their nutritional value, which included cheese, meat, egg, sardines, Marmite, peanut butter, dried fruits, and seasonal raw vegetables such as tomato, lettuce, mustard greens, or watercress.[159] In 1938, the LCC similarly experimented with a cold midday meal, taking as its model the "Oslo breakfast." The original Oslo breakfast was developed in Norway in the 1920s and introduced as a nourishing meal for schoolchildren in 1932.[160] The LCC modified what it renamed the "health dinner" to suit the apparently "conservative" tastes of English children: it included salad, brown bread, cheese, butter, a raw apple or orange, and two-thirds of a pint of milk.[161] The experiment proved successful both in terms of its health benefits and its appeal to the children, despite doubts that it would "satisfy English tastes," and by 1939, the Board began to advocate the adoption of an Oslo-style meal in places where providing a hot dinner was impractical.[162] It was only at the very end of the 1930s that the Board overcame its own conservatism as to what constituted a proper meal. This was despite the fact that scientific support for the Oslo breakfast had been widely available for almost a decade and its nutritional value advocated by some members of the ACN since the early 1930s.[163]

In fact, it was as much the cheapness and ease of the "health dinner," as the nutritional science behind it, that won the Board over in the end as variations in the quality of the hot dinners were partly due to local finances. The average gross cost to provide a meal across England and Wales in 1938 amounted to 5 pence, 3 pence of which covered the food itself. But some LEAs were spending as little as 2 pence per head on a cooked midday dinner, which the Board considered too little to provide what could be considered a "square meal."[164] Site visits made as part of the Board's routine inspections revealed that the LEAs who contracted with local cafés to feed the children (rather than running their own Feeding Centres) were often not getting the best value for their money. Contractors sometimes appeared to be "making a large profit" on the dinners they provided, which were often "unsatisfactory in quantity and quality." Cheap foods were widely utilized, such as dried vegetables and fruit, minced meat, and potatoes.[165] The Board's officials regularly found that the meals provided by contractors were "horrible" in appearance and "certainly not appetising enough to sample," suggesting that the funds might be adequate but the meal substandard due to an unscrupulous or unskilled caterer.[166] For these and other reasons, the Board typically advocated Feeding Centres run by the LEA itself (Figure 5.2). This did not necessarily solve the problem of poor quality

Figure 5.2 Trinity Street Feeding Centre: children eating in the dining room, Southwark, London, 1937. © City of London, London Metropolitan Archives, COLLAGE: The London Picture Archive, ref: 205146.

meals, however, as the Board provided almost no guidance as to the food itself; thus, the quality of meals in these institutions also varied widely.

In his 1931 Annual Report, Newman maintained that a school dinner should be treated as the child's main meal of the day. It should, therefore, provide two-thirds of the daily calories required for health and appropriate servings of protein, fat, and vitamins. He warned that cooks should not rely on soups for protein and insisted that the vegetable proteins found in peas, beans, and lentils were not equivalent to "first-class" animal proteins.[167] But throughout the 1930s, the Board offered little practical advice about the ideal components of a nutritious school dinner. Its officials generally cautioned LEAs that the meals should make good the deficiencies in the home diet and that menus should be formulated "in the light of modern knowledge of the science of nutrition," but they gave no concrete advice.[168] The question of whether the Board of Education should establish a minimum standard for the dietary was raised only in 1937. Glover felt that the Board's failure to provide "any guidance" as to the food values desirable in a school dinner was a clear weakness in the meals administration and suggested that the ACN should be asked to construct a school dietary based on their already extant minimum standards that could then be instituted by all LEAs. This suggestion was quickly dismissed, however, as others feared that this would require the mandating of meals that were too expensive for some districts to provide, leading some to opt out entirely. Rather than requiring a dietary conform to particular standards, examples of successful dietaries in place in LEAs with model meals programs, it was decided, would be provided to those who actively sought or clearly needed advice. But even this was a half-hearted effort because the Board never compiled a list of exemplary menus nor had any on hand as useful examples when LEAs wrote asking for them.[169]

In 1938, however, the Board appointed a dietician, initially on a short-term basis, to provide a report on how the meals services were operating nationwide.[170] E. M. Langley, who had served first as a domestic subjects instructor in Walthamstow and then as the LCC's organizer of school meals, took up the post of inspector of provision of meals arrangements.[171] In her first year, Langley visited 66 of the 150 LEAs that provided solid meals, focusing on those that seemed to be spending the least per child. She found that only a few of the dietaries in force reflected current scientific understandings of nutrition and that many had been introduced decades earlier and had not been altered since. These dietaries, she charged, had been drawn up on an "economic basis" and did not include the more expensive "protective" foods that were lacking in the children's home diets. Only in about 5 percent of the locations she visited were the meals really good; in 20 percent she maintained they were totally unsatisfactory.[172]

This appointment of a dietary inspector suggests that the Board was willing to chastise local authorities who provided poor quality dinners. But it also exposed its unwillingness to furnish them with any practical nutritional guidelines that could be immediately adopted, as even Langley did not provide any model dietaries. Ultimately, the Board's decision not to develop or provide LEAs with menus and recipes devised by nutritional experts undermined its contention that the school meals service was, even in the heyday of the nutritional sciences, effective at tackling the problem of malnutrition. For it was not until World War II was in full swing that the Board began to intervene in menu planning, directing local authorities as to the necessary nutritive components of school dietaries.

The End of Medical Selection and the Coming of War

Standards for the nutritional content of school meals were not established until 1941.[173] In fact, the Board admitted in the 1950s that it was only during World War II that the provision of school meals was "put on a sound nutritional basis," despite the availability of the necessary knowledge in the interwar period.[174] Although in the first months after the outbreak of hostilities there was a decline in the provision of school meals, it was the war that provided a context for the reconstitution of the school meals service along scientific, efficient, and humane lines. As Welshman has argued, by the 1940s, the Board began to accept the criticisms lodged at its meals program and to attend to the problems that had plagued the service in the 1920s and 1930s. By the middle of the war, the Board had abandoned its policy and practices of medical selection, increased its grants to LEAs, removed the distinction between canteens for paying children and Feeding Centres for the necessitous, and approved plans for the expansion of the number of LEAs offering solid meals rather than merely milk. Significantly, the Board also declared in 1943 not that its goal was to feed the right child, the mantra of the 1930s, but rather that "the Government's objective" was to feed at least 75 percent of schoolchildren. To achieve this, the 1944 Education Act turned the voluntary provision of meals into a compulsory service. It required all LEAs to provide meals and to employ an experienced school meals organizer, ensuring that the work was actually done and done properly.[175] It was thus only another crisis of national security that forced the state to take a more prominent role in preventing and treating malnutrition and not the social and economic crises wrought by the Depression.

Despite the availability of the "newer knowledge of nutrition," successful experiments with inexpensive and nutritious cold dinners, the administrative structures already in place to deliver meals to a large population of schoolchildren, and a demonstrated need for state feeding, the meals provided in the interwar period were substandard in quality and were not prepared according to any minimum dietary standards. Moreover, by the end of the decade, largely because of attempts to enforce medical selection and the substitution of milk for meals, they had reached only 4 percent of schoolchildren.[176] In the interwar period, the school meals service failed to fulfill the promise of the Lib-Lab agenda that had ushered in the state provision of free school meals as part of a series of progressive reforms aimed at those most vulnerable within the capitalist economy. Nor did the government deploy an instrumental approach to the feeding of dependent children as it had during the Indian famines. It failed to apply the logic that the state should feed all poor children (or even all malnourished children) at its own expense as part of its investment in the future efficiency of the nation. Without the wholehearted commitment from the Board to feed all those in need at a time of severe and widespread financial distress, many children continued, in the words of an SMO for a depressed area, to "bear on their bodies the marks of the economic hardships of recent years."[177]

6   Every Sort and Condition of Citizen
British Restaurants and the Communal
Feeding Experiment during World War II

The provision of school meals only lived up to the potential that had been conspicuously achievable in the 1930s once these services had become part of a broader wartime strategy of communal feeding, which considerably expanded the number of people eating government food. During World War II, the social researcher Tom Harrisson noted that "the State" seemed to be suddenly "taking an interest" in a much wider swathe of the population "getting decent food."[1] He was not only referring to rationing but to the government's introduction of a brand new institution: the communal feeding center. These not-for-profit government-run canteens provided nourishing, healthy, and warm midday meals for civilians at cost and off the ration. Unlike emergency feeding centers, communal feeding centers were open to the general public. Rebranded "British Restaurants" by Winston Churchill himself, these institutions represented a striking new phenomenon: for the "first time in the history of [the United Kingdom]," the government was providing nourishing and nutritious meals at below true market value to the "general public" on a "large-scale" in a manner that could not be classed as "charity."[2] This provision of communal feeding facilities for "the general public under Government auspices" was, according to the Ministry of Food (MOF), "an entirely new development since the War."[3] Unlike any of the other state-feeding programs that I have discussed, this one was open to "all comers," thus radically reconfiguring the nature of government food.[4]

Historians, even those such as Peter Atkins who have given these institutions serious consideration, have tended to argue that British Restaurants made only a marginal contribution to wartime feeding as they served a mere 618,000 meals across the United Kingdom per day and were far outnumbered by industrial canteens.[5] In the context of a wider history of state feeding, however, these institutions emerge as particularly significant. Initially targeted at the working poor in order to ameliorate their chronically deficient diets and boost wartime morale, British Restaurants were not in fact intended for all British citizens however much they might be "doing their bit" during wartime. That they came to serve a much broader cross section of the home front population was not the result of a coherent government policy. Instead, it was because a proactive public used these services for their own purposes and in the process became not merely passive recipients of government food control policies but "co-producer[s] of systems of provision."[6] The history of the British Restaurant illustrates how beneficiaries themselves shaped government programs, how malleable were the political ideologies that undergirded the state's food policies, and how initiatives conceived of as a form of war socialism could at the same time be deployed to instill market principles.

Poverty Diets and Target Populations

The idea of a communal feeding program targeted at the poor was not new in 1940. In the interwar period, a variety of experts concerned with poverty and malnutrition began to discuss the need for a national food policy that would remedy the deficiencies in diet wrought by economic inequalities. Communal feeding, including but not limited to school meals, was widely seen as an essential element of such a policy.[7] When the war broke out, John Boyd Orr, the leading expert on the relationship between poverty and malnutrition and a member of Churchill's Scientific Committee on Food Policy, cautioned that victory would depend upon the morale and endurance of the civilian population. This could not be maintained unless the whole population had access to a diet "good enough to maintain it in health." A wartime food policy, he argued, should be designed to meet the food requirements of those living in poverty.[8] "Equality of sacrifice," Orr and others argued, "must start only after the basic food requirements are met."[9]

These types of statements, however, took for granted that the state's food control policies would only be initiated to secure and equalize the food requirements of domestic British subjects as the sacrifices of colonial subjects did not merit such impassioned pleas. As Lizzie Collingham has demonstrated, in attempting to alleviate wartime hunger on the United Kingdom's home front, the British government precipitated the deaths by starvation and its concomitant diseases of three million Indian subjects during the Bengal Famine of 1943. Before and during the famine, Churchill and his War Cabinet resisted the implementation of rationing in India until it was too late to control the food supply, diverted foodstuffs elsewhere, and rejected international attempts at aid. In refusing to take seriously the desperateness of India's food situation, Collingham has argued that the British wartime state "determined that India would be the part of the empire where the greatest civilian sacrifices would have to be made, and displaced hunger on to the colony."[10]

The Bengal Famine was still three years away when concrete planning for the communal feeding initiatives that would come to be called British Restaurants began on June 24, 1940, several weeks after Winston Churchill assumed the position of prime minister and several months before the Blitz. But even as the state prosecuted a war to defend its version of empire, it never fully acknowledged that it was equally responsible for the food security of its colonial peoples. The first tentative conversations within the Food Policy Committee of the War Cabinet focused only on the need to provide adequate food for those within the United Kingdom who were living at the poverty line but were not dependent upon public assistance. Communal feeding was here discussed under the heading of "provision of cheap food for the poorer classes."[11] Lord Woolton, the minister of food, cautioned that experiments with communal feeding had not been particularly popular during World War I.[12] Given this, he proposed moving forward with one or two "National Kitchens" in "populous areas" rather than any "large scale" scheme aimed at the "general population."[13] In August of 1940, J. C. Drummond, the chief scientific advisor to the MOF and an expert on nutrition, supported such a plan, arguing that the deficiencies associated with "poverty diets" could be partly corrected cheaply and without disruption to food habits through well-planned communal meals.[14] The idea of a state-sponsored meals service was first formulated as a program for a necessitous target population: not the Blitzed, as many have assumed, but rather those civilians on Britain's home front whose diet was chronically deficient due to poverty conditions and made more so by wartime inflation and shortages.

The state's justification for communal feeding was not only that it would address chronic malnutrition and contribute to national efficiency. It was also deeply imbedded within concerns about the triangular relationship among civilian morale, the availability of foodstuffs, and social stability. Howard Marshall, director of public relations for the MOF from 1940 to 1943, stressed that the purpose of initiating a community feeding program was to "care for the poor" hit hard by the cost of living increase. Although Marshall would soon be accused of allowing his "heart" to "run away" with him,[15] he argued that "looked at from a hard-hearted point of view, the poor, who always exist, are not a serious danger to the state in peacetime, but in wartime their lack of morale may well be contagious and a grave danger." This morale, he posited, could best be built up by "adequate feeding and a sense of community." For Marshall, good cheap food was linked to national security. If the chronic malnutrition experienced by a large proportion of the population had not actually mobilized the government to take meaningful action during the Depression, low morale among the poorer quarters during wartime, Marshall implied, could destabilize the nation at a time when Britain could least afford internal fissures. "I regard communal feeding as the most important step we can take as a Ministry," argued Marshall, and there are "signs that unless we initiate it ourselves we shall be forced into it by public opinion."[16]

An example of effective communal feeding of the poorer population was already in operation in the summer of 1940, providing a reassuring model for the MOF to adopt. This "Communal Restaurant" was located in a working-class neighborhood of North Kensington and run by Flora Solomon, the staff superintendent for the department store Marks & Spencer, which had introduced subsidized staff canteens in every branch. Solomon's communal restaurant was financed by her employer Simon Marks.[17] Its customers represented a "typical cross section of a working class community," and it proved extremely popular with locals. Dining at this "people's restaurant" in July for the purposes of reconnaissance, a government official noted that, "in a poor district" such as this one, there were no commercial restaurants and that Solomon's canteen had allowed working people to eat well-cooked, nourishing meals for a price they could afford.[18] Seeing it in operation helped to convince the MOF that a collective feeding service for "the general public" could fill a real need, charge low tariffs, and still be self-supporting.

By "general public" the Ministry's officials clearly meant the poorer classes, for they argued that by placing collective feeding services in "poor urban areas, we should impose automatically a rough means test," fully cognizant of the fact that an actual means test was not on the table given how much it had been resented during the Depression.[19] When no suitable locations could be found for an experimental scheme run out of the MOF, Woolton urged local authorities to open and finance communal feeding centers themselves. The Ministry approached the London County Council (LCC) to take the lead in setting up feeding centers "in the very poorest quarters" to help the "poor classes," whose wages were not keeping up with rising price of foodstuffs.[20] If as Richard Farmer has argued, the British Restaurant was part of the government's "communalist gastronomic paradigm, which used food's association with mutuality, collectivity and consensus to integrate the private individual into the public body-corporate," this was an ideology that evolved slowly and intermittently over the course of the war in reaction to consumer demand for the meals services.[21] For the MOF initially paid scant attention to anyone its staff might have conceived of as "private individuals" and instead repeatedly returned to the working poor as the target population for its collective feeding experiments.

In September 1940, the need to move forward with some form of communal feeding came to a head as Germany's aerial bombardment of London began to destroy housing in the East End, rendering many working-class families homeless. Because of disruptions to municipal services, such as water and gas, and the closing of shops, many people were unable to cook even if their homes remained intact.[22] Solomon claimed that she stormed the MOF the morning after the first bombs fell, barged into Marshall's office, and demanded that food be provided to those now homeless in the East End, "or they'll rush this place and tear it to bits." Apparently, Marshall promptly introduced her to Woolton, who ultimately passed her on to W. J. M. "Jock" Menzies, whom he had put in charge of community feeding.[23] Whether or not Solomon was ultimately responsible for spurring the Ministry to action, Menzies quickly realized schemes for both shelter feeding and communal restaurants.

Launching and maintaining what were to become British Restaurants – cash-only eating establishments open to the general public that would provide cheap meals on a day-to-day basis rather than merely during an emergency – like many of the other feeding programs I have discussed, ultimately fell to local authorities. The MOF provided loans for capital expenditure related to start-up costs, which were to be paid back with no interest at an amortization rate of 1 percent per month.[24] It also reimbursed local authorities for unavoidable financial losses, such as those associated with emergency air raid feeding or the feeding of essential war workers under special arrangements. Otherwise, the Ministry required communal feeding centers to be conducted as businesses on a "self-supporting but not a profit-making basis."[25] They were not subsidized; indeed, the Ministry was firm that ratepayers were not being asked to "subsidize meals that benefit only a few people."[26] Rather, the cost of the meal was meant to reflect the price of the raw food, labor, rent, and incidentals required to produce and serve it, but not more.[27]

Communal feeding centers were encouraged to keep prices low and within reach of the target population by operating as self-service cafeterias. Customers queued to purchase tickets or tokens at a cash register and then joined a line to exchange these for food dished up at a counter. The food was in most cases cooked on-site, but some centers were supplied from "cooking depots" that delivered meals in thermal containers.[28] Patrons took their food to a communal table themselves and cleared their own dirty dishes when they were done. Occasionally, establishments employed servers to pour tea at the tables, but there was no other table service. Some staff were volunteers, largely middle-class members of the Women's Voluntary Service (WVS). The MOF, however, encouraged communal feeding centers to employ paid labor precisely to counter accusations that they were being subsidized and could not in fact be self-supporting.[29] However, some British Restaurants received perks that private caterers did not, such as produce from gardens owned by local authorities,[30] food that was damaged or nearing its expiration date from government emergency food stocks,[31] priority with regard to some unrationed foods in short supply,[32] equipment from a special MOF pool,[33] and most significantly, the ability to requisition buildings,[34] which meant that rent was often not an overhead to be factored into the prices charged. These advantages were often offset by the difficulties inherent in operating a restaurant in substandard facilities never intended for food service and the financial risk involved in opening them in neighborhoods with no track record of commercial cafés.[35]

With backing from the MOF, a funding model, and a special financial arrangement for London (that unlike the authorities that would follow suit held them totally unaccountable for any pecuniary losses), the LCC thus agreed to launch what it called the Londoners' Meals Service (LMS) as a model for other local governments.[36] By September 15, 1940, the LCC had set up a field kitchen and implemented cash-and-carry services from mobile canteens.[37] It opened the first dine-in restaurant in Woolmore Street, Poplar (a working-class district of the East End) on October 24, exactly four months after the War Cabinet had first raised the issue of providing "cheap food for the poorer classes" through some form of communal feeding.[38] The MOF urged other local authorities to follow London's example, arguing that these establishments were necessary for the "immediate benefit of the poorer sections of the population" and to "protect the morale of our poorest people."[39] It issued a circular to divisional food officers asking them set up "Community Kitchens" in working-class districts (particularly near factories) that would cater "primarily for working class people" who could afford to pay 6–8 pence for a good meal.[40] Some local authorities quickly followed suit, while others were slower to put plans into action. But many did clearly imbibe the government's message regarding the target population: a town councillor in Chatham maintained that, since these meals centers were for "the poor people," they deliberately put them in "poor districts."[41]

Although he did not mention communal feeding at all in his 1940 *Feeding the People in War-Time*, Orr's argument about morale, poverty, malnutrition, and the need for cheap nourishing food for the poorer classes did not therefore go unheeded. The communal feeding center was born out of this commitment to addressing nutritional deficiencies that were due to economic inequalities, though only those manifest within the British Isles. But unlike the Depression years, during which the government skirted the issue of its responsibility and refused to correlate poverty and malnutrition, the need to maintain civilian morale during wartime provided the necessary context for state action.[42] If, as R. J. Hammond has argued, in setting up British Restaurants the MOF demonstrated that its duty was to the population as a whole,[43] the inception and introduction of communal feeding centers during World War II in fact paralleled previous state-feeding programs targeted at specific populations. The government officials who launched the program had not anticipated that these meals services would in practice serve a much wider swathe of the public, and in the end, this owed as much to market principles as to a fair shares mentality.

Marketing the Meals Service

If the MOF had clearly articulated that communal feeding centers were intended for the large numbers of people who would be forced "below the poverty line" as prices rose, they were not meant for the "very poor" who were to be dealt with separately by the Public Assistance Authorities.[44] When the question was raised as to whether local Public Assistance Committees (that had essentially replaced the Boards of Guardians in 1930) could issue vouchers for those unable to afford the cash prices in British Restaurants, the consensus within the Ministry was that this should not be permitted as, they reasoned, it would only discourage other consumers from utilizing the restaurants.[45] W. J. O. Newton, the chief meals officer for the LCC, warned that any system where some customers presented public assistance tickets to obtain a meal was a "wrong system" because it would have the "taint of the poor law." "Decent people," he argued would not avail themselves of these restaurants if this arrangement was in place.[46] When the issue was raised again in 1941 as to whether those on public assistance should be issued a special identity card entitling them to reduced tariffs, the MOF stood firm. If the "poorer classes of the community" could not afford the cost of a three-course midday meal paid for in cash, argued the assistant director of operations for the Wartime Meals Division, they could nevertheless purchase soup, bread, and sweet only or just take a main course, all of which were separately priced. This would prevent some patrons being singled out as recipients of relief and would avoid linking these meals services in the public's mind to the government's income assistance programs.[47]

Thus, the MOF officials were more sensitive to the long and stigmatizing history of poor relief than the Board of Education had been in the previous decade and paid attention to the inducements that they believed would bring their target population through the doors without branding them as either charity cases or recipients of state assistance.[48] Woolton was a businessman who had been an executive at Lewis's department store in Liverpool before the war. But he was also a philanthropist. As a young man, he had lived among the Liverpool poor as warden of a charitable society; during World War I, he and his wife had also helped to run a feeding program for the wives and children of servicemen.[49] His personal experience structured his firm belief that public meals should only be provided as a cash service, as paying one's own way had been a central tenet of working-class respectability since the early nineteenth century. This had been corroborated early in the war when it became apparent that the emergency rest centers supervised by the Public Assistance Authorities, where food was given gratuitously, were not being fully utilized by the general public because of a "supposed poor law taint."[50] The MOF was adamant that there could be "no question of a Means Test" for those wishing to make use of the meals services, insisting that customers pay their own way.[51] In the first years of their operation, some centers charged as little as 6 pence for a main course; by 1944, most were charging 8 or 9 pence. The price for a three-course meal with a hot beverage (the typical meal consumed in a British Restaurant) cost on average 1 shilling and 3 pence in 1944, an extremely competitive tariff, although prices in the south west were consistently higher than in other parts of the country.[52] When Woolton presided over the opening of the first of Liverpool's communal feeding centers, one of the very first to be established outside of London, he proclaimed that it should not be interpreted as "charity" and that it was not intended to deal with "cases of destitution," thus separating the MOF scheme from any food aid provided either by do-gooders or by the Public Assistance Authorities.[53]

As a means of compensating for the fact that the prices might still be "beyond the purse of the people who need it most," and for added convenience, many centers had cash-and-carry services, which the MOF considered an "essential" part of the British Restaurant system.[54] Although the government frowned on the practice of dining in a restaurant and then bringing another meal home for oneself for later, taking home food for those who could not attend the center was sanctioned and encouraged.[55] These cash-and-carry services also allowed purchases of several meals, which could be shared among the household, something difficult to do on-site without stigmatizing those who could not afford a meal for each family member.[56] The provision of take-out services, however, required the MOF to bend its own rules as rationed meat could only be bought without surrendering a coupon if that meat was to be consumed on the premises, such as in a catering establishment. In order to encourage the poor to use the meals services, and by doing so extend their rations, the government decided to allow the cash-and-carry loophole to remain open throughout the war.[57] Affordable prices, separately priced items to allow patrons to pick and choose, and take-out services were all intended to encourage the poorer classes in particular to make use of the collective feeding services.

Although Orr had argued that the poor were not particularly susceptible to propaganda and chose to consume food that was priced within their means,[58] what to name these institutions was of paramount concern to a range of government officials who were well aware of the importance of public relations and the resistance to institutions of this nature. In the summer and autumn of 1940, the terms "National Restaurants," "National Kitchens," "People's Restaurants," "Community Feeding Centres," and "Communal Feeding Centres" were all being used indiscriminately to refer to nonemergency services that could undertake day-to-day feeding operations.[59] Marshall insisted that an alternative to "communal feeding" be coined as this term "repels a great many people." He favored something more "inspired" that could convey a "combined sense of happiness and friendliness."[60] Woolton concurred that the term "community feeding" needed to be "kill[ed]" because of its inherent "coldness."[61] According to the state's own Wartime Social Survey, housewives in Glasgow objected to the term "communal" precisely because it implied a soup kitchen.[62] Londoners, on the other hand, disliked the term "kitchens" for exactly the same reason. The government's adoption of the term "Community Kitchens" in November of 1940 was as equally problematic as "communal feeding centre."[63] Indeed, some even objected to the more innocuous term "community." According to the WVS, what these services were to be named was of vital importance in attracting people to them. The title "community feeding centre," this organization maintained, had "little appeal for the individualistic Englishman."[64]

The other problem with the term "communal" was that it evoked Soviet forms of state control. In 1942, F. Le Gros Clark, a leading expert on nutrition who had lobbied for an expansion of school meals during the 1930s, published a pamphlet detailing the Russian system of collective feeding. He entitled it "Soviet Forms in Communal Feeding."[65] His use of the term "communal" in this context reveals the strong association between this particular phrase and Communist regimes. Woolton had in fact chastised Solomon, a Russian émigré, for naming her feeding center a "Communal Restaurant." "Are you a Communist?" he queried.[66] In July of 1941, Mass Observation – which sought to compile a nongovernmental archive of everyday wartime experiences – reported that the term "communal kitchen" had been replaced precisely because some "sensitive people" had objected to the word "communal." It was quick to note, however, that this was before Russia entered the war as Britain's ally; presumably afterward, the British government needed to be more sensitive about its aversion to communism, though by this time the term "communal" had officially been retired.[67]

Some suggestions for a better name came both from local authorities and the public: council cafeteria, comfee café, potluck depot, victory restaurant, cookery nook, freedom restaurant, wooltaurant, Blitzaurant, and Family Fare Centres, among others.[68] In the end, it was Churchill himself who suggested the term "British Restaurant." "I hope the term 'Communal Feeding Centres' is not going to be adopted," he wrote to Woolton. "It is an odious expression suggestive of Communism and the workhouse. I suggest you call them 'British Restaurants.' Everybody associates the word 'restaurant' with a good meal, and they may as well have the name if they cannot get anything else."[69] The MOF thus officially adopted the name "British Restaurant" in April of 1941 and required it to be used by all local authorities, except the LCC, which was allowed to retain the term Londoners' Meals Service, having taken a firm stand on the importance of catering to local sensibilities.[70]

In naming them "British Restaurants," Churchill implied that the government could both invoke the wartime national spirit and capitalize on consumer expectations regarding the cultural cachet of dining out. In fact, the MOF had to overcome considerable public resistance to eating outside the home, which until the war, had been a practice largely confined to the middle and upper classes.[71] One of the problems posed by communal feeding was that it challenged the "tradition of the home meal" as a central part of "English home life."[72] In initial discussions about communal feeding, government officials feared that it would be extremely difficult to chip away at the "long established working-class habits of eating meals at home."[73] Solomon similarly argued that eating out was so foreign to the British people that it could be likened to replacing the brick walls of the Albert Hall with glass and "turning the place into a nudist colony."[74]

To counter these qualms, British Restaurants attempted to create a "home atmosphere."[75] This was about attractive but modest décor, friendly service, and securing the right staff. By all accounts, local authorities were fairly successful in creating a casual and unpretentious environment where all people could eat meals cooked by motherly women in a comfortable setting. As many patrons noted, you didn't need to dress up to go there, there was no fancy table service, and some even provided wireless sets, thus approximating the atmosphere of the British wartime home.[76] The domestication of the British Restaurant was intended to ease first time restaurant patrons into this new experience of public dining. At the same time, as Farmer has posited, it was part of a wider strategy of convincing the British people that they constituted a "family of 45,000,000" who, by sitting down to a meal together, were eating their way to victory.[77]

A Good Substantial Meal

If British Restaurants were to attract their target population and serve their dietary needs, creating a comfortable atmosphere was important, but by far the most critical element was the food itself. During World War II, the MOF took the advice of its nutritional experts much more seriously than it had during World War I.[78] Its scientific advisors attempted to implement a food policy that placed the nutritional health of the civilian population (though not those in the colonies) front and center. As Atkins has argued, British Restaurants were a central part of this policy of nutritional uplift.[79] MOF advisors were deeply engaged with the nutritional sciences and discussed and debated the nutritive qualities of the meals provided, which involved assessments of their calories, protein, fat, carbohydrates, vitamins, and minerals. For the first time, the state allowed its food scientists at least to attempt to put the "newer knowledge of nutrition" into practice. Although they were not always successful in implementing well-rounded meals throughout the British Restaurant system, a considerable amount of effort was expended on planning appropriate menus, surveying the establishments once they were up and running, and offering advice to local authorities both through site visits from wartime meals advisers and through MOF publications such as "Canteen Catering."

The scientific justification behind the British Restaurant meal was that it was to serve as the main meal of the day and provide one-third of the day's calories to those whose diets were chronically deficient.[80] Initially, the goal was for these meals to furnish 1,000 calories, but this was difficult to achieve. The Scientific Advisor's Division eventually determined that most people, except those working in heavy industry, were only prepared to eat about 630 calories at midday. On average, this was what a British Restaurant meal provided, given that customers tended to take all three courses on offer. Patrons thus fulfilled the government's goal that they should consume "a good substantial meal."[81] Not all calories were created equal, however, and nutrition (rather than merely bulk) was at the heart of menu planning. The idea of a modified "Oslo breakfast" dominated early discussions about what to serve in British Restaurants. The Oslo breakfast in its original form consisted of milk, salad, fresh fruit, cheese, and wholemeal bread. As Chapter 5 illustrated, by the eve of the war, the Board of Education had begun to promote these meals as cheaper, more nutritious, and easier to prepare than the cooked two-course hot dinner typically served to schoolchildren. Drummond similarly argued that adapting the Oslo ideal to British tastes and wartime conditions could "be done cheaply and without disturbing to any significant extent ordinary food habits."[82]

But if the goal was to make good "the deficiencies of the home diet" of the poor and working classes by attracting this population to the restaurants, the "ordinary food habits" of the working poor needed to be accommodated.[83] Thus, "purely nutritional considerations had to make way for national habit and tradition."[84] The Ministry's nutritional experts were careful that the food served in British Restaurants was familiar to working-class diners and "free from any suggestion of the influence of 'food cranks.'"[85] It was essential to avoid the appearance of trying to "thrust unusual articles of food or foodstuffs to which people are not accustomed" onto patrons, Menzies maintained, as this would only discourage those who most needed these services from utilizing them.[86] This meant that it was the presumed tastes, and not only the nutritional requirements, of working-class Britons that were reflected in the menus.

The wide assumption that "the working man likes his meat and two vegetables" set the standard for the British Restaurant meals.[87] The resulting menus, while basically nutritious and sometimes tested by food scientists for their nutrient quotients, were in the end quite far away from the Oslo ideal. Meal planners favored "homely fare," "plain" cooking, and traditional dishes built on the "meat-and-two veg" model.[88] These meals always included a pudding course (anathema to the Oslo breakfast), which almost all patrons consumed at least one portion of and, in the end, the MOF conceded was essential for providing heavy workers with additional calories.[89] Some restaurants, such as those run by the LMS, offered bread, butter or margarine, and cheese as an additional course, instead of the sweet, to cater to those who needed more calories and as a concession to the Oslo ideal.[90] A typical British Restaurant meal consisted of soup, a cooked main dish that included protein – such as roasted meat, fishcakes, stews, savory meat pies, or vegetarian offerings made with legumes or cheese – two vegetables (usually mashed potatoes and either cabbage, peas, carrots, or other roots vegetables), a traditional pudding, and either tea, coffee, or cocoa. Regional specialties (such as Lancashire hot pot and Cornish pasties) featured prominently in some locales, and the Ministry developed a set of menus to "meet Scottish tastes," which included Scotch broth, bubble and squeak, and haggis.[91] Some British Restaurants catered specifically to Jewish communities by serving only kosher food.[92] The MOF encouraged this local variation. Although the wartime meals advisers inspected British Restaurants regularly and offered advice about the nutritional content of food, its aesthetic appeal, and "satiety value," ultimately local authorities were left to be the final arbiters of local tastes.[93] The MOF only intervened in regards to menu planning in districts where nutritional standards were unusually low or when the inefficient use of food was leading to financial losses.[94]

Aside from the vegetarian dishes, most menu items did not stray too far outside the norms of the British working-class diet. In fact, part of the appeal for many customers was that the food was familiar: "You know what you are getting," was a common refrain.[95] Several British Restaurants chose to serve roast beef as their inaugural meal, a dish that as I have argued in Chapter 1, had long been regarded as the festive food of the British people. This established for patrons that British Restaurants would indeed be serving traditional British food.[96] The government's trepidation at offering anything that might be perceived as too fancy or too healthy was justified for, as one community feeding officer noted, patrons of British Restaurants were "very conservative in their taste." They tended to choose a hot dinner rather than a cold salad meal (even in the hottest weather) and consistently objected to eating raw vegetables however served.[97] While many customers in one British Restaurant that served mainly factory workers routinely ate pease pudding, a familiar dish, they discarded haricot beans and other unfamiliar, though similar, pulses.[98] In Manchester, there was, apparently, a strong dislike of cheese.[99] In Sheffield in 1942, no greens were served because of a belief that the public did not like them.[100] According to one patron who had frequented thirty different British Restaurants, greens were among the most often discarded food items and vegetarian dishes were regularly passed over.[101] Indeed some British Restaurants did not post their menus outside precisely to discourage the well-known practice of customers shopping around for the best meat meal and avoiding vegetarian offerings.[102] If already in the queue on meatless days, some customers opted instead to buy two soups and two puddings rather than partake of an unfamiliar and suspect vegetarian offering.[103]

If the MOF and the local authorities running British Restaurants recognized and catered to the unadventurous palate, they nevertheless also attempted to introduce new foods. In part, this was to enhance the nutritive value of their meals, but sometimes it was out of necessity as food shortages were common. This was done gingerly, however, so as not to "lose the confidence of the people."[104] The MOF maintained that the display of posters and conversations between the staff and the patrons was the best way to "overcome conservative food habits."[105] New foods were introduced alongside familiar ones – jacket potatoes beside peeled potatoes – to ease the public into new habits and preferences. The MOF recommended that British Restaurants treat the general public like a picky toddler, introducing "strange foods" into the meals "without the workers [i.e. the patrons] knowing they are there." For example, oatmeal could be sneaked into minced meat, and grated carrots into savory pies and even puddings. Anything new must be preceded or followed by something "known and liked," the Ministry cautioned, in order that change should come about slowly and imperceptibly, though the public stubbornly refused to take a liking to the government's National Wheatmeal Bread.[106]

Although its officials tried to expand the working-class diet, to inform the public about nutrition, and in the process, to use the British Restaurant as a "great opportunity for the re-education of people's tastes," the government's first priority was to bring customers through the doors – hence the focus on traditional and comforting foods.[107] While this meant that the nutritional content and quality of British Restaurant food varied, in general there was considerable praise for the meals they furnished. Most customers, though obviously not all, found them well-prepared, tasty, and hot. Surprisingly, few complaints about either the quality or the quantity of this food emerge from the historical record. Most Mass Observation diarists, who had no incentive to propagandize the British Restaurant and instead had been charged with accurately recording their own daily experiences, reported that they enjoyed the food.[108] That many customers ate at them on a regular basis suggests that British Restaurants offered consistently decent fare. In retrospect, some looked back on these meals as "all beige" and abysmal,[109] but during the war, most patrons seemed to have welcomed the availability of cheap, hearty, prepared food and found these meals not only convenient and economical but also satisfying.

From Charwoman to Hitler: Need, Desire, and Legitimate Usage

The MOF had done its best to provide nutritious but familiar food, to keep the prices reasonable, to discourage the respectable poor from associating British Restaurants with government relief, and to make them accessible by placing these new institutions within "poor districts" to "get the poor people," their target population, "to come for food."[110] Much as they tried, the government could not, however, entirely control the perception that the British Restaurant was just another "Government Depot" that smacked of the soup kitchen and the workhouse, a problem that had also befallen attempts at communal feeding during World War I and school meals during the Depression.[111] Indeed, some people were in the end too "proud" to eat at institutions that they thought were "demeaning," as they objected to "being fed by the government."[112] That said, the target population did come. But others did as well, which opened up public debate about who should be entitled to use these services.

When the Hampstead and Highgate restaurant opened in February of 1941, one housewife declared, "I don't think we'll get in...they'll want to see your identity card and your ration book and your rent book and your insurance card and your milk card and your benefit form, all the bag of tricks." This suggests that the public presumed that government feeding programs were only for particular groups and that stringent oversight would be practiced. Instead, the customers found that it was "completely open to anyone to walk in, from charwoman to Hitler." That one did not have to produce any documents or surrender any coupons, came as a surprise to these patrons. They nevertheless absorbed the message that British Restaurants were intended for those in the lower income groups. J. B. Priestley – a proponent of the concept of "community" and the voice that most embodied the English wartime spirit – had been engaged to open the Hampstead and Highgate center.[113] According to one attendee, while he gave the impression that he was indeed "just one of us," he nevertheless appealed to the "well-to-do" not to come too often "and take places needed more by the poor."[114] Patrons of another British Restaurant noted approvingly that it should not be used by "rich people with cars."[115] In Bradford, the residents of a "poor district" seemed to have looked upon their British Restaurant as "having been opened for their benefit entirely." The housewives of the district apparently resented the appearance of "clean, decently clad office workers and factory workers," implying that they were "intruders" and not legitimate users of these services, which these residents understood were intended solely for them.[116]

The idea that the British Restaurant was only for "the poorer section of the population [seeking] to obtain meals as cheaply as possible," however, did not take hold in the public mind despite initial apprehension about rights to use these meals services.[117] It quickly became apparent that "men and women, of all classes," were equally thankful for the affordable, hot, nutritious meal.[118] By February of 1941, Woolton informed the War Cabinet that while generally these centers were catering to the industrial section of the population, there could be "no doubt that better off people" were using those of the "more attractive type."[119] By June, he was reporting that "the Restaurants are used mainly by the working classes and the lower paid professional and clerical classes," a mixed population, many of whom were clearly not living at the poverty line.[120] A Mass Observation report in July of 1942 maintained that since "no selective control is exercised over customers," these services were "now patronized by better-off people" who may at first have been reluctant to use them.[121] In 1944, a survey of Birmingham British Restaurants found that all types of people – from manual industrial workers to high government officials and managers of industry – were customers.[122] While the "black-coated employee" appears to have been the LMS's major clientele, 34 percent of its patrons were industrial workers, rail workers, transport workers, or messengers, 26 percent were office workers, and 14 percent professional and managerial. These restaurants were "democratic" in their clientele: "The fusion of class types is very evident in many of them," noted one report. Another report found that rather than catering to the working poor, they served no "clear-cut clientele."[123]

The fact that many different kinds of people from across the class spectrum regularly ate at British Restaurants surprised many government officials and stimulated debate about legitimate usage. Although the MOF had been quite clear that British Restaurants were intended for the working poor, once in operation, it became harder to define what constituted legitimate use of these services and impossible, impolitic, and uneconomical to limit the general public's access. H. L. French, permanent secretary to the MOF, had argued in 1941 that British Restaurants were intended to provide "working class people" with a suitable meal for which they could afford to pay and must be established only to "fill a want," not necessarily a desire.[124] However, Woolton maintained that British Restaurants should be "open to all members of the public" and should be established by local authorities where a sufficient number of the population would be likely to take advantage of them. A memorandum on the matter did not insist that the needs or wants of only certain members of the population be taken as valid.[125]

The MOF had in fact encouraged the general public to make use of these services. Almost as soon as the British Restaurant system was initiated, a much more inclusive language emerged. In his November 5, 1940 letter to local authorities urging them to establish British Restaurants, Woolton diverged from the language of poverty to that of national efficiency: "If every man, woman and child could be sure of obtaining at least one hot nourishing meal a day, at a price all could afford, we should be sure of the nation's health and strength during the war, however long it may last, and of the fitness of the next generation."[126] Instead of arguing that the government was meeting the nutritional needs of the poor, Woolton here deployed populist language that promoted the British Restaurant as an institution that secured the health of every man, woman, and child, echoing earlier justifications for school meals. A 1941 Ministry of Information film produced to promote British Restaurants entitled *Eating Out With Tommy Trinder* similarly, and explicitly, encouraged all to use this service. In the film, Trinder, a well-known comedian, brings his fiancée and her middle-class family to a Liverpool British Restaurant. He then explains to them that these institutions were patronized by "all kinds of people": department managers, clerks, shop girls, and even performers like himself.[127] The MOF had thus justified communal feeding centers as a service for the poorer classes but once established had advertised them to the general public. That British Restaurants were in fact patronized by "every sort and condition of citizen," however, soon proved politically contentious.[128]

By the middle of the war, many within and beyond government circles argued for the need to prioritize the nutritional requirements of war workers, thus challenging the premise that British Restaurants were open to all on the same terms or that feeding the poor should be the state's number one priority. As British Restaurants began to be institutionalized, Menzies, who more than anyone else was involved in their day-to-day administration, argued that one of the principal planks of communal feeding was the provision of "feeding places" for "workers engaged on work of national importance."[129] In the summer of 1941, in response to concerns about access to British Restaurants, Gwilym Lloyd George, parliamentary secretary to the MOF who retained his affiliation with the Liberal Party, confirmed that they were being used "by the persons for whom they were intended, namely, the poorer classes, evacuees and those factory workers" without works canteens. Undoubtedly, Lloyd George continued, British Restaurants were patronized "by other people for whom they were not intended," but this was difficult to prevent. This suggested that British Restaurants were not in fact meant for all members of the public but rather these distinct populations, which now seemed to include factory workers.[130] When critics charged that British Restaurants were being used by the "general public as a means of cheap convenience" and that this "crowded out legitimate war workers," who, they argued, should receive priority, the government changed its tune.[131] In 1942, Lloyd George asserted that these services were not established for "any particular section of the community" but for anyone who, owing to wartime conditions, was finding it difficult to obtain hot and nourishing meals via the usual routes.[132]

This waffling irritated those who championed the industrial war worker, a figure who now began to compete with the working poor as the presumed target audience for communal feeding initiatives. Woolton deliberately kept the definition of the war worker vague. He responded to concerns about legitimate usage that while British Restaurants were intended for "people engaged on war work," he would "certainly deprecate any attempt by the Ministry to draw a line of distinction between the people who use British Restaurants." The "broad" issues remain "clear and obvious," he argued, but the "narrow ones of definition would, I think, cause great trouble."[133] The MOF thus continued to suggest that British Restaurants "ought to benefit" all those who have to take meals away from home including not only those engaged in industrial war work but also shop assistants, office workers, evacuees, housewives working part-time, and others for whom sandwiches are the only midday option.[134]

Manny Shinwell, chairman of the Labour Party, who had turned down a position in the MOF, challenged even the loosest definition of legitimate usage. He argued that if there was a greater demand by "the public" to make use of the British Restaurants, then there should be more British Restaurants rather than giving priority to "certain people." A trade unionist himself who supported the rights of laborers, Shinwell nevertheless argued that in serving the general public these institutions were catering for a "legitimate demand." While the government continued to assert that some British Restaurants were being "used by people for whom they are not really intended," suggesting that they were not actually for the home front population as a whole, Woolton tried to appease all parties.[135] Atkins has argued that Woolton intended British Restaurants to serve those doing war work, which was not restricted to fighting or producing munitions.[136] But Woolton did not deploy the rhetoric of "the People's War," which Priestley and others had used to configure all Britons as "doing their bit" for the war effort and allowed all citizens to be constituted as "war workers."[137] Instead, he avoided this readily available discourse and skirted the issue of who exactly was a "war worker." His solution was to encourage local authorities to make priority dining arrangements for factory workers and, in some cases office workers, which many quickly put into place.[138] This allowed him to pacify those who saw British Restaurants as essentially for industrial workers, but not necessarily for other civilians engaged in the war effort. At the same time, it allowed in practice for the broadest possible interpretation of who could make use of these services.

In the end, the MOF preferred a broad interpretation of who could be classed as a legitimate British Restaurant customer. Its officials nevertheless continued to configure these meals services as catering to the needs of a targeted population. In documents collated for the purpose of providing information on British Restaurants to American government officials, the MOF asserted that they were open to all members of the public. It stressed, however, that "the majority of those patronizing them are naturally in the lower income group, and include large numbers of the working classes."[139] By 1943, the government's official policy was that "all classes," but particularly war workers and other clearly necessitous populations, should be able to obtain proper meals through communal feeding arrangements.[140] Although British Restaurants were open to all members of the public, the MOF, in defending their importance, continued to maintain that they were frequented "mainly by the people for whom they are intended": the "wage and salary–earning classes in the lower income groups" and most particularly the "thousands of workers" who would not otherwise have a hot nourishing meal available to them at a reasonable price.[141] The British state thus clung to the idea of a necessitous target population in theory but was forced to abandon it in practice in order to make these institutions financially viable, socially acceptable, and to respond effectively to consumer demand.

Democratic Dining?

If there were to be no distinctions in regard to who could use British Restaurants, then they needed to be operated along democratic lines. The MOF insisted that patrons within each establishment must have access to the same meal and the same dining spaces.[142] In 1942, the Wembley High Road British Restaurant proposed having two classes and two prices in their meals service: one floor was to be set apart for "business meals" at 2 shillings and 6 pence, while the general lunch would be 1 shilling and 1.5 pence. Menzies cautioned that this practice was "dangerous" and immediately put a stop to it.[143] Some patrons noted that they liked that there was no "class distinction" or "favouritism" at play at these institutions and promoted the idea that "all people should have the same to eat, that is the idea of having a Communal Feeding centre."[144]

Equality was not always apparent when these principles were put into practice, however. One patron (who had used thirty different British Restaurants) noted that instead of servings being uniform in size, the staff tended to vary the amounts dished up according to the customer's "sex, size and clothes."[145] A Mass Observation diarist also claimed that in Sudbury the portions were equally distributed, while in Bury they decided how much customers should be given based on "your sex and size and whether you are still growing."[146] This practice favored young men as many assumed young women could not eat as much food unless they were obviously pregnant.[147] But as one district food officer noted, young girls were in fact growing faster than boys their age and were only just beginning to get the food they actually needed. I have never shown anyone around a British Restaurant, he stated, without hearing "look at the platefuls of potatoes those young girls can eat." Sometimes the amount they consume, he argued, was really "amazing."[148] In publicly eating their platefuls of potatoes, these young women were rejecting norms of female bodily sacrifice that had become magnified during the Depression. Instead, they demonstrated their ability to eat as much as men and declared their state-sanctioned right to do so at a moment when men's access to food was still privileged over women's, particularly within working-class communities.

Fair shares were not necessarily equal shares, and some British Restaurants did discriminate in favor of some portion of their clientele at the expense of others. In fact, as British Restaurants sprung up across the United Kingdom, differences in relation to the menu, the décor, and the clientele were in fact quite evident, particularly in cities with more than one of these establishments. In Reading, the British Restaurant in the center of town catered to laborers, porters, and van men. It offered a limited menu that consisted invariably of minced meat and enormous quantities of potatoes. Another that was located outside the town center offered varied menus, smaller helpings, higher prices, and a more "modern" décor. "This difference," noted one patron, "is said to be official policy in catering for different type [sic] of clientele."[149] The LMS argued that they too favored diversity in their restaurants, seeking to suit the tastes, needs, and pocketbooks of their different groups of customers. Newton maintained that the LMS provided the dockers in Poplar the "sort of meals we think they enjoy," while in London's financial district, the meals were geared to the tastes of office workers, which he claimed differed from those of East Enders.[150] According to Newton, an entirely "different class of customer" used the meals services located in the residential districts, suggesting that their tastes and price points were also accommodated.[151] Some British Restaurants even raised their prices when they discovered that a "better type of people" were using the services "than had been anticipated."[152]

The location of establishments, the food served, the amenities they provided, and the prices they charged sometimes contributed to a de facto class segregation in areas with multiple British Restaurants. A clerk with the Public Assistance Office in Bury St. Edmunds, who was a frequent customer of British Restaurants in her region, noted that the one in her hometown tended to attract "parsons" and others of "that class rather than the poor." The one in Sudbury, she noted, "caters more for the poor."[153] Two 1942 photographs of the Woolmore Street British Restaurant in London, the very first dine-in branch of the LMS, show an almost exclusively working-class male clientele dining with their caps on.[154] A photograph of another London establishment captured quite a different set of customers: several of the male diners wore suits and ties, while one woman sported a fur coat.[155] A report prepared by the London Council of Social Service (LCSS) noted that the LMS attracted primarily neighborhood business, thus they often had the character of an "intimate club" where fresh custom arrives "by introduction." In LMS restaurants, it argued, 75 percent of the clientele were regulars and self-selected the location where they felt most comfortable. The unskilled and "rough-handed worker," the LCSS argued, was likely "intimidated" by the sight of a queue of "white-collared diners" and chose to frequent other branches.[156] A retired policeman reiterated the assumption that patrons self-segregated: "I am afraid it would only be sheer necessity," he maintained, "that would compel the ordinary middle class flat dweller to dine with the working class and in their ordinary working clothes too. As the ladies would say—it simply couldn't be done."[157]

Some middle-class users of British Restaurants did express their disgust at the appearance and manners of the working classes where local facilities threw a mixed clientele together. The clerk from Bury proclaimed that one group of fellow diners were "a terrible lot of creatures" dressed in "dirty clothes" and Wellington boots and had "wild" unshaven faces. She surmised that they were a group of temporary workers, maybe even "ex-convicts" and "probably Irishmen," since some were "drink-sodden." According to this middle-class woman, while higher wartime wages may have bridged an economic divide, class was not merely about income. She herself made only £4 a week but lived "among Persian carpets and oil paintings," while they, she guessed, earned twice as much but "probably live on earth floors and have no pictures." Though she grudgingly acknowledged that they "behaved themselves all right," it gave her a "shiver inside," she reported, to think that before the war she had been "unaware almost such people inhabited the earth."[158] A female stenographer who visited one of Birmingham's many British Restaurants was dismayed to find that it was patronized by engineering workers whose clothes, she reported, smelled of oil and swarf and made her feel sick. She knew however that she was in no position to complain but felt put out nonetheless.[159] A housewife similarly noted that she and others were "disgusted" and irritated by youths making noise and "eating with their hats on" in her British Restaurant. She knew it was "snobby," but she and her friends, she insisted, couldn't help feeling that they should not have to tolerate it.[160]

The seating arrangements in some British Restaurants tended to exacerbate the discomfort felt by patrons wary of cross-class social interactions. Some establishments had four-seater tables, while others sat six, eight, twelve, or even more at long trestle tables.[161] While the LCSS asserted that the "average customer" found smaller tables more agreeable, in only one-quarter of the London restaurants it sampled for its study was the provision of tables for four or less a common practice. The "mess-room" feel of the longer tables, the report argued, would not accord with the "taste of most customers" under normal circumstances.[162] The MOF had initially proposed that long tables accommodating twelve people were the most preferable seating arrangements for communal feeding centers, affirming that its staff had anticipated that only working-class diners would be using these services and had paid little attention to the possibility of cross-class interactions occasioned by communal tables.[163] The film *Eating Out With Tommy Trinder* positioned the nuclear family eating at its own table, thus preserving the privacy of family life at the same time as it shared in a communal and patriotic experience, suggesting the government attempted to mitigate these qualms at least in its propaganda.[164] In his 1944 *Common Man and Colonel Bogus*, the humorist Michael Barsley lampooned these anxieties. Here, the fictional millionaire Colonel Bogus dines at a British Restaurant precisely in order to find a "Common Man." Reluctant to finish his plebeian plate of sausage toad, Bogus attempts to share his leftovers with the "typically English" Common Man seated across from him, who is visibly offended by the offer. "What – you probably dine at the Ritz and can't finish up a bit of Sausage Toad?" accuses Common Man, acknowledging the class tensions that may in fact have often been present in these shared-table interactions.[165]

In the end, more often than not, crowded dining rooms and long queues threw a mixed-class clientele together without incident. In

1941, the journalist Ritchie Calder described those queuing up at one LMS establishment as a mixture of bank managers, city councillors, local magnates, sewermen, navvies, women in fur coats, and "every sort and condition of citizen."[166] Similarly, Miss C. M. Edwards, who kept a wartime diary, noted that a visit to a British Restaurant revealed a "wonderful mixed bag" of patrons: "A parson and wife, some service men, working lads and girls, elderly clerks, mothers with small children, shopgirls, shoppers, etc." She noted that "all classes" were present, except the "smart or would-be smart set"[167] (Figure 6.1).

Figure 6.1 Miss E.D. Barry, her younger brother, and D.E.H. Murrells eating a meal at the Londoners' Meals Service canteen at Fishmongers' Hall, London, 1942. © Imperial War Museum (D 10503).

These customers were served in order with no deference paid to middle-class consumers waiting in the lineup or men who in working-class households were generally served before women and children. In fact, Mass Observation found that, once British Restaurants were operational, no one bothered much about whom they sat next to "or any nonsense of that sort."[168] The National Council of Social Service (NCSS) similarly reported that all members of the community were for the most part happy to have the same meals, often at the same tables.[169] Andrew Schuil, a civil servant in Stockton who was a regular at his local British Restaurant, was amused but not disgusted by the five "scruffy kids" whose "equally scruffy" older sister pulled a bottle of HP™ Sauce from her coat pocket with a slot punched in the metal cap and sloshed the sauce on their food, "licking the cap of the bottle after each application!!!," belying the sense that the food habits of the working class were necessarily revolting to their social betters.[170] Nor did the working poor take much notice of middle-class customers. A visit to a Wandsworth center in 1941 by a middle-class contributor to Mass Observation revealed that the patrons were "nearly all working men." They nevertheless showed "no suspicion" of the observer, despite his "middle-class appearance."[171] In Nottingham, only 3.8 percent of the respondents volunteered the suggestion that communal feeding centers should "keep social classes separate."[172] Some people not only tolerated the mixed-class clientele at these establishments but in fact preferred this environment given the choice. A married housewife and teacher living near Durham noted that she felt "much happier" in the British Restaurant among the "business girls and workmen" than among the "middle-class shoppers" at the store cafés whose "manners and beliefs" she could not stand.[173]

In fact, the seating arrangements in British Restaurants, far from causing anxieties about cross-class sociability, often resulted in convivial interactions. The NCSS found that in a few places there was segregation by occupational status, but more often "the office worker, the director, the student and the industrial worker are to be found not only eating at the same table, but discussing the day's news with each other."[174] A Mass Observation diarist noted that people at the same table seemed genuinely "willing to talk to each other."[175] An American observer admitted that, while it probably wouldn't outlast the war, the British public seemed in the midst of this disaster to be behaving "like a united family" and thus were "willing to sit beside each other regardless of station in life, the greasy overall beside the well cut suit, the unmannerly beside the fastidious."[176] At the very least, British Restaurants seem to have taught those that used them that sociability was possible across lines of class without fundamentally challenging the existing social order. In the words of one contributor to Mass Observation, you can still be "quite a lady or gentleman if you sit down at a long table next to someone you've never met before and have lunch and talk at the same time."[177] For others, it reinforced the message that distinctions of class were perhaps gradually becoming less marked. One patron noted happily that the "type of people" who frequented British Restaurants were in the end "neither too high nor too low, just sort of reasonable people."[178]

Given that many British Restaurants were crowded with "both sexes and all types," they provided ample opportunity not only for cross-class interaction but also for heterosocial encounters[179] (Figure 6.2). In Figure 6.2, a photograph of the Woolmore Street Restaurant, five young women employed as oil and grease fillers at a nearby factory are enjoying their meal in their work clothes. A jovial young man similarly dressed for factory work (sitting with a male companion who is just visible inside the frame of the photograph) looks happily over his shoulder at them, attempting to make eye contact.[180] More unmarried women used the British Restaurants run by the LCC than unmarried

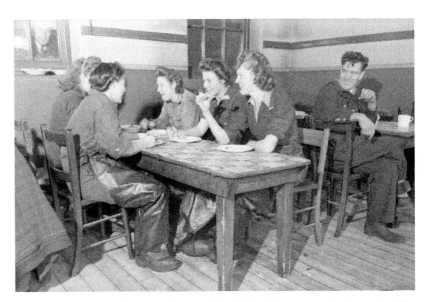

Figure 6.2 Women oil and grease fillers from a nearby factory eating a meal at the British Restaurant at Woolmore Street, 1942. © Imperial War Museum (D 10676).

men, a statistic that for the man in this photo clearly worked in his favor, given how eager he seems to initiate an interaction.[181] A customer in Stretford near Manchester made explicit the possibilities for hetero-social interaction that British Restaurants provided. He chose to eat at the British Restaurant instead of the works canteen precisely because a "Lady and a Gent can sit together" at the British Restaurant, which was not allowed at his canteen.[182] Unmarried women and men thus regularly ate together at these institutions, either by chance or by design. Some young people may have used them as spaces for court-ship, since they were cheaper than even the Lyons' Corner Houses, which in the interwar period had been a popular spot for an inex-pensive date.[183] British Restaurants provided young men and women with ample opportunity to socialize and were an ideal wartime pickup spot, which generated surprisingly little concern considering how much the war had refocused attention on unsupervised young women's sexuality.[184]

Although the British Restaurant did stimulate anxieties about the future of the British family and the gender politics of the midday meal, it was otherwise a surprisingly unproblematic institution.[185] In its opti-mistic 1946 study of the future of a government meals service, the NCSS concluded that British Restaurants were "inclusive" institutions that had resisted the "fissiparous tendency" of works canteens where mess rooms were divided by occupational group and thus by class and sex. Instead, the report maintained, the British Restaurant was "open to all comers." Despite the high proportion of industrial workers in some, there was "no distinction" between one type of worker and another: "The clerk, the managing director and the local clergy, boil-ermaker, apprentice and the schoolboy, are all to be found in the same queue selecting their food from the same counter and often obviously enjoying each other's company."[186] Thus, according to its supporters, the British Restaurant provided a mixed-class and mixed-sex clientele the "opportunity of meeting round a meal and sharing fellowship."[187] They succeeded in creating an atmosphere that was both "thoroughly democratic" and "thoroughly British."[188] The British Restaurant had brought all types of people together who were now "rubbing shoulders with any strangers and talking to them" and even helping themselves rather than being waited on.[189] These new institutions were to many the perfect example of the much-celebrated wartime spirit of the nation. They provided evidence that the British people were clearly willing, in Priestley's words, not only to "rough it together" but also to "trough it together."[190]

Socialism, Consumerism, and the Postwar Future

Whether or not they blunted or accentuated class differences, by 1942, Lloyd George was arguing that British Restaurants had already become an accepted and growing part of "our national life."[191] In fact, long before the war had ended, many citizens across the class spectrum began to agitate for the continuation of British Restaurants into the postwar period. The results of a Gallup poll released in January 1945 revealed that the majority of the British public had eaten at a British Restaurant: two-thirds of adults under 30 and 44 percent of those over the age of 50 had made use of these services. In fact, the poll reported that one-third of "well-to-do persons" had eaten at a British Restaurant, clearly establishing that in the end these were not merely "poor men's eating houses."[192] Satisfaction with the experience was overwhelmingly positive: less than one in five patrons reported that they would never go back; among the "poorer people," this figure dropped to below one in six. In fact, 60 percent of respondents wanted these meals services to continue after the war; only 17 percent categorically did not, leaving 23 percent undecided.[193] British Restaurants were surprisingly uncontroversial given that they represented the first time that food aid was given to the entire population – cooked meals at what was in almost all cases below true market value – regardless of whether recipients could be classed as "necessitous." That the MOF was able to justify what was a remarkable departure from previous feeding programs and contemplate its continuation into the postwar era, suggests that these services were able to be accommodated not only within the doctrine of war socialism but also within a variety of other political frameworks.

Those on the left of the political spectrum identified British Restaurants as a positive form of income redistribution and located these services outside the capitalist economy. The NCSS discouraged the use of the term "profit" in describing these institutions' financial successes, preferring "working surplus," given that their primary purpose was not to accumulate capital but instead was "social."[194] Both the NCSS and the LCSS had reported in their surveys that some patrons noted and liked that there was no profit motive in the running of the restaurants, suggesting that the "social values, which have accrued from this experimental social service," may have been as appealing to some customers as the food and the price.[195] A 1943 article argued that the MOF was the most popular government agency in Britain. This was in part, it argued, because the British Restaurant alongside other food controls had shown people that "better sharing *can* be brought about by the State."[196]

That cheap, nutritious food should be available to all through communal feeding schemes in peacetime became part of the Labour platform. As early as 1941, Clarice McNab Shaw, a Scottish Labour Party insider, praised the government's communal feeding initiatives, implying that they should outlast the war. She argued that "we now have a National Milk Scheme, a fine piece of real Socialist legislation; Communal Feeding Centres would help us to move in the direction of a National Food scheme."[197] Reporting on British food policy for an American audience three years later, Beatrice Gomberg argued that what underlay British successes in this area was "a strong sense of social responsibility with emphasis on equity as much as equality."[198] These were sentiments that were strongly linked to the 1942 Beveridge Report that was central to the Labour Party's postwar vision and would form the blueprint for the Welfare State. In fact by the end of the war, the promise to perpetuate British Restaurants had become part of the Labour Party's election strategy. Their manifesto, "Let Us Face the Future," declared that a Labour government would not only keep communal feeding centers but "improve and extend these services."[199] When the Labour Party won the 1945 election, the King's speech included an announcement of his government's intention to extend "the new food services for the workers established during the war," which appeared to cement the British Restaurant's place in the new Welfare State.[200] Labourites thus threw their support behind the British Restaurant both during and after the war as an institution that embodied their vision and version of a "responsible society."[201]

The MOF, initially headed by the nonparty affiliated Lord Woolton (who became chairman of the Conservative Party only when the Tories lost the 1945 election) and then the Conservative John Llewellin, used an entirely different political and economic framework to justify British Restaurants both during wartime and as a potential element of a postwar reconstruction plan. They repeatedly emphasized that British Restaurants were run on business principles, were not in fact subsidized by the state, and were closed if they could not remain solvent. The MOF assured retailers that British Restaurants did not engage in centralized purchasing of foodstuffs and received no special treatment from butchers or other suppliers.[202] Up to 60 percent of food used by LMS restaurants was in fact purchased in local shops.[203] The MOF was thus quick to clarify that British Restaurants were not a form of socialism but operated as much within the capitalist system as was possible in the context of wartime food controls. Woolton had argued in 1941 that there was no intention of transferring customers from private businesses to "State-subsidised" restaurants and that a balance between the rights of the private caterer and the requirements of the consumer must always be maintained if British Restaurants were to be defensible.[204] Even the LCSS deprecated socialism and similarly situated the British Restaurant within the model of a self-supporting business. Harkening back to an older language of the deserving and undeserving poor, its report argued that one could "scarcely imagine any form of society" where providing food for "an unselected and possibly undeserving portion of the general public" would be "tolerated" if they did not pay their way.[205]

Many British Restaurants more than paid their way. This allowed the MOF to concretely defend its meals services as profitable rather than a subsidized social service that was a drain on the nation's coffers. While they were not-for-profit, profits were not discouraged and, toward the end of the war, even encouraged by the MOF. In February of 1943, Woolton stated that British Restaurants were showing a profit of £27,000.[206] In fact, across the United Kingdom, it was only in its first year that the British Restaurant system operated at a loss. From their introduction to the end of the financial year 1943–4, the MOF, which retained the profits of most British Restaurants (though local authorities could choose to become independent once they had settled their debt to the Ministry), netted £90,000 from the scheme, excluding the LCC restaurants, which were separately financed.[207] Far from being a burden on taxpayers who unequally benefited from these services, British Restaurants generated revenue and benefitted British citizens whether they used the meals service or not.

Even some commercial caterers conceded that British Restaurants posed little threat to private business and situated them within the capitalist economy. This is not to discount serious opposition from the industry; a sustained critique of British Restaurants came from a segment of the catering trade that saw a state meals service as direct competition.[208] An irate business owner whose small cafés serviced transport workers, challenged British Restaurants as antithetical to British democracy, distinguishing little between forms of totalitarian state control. He denounced all methods of communal feeding as "Bolshevic" [sic] and argued that the British government was prosecuting a war against the fascist practices of "state controlled business," while at the same time, small British businessmen like himself were becoming victims of similar forms of "state control" on their home turf.[209] The Incorporated Association of Purveyors of Light Refreshments vigorously campaigned against British Restaurants and their continuation after the war, arguing that these services were an example of subsidized municipal trading.[210] The catering industry was not, however, uniformly resistant to British Restaurants. Although some traders had a "constitutional disapproval of municipal trading," many in fact argued that British Restaurants were justified if they could be financially self-supporting and were "not a charge on the rates or otherwise subsidized." For this, it was implied, would be honest competition within the capitalist system.[211] In fact, members of the catering industry, such as Major Montague Gluckstein of the Lyons Tea Rooms, a major competitor of British Restaurants, served as advisors to the MOF on communal and emergency feeding.[212]

The shrewder restaurateurs noted that in the long-term British Restaurants might in fact be good for business as they had introduced a whole new class of consumer to the conveniences of eating out, a habit that many hoped and predicted would outlast the war. The LCSS noted that it was not so much that the LMS restaurants attracted a particular clientele as that "a special type of diner" was actually "created through the existence of the restaurants."[213] This was a diner who might be eating out in public for the first time, and who might form the habit of eating out once accustomed to the procedure, food, and environment. The mayor of Canterbury, who owned a department store with a restaurant, maintained that British Restaurants were "creating an entirely new clientele for the commercial restaurant." These were "a new type of diners out," he declared, and his own restaurant, far from suffering from this competition, was doing a capacity business.[214] The *Daily Mirror* similarly proclaimed that the British Restaurant should be credited with having created this "social habit of eating out," a practice that it predicted was here to stay.[215] In addition, they had introduced commercial caterers such as Lyons to the self-service system, an innovation adopted by many to keep prices down, speed up service, and thus retain working-class clientele after the war.[216]

For free market capitalists, the British Restaurant was not understood as an experiment in municipal socialism. Instead, it was framed as an institution that was schooling the working classes as to the benefits of taking a proper midday meal in a restaurant and breeding a new population of consumers that would be integral to the postwar economy. In Birmingham, where British Restaurants were numerous and very well patronized, their superintendent testified that "working people" were unlikely to want to go back to "makeshift snacks" and would continue to eat out if they could obtain hot, inexpensive meals near their work.[217] The chairman of the Birmingham Reconstruction Committee agreed that British "social habits" had markedly changed during the war such that more people were getting "accustomed" to taking meals in restaurants.[218] In preparing for discussion on the future of the British

Restaurant, the chief officer of the LMS similarly maintained a considerable number of Londoners had since the outbreak of hostilities acquired the habit of taking a midday meal at restaurants.[219] If initially, as one customer noted, it felt "strange eating out," by enabling workers to eat a "good meal" on a regular basis in their working clothes without being "bothered by frills," the British Restaurant had trained the working classes no longer to feel embarrassed and uncomfortable eating out in commercial cafés.[220] If the working classes could be made more comfortable dining in public, and no longer brought their own bread and cheese to work or to the football match,[221] they would become more imbedded within the capitalist system and contribute to a healthy post-war economy.

The government's communal feeding experts understood that post-war reconstruction could be facilitated through mobilizing this new group of consumers. The Sub-Committee on Nutritional Policy of the wartime government's Informal Post-War Plans Committee identified British Restaurants as the basis for "building up consumption habits of wide and economical utilization of foodstuffs."[222] Given that this committee imagined that government-sponsored communal feeding would continue after the war only for a limited number of necessitous populations, the implication was that British Restaurants had introduced the working class to consumer behaviors that might well benefit a market or mixed economy after the war. Unlike the Labour Party, Conservatives hedged their bets as to whether local authorities should be given the powers after the war to continue to operate British Restaurants.[223] They recognized that the future of British Restaurants was a "highly contentious political issue" that might pit the interests of some vocal commercial traders against the powerful Trades Union Congress, which advocated for the continuation of the British Restaurant system.[224] In the end, Churchill's advisors cautioned him not to make a "premature announcement"; thus, he did not comment on this issue in the Conservative Party's election manifesto whose passages dealing with the future of wartime controls had an "exceptional vagueness" that reflected a lack of consensus within the Party itself.[225] The opinion that British Restaurants were good for the nation during wartime and would have positive repercussions into peacetime was however widely shared across political lines. Whether they should continue after the war was more contentious, though the two political parties were not as "sharply divided" on the issue as some historians have assumed.[226] That even Churchill was prepared to support this measure suggests that the institutionalization of the British Restaurant could be absorbed into a multitude of political worldviews.

Churchill may or may not have preserved the meals services had he won the July 1945 election. The Labour victory, however, did lead to an extension of these services. The powers given to local authorities to run British Restaurants and the financial arrangements that had made this possible had already been extended into the spring of 1947 to allow for a transitional period while permanent legislation was pending.[227] In 1947, the Labour government passed the Civic Restaurants Act, allowing local authorities to continue to run their British Restaurants as self-supporting businesses but without any ties to the central government. Under this act, Civic Restaurants could not be subsidized by the local authority and would be closed if they could not remain solvent, thus confirming that these meals services were not intended to be part of a municipal socialist agenda. Rather, according to historian Ellen Leopold, they "implicitly restored the market mechanism as the appropriate means for distributing resources."[228] In the wake of this legislation, 465 local authorities closed down their meals services, while 300 continued them.[229] By March 1947, there were 1,098 Civic Restaurants in operation.[230] The end of rationing, however, spelled decline for these once popular institutions, and except in Birmingham (where they lasted into the 1970s), most shuttered once foodstuffs became more widely available in the post-austerity age.[231]

In his 1956 study of food control during the war, R. J. Hammond argued that the value of British Restaurants should not be measured solely in terms of the facilities they provided. Rather, he argued, they were an "emblem of 'fair shares'" that helped "to give substance to the claim that there was no part of the community that was not the Ministry [of Food]'s especial care."[232] The implementation and success of British Restaurants during the war, and their ability to be accommodated within a variety of postwar reconstruction plans, cannot however be explained merely by situating them within the context of the fair shares mentality of "the People's War," an understanding of wartime food policy that historians have increasingly challenged.[233] In practice, they were an entitlement for those "doing their bit" and should be understood alongside rationing as a form of war socialism that helped to generate buy-in for what would become the Welfare State and the new vision of "social citizenship" it embodied.[234] But the British Restaurant also participated in creating a market to be "exploited and developed by private caterers."[235] Indeed, historian John Burnett has credited the British Restaurant, alongside the industrial canteen and other forms of wartime communal feeding, with significantly changing eating habits. If before the war, dining out in public had been a luxury restricted to the few, the wartime meals services had "familiarised and democratized" the practice, he argued, creating "new styles" of dining and "new places" that in the postwar period catered to "an emerging mass market."[236]

The British Restaurant was therefore part of a government-led process of transforming the poor from capitalism's pariahs whose food, as Chapter 1 has argued, had to be strictly controlled to a different kind of consuming public whose social and economic habits were no longer merely parasitic on, but productive for, the nation. Working-class consumerism was nurtured in the postwar period, and it was this spirit that was to have transformative effects not only on working-class culture but also on the political and social life of the British nation, something not yet visible to Hammond in 1956.[237] By 1994, when Tony Blair assumed leadership of the Labour Party, he was acutely aware of and animated by the fact that, in the words of his strategy and polling advisor, "the old working class was becoming a new middle class; aspiring, consuming, choosing what was best for themselves and their families. They had outgrown crude collectivism and left it behind in the supermarket car park."[238] Although the "communal feeding centre" was not instituted for this purpose, the "British Restaurant" was nevertheless a meaningful part of this process.

7   Nations Out of Nurseries, Empires into Bottles
The Colonial Politics of Welfare Orange Juice

If World War II gave rise to the British Restaurant, an institution that in catering to "all comers" profoundly changed the politics of government food, the war was also the origin of the Ministry of Food's (MOF) Welfare Foods Service (WFS),[1] which continued to target specific populations for additional nourishment. Introduced in 1942, the WFS provided concentrated orange juice, cod liver oil, and milk, which were vitamin-rich food products, to all pregnant women and young children. This food program, which lasted in this form until 1971, had strong links both to the relief of child famine victims and to the school meals service as in each of these cases the state provided nourishment to the youngest and thus most vulnerable subjects of the nation and the empire. But the idea that the state should furnish all children with these nutritional supplements, not merely those whose parents had failed to provide for them, was relatively new. If this philosophy had emerged in a wartime economic and political context in which market solutions to the problem of access to ample and nutritious foods were inexpedient, the decision to extend these services into the peace represented a profound ideological shift. Although both major political parties pledged to continue the WFS after the war, it was the Labour Party that most succinctly integrated it into its larger plan for a Welfare State. This new vision, however, was predicated on and perpetuated older colonial relationships. Since orange juice could not be produced in sun-starved Britain, the government jump-started an orange-growing industry and juice concentrating plants in the British West Indies. The United States' national school lunch program had been started to benefit the agricultural sector, in that it provided a way to dispose of surplus commodities at a time when farm prices were depressed.[2] But the British state turned this relationship on its head, initiating a colonial agricultural scheme entirely to serve the needs of a domestic welfare program.

As the previous chapter noted, historians have stressed that wartime food policy in the 1940s took place in the long shadow cast by the Bengal Famine and the prioritizing of domestic rather than colonial subjects' food needs. They have also exposed the ways in which the United and Standard Fruit Companies practiced a form of economic imperialism to render Latin American and Caribbean banana growers dependent on these corporations.[3] The Big Fruit companies were an example of the exploitation inherent in profit-driven global capitalism. In contrast, the economic dependencies created by welfare orange juice were the result of government investment in a commodity that was explicitly not-for-profit. Its production, ironically, embodied the British state's commitment to a new form of social democracy that stood in direct opposition to the liberal doctrines so central to capitalism. It was not therefore only that the entitlements of metropolitan citizens continued to take precedence over those of Britain's colonial subjects; in the post-war period, colonial subjects were also expected to produce nutritious foods for the Welfare State without partaking of its benefits.

Vitamin Foods, Wartime Shortages, and Lend-Lease Orange Juice

In November 1941, the MOF announced a "Vitamin Scheme" aimed at compensating for the shortage of fresh fruit during the war. The new program was more targeted than the British Restaurant in that it sought to provide cod liver oil, which was rich in vitamins A and D, and blackcurrant or rose hip products high in vitamin C to children under two years old. (Notably absent was any product rich in vitamin B, a nutrient heavily promoted in wartime America.[4]) In 1942, the Vitamin Scheme substituted orange juice for local products, amalgamated with the government provision of cheap and free liquid and dried milk, expanded to include both pregnant women and children up to five years old, and was renamed the Welfare Foods Service. The WFS was born out of widespread concerns about nutritional deficiencies during wartime.[5] As we saw in Chapter 5, the 1920s and 1930s witnessed an explosion of research into malnutrition. In spite of substantial disagreements within the scientific community, nutritionists used this new expertise to wield greater influence over government policy during World War II than they had had during World War I.[6] This had resulted in schemes such as the British Restaurant that provided the general public access to ample, healthy, and inexpensive prepared foods, and it focused the state's attention more narrowly on the problem of specific vitamin deficiencies and the toll these took on the developing bodies of young children, hence the introduction of fortified foods such as vitaminized margarine.[7]

The body's need for what would come to be labeled vitamin C had been recognized since the mid-eighteenth century when James Lind, a naval surgeon, had demonstrated that regular intake of citrus juices could prevent scurvy. The antiscorbutic properties of citrus (as well as potatoes and other fruits and vegetables) were the subject of experiment in the interwar period, and ascorbic acid, also known as vitamin C, was finally isolated in 1928. In 1940, Geoffrey Bourne, an Australian expert in vitamin C, was residing in the United Kingdom as a Beit Memorial Medical Research Fellow and was well known to J. C. Drummond, the MOF's chief scientific advisor. Bourne theorized that the global influenza pandemic that had followed World War I had been particularly deadly because of the lowered nutritional state of much of the world population due to the effects of wartime food shortages. Thus, he proposed that nutritional levels must be maintained or raised during the current war through a national scheme for making vitamin-rich foods widely available, particularly for growing children, a position endorsed by John Boyd Orr, the nation's leading nutritional expert.[8]

Based on these and other recommendations from nutritionists, Lord Woolton, as minister of food, moved to make a reliable supply of cheap and free food products known to prevent nutritional diseases (such as rickets and scurvy) available to pregnant women and small children, populations most likely to benefit from early and frequent dosages of these dietary supplements. Having already taken upon itself the responsibility for feeding a family of 45,000,000 through its food control policies and British Restaurants, the MOF now declared its priorities: "In this family THE CHILDREN COME FIRST."[9] The WFS assumed responsibility for procuring and distributing these vitamin foods among the entire population of unborn and young children – the future citizens on the nation – who from its (and their) inception were the target population for this government service. According to Richard Titmuss, what set the WFS apart from prewar social policies was precisely its "universal character": it was "free of social discrimination and the indignities of the poor law."[10] In many ways, it was a model both for a plethora of social services that in the postwar period would come to define the Welfare State and for the ways its benefits were significantly reworked by both major political parties in the 1950s and 1960s.[11]

The WFS had little trouble providing liquid and dried milk and cod liver oil to beneficiaries. The United Kingdom had a well-developed dairy industry and did not have to rely on any imported milk either during World War II or in its aftermath. Although initially cod liver oil was imported from Iceland, it quickly became a domestic product supplied exclusively to the government by British Cod Liver Oil Producers, Ltd., a cooperative of trawler owners based out of Hull.[12] The question of vitamin C products was, however, more complicated. While there was a glut of oranges in Cyprus, Britain did not wish to waste limited shipping space for the importation of fruit.[13] For the first few months of the program, the WFS provided blackcurrant purees and syrups and rose hip syrup, products that were manufactured in Britain from locally grown produce. These had limited long-term potential, however. No commercial crops of rose hips were under cultivation (indeed the hips used in 1941 had been collected by volunteers from wild plants) and the syrup required a lot of sugar to make it palatable to children; thus, making it an expensive product to manufacture. The blackcurrant products were more viable, but these fruits were also earmarked for much-needed jam during the war. Additionally, the cultivated crops had inconsistent annual yields, the products were sometimes poorly tolerated by young children, and they were more expensive to produce than orange juice. In January 1942, these local products were abandoned as supplies of concentrated orange juice (COJ) – a shelf-stable liquid meant to be diluted with water before consumption – began arriving in the United Kingdom from the United States. This COJ was exclusively for the WFS and had been sent under the Lend-Lease program whereby the United States lent military supplies, food, oil, and other items necessary to the war effort to the Allies in exchange for leases on military bases in the Allied countries.

Welfare Foods were heavily subsidized and thus affordable for beneficiaries who were charged 5 pence per bottle of juice, each of which contained a supply lasting ten days to two weeks, depending on the dosage.[14] A six-week supply of cod liver oil was sold at 10 pence.[15] These government-subsidized products were much cheaper at the point of purchase than the proprietary product Haliborange™, which contained both orange juice and halibut liver oil and retailed at 2 shillings and 6 pence.[16] The MOF and Ministry of Health (MOH) had agreed that nominal charges, which remained constant until the subsidy was removed in 1961, were likely to encourage take-up as their officials believed that the public tended not to value things they got for free.[17] Free supplies, however, were still made available to those receiving government income assistance and those eligible based on a variety of financial calculations that were flexible enough, it was hoped, to catch all those truly in need.[18]

The MOF had expected take-up of welfare orange juice (WOJ) to be high as response to the milk scheme had been very positive, but this was not the case at all.[19] For reasons that it was not always possible for the government to discern, the use of WOJ was limited and cod liver oil turned out to be "a ghastly failure."[20] During the war, the uptake of WOJ varied from a low of 23.3 percent to a high of 52.5 percent.

In the two years after the war, its consumption hovered around 40 percent.[21] What these statistics failed to reveal, however, was whether this consumption average of about one-third of the entitlement meant that only one-third of beneficiaries were making using of the product or that individuals were taking only a third of their full entitlement. This made any interpretation of the numbers, and the solution to the problem, difficult for the ministries involved to identify.[22] In the first few months of their provision, some parents objected to being issued free or subsidized government products, viewing these as a form of "charity" that smacked of stigmatizing forms of welfare. This "give, give, give," argued one mother, "assumes we are all paupers."[23] An article in the *Daily Mirror* noted that ironically the response to these products is lowest "where the need of the children is greatest – in the industrial areas, in the crowded city boroughs of working-class homes."[24] Whether the low uptake of these nutritional supplements was because of active resistance to government programs, or merely to collection difficulties, lack of awareness of the new program, or food habits, was, however, difficult for both local and central authorities to establish.

The inconvenience associated with the collection of WOJ, which unlike the milk was not delivered to the door, clearly shaped consumption and the government faced criticism from the press, parliament, and consumers about distances, opening hours, the constant production of ration books (which lasted until 1954), product unavailability, and other inconveniences associated with procuring Welfare Foods.[25] The MOF took these concerns seriously. In the war years, it had simplified the paperwork required to apply for Welfare Foods, introduced postage stamps as a convenient form of payment, and opened 12,000 distribution points across the United Kingdom to make these food benefits more accessible. It experimented with making Welfare Foods available for pick up in large factories where many mothers worked full-time, encouraged mothers to take turns collecting each other's supplies, and unlike the food rationing system, allowed beneficiaries to obtain these products wherever it was convenient without having to use the same distribution point each time.[26] In 1947, as Figure 7.1 illustrates, the WFS also introduced a van that traversed London as a mobile distribution center in order to address these concerns about accessibility[27] (Figure 7.1). Local distribution centers resorted to other methods to attract beneficiaries. At one center, parents who collected both WOJ and the even less popular cod liver oil were entered into a raffle for a portrait of their baby, although the MOF discouraged this practice fearing that the prize winners were invariably "bouncy, fat, flabby infant[s]" raised on proprietary baby foods.[28]

Figure 7.1 A. E. Johnson, mayor of the Municipal Borough of Tottenham (third adult from the left) holds Susan Farwick at age 13 months and a bottle of welfare orange juice in front of the Ministry of Food's Welfare Foods Service mobile van, Tottenham High Road, London, September 27, 1948. Courtesy of Susan Farwick.

The MOF also released copious propaganda extolling the health benefits of Welfare Foods. This included short "Food Flash" films, posters for use at collection points and in infant welfare clinics, and "Food Facts" advertisements in daily papers. One "Food Flash" shamed mothers into using WFS products by arguing that these were essential supplements "unless, of course," it threatened, "you want a rickety child, a bandy, knock-kneed, large-headed pale and rickety article."[29] Other propaganda figured the consumption of Welfare Foods as a collective enterprise – the duty of all citizens – in order to build "Nations out of Nurseries" together. "The Government is doing its part in protecting your child's health by *providing* these vitamin foods. Do your part by seeing that he *gets* them," instructed a "Food Facts" bulletin.[30]

Despite the limited uptake of WOJ and cod liver oil, many members of the public as well as politicians and civil servants did credit the WFS with sustaining the health of all children during wartime,

some contrasting bonny British babies with their Continental counterparts, thus imbibing the rhetoric of nurturing the national body.[31] The
egalitarian nature of the program was also highly appealing to many
who saw in it, as in the 1942 Beveridge Report, the means of level-
ing the playing field. Instead of "half the working-class children being
brought up in poverty and malnutrition," a Mass Observation broad-
cast asserted in 1942, harkening back to the very recent experiences
of the Depression years, the WFS ensures that "everyone gets a level
break of at least the minimum requirements for life and health and
happiness."[32] This view was widely shared by those across the political spectrum who promoted its continuation into the peace as a highly
effective and relatively inexpensive route to national efficiency.[33] Before
the war was even over, the MOF began planning for future supplies of
COJ by "encouraging [its] production" in Palestine, Jamaica, Southern
Rhodesia, and South Africa. The ability to sustain the WFS, the MOF
maintained, was dependent upon these "Empire sources."[34]

Postwar Provision and the Search for Empire Sources

Even two years after the war had ended, however, almost all of the
COJ imported into the United Kingdom still came from the United
States (at this point, as part of the Marshall Plan) with negligible
amounts from Palestine.[35] This foreign aid in kind was temporary,
and the currency crisis of 1947 made the shoring up of supplies of
COJ within the bloc of countries that either used the pound sterling
as their currency or pegged their currencies to the pound sterling an
issue of paramount concern for the Labour government, whose 1945
election campaign had included the perpetuation of the WFS. While
the empire production of orange juice could not earn dollars, since
the United States already manufactured an abundant supply of COJ,
it could save dollars, which was crucial to Britain's postwar economic
recovery plan. During the war, many state officials had assumed that
Palestine could provide a steady supply of COJ creating a mutually
beneficial arrangement that could contribute to the "rehabilitation of
Palestine and thus the economic reconstruction of the Middle East."[36]
When a West Indian delegation arrived in the United Kingdom in
1947 to discuss bananas, the MOF urged them to consider expanding
the citrus industry for the purpose of producing COJ.[37] If, as historians have argued, the scientific identification of nutritional deficiencies had taken place largely in the context of the colonial laboratory,
and malnutrition identified as a key target of colonial development

programs,[38] in the immediate postwar period, it was "colonial development" itself that offered Clement Atlee's administration a solution to the dilemma of metropolitan malnutrition that its Welfare State had pledged to address.

In 1947, the Colonial Primary Products Committee (CPPC) took up the question of COJ.[39] The CPPC had been set up in May 1947 to investigate increasing the colonial production of specific commodities with regard to the interests of the empire, the present and future needs of the world market, and the desirability of increasing foreign exchange resources. The CPPC concluded that Palestine and Jamaica could together meet the needs of the WFS and that the MOF should contact the Colonial Office and spell out the assurances it was willing to provide for citrus growers so that the next steps could be taken in developing these colonial industries.[40] The CPPC warned, however, that in promoting colonial development it was necessary to bear in mind "the doctrine of trusteeship." The colonies are not, the CPPC Interim Report concluded, "British estates which can be exploited by the U.K. for her own advantage." This directly challenged the theory of Joseph Chamberlain, secretary of state for the colonies between 1895 and 1903, which had maintained that colonial territories were "great estates" to be exploited by their British landlord. "The primary concern of Colonial agricultural policy," the report advanced, "must be the benefit of Colonial peoples themselves." It recognized, however, that some government ministries were "anxious to encourage particular lines of production in the Colonies" and encouraged them to do so, provided that they gave "some form of long term assurance to producers which would at least guarantee a reasonable return on capital expenditure."[41]

From the CPPC's first meeting, the tension between the exploitation of colonial territories in order to serve Britain's needs and economic development projects intended to set colonial peoples on the path to economic security (and then responsible self-government) was palpable.[42] This conflict was typical of the immediate postwar period, that "strange Indian summer of the old imperial economy."[43] Despite its commitment to phase out Imperial Preference, in this moment of economic crisis, Britain faced both a shortage of food and a rise in import prices that encouraged it to renew its commercial bond with the empire. This precarious situation required the British government to provide increased economic support to its colonial territories while, at the same time, expecting them to contribute to the United Kingdom's own financial recovery.[44] In the wake of the currency crisis during the summer of 1947 – when Britain reneged on its commitment to the United States to make the pound sterling a fully convertible currency – Atlee's administration decided to place an even greater emphasis on the use of colonial resources in its program of economic reconstruction. It was in this moment that many government agencies began to reconfigure "colonial development" almost exclusively in terms of the expansion of either dollar-saving or dollar-earning colonial commodities.[45] In the aftermath of World War II, as Nick Cullather and Sherene Seikaly have argued, colonial subjects were transformed into developmental subjects largely for the welfare and stability of already "developed" nations.[46]

What made the production of COJ particularly problematic as a colonial development scheme was that, unlike the other agricultural produce the CPPC promoted, it was a highly specialized product, not already under large-scale production, with a very limited commercial world market and no buyer on the horizon beyond the MOF, which only distributed it through the WFS. Far from jump-starting the manufacture of a globally marketable commodity that could lead to a stable industry for the colonies themselves, the empire production of COJ benefitted primarily the British government that desperately needed a nondollar source of juice in order to continue to build its nation out of its nurseries. The history of Britain's Welfare State must therefore be understood, as Jordanna Bailkin has argued, as part of broader imperial dynamics.[47]

Long-Term Contracts and West Indian Citrus

The CPPC's recommendations to move forward with more concrete plans for procuring COJ from the sterling area came not a moment too soon for the MOF. In late April 1948, the Treasury was pressuring the Ministry to cut back the distribution of WOJ in order to reduce imports from the United States.[48] But just as it was anticipating turning to Palestine, which had seemed the most reliable nondollar source of juice, this British Mandate was plunged into turmoil with the eruption of the Arab-Israeli war. The orange groves in Jaffa became a site of heightened tension as the *Haganah* – the army of the newly pronounced State of Israel – seized the town, forcing the exodus of the majority of the Arab population and resulting in the occupation of their citrus groves. The MOF had every reason to fear that the "troubles" in Palestine would limit the production of COJ and Britain's access to it.[49] Future supplies of juice from the region seemed extremely uncertain, and it was increasingly apparent to the British government that other nondollar sources of COJ would have to be found or else risk the reduction, or even cancellation, of this component of the WFS. Suggestions to turn back to blackcurrant and rose hip products, even though this would have helped to "foster a struggling native industry," were few and far between and never seriously pursued as COJ, however difficult to procure, remained the cheapest source of vitamin C.[50] Given this situation, Jamaica began to look like a very appealing source for juice.

The plan to "stimulate" production in the West Indies by means of a long-term contract became the new focus of the MOF's efforts to secure nondollar sources of COJ for the foreseeable future. In 1948, S & S Services Ltd., a newly formed firm acting as the sales agents and technical advisers of the Jamaican citrus producers,[51] proposed to the MOF that an industry in COJ could be cultivated in Jamaica and Trinidad. The firm was run by G. T. Shipston and J. W. Seymour who until the previous year had been, respectively, the MOF's director and assistant director of fruit juices and pectin and as such had managed the sourcing and bottling of WOJ. Before the war, Shipston had worked for the California Fruit Growers Exchange (that marketed some of its fruit under the name Sunkist), which had been making COJ since the 1920s.[52] As a paid temporary officer of the wartime MOF, he had built up production of WOJ from the start of the scheme (much of which appears to have come directly from Sunkist), had been in charge of quality control, and was the chief contact with the British bottlers.[53] It was Shipston who had presented to the CPPC the Ministry's need for sterling supplies of juice. The Ministry felt highly reassured by the fact that Shipston and Seymour – who until that year had been the MOF's own WOJ experts – were claiming that within ten years the British West Indies could produce enough to supply two-thirds of the needs of the WFS.[54] S & S Services, as former employees of the MOF, as both technical advisers to the Jamaican citrus growers and their sales agent in the United Kingdom, and as central players in negotiations been the growers and the various UK Ministries that oversaw procurement of WOJ, smoothed the way for the MOF to commit to a long-term investment in the nascent Caribbean COJ industry.[55]

While initially wary of plans for the empire production of COJ, by the summer of 1948, the Colonial Office was also fully committed to procuring the product from the British West Indies. In July, Parliamentary Under-Secretary of State for the Colonies David Rees-Williams promoted the advantages to the Caribbean colonies of a long-term WOJ contract, which the CPPC had already identified as essential for industries such as citrus tree crops given the lag time between first planting and full bearing.[56] His confident statements about the financial potential of the West Indies and WOJ's role in strengthening the Caribbean economies, were also an explicit rejoinder to the arrival of the *Empire Windrush*. Only weeks earlier, the ship had brought some 500 hopeful

Jamaican migrants to Britain and, in the process, raised alarm about the United Kingdom's permissive immigration policy and its generous social services at a time when many felt the outlook for colonial economies was bleak. WOJ thus promised not only to build healthy bodies at home but healthy economies abroad. British colonial subjects, Rees-Williams implied, would also benefit from the Welfare State but not by journeying to the United Kingdom to become dependent upon it.[57] Stimulating the Caribbean economy through the development of a COJ industry, Rees-Williams seemed to be arguing, was an effective way to keep everyone exactly where they belonged.

In this climate, some officials within the Colonial Office wanted the MOF to provide more than just a vague long-term contract for WOJ. Eugene Melville, the Colonial Office's assistant under-secretary, stressed the importance of understanding COJ production in the British West Indies from the "Colonial political angle." "The Colonies are constantly urged to increase their production of things which the U.K. needs," he wrote, and thus colonial producers must be supported up to the limit of their production capacities. To encourage foreign competition for the products the British government urged its colonies to grow, would breed "mistrust of H.M.G.'s sincerity and ... weaken the production effort." Melville argued that the United Kingdom needed to provide a ten-year contract that allowed the West Indian juice producers to feel secure that the government would commit itself to purchasing, at a reasonable price, their maximum output of the product.[58] Indeed, in the summer of 1948, West Indian growers constructed the impending contract as a "family affair" between Britain and its colonies, downplaying the commercial nature of the transaction.[59] Melville's colleague, H. F. Heinemann, however, foregrounded market concerns. He warned that even in the long run the British West Indies might prove to be a more expensive producer than other suppliers and paying more at the outset might send the wrong message. "Indeed we should not be altogether happy about establishing the industry," he argued, "if there were not a prospect that it would become able to produce on competitive terms."[60] Some Colonial Office officials were from the outset concerned about the nature of a colonial development program that was instigated first and foremost to serve the needs of a British government ministry. These doubts were cast aside as a contract that seemed to solve the immediate problem of juice supply was eagerly drawn up, but they would return to haunt the WFS for decades to come.

The terms of the long-term contract that was eventually negotiated specified that the MOF would purchase 75 percent of the output of COJ from the British West Indies up to a maximum of 5,000 tons per annum, which was about half of what the WFS predicted it would require. The rest would come from other sources because to achieve a consistent flavor and level of vitamin C in all batches of WOJ it was necessary to blend juices. Quotas were to be divided among Jamaica, Trinidad, and British Honduras. This was a joint contract stating that if any of these colonies could not meet its quota, the others would be allowed to supply COJ in its stead. Prices for COJ were to be negotiated each year but were limited to increases or decreases of not more than 12.5 percent from the previous year's price.

The plan to procure COJ from colonial territories had been initiated by the demands of the WFS; indeed, the Colonial Office explicitly thanked the MOF for "fixing it up," taking none of the credit itself.[61] The scheme was nevertheless sold and publicized as good for all parties. In October 1948, the secretary of state for the colonies sent a telegram to the relevant West Indian colonies alerting them to the ten-year contract for COJ and stressing its mutual benefits. It stated that, "supplies from the Colonies of concentrated orange juice of which substantial purchases are at present made in the United States for the U.K. Welfare service will be of great benefit to the U.K. In providing a steady outlet for a high quality and specialized product, the proposed arrangement would clearly also benefit the producing Colonies."[62] According to the MOF, the British West Indies were pleased with the outcome of the negotiations and accepted the ten-year contract "as a very important piece of Colonial development" that "will materially assist in solving many of the problems which exist in the territories today."[63] In announcing the ten-year contract to the House of Commons in November of 1948, John Strachey, the minister of food (and great-nephew to the Indian civil servants Sir John and Sir Richard Strachey), maintained that he hoped the contract would increase Britain's access to WOJ supplies, while at the same time, reduce "our dollar expenditure," statements which were published on the front page of Jamaica's most prominent newspaper.[64] It was hard not to conclude that the ten-year contract for COJ was extremely beneficial for all parties concerned. In retrospect, however, this moment proved to be the high point of a relationship between the WFS and West Indian juice producers that was anything but unproblematic.

Despite this initial enthusiasm, COJ from the British West Indies was slow to start flowing down throats of British children. It took another nineteen months before the contract that had been agreed to could be signed. The Jamaican citrus growers – most of whom were small farmers producing less than fifty boxes of oranges per year (with 400 boxes required for a single ton of COJ)[65] – first had to establish themselves as an approved association under the Agricultural Marketing Law of Jamaica before jointly committing to the contract. It was this organization that would sell its product directly to the MOF. It was not until April 1950 that the contract was finally signed.[66] Even then pickings were slim as the COJ industry struggled to get off the ground and the WFS had to tap other sources of supply.[67] When the Treasury suggested that it would not authorize further dollar purchases of COJ, tensions emerged between the "well-being" of "mothers and children" and economic considerations.[68] WOJ had already been enshrined as a benefit available to all, and its consumption constructed as part of the ritual of becoming a British child citizen. When Princess Anne was born in August 1950, the Westminster Food Office had publicly bestowed on the Duke of Edinburgh Anne's entitlement of Welfare Foods.[69] To curtail the scheme now would thus prove an embarrassment to the Labour government that had narrowly won a majority of seats in the House of Commons in the February 1950 election and was eager to uphold its campaign promises. These included not only the perpetuation of cheap and free food supplements but also the amelioration of colonial economic conditions through "long-term contracts and bulk purchase agreements" to properly prepare them for democratic self-government.[70] That these two promises were linked through the procurement of WOJ from the British West Indies was likely lost on most Labour voters, as the product was never advertised to beneficiaries as an empire good.[71] But it was front and foremost for MOF and Colonial Office officials as were the recent failures of other colonial development schemes. In 1950, the Gambia Poultry Farm program, initiated to supply the British market with dressed chicken and eggs, had collapsed. Early in 1951, the MOF had finally pulled the plug on the equally disastrous Tanganyika groundnut scheme that had been launched to provide more cooking fats for the "harassed housewives of Britain." Neither of these initiatives had been developed primarily in the interests of colonial subjects, but like COJ they were intended to meet Britain's needs.[72] When Winston Churchill won the October 1951 election, he inherited the legacy of these recent failed colonial development projects, on the one hand, and assumed power with a different vision regarding social services, on the other.

The Conservative Party and Cuts to the Welfare State

Although some historians have argued that between 1951 and 1964 the Conservatives did little to undo the structure of the Welfare State and instead maintained the status quo,[73] others have emphasized the

Conservative Party's continued commitment to targeted social services but not to the egalitarian distribution so central to the Labour Party's vision.[74] While the Conservatives did not jettison the WFS, this period saw significant changes to it in terms of both the number of entitled beneficiaries and the cost of the products to the consumer. In 1951, the MOF and MOH were in fact already in discussions about reducing the provision of WOJ for children over two years old as the promised West Indian supplies were limited and other cheap sources of vitamin C had not been found. The hurricane season in the Caribbean that year had led to limited production. The British government received no Caribbean juice in 1951 and instead had been required to furnish replanting grants.[75] Prospects for a sustainable industry in Trinidad looked doubtful and it eventually withdrew from the contract (having provided no juice at all), while British Honduras could provide only 3 tons of COJ to the United Kingdom in 1952.[76] The established industry in the United States with plentiful and cheap juice made it difficult for the upstart British West Indies to compete with either California or Florida producers in sales outside the United Kingdom. Prices for West Indian COJ were also consistently higher than those obtained by the MOF for Spanish, Israeli, and American juice, largely because of higher shipping costs.[77] Whether the British government should be obliged to pay more for West Indian juice in order to stabilize these economies became a highly contentious issue that the ten-year contract had not actually resolved and meant that hostility to West Indian COJ was evident almost as soon as it became available. By the early 1950s, the enthusiasm for Caribbean COJ had faded along with the sense that the WFS continued to be of much value to the general population, since a wide variety of fresh fruit was now readily available for purchase in the United Kingdom.

Even the Conservatives feared in these early days of the Welfare State, however, that altering the beneficiaries of WOJ might provoke public censure unless scientific evidence could be furnished that supported the contention that the product was no longer necessary. The scientific literature on nutritionally appropriate vitamin C intake for children was limited and inconsistent. Magnus Pyke (who had worked under Drummond during the war) pointed out in retrospect that recommended dietary allowances "occupy a curious and interesting position midway between science and politics."[78] The League of Nations Technical Commission had recommended 5–15 mgs per day in 1938. In 1941, the American National Research Council had recommended 30–50 mgs, depending on age. Eight years later, the British Medical Association (BMA) proposed that only 10–15 mgs were necessary.[79] Thus, in 1951, the Standing

Committee on Nutrition requested that a social survey of the national diet be undertaken with particular attention to vitamin C intakes of children for the explicit use of the MOF and MOH in further discussions on the future of WOJ.[80] It found that the average daily intake of vitamin C ranged from 14 mgs for children under a year up to 28 mgs for children aged 4–5 years old. On average, only an additional 5 mgs per day was obtained from WOJ and 2 mgs from other vitamin preparations.[81] Thus, even without these supplements factored in, the diets of young children exceeded both the League of Nations' and the BMA's recommended intakes. (They did not, however, come close to meeting the standards of the National Research Council, although some of the American nutritional research on the health benefits of oranges had been "fostered and supported" by Sunkist itself.)[82]

In 1953, E. R. Bransby, an MOH official, moved to publish a scientific paper that he had written with J. E. Fothergill of the Social Survey based on these findings. This paper, which used the BMA recommendations as definitive, could be utilized as the most up-to-date scientific support, suggested Bransby, should the government move to withdraw WOJ from children over two years old.[83] H. E. Magee, the chief medical officer to the MOH, approved this course of action, citing the need for some reason to be given once the benefit was withdrawn. He initially suggested that the paper be published before any announcement was made regarding a reduction in WOJ benefits and without any reference to why the survey was conducted in the first place. "Simple reference to the paper," he argued, "would suffice to answer questions and much official time would thereby be saved."[84] Bransby suggested that, should it be decided to withdraw WOJ from children over two, then the paper would appear somewhere prestigious such as the *Lancet* or the *British Medical Journal*, implying that this would provide further confirmation from the scientific community that WOJ was no longer necessary for older toddlers. Should that decision not be taken, the article could still be sent to the *British Journal of Nutrition*, he concluded.[85]

This planting of scientific evidence for a decision not yet taken began to feel problematic to a variety of officials, and Magee backpedaled on the decision to publish in advance of any official announcement.[86] Within a week, a report on the survey had been leaked to the press, possibly by the Treasury who sought to reduce the cost of WOJ by cutting beneficiaries but wished first to "test public opinion."[87] An article in the *Daily Express* disclosed that the survey had found that WOJ brought little measurable benefit to children over two years and that the MOF had wasted millions of pounds by supplying it for children up to five, a policy that had benefitted only "American orange growers." Armed with this new information, argued the *Daily Express*, the chancellor of the exchequer will surely wish to economize by ending the supply of juice to children over two. "But such a move," it concluded, "might be misconstrued as a Tory attack on the Welfare State," thus reinforcing the delicate domestic politics of WOJ.[88]

The MOF was "extremely embarrassed" by this newspaper coverage and warned the MOH to be wary of publishing Bransby and Fothergill's study before the Standing Committee on Medical and Nutritional Problems had itself reached a decision on the future of WOJ.[89] Norman C. Wright, the chief scientific advisor to the Ministry of Food, objected to Bransby and Fothergill's findings. He cited major scientific differences of opinion as to the vitamin C requirements of children and questioned the conclusions drawn from the survey itself, which he suggested were far from transparent.[90] Minister of Food Gwilym Lloyd-George (a Liberal within Churchill's Conservative administration who was now choosing to hyphenate his last name) was similarly "uneasy" about the proposition. He refused to withdraw the provision until he had convinced himself "that we have a political defence for any action we take which is not only well based scientifically but which can be made really convincing to the public." WOJ was not merely intended to provide the bare minimum of vitamin C, Lloyd-George argued. Instead, it was an "over-insurance," which we cannot disavow now based on "inferential" supporting evidence that is open to "technical doubt and certainly not convincing to the layman." If the MOF withdrew subsidized WOJ, Lloyd-George reasoned, comparable vitamin C was only obtainable at a cost of four to seven times as much. This was "awkward in the present atmosphere of public sensitiveness to price levels," particularly food prices, which were rising each year during the first half of the 1950s.[91]

In the end, the MOF dragged its feet and ultimately did not accept the recommendation of the MOH, headed by the Conservative Iain Macleod, to terminate the benefits of children over two years old.[92] This prompted the *Daily Express*, citing the Bransby and Fothergill study (which had appeared in 1954 in the *British Journal of Nutrition* as had been previously arranged) to continue to complain that, "the cut-price orange juice is doing little more than provide [sic] an enjoyable drink at the taxpayers' expense."[93] This apparent lack of unity within and between the Ministries of Food and Health on the issue of WOJ suggested that it had received only a temporary reprieve, its future was far from assured, and its provision a highly politicized issue, which was about to get even more contentious. For, when rationing ended in July 1954, the uptake of WOJ declined even further, hovering around 28 percent of entitlement, which severely undermined the case for its continued provision.[94]

Free Trade, Dependencies, and West Indian Juice

Initially, the West Indian suppliers seemed unperturbed by the steady decline in the consumption of WOJ and even suggested that growers could currently get better prices on the open market for their orange juice and might need to be released from their obligation to provide the WFS 75 percent of the juice available from their fruit.[95] But when the British government began to consider issuing an Open General Licence for nondollar and nonsterling fruit juices, the Jamaican Citrus Growers Association (JCGA) advocated for protections for their industry. The JCGA feared that, in this climate of increasing trade liberalization, juice from other countries would become widely available, thus driving prices down, and that the British government could congratulate itself on starting a now commercially viable industry and, in good faith, walk away from its long-term contractual obligations.

To pacify the West Indian citrus growers who insisted that trade liberalization would negatively impact their industry and to obtain a better understanding of the outlook for Caribbean citrus, the secretary of state for the colonies initiated a fact-finding mission into the economic viability of the industry at the end of 1954.[96] While awaiting the findings, the Colonial Office tried to deflate what it feared were mounting tensions at a delicate political moment. The Social Democrat Norman Manley was being installed as the new chief minister in Jamaica; at the same time, negotiations over Federation – the political union of Caribbean islands that together sought independence from Britain as a single state – were ongoing and tense. The Colonial Office thus encouraged the Welfare Foods Procurement Division to purchase more COJ from the West Indies, which was now retreating from its earlier assertion that it might prefer to sell its juice elsewhere on the open market. There was no "commercial" justification for this purchase, argued the Procurement Division, which had already obtained supplies elsewhere. Instead, its officials claimed, the issue was "entirely political."[97] Precisely because it was political, within two days, the newly amalgamated Ministry of Agriculture, Fisheries, and Food (MAFF), now under the leadership of the Conservative Derick Heathcoat-Amory, had reluctantly agreed to the Colonial Office's request to purchase an additional 100 tons of COJ from the West Indies but put the onus on the Colonial Office to convince the Treasury to sanction a transaction that was so patently uneconomic.[98]

By the spring of 1955, the fact-finding mission was complete. It found that orange juice prices had dropped since the introduction of the Open General Licence for nondollar fruit juices, which had allowed these goods to be imported into the United Kingdom more easily after 1954. Only British Honduras could currently obtain a reasonable return for the production of COJ at present market prices. The fact-finding mission projected that the future for Jamaican juice was particularly bleak because its COJ was uneconomical and unprofitable, and "its future prospects against U.S. competition" were "very poor."[99] The fact-finding mission, however, strayed from providing just the facts. Its report concluded that the Caribbean growers could rightly argue that Her Majesty's Government had "a moral obligation to pay the West Indies an economic price for the juice which it is producing in response to a United Kingdom request and to continue the contract beyond 1960 until at least the capital cost of establishing groves has been recovered."[100] It claimed that, unlike in other colonial industries with bulk purchase agreements, the orange trees in Jamaica and British Honduras had been planted almost entirely for the purpose of producing WOJ, and without the security of that contract, the planting, which had increased by 12,000 acres by the end of 1954, would not have developed "to anything like the extent that it has."[101] The report of the fact-finding mission, which was also published in Jamaica's daily newspaper, underscored that the West Indian industry was not yet competitive and would require continued support.[102] It presented the West Indies as dependent colonies whose COJ industry had been developed entirely for the purposes of the WFS and whose orange growers would need to be backed by the United Kingdom indefinitely. The alternative, the report predicted, was the eventual collapse of the industry, a situation that would have significant political ramifications.

In May of 1955, after the results of the fact-finding mission had been disseminated to the relevant departments, F. Hollins, under-secretary of the MAFF, pushed back against the Colonial Office, which he maintained seemed to be implying that "H.M.G. must be regarded as under an obligation to support the citrus industry even if the conclusion to be drawn from the report of the Mission is that it is incurably uneconomic." Hollins countered that the United Kingdom should not be forced to pay an "uncompetitive price" for its WOJ. The knowledge that the contract would end and the demand for WOJ was diminishing, should stimulate "the more efficient elements of the industry" to develop new outlets for products likely "to hold their own in a competitive world." If money was to be expended on the West Indian citrus industry, Hollins reasoned, then it should be invested into research regarding the transportation of agricultural products to "different overseas markets."[103] Hollins seemed to be implying that hard work and initiative would buoy the citrus producers willing to put the effort into making themselves competitive and that the others should be left to reap what they had sown. The WFS, Hollins suggested, subsidized the WOJ provided to its British beneficiaries, but it had no responsibility to subsidize the West Indian producers of the product, despite the fact that they too were British subjects.

The argument that the MAFF was building against more investment in the Caribbean citrus industry in the spring of 1955 was undermined by a surprising 22 percent increase in the uptake of WOJ during the unexpectedly warm and dry months of July and August that followed.[104] This increased consumption in the summer seemed to confirm what the government had long suspected: that WOJ was not necessarily being consumed as a nutritional supplement but rather as "an enjoyable and refreshing drink" (some parents reportedly used it as a cocktail mixer!).[105] Despite known abuses, the product was nevertheless an entitlement, and this spike in demand proved problematic. The new crop of juice from Israel, Spain, and the United States would not be available before February 1956, so the WFS was forced to turn again to Jamaica whose orange crops began to be harvested in October. This was embarrassing, having represented recent purchases as merely a political concession. In this climate, the Jamaicans moved to demand a higher price than the MAFF usually paid: 33 shillings and 9 pence per gallon as opposed to 30 shillings. This was still within the allowable 12.5 percent markup and, according to S & S Services, well below the current market price of 38 shillings. But the MAFF balked at what it considered an inflated price, arguing that it placed large and reliable orders in return for low prices and were even prepared to buy early season juice, which "although admirably suited to the purpose for which it is required, is less attractive to some other buyers."[106] Robert Kirkwood – a key player in the sugar industry and head of the JCGA at this time[107] – pressed the Ministry to reconsider their purchase price. He argued it should reflect the British government's historical investment in the industry and its future plans for the economic viability of an independent West Indies, not merely the WFS's current needs.[108]

Kirkwood found little support for this position even from the Colonial Office, which felt that it was not in the West Indies' best interests to maintain artificially high prices and that its citrus industry needed to be made more competitive in relation to the world market. The United Kingdom was also concerned about its commitment to the General Agreement on Tariffs and Trade (GATT) and felt considerable pressure from the Americans to encourage freer global trade rather than protecting its own and its colonial industries, hence the Open General Licence issued in 1954. In order to assuage the citrus industry, and others that were equally hanging in the balance, the United Kingdom nevertheless conceded to seek the amendment of GATT to include a Colonial Waiver that permitted Britain to help its colonial industries on the same terms as its domestic industries.[109] The Colonial Office continued to stress, however, that although the British government was willing to help to "create the conditions in which colonial industries can flourish" it could not support unfair methods of competition. It insisted that it was now up to the industry itself to make itself competitive in a global citrus market. All future aid must instead be sought from the Colonial Development and Welfare Fund that since 1940 had provided grants to ameliorate the standard of living in colonial territories and had been introduced in part as a response to agricultural depression and social unrest in the West Indies.[110] The British government insisted that the West Indies free itself from dependency on the WFS, casting the citrus growers, rather than the consumers of their juice, as welfare recipients.

The recent surge in uptake of WOJ, however, placed the WFS in a precarious position in these price negotiations, since its officials knew it would be hard to meet demand without additional West Indian juice. The WFS thus proposed buying a token amount of juice, 200 tons, at the higher price to meet what it understood to be merely a temporary demand. Kirkwood, however, demanded that the MAFF procure 750 tons, 75 percent of their yield, which was in accord with the long-term contract.[111] Reminding the government of the origins of the contract, he rightly asserted that the British West Indies' provision of COJ had never been merely a commercial transaction. The development of an industry in COJ had been born in the context of the "*the economic and agricultural advancement of the Colonial Empire*" and the diversification of colonial industries, on the one hand, and "the *special balance of payment difficulties* in the sterling area" in the wake of the war, on the other, Kirkwood claimed, spitting its own 1948 rhetoric back at the British government. From an "entirely non-political view," Kirkwood asserted, the "threat of purchase of dollar concentrate in order to drive down prices would be hardly consistent with the original intention of the Contract," he reasoned, "which was to build up a Colonial industry which would gradually replace dollar Concentrate with Sterling Concentrate." This was not merely an economic issue, he reasoned. If the contracts were abrogated, this would make it impossible to establish the industry on a sound economic basis, which Kirkwood declared had repercussions that took the entire "matter into the political field."[112] For the JCGA, these discussions were about reestablishing the British government's enduring obligations to the West Indian orange growers.

Given the terms of the contract, the MAFF was obliged to commit to the purchase of all 750 tons of West Indian juice, and because their need for stocks was now urgent, they had little room to negotiate price. Although the Procurement Division badly needed this COJ, and had itself been caught in a market transaction, it nevertheless took up Kirkwood's own rhetoric in order to cast its willingness to pay what its officials considered an inflated price as helping a colonial industry. It needed to be made clear to the JCGA, argued the MAFF, that the prices currently paid were not conceded to on "commercial" grounds but as an interim measure of assistance to the industry, and in the future, the 30 shilling price would be paid.[113] While the use of this language served the West Indian growers who clearly wanted the British government to feel obliged to invest in their industry, it also reasserted the colonial relationship between the United Kingdom and the British West Indies by clarifying exactly who was dependent on whom at a time when this relationship was in fact much less obvious.

By the start of the 1955–56 West Indian juice season, the annual negotiations with the Caribbean citrus delegation had transformed, as Kirkwood had feared, into more significant debates about the future of the contract. When the Colonial Office and the MAFF met to discuss the issue at the end of September 1955, a senior official of the MAFF declared that, although the ten-year contract had "doubtless been conceived in a spirit of helpfulness towards the Colonies," it was economically "bad" for both parties. It bound the government to buy more juice than it needed and required the producers to accept a price below market value. It would be best, he stated, if the colonies could be brought to recognize that it was mutually advantageous to terminate these agreements.[114] Alan Lennox-Boyd, secretary of state for the colonies, argued that the West Indies should turn to the free market, since full employment and an expanding economy created by his administration had led to opportunities for the sale of West Indian goods. "The market is there for those who wish and are ready to build it up," Lennox-Boyd claimed, returning to the idea that committed and efficient growers could not only make ends meet but turn a profit. "I am quite sure that it is in the industry's own interests to build its market in this way," he argued, "rather than to become largely dependent for its outlet on Government schemes."[115] Lennox-Boyd suggested that those who were willing to take responsibility for modernizing their production could take advantage of the expanding opportunities provided by embracing the free market and free themselves of their servility to the British government.

The British Caribbean Citrus Association (BCCA) – newly formed in 1955 to eliminate competition among the West Indian citrus-producing territories themselves and to improve quality and production[116] – maintained, however, that when the contract had been negotiated, the then (Labour) government had indicated that there should be an "expanding demand for the product." We were given to understand that there would be a "permanent future for this business," the BCCA maintained, otherwise we would never have "persuaded growers to plant trees which take 5 years to come into bearing, and which have a life expectancy of 35 years." (And they might have added would increase in productivity between 1955 and 1960 by 335 percent in British Honduras and 102 percent in Jamaica.[117]) It is a "revolutionary suggestion," the BCCA asserted, that the British government should embark upon a change of policy without considering how growers should market the orange production "created solely as a result of this Contract."[118]

Norman Manley, the chief minister of Jamaica, and Albert Gomes, Trinidad's minister of labour, industry, and commerce, were at that time in London and in talks with Lennox-Boyd presumably on issues relating to the proposed Federation of the West Indies. They similarly decried the idea that the long-term contract could be canceled and insisted that the British government was obliged to keep the West Indian citrus industry afloat. In a letter to Lennox-Boyd signed also by Gomes, Manley asserted that from the very beginning the citrus industry in the British West Indies had been intimately tied to the WFS and had not been conceived of primarily as part of a diversification of colonial agriculture. Manley cited the 1948 telegram sent from the then secretary of state for the colonies to the governor of Jamaica that made it patently clear that it had been a "deliberate policy of the British Government to encourage the production of concentrated orange juice within the Caribbean area" in "the interest of plans which England had for the Welfare State and for the avoidance of dollar difficulties." "I should doubt very much if there is any other case in which a Colonial industry has been stimulated in this deliberate way," insisted Manley, "with full appreciation of all that it would involve in long term capital investment, as a result of considerations arising from British policy and dollar difficulties." "Consequently," he concluded, "the contention that there is a unique situation which has every moral claim for protection at this moment of critical difficulty, this turning point of the whole future development of the industry, is clear beyond question."[119] Manley could not have made Britain's moral obligation to the Caribbean citrus industry any clearer and had the documentation – namely the original telegram announcing the contract – to back up his assertion. Within three days of this letter that so clearly laid out the history of the Caribbean citrus scheme in relation to the WFS, the MOH, MAFF, Colonial

Office, and Treasury were compelled to agree that the ten-year contract could not be abrogated. But they insisted that it would continue on "strictly commercial principles."[120]

Reducing Beneficiaries and Removing the Subsidy

If WOJ raised these vexing problems in relation to its procurement from the colonies, at the same time it continued to be a target for Conservatives seeking to cut expenditures on the Welfare State. To many Conservatives, WOJ epitomized the indiscriminate subsidization of products that most people could afford to buy for themselves and served as a symbol of an age that Conservatives felt was breeding a generation dependent on the state. But making cuts to its provision would not in fact save the government much money. In 1955, the cost of WOJ was a mere 4 percent of the entire cost of the WFS.[121] In addition, the WFS was linked to the Family Allowance Scheme as a benefit in kind.[122] If the subsidy for WOJ was reduced, compensation might have to come in the form of raising family allowance payments. Decreasing the subsidy on WOJ was therefore not necessarily a financial benefit to the government. However, reducing the entitled beneficiaries remained a possibility, but only if backed by "the most authoritative recommendation."[123] The MOH decided to remit the matter to the Standing Medical Advisory Committee in consultation with the Medical Research Council. The Ministry asked Sir Henry Cohen, chairman of the committee, to work jointly with the Scottish Medical Advisory Committee and prepare a "reasoned report" on the present needs of pregnant women and young children for orange juice and cod liver oil, paying particular attention to children aged two to five. The report could then be used by the MOH to determine the best course of action in regard to the provision of WOJ in particular.[124]

The Cohen Committee began its deliberations in 1956 and was asked by the MOH to release an interim report that summer because contracts for COJ had to be placed in advance and the purchasing season was approaching.[125] Having determined that the MOF's most recent decision to continue to provide WOJ to children over two years old was made on "administrative, not nutritional, grounds," the Committee turned its attention to the medical evidence before them. This included Bransby and Fothergill's *British Journal of Nutrition* publication – which had been published precisely in order to provide scientific evidence for just such a policy change – and a series of experiments in vitamin deprivation undertaken by the Medical Research Council that had concluded that requirements might not be as high as previously supposed.[126] Two members of the Cohen Committee favored the continued provision of WOJ for all children up to the age of five, but the majority position parroted just what the MOH had hoped to hear: that there was now adequate evidence that COJ was no longer required for children over two. The report concluded that the beneficiaries of WOJ could safely be substantially reduced.[127]

The Cohen Committee's final report was not scheduled for release until the end of July 1957, and in the interim, the Colonial Office moved to be included in all discussions of the future of WOJ that might result from its findings given the "political difficulties of the most unpleasant kind" that might arise in relation to the future of the long-term contract.[128] One WFS official anticipated that the Colonial Office would object to any reduction of beneficiaries, "waving the flag of Empire, etc.," and in the end, he was correct.[129] When the MOH and the MAFF received the results of the Cohen Committee, they conferred with the Home Affairs Committee of the Cabinet, the Treasury, the secretary of state for the colonies, and the prime minister as to what action to take. Lennox-Boyd argued that while WOJ should not continue to be supplied to children aged two to five "merely in order to provide a market for West Indian orange juice," West Indian interests were nevertheless one of several factors that should be taken into account in relation to the Cohen Committee's recommendations.[130] "There is no question of the contract being operated as a political instrument to boost the industry artificially," Lennox-Boyd insisted, but any "attempt on the Ministry's part to offer the producers minimum and unacceptable prices in an attempt to kill the contract would be bitterly resented in the producing Colonies and might well have serious political repercussions," suggesting that the MAFF had its own plans to decrease consumption of WOJ besides the cut in beneficiaries.[131]

When Harold Macmillan became prime minister in January 1957, after the resignation of Anthony Eden in the wake of the Suez Crisis, he made it abundantly clear that he was in favor both of limiting the beneficiaries of WOJ to those under two years old and of removing the subsidy so that the product could be sold at cost. Although he would later claim that the WFS had been part of his "political philosophy,"[132] Macmillan advised Peter Thorneycroft, the chancellor of the exchequer, who was adamant about trimming public expenditure especially to health and welfare services, to take "full advantage" of the Cohen Committee's recommendations to reduce beneficiaries and at the same time to seize the "opportunity of getting rid of this subsidy." Most people didn't need this kind of government assistance, Macmillan insisted. Indeed, "most of our people have never had it so good," he intoned in

July of 1957.[133] The prime minister found it trying that anyone thought the views of the West Indian producers should be heard: "We did not have to get [gin magnate] Godfrey Nicholson's agreement before stopping the supply of gin to babies," Macmillan grumbled.[134] Ironically, Macmillan's "never had it so good" speech was made at a celebration of Lennox-Boyd's political career.[135] But as was to become apparent, the decisions made first about the reduction of benefits, and a few years later about the withdrawal of the subsidy, meant that the colonial subjects that the secretary of state for the colonies at least nominally represented were not in fact entitled to share in this so-called economic prosperity. Lennox-Boyd could do little in this instance but cable Jamaica and British Honduras to inform them in advance of the public announcement that the Cabinet had decided to withdraw WOJ from two to five year olds effective November 1, 1957.[136]

The decision to reduce the beneficiaries of WOJ came at a tense political moment. The ten-year contract was due to expire at the end of the 1959–60 juice season, leaving the Caribbean citrus industry with no more guarantees from the British government. At the same time, the West Indies was moving toward decolonization: its Federation had finally been formed in January of 1958 after years of negotiation. At the end of the 1958–59 growing season, with only one more year on the contract, the West Indian citrus delegation pushed for further commitments from the MAFF, arguing that the trade liberalization policy of the British government had left the Caribbean citrus industry unprotected at just the moment that it was reaching maximum output. While the Colonial Office all but begged the MAFF to at least give their "blessing in principle" to such an agreement,[137] the MOH and MAFF were seeking further to curtail the distribution of WOJ and decried any attempt to continue the supply based on the economic and political condition of the Caribbean colonies. Officials within these ministries maintained that the "appeasement" of the West Indies through WOJ purchases had "gone too far as it is."[138] The WFS, they insisted, could not be used as a "permanent attempt to sustain the citrus industry in the West Indies."[139] A memorandum by John Hare, the minister of agriculture, fisheries, and food, explicitly stated in July 1959 that to ensure low prices, protect against crop failure, and diversify sources for the purposes of blending in order to maintain a uniform product, his procurement department needed to spread its purchases around the globe without giving preference to West Indian growers. While the secretary of state for the colonies might wish the MAFF to purchase specified quantities of juice from the West Indies, he insinuated, the WFS was "not an appropriate means of providing aid for their citrus industry."[140]

These arguments were articulated in a climate of increased concerns not only about the economics of decolonization but also about its effects on immigration. A 1955 newsreel entitled, *Our Jamaican Problem*, had attributed the recent increase in Jamaican immigration in part to depressed agricultural industries and offered more economic development programs as a solution to the implied "problem" of the "influx" of West Indians. Many feared that those who purportedly came "in search of hope" were merely cashing in on Britain's generous Welfare State.[141] The Nottingham and Notting Hill race riots of 1958 had exposed the deep tensions around West Indian immigration to the British Isles and could only have provided further stimulus to keep as many Caribbean subjects as possible on their own islands by propping up their failing industries. When the ten-year contract did in fact terminate in July 1960, the BCCA tapped these anxieties and used the government's own postwar rhetoric of "Colonial Development, and agricultural diversification" and the more recent policy of providing assistance to "economically backward areas within the Commonwealth" to argue for continued purchases of COJ.[142] This strategy led Hare, as one of his final acts as head of the MAFF, to sign a "Statement of Intent" that bound the WFS to purchase from the West Indies in each of the subsequent four crop years at least 60 percent of their requirements of WOJ at a price to be agreed upon each year.[143]

At the same time that the MAFF was brokering this new Statement of Intent, Macmillan reshuffled his cabinet and appointed Enoch Powell minister of health. The MOH had been in charge of the distribution of Welfare Foods since 1955. In 1961, they were also scheduled to take over the procurement of COJ from the MAFF, consolidating the administration of the service. Powell was adamantly opposed to the government's subsidization of WOJ and had little sympathy for what he interpreted as the use of the WFS to subsidize the West Indian economy. As members of the Conservative One Nation Group, Powell and Macleod (who had become secretary of state for the colonies the previous year) had articulated the philosophy that one should first help those in need rather than providing the same benefits to everyone. In a "responsible society," One Nation members argued, people paid for themselves whenever they could and should be encouraged to do so.[144] In fact, Powell had resigned alongside Thorneycroft in 1958 over the issue of government over spending on social services.[145] For Powell, removing the subsidy was at least in part ideological. Although Macleod shared these sentiments in theory, the Colonial Office explained to the MOH that WOJ was not merely a domestic benefit program that could be administered like any other. Rather, it was linked to colonial issues. This was a particularly tense time in the Caribbean, its officials explained, as the "whole future of the Federation is at stake." There was a "difficult" constitutional conference upcoming, followed by a referendum in Jamaica, and W. L. Gorell Barnes, deputy permanent under-secretary for the Colonial Office, argued that they should try not to "rock the boat."[146]

The MOH chose not to heed these warnings. Knowing that without the subsidy the normal uptake of WOJ would likely be "appreciably lower," Powell nevertheless removed "the indiscriminate subsidy" on WOJ effective June 1, 1961. Hereafter, the juice would be sold at the cost of 1 shilling and 6 pence, although free supplies would still be available to those that met the income qualifications. Since the government would be offering the product at cost, the MOH conceded that it was willing to return to the policy of making COJ available to all children up to the age of five as well as to "handicapped" children.[147] As Figure 7.2 illustrates, it launched a new advertising campaign to clarify its beneficiary policy (Figure 7.2).

Figure 7.2 Ministry of Health, Welfare Orange Juice poster. Color lithograph by Eileen Evans, c. 1961. Wellcome Collection. CC BY.

Concentrated Orange Juice in a Cold War World

The removal of the subsidy led to a drastic and immediate decline in the consumption of WOJ. In 1960, 21.48 million bottles of WOJ had been sold in England and Wales; in 1962, that number plummeted to 8.82 million.[148] While the MOH declared that it was more than satisfied that the "vitamin state of the nation was at present satisfactory, despite the fall in Welfare Foods consumption,"[149] this could not have come at a more inconvenient political moment for the British government, as Gorell-Barnes had warned. Jamaica seceded from the Federation after a referendum in September 1961 and began preparing for independence. Its first election, held on April 10, 1962, returned Alexander Bustamante as prime minister who was to assume his position with the coming of independence on August 6. In the summer of 1962, the West Indian citrus delegation, now representing the producers of a newly independent nation, pushed the MOH to buy more COJ in the coming season than it had the previous year. But given the drastic drop in WOJ uptake, the requirements of the WFS were now for only 200 tons of juice for blending purposes.[150]

In discussions that extended into the autumn, the issue of the "moral obligation" reemerged. Some of the staff of the Commonwealth Relations Office and of the Colonial Office were prepared to admit that the British government had been responsible for encouraging the West Indians to plant orange trees for the production of WOJ. The contracts had been terminated, they acknowledged, just as the trees had come into full bearing, and these officials conceded that Her Majesty's Government had "let [the colonial producers] down pretty badly" and could "hardly be proud of this."[151] The official position voiced by the Commonwealth Relations Office, however, was that, as far back as 1955, the growers had been told that the contract would not be renewed; instead, it would run its course on the understanding that it would be regarded as a "primarily commercial commitment – i.e. but not as an additional means of subsidy by H.M.G. of Jamaican Industry."[152] Upon assuming the role of prime minister, Bustamante nevertheless wrote to Duncan Sandys, the secretary of state for both the colonies and commonwealth relations, asking the British government to assist Jamaica to find markets for "thousands of acres of citrus planted through encouragement of Her Majesty's Government specifically to provide the vital source of vitamin C" for British children.[153] The assistant under-secretary of state for commonwealth relations, drawing on both a stereotype of the slow-paced West Indian and the rhetoric of dependency, figured this and other requests as typical of the Jamaicans, who he claimed did not seem to be "bestirring them-selves" to find alternative outlets for their product.[154] In meetings with the West Indian citrus producers, the Commonwealth Relations Office thus continued to reiterate that there was "no obligation, legal or moral, on us to continue to take supplies of concentrated orange juice."[155]

Despite having rebuffed the accusation that there was any moral obligation to purchase more juice, both the Colonial Office and the Commonwealth Relations Office felt strongly that "from the political standpoint this, at the time of Jamaica's independence," was a "sin-gularly inappropriate moment" to turn down their request.[156] The Commonwealth Relations Office admitted that there was no need for additional stocks of juice, and thus the argument for purchasing more was purely "political" and hinged on "being nice to the Jamaicans in the early months of their independence."[157] The Duke of Devonshire, minister of state for the Commonwealth Relations Office, stressed that political stability in Jamaica was essential and that the small farmers who grew the bulk of Jamaica's oranges were Bustamante's keenest sup-porters. To undercut this industry, he implied, might have devastating political results.[158] Sandys thus urged Powell to reconsider his decision to buy only 200 tons of COJ from Jamaica. If we stop buying juice this year, Sandys argued, Bustamante "will say that it shows that we have lost interest in Jamaican welfare at the moment of her indepen-dence: and I should like to avoid a deterioration of relations at such a time."[159] The Commonwealth Relations Office was keen to help the cit-rus industry at this tense moment. Its officials were careful to construct any forthcoming aid, however, not as blood money that reinforced the United Kingdom's primary role in the death of the COJ industry but as stemming purely from "a political desire to help Jamaica through the first months of Independence and our general policy of assisting under-developed countries."[160]

Even if construed in these terms, these proposed juice purchases were not merely about being "nice" to a newly independent and "under-developed" Jamaica. They were also part of a wider strategy aimed at preserving the balance of power in a Cold War world, given that since the early 1950s the United Kingdom had been waging an extensive anti-communist campaign in the Caribbean.[161] The British high commissioner at Kingston suggested that the Jamaicans were cur-rently "extremely friendly to Britain and to the West in general." He felt there was "a very good chance of Jamaica aligning itself with the Western powers in debates at United Nations."[162] Devonshire similarly stressed "how desirable it would be for us to have a country, the major-ity of whose people are of Afro-Asian descent, supporting Britain in international disputes." "I do not think it is an exaggeration to say," he maintained, "that if we cannot meet the Jamaicans over concentrated orange juice we will be in danger of losing the friendship of the Jamaican Government."[163] Devonshire's allusion to those of "Afro-Asian descent" was a direct reference to the Afro-Asian (or Bandung) Conference of 1955 that was generative of the Non-Aligned Movement, which viewed the Cold War blocs as a form of neocolonialism, a reassertion of the old world order that decolonized Asian and African peoples had newly freed themselves from. Devonshire thus warned that Jamaica must be cultivated as a "friend to ourselves and the West," lest its government chose either to join the Non-Aligned Movement or, worse still, to go the way of Cuba, its closest neighbor.[164] The Cuban Revolution had ushered in a Communist government in 1959, whose strength was tested during the disastrous Bay of Pigs invasion in 1961, during which ships provided by the United Fruit Company formed part of the fleet that attempted to overthrow Fidel Castro.[165] That Jamaica might follow suit was not unthinkable. In September of 1962, Bustamante insisted that the British government should not leave the orange growers "in the lurch" and threatened to sell Jamaican COJ to Cuba and to Russia. It was not the first time he had raised this as a possibility. Though the British high commissioner had initially thought Bustamante was "pulling [his] leg," the Commonwealth Relations Office and the Foreign Office were rattled by the statement and worried that this might prove embarrassing to the British government, particular in terms of its own relations with the United States, its most important Cold War ally.[166] The MOH was nevertheless prepared to call Bustamante's bluff, and in the end, Powell sanctioned the purchase of only the 200 tons needed for blending purposes, which was nowhere close to the 6,000 tons the Jamaicans had on offer.[167]

The Bitter End of Welfare Orange Juice

Despite these Cold War concerns and his own mounting fears about West Indian immigration (later made explicit in his infamous 1968 "Rivers of Blood" speech), Powell refused to use WOJ to (as he saw it) artificially sustain the Caribbean economy. In the 1963–64 juice season, the MOH purchased another minute amount from the West Indies: 200 tons from Jamaica and 100 tons from British Honduras.[168] Had the MOH not needed the low-acid Caribbean juice for blending purposes, no orders might have been forthcoming at all in these last two years of the Statement of Intent.[169] For unlike the ten-year contract that obliged the United Kingdom to purchase up to 75 percent of the West Indian juice crop, the Statement of Intent only required the government to acquire 60 percent of what it actually needed. That the Jamaicans had estimated that 60 percent would work out to 2,000 tons per year, not the "pathetically small" 200, was not the responsibility of the MOH, Powell insisted.[170] The only bright side for the West Indian orange growers was that, even before the Labour Party won the election later that year, in February 1964 the government renewed its commitment to the WFS, and thus the purchase of COJ for consumption in 1965–66 could move forward with approximately 1,200 tons allocated to the West Indies.[171] When Kenneth Robinson was installed as the Labour Party's new minister of health, he declined, however, to enter into any further long-term contracts. The MOH claimed that it would continue to order from both Jamaica and British Honduras, but only if the price was satisfactory. Harold Wilson's newly elected Labour government thus supported the continuation of the WFS, but did not think it was "appropriate for the Welfare Foods Scheme to be used as a medium for giving special support to the economies of overseas territories."[172] The Labour Party, while committed to the domestic beneficiaries of WOJ, was no more willing to concede its responsibility to the producers of the product than the Conservatives had been.

In the spring of 1969, before negotiations could commence regarding the next West Indian juice season, the newly created Department of Health and Social Security (DHSS) released a report linking WOJ to tooth decay. Rather than WOJ improving children's teeth – "that terrible black spot" in British health –, as some had earlier hoped,[173] the misuse of undiluted juice in children's pacifiers and reservoir feeders, the report uncovered, had significantly increased dental disease among young children.[174] The report was written by the Panel on Cariogenic Foods that had been formed by the chief medical officer's Committee on Medical Aspects of Food Policy in 1967 to investigate the use of vitamin preparations in babies' pacifiers and feeding bottles. It came as a direct response to a series of letters to the editor and an editorial that had appeared in the *British Dental Journal* in the summer and fall of 1967, which blamed WOJ and rose hip syrup for the marked increase in acid erosion and cavities in young children.[175] The DHSS responded by printing warning labels on WOJ bottles that cautioned parents not to use the juice in its undiluted form and by investigating alternatives to the sucrose, which they used to make the product consistent and palatable, though it concluded that this latter problem was "insurmountable."[176]

As had Bransby and Fothergill's *British Journal of Nutrition* publication and the Cohen Committee's report, this scientific study furnished the DHSS with an opportunity to revisit the whole question of WOJ and

not merely its misuse. It provided scientific and seemingly apolitical support for retrenchment in a financial climate in which no aspect of the
Welfare State could afford to be held sacred, even for the Labour government. The late 1960s were a challenging time for Wilson's administration, which had been returned to power in an easily won 1966 snap
election only to be faced with a faltering economy. His cabinet devalued
the pound in 1967, raised taxes, announced a spending cut of £716 million, hiked the cost of school meals, and ironically even reintroduced
prescription charges, an issue that had led Wilson to resign from Atlee's
government in 1951.[177] Given that new synthetically combined vitamin
drops and tablets were cheaper than WOJ and cod liver oil, the government could no longer justify the continuation of these older products.
That cheap milk, which had not been found to be unsafe, was withdrawn
at the same time suggests that the decision to discontinue WOJ was as
much about the larger goals of reducing expenditures as about dental
health, which merely provided a convenient rationalization for a position
that had likely already been taken.[178] The DHSS could thus confidently
move forward with what their secretary of state lauded as a "more modern method" of providing vitamins.[179]

These decisions were also easier to justify by 1970 because the child
life of the British nation itself was, like its budget, under intense scrutiny.
WOJ had contributed to the goal of building "Nations out of Nurseries."
Many people credited the WFS with transforming British infants into
"miniature Samsons."[180] This "milk-and-orange-juice-generation,"
however, had also been responsible for the Swinging Sixties, which had
challenged traditional British values.[181] Argued one reporter in 1962,
these smoking, illiterate, cursing teenagers seemed "a poor return for
all that orange juice and vitaminised milk."[182] Moral reformer Malcolm
Muggeridge's 1967 attack on the "Permissive Society," and the youth
whose culture had reshaped, even revolutionized, Britain in the 1960s,
contained oblique references to youth washing down their newly available birth control pills with WOJ.[183] In June of 1970, with an election
looming, Home Secretary James Callaghan, notorious for voicing his
own traditional values, articulated this disillusionment with his own
Labour Party's investment in the welfare of Britain's youngest citizens.
Responding to critiques about rising prices from skinny, long-haired,
newly enfranchised teenagers, he declared, "When I think of the welfare orange juice that was given to you I can only say it was wasted."[184]
By 1970, WOJ was no longer tied to a sentimentalized vision of bonny
British war babies and had come to stand – even for some of the staunch-
est supporters of the Welfare State – for a cynical youth population who
many were loath to let take control of the wheel.

The question of whose welfare was at stake in decisions about WOJ died a slow death, but by 1971, this issue, like the product itself, was dead in the water.[185] These and other cuts to the Welfare State had led to an outpouring of criticism that Wilson had betrayed the Labour Party's mission, reneging on the promise of cradle-to-grave care. A few members of the House of Lords continued into the spring of 1971 to raise the alarm over the West Indian economy and blamed the withdrawal of WOJ for this bleak state of affairs.[186] But the decision to withdraw the juice at the close of that year was final and in the end supported by both political parties.

To bring closure to relationship between the WFS and the West Indian citrus industry in January of 1971, B. J. Crisp of the Supply Division of the DHSS undertook a trip to Jamaica and British Honduras to express his agency's gratitude in person for the services rendered by the growers and producers of WOJ. While the Jamaicans and British Hondurans pressed him for help with the economic impact of the withdrawal of WOJ, Crisp maintained that even if their economic difficulties were in fact real, they were, at least in the case of Jamaica, "far more likely" to stem from their "own organizational and political policies than from the ending of our contracts." In the end, Crisp blamed the "easy-going Caribbean attitude to life" that eschewed competition and their long-term reliance on UK business that had "blunted the initiative" to seek other markets for any economic difficulties the West Indians might be experiencing in relation to their citrus industry.[187] He comfortably asserted that it was the national character and habitual behaviors of West Indians themselves, which both led to dependence, and not the policies of the British government that were to blame for any economic decline in the region. Crisp's report of his visit, which served as the final official word on WOJ, rehearsed a narrative deeply imbedded by the early 1970s of West Indians as unambitious malingerers with a "mendicant mentality" who, rather than contributing to the Welfare State, had become dependent upon it.[188] But the archival evidence clearly points in a different direction. It exposes Britain's own dependency on its colonial subjects to provide the means of furnishing welfare benefits to its metropolitan citizens. The history of WOJ thus opens up a much more complex understanding of the politics and economics of the Welfare State and its relationship both to colonial development projects and the uneven processes of decolonization.

Conclusion
How the Sausage Gets Made

The introduction of the New Poor Law and the workhouse system in the 1830s allowed the British government to argue that it had solved the problem of poverty by inducing the able-bodied to work and by providing for the basic maintenance of those that did not. At the same time, Britain introduced the civil registration of births and deaths. This made it possible for the state to track mortality rates and causes. The confluence of these policies led to debates over the extent to which deaths due to starvation and exposure could and should be registered because to do so was an embarrassment to the state. It implied either that relief had been withheld from the destitute or that some had chosen to starve to death rather than to partake of government services.[1]

In 1871, in an attempt to make certain that the poor law authorities were not shirking their responsibilities to provide relief, an annual parliamentary return of "Deaths from Starvation or Accelerated by Privation" was introduced. This provided details of select cases across the nation that local Boards of Guardians had investigated in response to coroners' inquests that had determined that the individual's death was due to starvation, exposure, and/or privation. These were discontinued in 1919, in part because they had ceased to serve their intended purpose as many of the deaths that might technically be classed as due to starvation or exposure (such as mountaineering accidents) were totally unrelated to destitution. The continued reporting of these statistics only proved embarrassing to the government because they provided an occasion for the press to critique the poor law administration by capitalizing on the public's assumption that the parliamentary return contained only cases where poverty had been the defining factor. The Home Office, the Registrar General, and the Ministry of Health, however, continued to consult on these cases at least through the 1920s because its officials believed that in a "civilised state there ought to be some record of the failures of the social organisation to meet the elementary needs of life." But they also well understood the "inherent difficulties of the subject-matter" that was purportedly expressed

244

through these statistics and were resistant to making even the small number of cases that came to light each year too readily available for public consumption.[2] For as long as they were easily accessible to the public and the press, it was very difficult for the state to control the narrative about the extent of its responsibility to ensure that all British citizens were being properly fed.[3]

In the immediate aftermath of World War I – during which the German population had been nearly starved to death as a deliberate British policy – the British state acknowledged its obligation to provide its own citizens with the "elementary needs of life." While government officials expressed confidence that the social services they administered were sufficient, their anxieties about public opinion suggest that the government's role in reducing starvation deaths over time was much more contested. Organizing these case studies chronologically has underscored that in fact no arc of progressive change is discernable in relation to more and better food being dispersed by the British government to needy populations. Ironically, the local officials who actually oversaw the New Poor Law often treated the poor in their care humanely, overriding draconian central policies in order to feed them as fellow subjects. Conversely, rather than actually providing cradle-to-grave care as part of a new vision of the rights of British citizens, the food program of the Welfare State was eroded almost immediately after it was established, since succeeding governments sought to diminish the number of UK residents eligible for Welfare Foods and to undercut an entire colonial industry that was itself predicated on the Welfare State. In theory and on paper, the Welfare Foods Service (WFS) appears to be a progressive program that underscored the right of the youngest citizens to be properly nourished by the state. In practice, the provision of roast beef by some empathetic Boards of Guardians under the New Poor Law may have actually done more than the WFS to enhance the recipients' feelings of national belonging.

The outcomes of government food schemes were not only incongruous but also inconsistent because each decision to feed a target population emerged from particular circumstances and took shape in response to the political, economic, social, and cultural problems posed by the situation. The British government never developed a coherent policy of state feeding that was based on cumulative knowledge and/or practical experiments because the state agencies initiating, and ultimately responsible for, each of these programs were various and had different mandates: the policies and practices they generated differed from each other and were sometimes at odds. Indeed, they frequently failed to take into consideration the existence or history of other initiatives. This meant that a baffling array of government departments were involved in feeding British subjects over the nineteenth and twentieth centuries. They sometimes conferred with each other, the result being that some experience became transferable, such as (for better or for worse) the use of prison dietaries in relation to famine relief. But in other cases, the government stubbornly refused to learn the lessons of its own administrative history. Parents' resistance to school meals in the 1920s and 1930s clearly owed much to the legacy of the New Poor Law, which a century earlier had intentionally stigmatized the receipt of government relief. That the implementation of the school meals service had perpetuated these meanings attached to state feeding, suggests that, even with a hundred years of experience, the British government had not accounted for the legacies of its policies and practices in relation to the expected uptake of its services. In short, it often failed to understand beneficiaries as consumers whose response to the food itself, to its mode of delivery, and to its packaging as a public service all contributed to the success or failure of any feeding program. This was true even when the intended recipients were desperately hungry, actually starving, seriously malnourished, and/or a captive population.

This book has focused on the cultural politics surrounding particular state-feeding initiatives, arguing that the production, consumption, and distribution of the scarce and vital resource of food within Britain and its empire sheds critical light on the relationship between the citizen and the state at significant moments in modern British history. In part, this has been a study of biopolitics. The British government's provision of food to certain segments of the population, but not others, was often part of wider initiatives that involved harnessing these groups as resources for the purposes of nation and empire building. In these cases, the government did not necessarily see food as a basic right but as a means to an end. The provision of gratuitous food to Indian child famine victims was part of the humanitarian imperative to save the lives of the Queen's subjects. But this was not incompatible with investing in these children as the agricultural laborers of the future who would be revenue producers for the empire. Similarly, the origins of school meals lay in anxieties about the capacity of future generations to defend the nation in times of war. It is no surprise that World War II breathed new life into the school meals service. At the same time, although they ended up serving a much broader cross section of the population, the British Restaurant emerged out of fears of low morale among the working classes on the home front who might foment discontent and present a threat to national security if their material needs were not being met.

Thus, these populations had political value to the state and were fed in moments when this relationship needed to be nurtured. When British subjects were denied food, as in the case of festive meals in workhouses, it was because they were not seen by the state as assets.

The public well understood that food was part of an exchange relationship between the subject, or citizen, and the state that underscored the recipients' value to the nation. Paupers' demands for roast beef in the 1830s and 1840s and Carolyn Steedman's relationship to welfare orange juice, though separated by more than 100 years, both confirm that recipients saw the provision of these government foods as an expression of their place within the national community. Individuals and groups thus used the language of rights to make their own demands upon the state for food. The servicemen and civilians held in POW camps during World War I used the roles they played in the national war effort as loyal citizens to underscore their right to receive proper British foodstuffs sent from home. Those whose claims on the state were more tenuous, such as criminal prisoners, nevertheless also demanded more or different food as part of the state's obligation to maintain their bodies in health both because they were subjects under its care and because their productivity remained a central concern. Even famine victims, whose imminent starvation left them little room to negotiate, insisted that the food provided as relief conform to their religious and cultural practices, drawing the government's attention to its various obligations toward and articulating their own rights as Her Majesty's subjects.

There were nevertheless clear limits to food's role as a tool of statecraft. These case studies reveal that recipients of food aid were rarely "docile bodies";[4] they sometimes resisted, and always reshaped, government food policies. But what is of equal significance is that many of these cases seem like missed opportunities to maximize the "utility" of populations through state feeding. The half-hearted school meals program in the interwar period and the WFS instituted in the postwar years might have effectively nourished generations of children in service of national defense had the government not been so dilatory in its ideological and financial commitment to these programs. In contrast, the British Restaurant, which in effect served a similar purpose to these other programs as feeding became linked not only to a fitter citizenry but increased morale during wartime, served a target population not initially identified by the state when it introduced the services. This suggests that the state's vision was often much narrower than it might have been, and that there was no necessary correlation between advances in nutritional knowledge that could be harnessed by the state and tangible government action.

The nutritional sciences were heavily contested in this period, and this meant that they were easily deployed for economic and political ends. Over the 140 years covered by this book, there were clear developments in the sciences of food. Food provided energy, and by the end of the nineteenth century, it was common to calculate this in calories, making diets comparable with each other. But the components of those diets also mattered. From the middle of the nineteenth century, scientists had determined that it was not merely the quantity of food that led to adequate health but its quality. By the 1860s, medical research had demonstrated that protein, carbohydrates, and fat were all essential to the maintenance of health and fitness. The discovery of vitamins in the early twentieth century heralded a period when diets could be more carefully tailored to specific populations as malnutrition rather than undernourishment became an increasingly significant means to assess the health of the nation. This book has not, however, been a story of the rise of the "newer knowledge of nutrition" and how it was subsequently applied to different target populations. Rather, *Many Mouths* has demonstrated that developments in nutritional research rarely provided the impetus for state feeding. In fact, this scientific knowledge was frequently ignored or reinterpreted when it did not suit the policies and/or practices that had already been determined to be expedient. In the case of Indian famine relief, the food provided either as payment on the public works or gratuitously was sometimes exclusively rice, despite the fact that senior administrators knew that some form of protein was also necessary for survival. In the case of school meals, although there was no way to test definitively for malnutrition, the Board of Education used this seemingly scientific diagnosis to limit the number of children being fed. Similarly, government scientists deliberately manipulated medical research in the 1950s and 1960s to justify ending a program that provided supplemental vitamin C to the nation's children.

This meant that even the feeding programs explicitly intended to combat the undernourishment and malnourishment associated with poverty diets made little appreciable difference to populations that, even well into the twentieth century, continued to experience the effects of poverty. During the interwar period – a time when many regions suffered from chronic unemployment – the school meals service reached only a fraction of the children in need. It certainly contributed to improved health and wellness for the individual schoolchildren who qualified for free meals in the Local Education Authorities (LEAs) that provided ample and nutritious food. But in the aggregate, school meals cannot be said to have made a significant difference to the health of British schoolchildren as a whole until well into World War II. Similarly, the low voluntary uptake of welfare orange juice (WOJ) and the government's continued attempts to scale back the program meant that this element of the WFS might have led directly to gains in health for a proportion of the target population but certainly not for the majority. Although the government failed to identify why uptake was so low, the stigma of state feeding, which also impacted the take up of school meals, must have been part of the problem. This meant that precisely those families that would have significantly benefited from initiatives that explicitly remedied the problems of poverty diets often refused the services. In other cases, because of the ways in which the program was administered, the food provided by the state came in lieu of other forms of income assistance and did little to ameliorate the root problem that families lived in poverty and the provision of services to one member often came at the expense of another. It is difficult therefore to argue that the government's provision of food to a range of target populations over the course of the nineteenth and twentieth centuries materially improved the standard of living for the British people as a whole by supplementing their diets. Indeed, the recent expansion of food banks run by voluntary associations across the United Kingdom testifies to the British government's ongoing practical and ideological struggles with ensuring the population's food security.[5] The significance of state feeding should not therefore be measured either by its material effects alone or by the stated intentions of its initiatives.

These programs nevertheless had important cultural effects on how a range of British subjects experienced the state at the intimate site of their own or their children's bodies. The stories that *Many Mouths* has told about the politics of food reveal that the state was far from monolithic. In fact, one of the central themes of this book has been the tension that existed between national policies and local implementation. For beneficiaries of these programs, the values and behavior of local officials was of paramount importance because how these state agents interpreted or reacted to directives emanating from London had a major impact on how and what food did or did not become available to whom. State feeding was always experienced as a local phenomenon, and this meant that even though policies were national, beneficiaries often had vastly different encounters with and attitudes toward the services. It was the belief systems of local Boards of Guardians that ultimately determined whether workhouse inmates would receive roast beef on Christmas, despite the clear directive from the central Poor Law Commission (PLC) that they should not. In terms of famine relief, local officials often overrode the viceroy's orders and used their own assessments as to how to balance cost saving and lifesaving when deciding who was entitled to gratuitous relief and how much and what food should be dispensed. Despite the fact that the central government paid 50 percent of the cost of school meals, it was the LEAs that decided whether or not they would offer the service at all and how they would select the children who qualified for free meals. Not only were British Restaurants run by local authorities during World War II, it was often cooks and servers that determined the menus and portions so that the nature and amount of food a patron might receive on any given day varied considerably among the establishments. That vehement disagreements about state feeding often erupted between the local and central authorities meant that the policies made in London were not always implemented in identical ways in every community. The public thus experienced the state, the nation, and their identities as subjects and citizens in a variety of different ways, which depended not just on their social, but also on their geographical, location.

Local authorities had their own responses to central policies that influenced how they implemented the feeding of target populations. However, local implementation and in fact the national policies themselves were also shaped by the consumers of these services. Far from merely passive and grateful recipients of the government's largesse, the beneficiaries of these initiatives also significantly influenced the programs. Even the most vulnerable populations – such as those incarcerated in prisons, workhouses, and POW and famine camps – made demands on the state in relation to the amount and type of food they were prepared to eat. Paupers demanded festive meals, prisoners rejected stirabout, famine victims refused food unless prepared by members of their own caste, and POWs asserted their right to white bread. In each of these cases, the government conceded and honored the claims of these populations to the kind of nourishment they felt they required and deserved. In some cases, the target populations rejected state food outright, as in the cases of many needy families that refused to take advantage of the school meals service or the large proportion of mothers that did not collect WOJ either for themselves or for their children. This meant that the way these services were delivered had to be rethought, sometimes multiple times, precisely because they did not meet the needs of consumers. The reverse was also true. In the case of the British Restaurant, these wartime meals services had to be repositioned ideologically in response to the fact that the consumers of this food were not exclusively the populations that had been targeted by the program in the first place. It was the surprising uptake of these services by a wide range of British subjects that forced the government to alter its own justification for them both during the war and in its aftermath.

It is for these reasons that this study of the cultural politics of state food has provided a close reading of selected cases. This has allowed for an examination of how policies around governmental responsibility for the feeding of British subjects emerged from particular historically contingent contexts. It has insisted on understanding these policies in practice because they were implemented by local authorities and then reformulated in response to reactions from actual and potential beneficiaries. There was always a tension between the ideology behind the feeding of target populations and the practical need to implement these programs, which required thinking beyond expedience and financial concerns to questions of culture and consumer behavior. *Many Mouths* has thus demonstrated that state feeding was the result of complex negotiations among central policy makers and administrators, local government officials, and the publics who did and did not consume the services provided. All groups shaped the material outcomes of government feeding programs and the cultural meanings attached to them. This has therefore been a study of how the sausage really gets made.

Notes

Introduction

1 M. Pyke, *Food and Society* (London: John Murray, 1968), pp. 8–9.

2 M. Bruegel, "Introduction: Locating Foodways in the Nineteenth Century" in M. Bruegel (ed.), *A Cultural History of Food in the Age of Empire* (London: Bloomsbury, 2016), pp. 11–17.

3 P. Carroll, *Science, Culture, and Modern State Formation* (Berkeley: University of California Press, 2006).

4 C. Hamlin, *Public Health and Social Justice in the Age of Chadwick: Britain, 1800–1854* (Cambridge: Cambridge University Press, 1998), pp. 335–7.

5 I. Miller, "Food, Medicine, and Institutional Life in the British Isles, *c.* 1790–1900" in C. Helstosky (ed.), *The Routledge History of Food* (London: Routledge, 2015), p. 216.

6 C. Biltekoff, *Eating Right in America: The Cultural Politics of Food and Health* (Durham: Duke University Press, 2013), pp. 5–7; D. F. Smith, "The Politics of Food and Nutrition Policies" in A. Murcott, W. Belasco, and P. Jackson (eds.), *The Handbook of Food Research* (London: Bloomsbury, 2013), pp. 298–305; H. Kamminga and A. Cunningham (eds.), *The Science and Culture of Nutrition, 1840–1940* (Amsterdam: Rodopi, 1995); N. Cullather, "The Foreign Policy of the Calorie," *American Historical Review* 112(2) (2007), 337–64. On the history of the modern fact see M. Poovey, *A History of the Modern Fact: Problems of Knowledge in the Sciences of Wealth and Society* (Chicago: University of Chicago, 1998).

7 Pyke, *Food and Society*, pp. 8–9; A. F. Wilt, *Food for War: Agriculture and Rearmament in Britain before the Second World War* (Oxford: Oxford University Press, 2001), p. 188.

8 Talk to Birmingham Canteen Supervisors and Caterers. Wartime Menus and Cooking for Canteens and Catering Firms, The National Archives, UK [hereafter TNA] MAF 98/55. For food as a weapon during World War II see L. Collingham, *The Taste of War: World War II and the Battle for Food* (New York: Penguin Press, 2012).

9 C. Lévi-Strauss, *Totemism*, trans. Rodney Needham (Boston: Beacon Press, 1963), p. 89.

10 A. Nützenadel and F. Trentmann, "Introduction: Mapping Food and Globalization" in A. Nützenadel and F. Trentmann (eds.), *Food and Globalization: Consumption, Markets and Politics in the Modern World*

(Oxford: Berg, 2008), pp. 1–2; A. Bentley, *Eating for Victory: Food Rationing and the Politics of Domesticity* (Urbana: University of Illinois Press, 1998), p. 1; K. M. Guy, "Food Representations" in M. Bruegel (ed.), *A Cultural History of Food in the Age of Empire* (London: Bloomsbury, 2016), p. 190; D. Wylie, *Starving on a Full Stomach: Hunger and the Triumph of Cultural Racism in Modern South Africa* (Charlottesville: University Press of Virginia, 2001), p. 23.

11 C. Helstosky, *Garlic and Oil: Food and Politics in Italy* (Oxford: Berg, 2004), p. 9.

12 G. Agamben, *Homo Sacer: Sovereign Power and Bare Life*, trans. D. Heller-Roazen (Stanford: Stanford University Press, 1998).

13 S. W. Mintz, *Sweetness and Power: The Place of Sugar in Modern History* (Harmondsworth: Penguin, 1985), p. 3; D. Arnold, *Famine: Social Crisis and Historical Change* (Oxford: Basil Blackwell, 1988), pp. 3–4; Bentley, *Eating for Victory*, pp. 1–2; A. Warde, *Consumption, Food and Taste: Culinary Antinomies and Commodity Culture* (London: Sage, 1997), p. 22; A. Weinreb, *Modern Hungers: Food and Power in Twentieth-Century Germany* (Oxford: Oxford University Press, 2017), p. 6.

14 C. Otter, "Feast and Famine: The Global Food Crisis," *Origins* 3(6) (2010) http://origins.osu.edu/article/feast-and-famine-global-food-crisis/page/0/1.

15 A. Drewnowski, "Poverty and Obesity: The Role of Energy Density and Energy Costs," *American Journal of Clinical Nutrition* 79(1) (2004), 6–16; NHS Digital, *National Child Measurement Programme, England 2015–16 School Year* (November 3, 2016). https://digital.nhs.uk/services/national-child-measurement-programme/.

16 There exists a large and growing literature on food and power. The monographs that have been most helpful to me have been Mintz, *Sweetness and Power*; J. Vernon, *Hunger: A Modern History* (Cambridge: Harvard University Press, 2007); E. Rappaport, *A Thirst for Empire: How Tea Shaped the Modern World* (Princeton: Princeton University Press, 2017); R. L. Spang, *The Invention of the Restaurant: Paris and Modern Gastronomic Culture* (Cambridge: Harvard University Press, 2000); J. M. Pilcher, *Que Vivan Los Tamales!: Food and the Making of Mexican Identity* (Albuquerque: University of New Mexico Press, 1998); H. Diner, *Hungering for America: Italian, Irish, and Jewish Foodways in the Age of Migration* (Cambridge: Harvard University Press, 2003); C. W. Bynum, *Holy Feast and Holy Fast: The Religious Significance of Food to Medieval Women* (Berkeley: University of California Press, 1988); R. P. Tucker, *Insatiable Appetite: The United States and the Ecological Degradation of the Tropical World* (Berkeley: University of California Press, 2000); J. Carney, *In the Shadow of Slavery: Africa's Botanical Legacy in the Atlantic World* (Berkeley: University of California Press, 2010); and W. Cronon, *Nature's Metropolis: Chicago and the Great West* (New York: W. W. Norton, 1991).

17 Helstosky, *Garlic and Oil*, p. 66; Weinreb, *Modern Hungers*, pp. 4–5.

18 J. M. Pilcher, "The Embodied Imagination in Recent Writings on Food History," *American Historical Review* 121(3) (2016), 861.

19 P. Joyce, *The State of Freedom: A Social History of the British State since 1800* (Cambridge: Cambridge University Press, 2013), p. 10.

20 Helstosky, *Garlic and Oil*.

21 Helstosky, *Garlic and Oil*; Weinreb, *Modern Hungers*.

22 Vernon, *Hunger*, p. 3.

23 C. Dickens, *Oliver Twist*, 2nd ed., Vol. I (London: Richard Bentley, 1839), pp. 27–9.

24 O. MacDonagh, "The Nineteenth-Century Revolution in Government: A Reappraisal," *The Historical Journal* 1(1) (1958), 52–67; H. Parris, "The Nineteenth-Century Revolution in Government: A Reappraisal Reappraised," *The Historical Journal* 3(1) (1960), 17–37; V. Cromwell, "Interpretations of Nineteenth-Century Administration: An Analysis," *Victorian Studies* 9(3) (1966), 245–55.

25 P. Harling, *The Modern British State: An Historical Introduction* (Cambridge: Polity, 2001), pp. 71–3; G. Finlayson, *Citizen State, and Social Welfare in Britain, 1830–1990* (Oxford: Clarendon Press, 1994).

26 O. MacDonagh, *Early Victorian Government* (London: Weidenfeld and Nicolson, 1977).

27 D. Eastwood, "'Amplifying the Province of the Legislature': The Flow of Information and the English State in the Early Nineteenth Century," *Historical Research* 62(149) (1989), 276–94; E. Higgs, *The Information State in England* (Houndmills: Palgrave, 2004); D. Fletcher, "Government Boundary Mapping and the Knowledge Apparatus of the British State, 1841–1889," *Journal of Policy History* 25(4) (2013), 512–37.

28 G. Savage, *The Social Construction of Expertise: The English Civil Service and Its Influence, 1919–39* (Pittsburgh: University of Pittsburgh Press, 1996); J. Vernon, *Distant Strangers: How Britain Became Modern* (Berkeley: University of California Press, 2014), pp. 61–5.

29 G. F. Langer, *The Coming of Age of Political Economy, 1815–1825* (New York: Greenwood Press, 1987); R. G. Cowherd, *Political Economists and the English Poor Laws* (Athens: Ohio University Press, 1977).

30 S. Auerbach, "'Some Punishment Should Be Devised': Parents, Children, and the State in Victorian London," *The Historian* 71(4) (2009), 757–79; N. Durbach, *Bodily Matters: The Anti-Vaccination Movement in England, 1853–1907* (Durham: Duke University Press, 2005); J. Walkowitz, *Prostitution and Victorian Society: Women, Class, and the State* (Cambridge: Cambridge University Press, 1980).

31 E. Hadley, *Living Liberalism: Practical Citizenship in Mid-Victorian Britain* (Chicago: University of Chicago Press, 2010), p. 7.

32 S. Gunn and J. Vernon (eds.), *The Peculiarities of Liberal Modernity in Imperial Britain* (Berkeley: University of California Press, 2011); P. Joyce, *The Rule of Freedom: Liberalism and the Modern City* (London: Verso, 2003); Hadley, *Living Liberalism*.

33 P. Weiler, *The New Liberalism: Liberal Society Theory in Great Britain, 1889–1914* (New York: Garland, 1982).

34 G. Claeys, "Political Thought" in C. Williams (ed.), *A Companion to Nineteenth-Century Britain* (Oxford: Blackwell, 2004), p. 197.

35 G. R. Sims, *How the Poor Live and Horrible London* (London: Chatto & Windus, 1889), p. 108.

36   H. Pelling, *The Origins of the Labour Party, 1880–1900* (Oxford: Clarendon Press, 1965); N. Thompson, *Political Economy and the Labour Party* (London: University College London Press, 1996).

37   S. Pennybacker, *A Vision for London 1889–1914: Labour, Everyday Life, and the LCC Experiment* (London: Routledge, 1995).

38   D. Powell, "The New Liberalism and the Rise of Labour, 1886–1906," *The Historical Journal* 29(2) (1986), 369–93.

39   R. Mackay, *The Test of War: Inside Britain, 1939–1945* (London: Routledge, 1999), pp. 23–8.

40   I. Zweiniger-Bargielowska, *Austerity in Britain: Rationing, Controls, and Consumption, 1939–1955* (Oxford: Oxford University Press, 2000).

41   C. K. Steedman, *Landscape for a Good Woman: A Story of Two Lives* (New Brunswick: Rutgers University Press, 1987), p. 122.

42   Joyce, *State of Freedom*.

43   J. Innes, "Changing Perceptions of the State in the Late Eighteenth and Early Nineteenth Centuries," *Journal of Historical Sociology* 15(1) (2002), 111.

44   R. M. Gutchen, "Local Improvements and Centralization in Nineteenth-Century England," *The Historical Journal* 4(1) (1961), 87, 91, 96; M. R. Maltbie, *English Local Government of Today* (New York: Columbia University Press, 1897), pp. 18–19; E. L. Hasluck, *Local Government in England* (Cambridge: Cambridge University Press, 1936), pp. 96, 99, 338–9; T. Crook, *Governing Systems: Modernity and the Making of Public Health in England, 1830–1910* (Berkeley: University of California Press, 2016), p. 24; A. Brundage, *England's "Prussian Minister": Edwin Chadwick and the Politics of Government Growth* (University Park: Penn State University Press, 1988), p. 10; P. E. Carroll, "Medical Police and the History of Public Health," *Medical History* 46 (2002), 461–94.

45   Vernon, *Distant Strangers*, pp. 14–15, 51–3.

46   H. Finer, *English Local Government*, 4th ed. (London: Methuen and Co., 1950), p. 6.

47   C. Hamlin, "Nuisances and Community in Mid-Victorian England: The Attractions of Inspection," *Social History* 38(3) (2013), 377.

48   J. A. Chandler, *Explaining Local Government: Local Government in Britain since 1800* (Manchester: Manchester University Press, 2007).

49   Crook, *Governing Systems*, p. 16.

50   Joyce, *State of Freedom*, pp. 144–84.

51   E. V. McCollum, *The Newer Knowledge of Nutrition: The Use of Food for the Preservation of Vitality and Health* (New York: Macmillan, 1919).

52   Vernon, *Hunger*, p. 3.

Chapter 1

1   L. Charlesworth, *Welfare's Forgotten Past: A Socio-Legal History of the Poor Law* (London: Routledge, 2010), p. 60.

2   P. Brears, "Bastille Soup and Skilly: Workhouse Food in Yorkshire" in C. A. Wilson (ed.), *Food for the Community: Special Diets for Special Groups* (Edinburgh: Edinburgh University Press, 1993), pp. 116–50; A. Brundage,

The English Poor Laws, 1700–1930 (Houndmills: Palgrave, 2002), p. 80; M. A. Crowther, *The Workhouse System, 1834–1929* (London: Batsford, 1981), pp. 213–21; D. Englander, *Poverty and Poor Law Reform in Nineteenth Century Britain, 1834–1914* (London: Pearson, 1998), pp. 39–40; I. Miller, "Feeding in the Workhouse: The Institution and the Ideological Functions of Food *c*. 1834–1870," *Journal of British Studies* 52(4) (2013), 940–62.

3 E. M. Crawford, "The Irish Workhouse Diet, 1840–90" in C. Geissler and D. J. Oddy (eds.), *Food, Diet and Economic Change Past and Present* (Leicester: Leicester University Press, 1993), pp. 83–100; A. Digby, *Pauper Palaces* (London: Routledge & Kegan Paul, 1978), pp. 13, 146; U. Henriques, "How Cruel Was the Victorian Poor Law?" *The Historical Journal* 11(2) (1968), 365–71; V. J. Johnston, *Diet in Workhouses and Prisons 1835–1895* (New York: Garland, 1985); D. Roberts, "How Cruel Was the Victorian Poor Law?" *The Historical Journal* 6 (1) (1963), 97–107; P. Wood, *Poverty and the Workhouse in Victorian Britain* (Stroud: Sutton, 1991), pp. 100–1.

4 Hamlin, *Public Health and Social Justice*, p. 5.

5 Cowherd, *Political Economists*, p. 284; A. Brundage, *The Making of the New Poor Law: The Politics of Inquiry, Enactment, and Implementation, 1832–1839* (New Brunswick: Rutgers University Press, 1978), p. 4.

6 P. Dunkley, "Whigs and Paupers: The Reform of the English Poor Laws, 1830–34," *Journal of British Studies* 20(2) (1981), 125–6; Cowherd, *Political Economists*, p. 250.

7 Over 300 workhouses were either built or under construction within the first five years of the passage of the New Poor Law. For these statistics see K. Williams, *From Pauperism to Poverty* (London: Routledge & Kegan Paul, 1981), p. 77.

8 Charlesworth, *Welfare's Forgotten Past*.

9 Cowherd, *Political Economists*, p. 278.

10 Charlesworth, *Welfare's Forgotten Past*, p. 14; Cowherd, *Political Economists*, pp. 20, 122.

11 Brundage, *England's "Prussian Minister,"* p. 38.

12 Quoted in Cowherd, *Political Economists*, p. 271.

13 Brundage, *England's "Prussian Minister,"* p. 6; Cowherd, *Political Economists*, p. 86.

14 Digby, *Pauper Palaces*, p. 54; F. Driver, *Power and Pauperism: The Workhouse System, 1834–1884* (Cambridge: Cambridge University Press, 1993), p. 34; L. H. Lees, *The Solidarity of Strangers: The English Poor Laws and the People, 1700–1948* (Cambridge: Cambridge University Press, 1998), pp. 145–8; S. Webb and B. Webb, *English Poor Law Policy* (Hamden: Archon, 1963), pp. 1–3.

15 Cowherd, *Political Economists*, p. 252.

16 Brundage, *England's "Prussian Minister,"* pp. 14–16; Harling, *The Modern British State*, p. 78.

17 Hamlin, *Public Health and Social Justice*.

18 Brundage, *Making of the New Poor Law*, pp. 81–8.

19 A. Brundage, "The Landed Interest and the New Poor Law: A Reappraisal of the Revolution in Government," *The English Historical Review* 87(342) (1972), 27–48.

20 Quoted in S. Webb and B. Webb, *English Poor Law History. Volume II: The Last Hundred Years* (Hamden: Archon, 1963), pp. 119–21.

21 Brundage, "The Landed Interest," 30–2.

22 Brundage, *England's "Prussian Minister,"* pp. 35–55.

23 Letter from Edwin Chadwick [hereafter Chadwick] to the Poor Law Commission [hereafter PLC], December 4, 1835, TNA MH 10/7; G. Nicholls, *A History of the English Poor Law*, Vol. II (London: P. S. King & Son, 1898), p. 301.

24 Johnston, *Diet in Workhouses and Prisons*, p. 16.

25 Quoted in Cowherd, *Political Economists*, pp. 232–3.

26 Cowherd, *Political Economists*, pp. 234–5.

27 C. Hamlin, "The 'necessaries of life' in British political medicine, 1750–1850," *Journal of Consumer Policy* 29 (2006), 373–97.

28 Miller, "Food, Medicine and Institutional Life."

29 Johnston, *Diet in Workhouses and Prisons*, p. 16.

30 Letter from Chadwick to PLC, December 4, 1835, TNA MH 10/7; Nicholls, *A History of the English Poor Law*, pp. 314–15.

31 Draft Letter from PLC to Clerk to the Aberayron Union, April 8, 1841, TNA MH 12/15783; Chris Otter, "The British Nutrition Transition and Its Histories," *History Compass* 10(11) (2012), 812–25; R. Perren, *The Meat Trade in Britain 1840–1914* (London: Routledge & Kegan Paul, 1978), p. 1. However, when the New Poor Law was extended to Ireland in 1838, the dietaries for agricultural laborers were meatless. See Crawford, "The Irish Workhouse Diet."

32 *Eight Report from the Select Committee on the Poor Law Amendment Act*, 1837 (PP 278), pp. 24–25; *Ninth Report from the Select Committee on the Poor Law Amendment Act*, 1837 (PP 296), p. 2.

33 Letter from Chadwick to PLC, December 4, 1835, TNA MH 10/7.

34 Draft Letter from PLC to Clerk to the Boston Union, January 9, 1838, TNA MH 12/6630; Draft Letter from PLC to Henry Neale, December 28, 1836, TNA MH 12/10971; Draft Letter from PLC to Joseph Carter, January 5, 1838, TNA MH 12/4074; Report of Audit, Bolton Union, for Half-Year Ended March, 25, 1855, TNA MH 12/5601.

35 Draft Letter from PLC to Joseph Rider, December 22, 1837, TNA MH 12/14639; Draft Letter from PLC to J. Forrest Lesingham, December 17, 1838, TNA MH 12/4074.

36 I. Anstruther, *The Scandal of the Andover Workhouse* (London: Bles, 1973); Webb and Webb, *English Poor Law History*, pp. 179–82.

37 Pilcher, *Que Vivan Los Tamales!*; Rappaport, *A Thirst for Empire*; Mintz, *Sweetness and Power*; N. Fiddes, *Meat: A Natural Symbol* (London: Routledge, 1991); F. Trentmann, "Bread, Milk and Democracy: Consumption and Citizenship in Twentieth-Century Britain" in M. Daunton and M. Hilton (eds.), *Politics of Consumption: Material Culture and Citizenship in Europe and America* (Oxford: Berg, 2001), pp. 129–63; D. Valenze, *Milk: A Local and Global History* (New Haven: Yale University Press, 2011).

38 C. Muldrew, *Food, Energy and the Creation of Industriousness: Work and Material Culture in Agrarian England, 1550–1780* (Cambridge: Cambridge University Press, 2011), pp. 36–42, 83–102.

39 B. Rogers, *Beef and Liberty: Roast Beef, John Bull and the English Nation* (New York: Vintage, 2004), pp. 77–8.

40 Rogers, *Beef and Liberty*, pp. 87–109, 163; M. Taylor, "John Bull and the Iconography of Public Opinion in England *c.* 1712–1929," *Past and Present* 134 (1992), 93–128; S. Shapin, "'You Are What You Eat': Historical Changes in Ideas About Food and Identity," *Historical Research* 87(237) (2014), 385–9.

41 J. Twigg, "Vegetarianism and the Meanings of Meat" in A. Murcott (ed.), *The Sociology of Food and Eating* (Aldershot: Gower, 1983), p. 23.

42 Lees, *Solidarity of Strangers*, p. 163; J. Vernon, *Politics and the People: A Study in English Political Culture, c. 1815–1867* (Cambridge: Cambridge University Press, 1993), p. 300.

43 M. Mauss, *The Gift*, trans. W. D. Halls (New York: Routledge, 1990).

44 M. Connelly, *Christmas: A Social History* (London: I.B. Tauris, 1999), pp. 12–14; J. A. R. Pimlott, *The Englishman's Christmas* (Hassocks: Harvester Press, 1978), p. 31.

45 D. Cressy, *Bonfires and Bells: National Memory and the Protestant Calendar in Elizabethan and Stuart England* (Berkeley: University of California Press, 1989), pp. 46–9; Pimlott, *Englishman's Christmas*, pp. 49–58.

46 Pimlott, *Englishman's Christmas*, pp. 85–96.

47 C. Dickens, *A Christmas Carol* (London: Bradbury & Evans, 1858 [1843]), pp. 8–9.

48 Dickens, *A Christmas Carol*, pp. 5–6.

49 Connelly, *Christmas*, p. 18; Pimlott, *Englishman's Christmas*, p. 88; M. Johnes, *Christmas and the British: A Modern History* (London: Bloomsbury, 2016), pp. 114, 124.

50 Quoted in N. Armstrong, *Christmas in Nineteenth-Century England* (Manchester: Manchester University Press, 2010), p. 9.

51 Armstrong, *Christmas in Nineteenth-Century England*, pp. 99–101; J. M. Golby and A. W. Purdue, *The Making of the Modern Christmas* (Athens: University of Georgia Press, 1986), p. 51; D. Roberts, *Paternalism in Early Victorian England* (New Brunswick: Rutgers University Press, 1979), pp. 114–16.

52 T. Moore, "Starvation in Victorian Christmas Fiction," *Victorian Literature and Culture* 36(2) (2008), 501.

53 Johnes, *Christmas and the British*, pp. 97–9.

54 Rogers, *Beef and Liberty*, pp. 19–24; Twigg, "Vegetarianism," pp. 25–6.

55 *John Bull*, December 25, 1847, p. 828.

56 Quoted in Pimlott, *Englishman's Christmas*, p. 67.

57 E. Hobsbawm and T. O. Ranger (eds.), *The Invention of Tradition* (Cambridge: Cambridge University Press, 1983); B. Anderson, *Imagined Communities*, rev. ed. (London: Verso, 1991); Johnes, *Christmas and the British*, p. 145.

58 M. Pitts, C. Pattie, and D. Dorling, "Christmas Feasting and Social Class," *Food, Culture & Society* 10(3) (2007), 409; J. Goody, *Cooking, Cuisine, and Class* (Cambridge: Cambridge University Press, 1982), pp. 140–2.

59 H. Newby, C. Bell, D. Rose, and P. Saunders, *Property, Paternalism and Power: Class and Control in Rural England* (Madison: University of Wisconsin Press, 1978), p. 29.

60 Johnes, *Christmas and the British*, p. 125.

61 Letter from Joseph Rider to Chadwick, December 16, 1837, TNA MH 12/14639.

62 *Morning Chronicle*, December 30, 1808, p. 3; *Morning Post*, January 4, 1822, p. 1.

63 *Morning Post*, January 2, 1827, p. 3; *Liverpool Mercury*, December 31, 1824, p. 6.

64 *Ipswich Journal*, December 29, 1827, p. 2; *Sheffield Independent and Yorkshire and Derbyshire Advertiser*, December 27, 1828, p. 3.

65 *The Satirist*, December 25, 1842, p. 415.

66 Draft Letter from PLC to Henry Neale, December 28, 1836, TNA MH 12/10971.

67 Draft Letter from PLC to Joseph Rider, December 22, 1837, TNA MH 12/14639.

68 Draft Letter from PLC to J. Forrest Lesingham, December 17, 1838, TNA MH 12/4074.

69 Brundage, *Making of the New Poor Law*, p. 2.

70 A. Kidd, *State, Society and the Poor in Nineteenth-Century England* (Houndmills: Palgrave Macmillan, 1999), pp. 13–14.

71 Norman McCord, "The Poor Law and Philanthropy" in D. Fraser (ed.), *The New Poor Law in the Nineteenth Century* (Basingstoke: Macmillan, 1976), pp. 87–110; Roberts, *Paternalism in Early Victorian England*.

72 Dunkley, "Whigs and Paupers," 141; D. Hay, "Property, Authority, and the Criminal Law" in D. Hay, P. Linebaugh, J. G. Rule, E. P. Thompson, and C. Winslow (eds.), *Albion's Fatal Tree: Crime and Society in Eighteenth Century England* (London: Allen Lane, 1975), p. 62.

73 Letter to Chadwick from Clerk to the Eastry Board of Guardians, December 19, 1839, Copy of Petition to Eastry Board of Guardians, and Draft Letter from PLC to Clerk to Eastry Board of Guardians, December 21, 1839, TNA MH 12/4992.

74 E. P. Thompson, *Customs in Common* (New York: The New Press, 1993), pp. 97–184.

75 *Times*, December 28, 1838, p. 2.

76 *Times*, December 29, 1836, p. 2, November 27, 1837, p. 5, December 26, 1838, p. 5, December 13, 1839, p. 3, December 27, 1839, p. 8. For the unions established and maintained under the Local Acts or Gilbert's Act see Driver, *Power and Pauperism*, pp. 42–7.

77 On gender and the New Poor Law see L. F. Cody, "The Politics of Illegitimacy in an Age of Reform: Gender, Reproduction and Political Economy in England's New Poor Law of 1834," *Journal of Women's History* 11(4) (2000), 131–56; Lees, *Solidarity of Strangers*, pp. 135–45; M. Levine-Clark, "Engendering Relief: Women, Ablebodiedness, and the New Poor Law in Early Victorian England," *Journal of Women's History* 11(4) (2000), 107–30; P. Thane, "Women and the Poor Law in Victorian and Edwardian England," *History Workshop Journal* 6(1) (1978), 29–51.

78 Brundage, *English Poor Laws*, p. 86. For statistics on the categories of people receiving relief see Williams, *From Pauperism to Poverty*.

79 Letter from Henry Neale to Chadwick, December 26, 1836, TNA MH 12/10971; *Times*, December 28, 1838, p. 2.

80 *John Bull*, January 1, 1837, p. 8.

81 *The Satirist*, January 1, 1837, p. 423.

82 *Times*, July 24, 1821, p. 3, September 7, 1831, p. 3.

83 *Times*, December 28, 1838, p. 2, June 25, 1838, p. 5, June 28, 1838, p. 4; G. R. Wythen Baxter, *The Book of the Bastiles: Or, the History of the Working of the New Poor Law* (London: John Stephens, 1841), p. 113; G. B. Hodgson, *The Borough of South Shields: From the Earliest Period to the Close of the Nineteenth Century* (Newcastle: A. Reid, 1903), p. 174; Extract from Minutes of Meeting of Boards of Guardians, Macclesfield Union, June 26, 1838, TNA MH 12/968.

84 Letter from Thomas Marriott to PLC, June 19, 1838, TNA MH 12/9525/77/2. Interestingly, George Nicholls, one of the Poor Law Commissioners who was himself closely associated with the principle of "less eligibility" and the workhouse test, had been an overseer for the poor in Southwell in the early 1800s. He was one of the "Nottinghamshire Reformers" whose model of poor relief formed the backbone of the New Poor Law. The about face of Southwell in regards to these kinds of treats, which Nicholls condemned, reinforces how much depended on local administration, which given the elected nature of Boards of Guardians, was subject to change quite regularly. See Brundage, *English Poor Laws*, pp. 53–5; D. Fraser, "The Poor Law as a Political Institution" in D. Fraser (ed.), *The New Poor Law in the Nineteenth Century* (London, 1976), pp. 111–27; Nicholls, *A History of the English Poor Law*, pp. 228–36; J. R. Poynter, *Society and Pauperism: English Ideas on Poor Relief, 1795–1834* (London: Routledge & Kegan Paul, 1969), pp. 313–16.

85 Draft Letter from PLC to J. H. Jardine, June 27, 1838, TNA MH 12/11955; Draft Letter from PLC to Edwin Unwin, June 25, 1838, TNA MH 12/9357.

86 Draft Letter from PLC to Thomas Marriott, June 21, 1838, TNA MH 12/9525; Draft Letter from PLC to J. Forrest Lesingham, June 21, 1838, TNA MH 12/4074; Draft Letter from PLC to J. S. Clay, June 14, 1838, TNA MH 12/2125; Draft Letter from PLC to W. Shilson, June 19, 1838, TNA MH 12/1407; Draft Letter from PLC to Benjamin Ellis, June 21, 1838, TNA MH 12/10428; Draft Letter from PLC to Clerk to the Medway Union, June 22, 1838, TNA MH 12/5249.

87 Draft Letter from PLC to Richard Loxdale, October 12, 1838, TNA MH 12/9822; Letter to PLC from George Hewett, July 12, 1838, TNA MH 12/10805.

88 McCord, "The Poor Law and Philanthropy," p. 94.

89 P. Stallybrass and A. White, *The Politics and Poetics of Transgression* (Ithaca: Cornell University Press, 1986).

90 L. Colley, *Britons: Forging the Nation, 1707–1837* (New Haven: Yale University Press, 1992).

91 Hansard HC Deb July 27, 1838, vol. 44 cc. 722–7. I have not been able to trace this newspaper or article or determine which workhouse master it referenced.

92 *Hampshire Advertiser and Salisbury Gazette*, January 7, 1837, p. 4.
93 Durbach, *Bodily Matters*, p. 82; R. Gray, *The Factory Question and Industrial England, 1830–1860* (Cambridge: Cambridge University Press, 1996), pp. 21–47.
94 J. Belchem, "Republicanism, Popular Constitutionalism and the Radical Platform in Early Nineteenth-Century England," *Social History* 6(1) (1981), 1–32; J. Epstein, *Radical Expression: Political Language, Ritual, and Symbol in England, 1790–1850* (Oxford: Oxford University Press, 1994); P. Joyce, "The Constitution and the Narrative Structure of Victorian Politics" in J. Vernon (ed.), *Re-Reading the Constitution: New Narratives in the Political History of England's Long Nineteenth Century* (Cambridge: Cambridge University Press, 1996), pp. 179–203; J. Vernon, "Notes Towards an Introduction" in J. Vernon (ed.), *Re-Reading the Constitution: New Narratives in the Political History of England's Long Nineteenth Century* (Cambridge: Cambridge University Press, 1996), pp. 1–21; Vernon, *Politics and the People*.
95 Letter from Benjamin Ellis to PLC, June 19, 1838, TNA MH 12/10428; Letter to Chadwick from John Davenport, June 16, 1838, TNA MH 12/6387.
96 Extract From Minute Book, Northampton Board of Guardians, June 12, 1838, TNA MH 12/8781.
97 Extract from Minute Book, Bridgwater Board of Guardians, June 8, 1838, TNA MH 12/10244.
98 Extract of Minutes of Meeting of Board of Guardians, Bridgnorth Union, June 16, 1838, TNA MH 12/9851. Unmarried mothers were also excluded from the Coronation dinner hosted on the Workhouse Green in the Swaffham Union. See Digby, *Pauper Palaces*, p. 153.
99 Letter to PLC from the Risbridge Board of Guardians [June 24, 1838], TNA MH 12/11955.
100 For roast beef in the workhouses on Victoria's wedding day see Letter to Chadwick from J. H. Jardine, February 11, 1840, TNA MH 12/11955; PLC Minute Books Volume 22, Entry 611, TNA MH 1/22; Letter to PLC from R. N. Shawe, April 7, 1840, TNA MH 12/12079; *Times*, February 20, 1840, p. 3; Baxter, *Book of the Bastiles*, p. 126; Hodgson, *Borough of South Shields*, p. 174.
101 Draft of Circular Letter from George Coode, April 23, 1840, TNA MH 12/12079; Circular Letter from Chadwick, March 18, 1840, TNA MH 10/99.
102 Draft Letter from PLC to Clerk to the Bourn Union, January 25, 1841, TNA MH 12/6658.
103 *Times*, December 23, 1840, p. 3, December 25, 1840, p. 6.
104 Letter to Chadwick from John Dallenger, November 29, 1841, TNA MH 12/11935; Letter to PLC from Charles Hammond, December 11, 1841, TNA MH 12/14598; *Times*, December 22, 1846, p. 5; *The Age*, December 27, 1840, p. 415.
105 *Times*, December 16, 1841, p. 3.
106 *Times*, December 25, 1841, p. 6.
107 *The Satirist*, January 7, 1844, p. 2. The song is officially entitled "The Battle of the Nile" and dates to the Napoleonic Wars.

108 D. R. Green, "Pauper Protests: Power and Resistance in Early Nineteenth-Century London Workhouses," *Social History* 31(2) (2006), 137–59; Lees, *Solidarity of Strangers*, pp. 153–76.

109 Letter from R. D. Thurgood to Chadwick, January 29, 1841, TNA MH 12/3708; Letter from Frederick Inskipp to PLC, January 21, 1841, TNA MH 12/12951; Copy of Letter from Thomas Kelsall to Board of Guardians, Fareham Union, January 29, 1841, TNA MH 12/10768; Copy of Resolution of Board of Guardians, Launceston Union, December 23, 1840, TNA MH 12/1407; Letter from Edward Senior to PLC, December 29, 1840, TNA MH 12/6422; Letter to PLC from S. R. Strode, December 16, 1840, TNA MH 12/4236; Auditor's Report for Bosmere and Claydon, Stow, and Cosford, Quarter Ending Christmas, 1840, TNA MH 12/11765; S. I. Richardson, *A History of the Edmonton Poor Law Union, 1837–1854*. Edmonton Hundred Historical Society, Occasional Papers New Series Number 8, n.d., p. 46.

110 *Dudley Union. Copy of Correspondence between the Guardians of Dudley Union and the Poor-Law Commissioners Respecting the Disallowance of the Money Paid for the Last Christmas-day Dinner Given to the Paupers*, 1847 (PP 276), p. 2.

111 Letter to PLC from John Scoones, December 17, 1841, TNA MH 12/5372.

112 Letter to Chadwick from Clerk to the Bourn Union, January 7, 1841, TNA MH 12/6658. Emphasis in original.

113 Letter to Chadwick from Clerk to the Bourn Union, January 7, 1841, TNA MH 12/6658.

114 *Dudley Union*, p. 3.

115 Letter to PLC from John Scoones, December 17, 1841, TNA MH 12/5372.

116 Resolution of the Crickhowel Board of Guardians, April 20, 1840, TNA MH 12/15747; Letter to Chadwick from Clerk to the Bourn Union, January 7, 1841, TNA MH 12/6658; Letter to PLC from Robert Sarjeant, December 12, 1846, TNA MH 12/14204.

117 *The Age*, December 27, 1840, p. 415.

118 Letter to Chadwick from Clerk to the Bourn Union, January 7, 1841, TNA MH 12/6658.

119 *Dudley Union*, p. 1.

120 N. C. Edsall, *The Anti-Poor Law Movement, 1834–44* (Manchester: Manchester University Press, 1971).

121 Nicholls, *A History of the English Poor Law*, p. 340.

122 Brundage, *English Poor Laws*, p. 71; Nicholls, *A History of the English Poor Law*, pp. 338, 340.

123 Letter to Chadwick from Clerk to the Bourn Union, January 7, 1841, TNA MH 12/6658. Emphasis in original.

124 *Dudley Union*, p. 4. See also Hansard HC Deb May 17, 1847, vol. 92 cc. 978–9.

125 Brundage, *English Poor Laws*, p. 112.

126 P. Harling, "The Power of Persuasion: Central Authority, Local Bureaucracy and the New Poor Law," *The English Historical Review* 107(422) (1992), 38.

127 Nicholls, *A History of the English Poor Law*, p. 299.

128 Harling, "The Power of Persuasion," 37–40; Nicholls, *A History of the English Poor Law*, pp. 361–2.
129 For debates over tensions between local and central control see P. Dunkley, "The 'Hungry Forties' and the New Poor Law: A Case Study," *The Historical Journal* 17(2) (1974), 329–46; Harling, "The Power of Persuasion"; Crowther, *The Workhouse System*, p. 46; Englander, *Poverty and Poor Law Reform*, pp. 84–5; Wood, *Poverty and the Workhouse*, p. 98. For the persistence of these sentiments into the 1850s see the correspondence on a Wakes week celebration in Stoke-on-Trent in TNA MH 12/11463; TNA MH 12/11464.
130 *Report from the Select Committee on the Andover Union*, 1846 (PP 663), p. 368.
131 Baxter, *The Book of the Bastiles*, p. 130.
132 *Fourteenth Report of the Poor Law Commissioners*, Appendix A, 1847–48 (PP 960), p. 16.
133 Letter from Clerk to the Bridgwater Union to PLC, December 21, 1843, TNA MH 12/10246.
134 Letter from the Board of Guardians, Bolton Union, to the Poor Law Board [hereafter PLB], August 4, 1855, TNA MH 12/5601.
135 Letter to PLB from J. C. Anwyl, June 17, 1864, TNA MH 12/16095.
136 *Metropolitan Workhouses.* 1850, (PP 133), p. 104.
137 Miller, "Feeding in the Workhouse."
138 Letter from Joseph Spencer to PLB, September 24, 1855, TNA MH 12/15474; Letter to Lord Courtenay from Thomas Field, May 15, 1856, TNA MH 12/10647.
139 Letter from J. E. Jackson Riccard to PLB, November 29, 1856 and Draft Letter from PLB to Board of Guardians, South Molton, January 12, 1857, TNA MH 12/2500.
140 Letter from John Tryas to PLB, November 26, 1856 and Extract for Minutes of Board of Guardians Meeting, Barnsley Union, May 27, 1856, TNA MH 12/14677; Draft Letter from PLB to W. John Wright, January 23, 1857, TNA MH 12/14678.
141 *Times*, January 22, 1858, p. 6.
142 Draft Letter from PLB to Clerk to the Leominster Union, July 23, 1858, TNA MH 12/4390; Letter to PLB from Chairman, Board of Guardians, Sheffield, January 18, 1858, TNA MH 12/15475; Letter from W. Stewart to PLB, January 21, 1858, TNA MH 12/15574.
143 Letter to PLB from Downing Evans, February 14, 1863, TNA MH 12/8096.
144 Letter from Saul Speedy to PLB, May 6, 1863, TNA MH 12/15556.
145 Copy of Letter from Humphry England to PLB, undated, TNA MH 12/10384.
146 Letter from Walter J. Reed to PLB, February 16, 1863, TNA MH 12/14309.
147 Letter to PLB from Robert White, February 13, 1863, TNA MH 12/6825.
148 On the tensions between moral economy and political economy see G. S. Jones, *Languages of Class: Studies in English Working Class History, 1832–1982* (Cambridge: Cambridge University Press, 1983); Thompson, *Customs in Common*.

149 For debates over continuity and change in poverty relief see M. E. Rose, *The Relief of Poverty, 1834–1914* (Houndmills: Macmillan, 1986).

Chapter 2

1 H. Mayhew and J. Binny, *The Criminal Prisons of London and Scenes of Prison Life* (London: Frank Cass and Co., 1968 [1862]), p. 131.

2 Johnston, *Diet in Workhouses and Prisons*, pp. 37, 49, 58; A. Brown, *English Society and the Prison* (Woodbridge: Boydell Press, 2003), p. 80; M. J. Wiener, *Reconstructing the Criminal: Culture, Law, and Policy in England, 1830–1914* (Cambridge: Cambridge University Press, 1990), pp. 103–9; S. McConville, *A History of English Prison Administration*, Vol. I (London: Routledge & Kegan Paul, 1981), pp. 374–80; W. J. Forsythe, *The Reform of Prisoners, 1830–1900* (New York: St. Martin's Press, 1987), p. 159.

3 E. Ruggles-Brise, *The English Prison System* (Maidstone: H.M. Convict Prison, 1921), p. 189.

4 *Minutes of Evidence Taken by the Departmental Committee on Prisons* (London: Her Majesty's Stationary Office [hereafter HMSO], 1895) (PP c. 7702 – I), Q: 1332–62, 3332, 8537.

5 M. J. Wiener, "The Health of Prisoners and the Two Faces of Benthamism" in R. Creese, W. F. Bynum, and J. Bearn (eds.), *The Health of Prisoners* (Amsterdam: Rodopi, 1995), pp. 47–8.

6 *1835. Gaols. Copies of All Reports and of Schedules (B).* February 17, 1836 (PP 31), p. 5.

7 Johnston, *Diet in Workhouses and Prisons*, pp. 37–9, 45.

8 *Report Relative to the System of Prison Discipline &c. by the Inspectors of Prisons* (London: HMSO, 1843), p. 12.

9 *Report from the Select Committee of the House of Lords on the Present State of Discipline in Gaols and Houses of Correction Together With the Proceedings of the Committee, Minutes of Evidence, Appendix and Index,* July 24, 1863 (PP 499), p. iv; *Prison Discipline. Copies of Correspondence between the Secretary of State for the Home Department and the Inspector of Prisons Relating to the Report of a Select Committee of the House of Lords on Prison Discipline; And of the Report of a Committee Appointed by the Secretary of State to Inquire into the Dietaries of County and Borough Prisons,* May 20, 1864, (PP 313), p. 3.

10 R. Wilkinson, *The Law of Prisons in England and Wales* (London: Knight and Co., 1878), p. vii.

11 *Dietaries in Prisons (England and Wales) (Acts 1865 and 1877). Copy of the Report of the Committee Appointed to Inquire into the Dietaries of the Prisons in England Wales Subject to the Prison Acts 1865 and 1877, With the Memorandum of Instruction of the Prison Commissioners,* March 19, 1878 (PP 95), pp. 8, 14; Report to Edmund Du Cane from R. M. Gover, May 6, 1882, TNA HO 45/9554/66373.

12 Ruggles-Brise, *The English Prison System*, pp. 69, 72.

13 Minutes by Home Department, March 8, 1878, TNA HO 45/9554/66373.

14 *Dietaries in Prisons (England and Wales) (Acts 1865 and 1877)*, p. 19; Wilkinson, *The Law of Prisons*, p. 45.

15 M. Ignatieff, *A Just Measure of Pain: The Penitentiary in the Industrial Revolution, 1750–1850* (New York: Pantheon, 1978), pp. 175–7.

16 Agamben, *Homo Sacer.*

17 E. Smith and W. R. Milner, "Report on the Action of Prison Diet and Discipline on the Bodily Functions of Prisoners, Part I," *Report of the Thirty-First Meeting of the British Association for the Advancement of Science, September, 1861* (London: John Murray, 1862), pp. 44–81; P. Higginbotham, *The Prison Cookbook* (Stroud: The History Press, 2010), p. 84; Miller, "Food, Medicine, and Institutional Life," p. 212; K. J. Carpenter, "Nutritional Studies in Victorian Prisons," *Journal of Nutrition* 136(1) (2006), 1–8.

18 J. Burnett, *Plenty and Want: A Social History of Food in England from 1815 to the Present Day*, 3rd ed. (London: Routledge, 1989), pp. 111–12, 139–44, 162–5, 171–4; T. Cardwell Barker, D. J. Oddy, and J. Yudkin, *The Dietary Surveys of Dr. Edward Smith, 1862–3: A New Assessment* (London: University of London Department of Nutrition, 1970); E. V. McCollum, *A History of Nutrition* (Boston: Houghton Mifflin, 1957), pp. 122–5.

19 Johnston, *Diet in Workhouses and Prisons*, pp. 53–7; A. Hardy, "Development of the Prison Medical Services, 1774–1895" in R. Creese, W. F. Bynum, and J. Bearn (eds.), *The Health of Prisoners* (Amsterdam: Rodopi, 1995), pp. 62–66; Wiener, "Health of Prisoners," pp. 44–58.

20 *Prison Dietaries Committee. Report of the Departmental Committee on Prison Dietaries* (London: HMSO, 1899) (PP C. 9166), pp. 3, 10.

21 *Prison Commission for Scotland. Report on Prison Dietaries by James Craufurd Dunlop* (London: HMSO, 1899) (PP C. 9514), pp. 11, 14.

22 J. L. Hargrove, "History of the Calorie in Nutrition," *Journal of Nutrition* 136(12) (2006): 2957–61.

23 *Prison Dietaries Committee*, 1899, p. 10.

24 Minute from H. B. Simpson, December 6, 1900, TNA HO 45/10037/A60059.

25 Copy of Report by Dr. Smalley, Medical Inspector, TNA HO 45/10037/A60059.

26 *Minutes of Evidence*, 1895, QQ 1333–4.

27 *Prison Commission for Scotland*, pp. 9, 65–7, 103; *Prison Dietaries (Scotland). Rules Made by the Secretary of State for Scotland under the Prisons (Scotland) Act, 1877, establishing New Rates of Dietaries for the Several Classes of Prisoners*, June 15, 1900 (PP 205).

28 McConville, *A History of English Prison Administration*, pp. 349–51, 396–9.

29 *Report Relative to the System of Prison Discipline*, 1843, pp. 3, 12.

30 Gaol Regulations for the Prisons of the City of London Allowed by the Secretary of State Sir James Graham, March 18, 1843, with New Dietary as Transmitted by Sir James Graham August 26, 1843, London Metropolitan Archives [hereafter LMA] CLA/032/01/028.

31 Smith and Milner, "Report on the Action of Prison Diet," p. 47; *Report from the Select Committee*, 1863, pp. iii–iv, vii; *Convict Prison Dietaries. Copy of the Reports of a Committee Appointed to Inquire into the Dietaries of Convict Prisons*, July 8, 1864 (PP 467); *Prison Discipline. Copies of Correspondence*, 1864, p. 73.

32 E. Smith, "Gaol Dietary – The Operations of the Recent Committees," *Journal of the Society of Arts*, September 2, 1864, pp. 669–70.

33 New Bailey Prison Dietary, 1864. Lancashire Archives, QSP 3693/32; Middlesex. House of Correction, Cold Bath Fields. Dietary Table, LMA MJ/SP/1864/01/19.

34 *Copy of the Rules for the Dietaries of the Prisons in England and Wales*, March 18, 1878 (PP 93).

35 *Prison Rules (Convict Prisons). Draft of Rules Proposed to be Made under the Prison Act, 1898, March 1901* (London: HMSO, 1901), TNA PCOM 7/345; Standing Order, September 2, 1901, TNA HO45/10037/A60059; *Prison Dietaries Committee*, 1899, p. 15.

36 *Prison Dietaries Committee*, 1899, p. 8.

37 *Prison Dietaries Committee*, 1899, p. 8.

38 *Prisons (Rules for Local Prisons). Draft of Rules Proposed to be Made by the Secretary of State for the Home Department under the Prison Act, 1898, with Regard to the Dietary of Prisoners*, May 16, 1901 (PP 187); *Minutes of Evidence*, 1898, QQ: 101, 167–70, 212, 221, 971, 1219.

39 E. Smith, "On the Principles Involved in a Scheme of Prison Dietary," in *Transactions of the National Association for the Promotion of Social Science, 1857* (London: John W. Parker and Son, 1858), p. 297.

40 *Minutes of Evidence*, 1898, Q: 1720.

41 Copy of Report to Prison Commissioners by the Committee Appointed to Consider the Resolution of the Prison Conference of 1882 as to Dietaries of Certain Prisoners c. May 1883, by Henry Brisco, C. H. Braddon, R. M. Gover, TNA HO 144/111/A24267.

42 Departmental Committee on Prison Dietaries. Interim Report, June 14, 1898, TNA HO 45/10037/A60059.

43 *Report Relative to the System of Prison Discipline*, 1843, pp. 4–5, 27–29.

44 Surrey House of Correction, Brixton, Rules 1843, TNA HO 45/2149.

45 *Report of the Commissioners Appointed to Inquire into the Management of Millbank Prison*, January 20, 1847 (PP 8), p. 32.

46 Class 1, 2 and 3 Dietaries, LMA WA/GP/1857/017; *Dietaries for Convicts, &c. Returns of the Dietaries Sanctioned by the Government for Convicts at Gibraltar, Bermuda, and the Different Convict Establishments of Every Class in England, Wales, and Ireland*, March 21, 1857 (PP 154), pp. 41, 54, 110, 124, 133; Mayhew and Binny, *Criminal Prisons*, pp. 597, 617; Sir Joshua Jebb, *General Report on the Convict Prisons, 1860–1* (London: HMSO, 1862) (PP 5178), p. 99; Middlesex House of Detention. Daily Diet List. 1861, LMA MA/G/GEN/662.

47 *Prison Discipline. Copies of Correspondence*, 1864, p. 27.

48 *Report from the Select Committee*, 1863, p. xi; *Prison Discipline. Copies of Correspondence*, 1864, p. 73; *Convict Prison Dietaries*, 1864.

49 Smith, "Gaol Dietary," p. 669; Smith, "Gaol Dietary – The Operations of the Recent Committees (continued)," September 9, 1864, pp. 683–4.

50 Copy of Report by Dr. Smalley, Medical Inspector, TNA HO 45/10037/A60059; *Minutes of Evidence*, 1898, QQ: 703, 705, 781–3.

51 *Prison Commission for Scotland*, pp. 9, 14, 67–8; *Prison Dietaries (Scotland)*, 1900.

52 Letter from William Baly to the Inspectors of Millbank Prison, January 27, 1844, TNA HO 45/388.

53 Letter from W. Harris, June 5, 1848, and W. A. Wilkinson, Resolution, March 27, 1848, TNA HO 45/2149; Colonel Jebb, *Report on the Discipline of the Convict Prisons for 1856 and 1857* (London: HMSO, 1858), p. 137; *Dietaries for Convicts*, 1857, pp. 30–1, 55, 100, 129; *Report of the Commissioners Appointed to Inquire into the Acts Relating to Transportation and Penal Servitude, Vol. I.* (London: HMSO, 1863) (PP 6457), pp. 195–6; Mayhew and Binny, *Criminal Prisons*, pp. 183–4; Westminster Regulations, 1866, LMA MA/G/GEN/1253.

54 *Convict Prison Dietaries*, 1864.

55 *Instructions to be Followed in the Carrying out of the Rules Approved by the Secretary of State for the Home Department for the Government of Convict Prisons* (London: HMSO, 1896), TNA PCOM 7/189.

56 *Dietaries in Prisons (England and Wales) (Acts 1865 and 1877)*, p. 15.

57 *Minutes of Evidence*, 1898, QQ: 1215–7, 1313–4.

58 For photographs of women engaged in laundry work see TNA COPY 1/420/173, COPY 1/525/181, COPY 1/525/194.

59 *Prisons (Rules for Local Prisons)*, 1901.

60 *Prison Rules (Convict Prisons). Draft of Rules Proposed to be Made under the Prison Act, 1898* (London: HMSO, 1898) (PP C. 8771), pp. 36–7.

61 *Prison Dietaries (Scotland), 1900*; *Prison Commission for Scotland*, p. 15.

62 E. Showalter, *The Female Malady: Women, Madness, and English Culture, 1830–1980* (New York: Pantheon, 1985); J. Sim, "The Prison Medical Service and the Deviant, 1895–1948" in R. Creese, W. F. Bynum, and J. Bearn (eds.), *The Health of Prisoners* (Zedner), p. 111; L. Zedner, *Women, Crime, and Custody in Victorian England* (Oxford: Clarendon, 1991), pp. 184–5; Forsythe, *Reform of Prisoners*, pp. 128–31.

63 *Convict Prison Dietaries*, 1864.

64 *Dietaries in Prisons (England and Wales) (Acts 1865 and 1877)*, p. 15.

65 *Convict Prison Dietaries*, 1864.

66 *Minutes of Evidence*, 1898, QQ: 281, 285, 288. For a photograph of women engaged in laundry work at Wormwood Scrubs see TNA COPY 1/420/173.

67 *Minutes of Evidence*, 1898, QQ: 2145. For a series of 1908 photographs of women engaged in laundry work at Aylesbury see TNA COPY 1/525/181, COPY 1/525/194.

68 *Minutes of Evidence*, 1895, QQ: 639–40, 1269–1, 1481–3, 3757–9, 3899, 5380–4, 5840–1, 6325; Letter from E. Du Cane to Under-Secretary of State, Home Office, November 20, 1894, Minute from A.G.E., November 23, 1894, and Prisons (England and Wales). Rules made by the Secretary of State with respect to the Diets of Prisoners, March 21, 1895, TNA HO 45/9744/A56503.

69 *Prison Dietaries Committee*, 1899, pp. 14–15.

70 W. J. Forsythe, *Penal Discipline, Reformatory Projects and the English Prison Commission, 1895–1939* (Exeter: University of Exeter Press, 1991), p. 98.

71 K. Grant, "British Suffragettes and the Russian Method of Hunger Strike," *Comparative Studies in Society and History* 53(1) (2011), 113–43; L. Tickner, *The Spectacle of Women* (Chicago: University of Chicago Press,

1988); C. Howlett, "Writing on the Body? Representation and Resistance in British Suffragette Accounts of Forcible Feeding," *Genders* 23 (1996), 3–41; J. F. Geddes, "Culpable Complicity: The Medical Profession and the Forcible Feeding of Suffragettes, 1909–1914," *Women's History Review* 17(1) (2008), 79–94; I. Miller, "A Prostitution of the Profession? Forcible Feeding, Prison Doctors, Suffrage and the British State, 1909–1914," *Social History of Medicine* 26(2) (2013), 225–45.

72 Memorandum to all Local Prisons from B. H. Thomson, July 5, 1910, TNA PCOM 7/297.

73 Memorandum sent to E. Ruggles-Brise, February 3, 1910, TNA PCOM 7/297.

74 Memorandum, February 9, 1910 and Memorandum from E. Ruggles-Brise, May 26, 1910, TNA PCOM 7/297.

75 Minute from Winston Churchill, May 20, 1910 and Minute from Winston Churchill, June 19, 1910, TNA PCOM 7/297.

76 Copy of Draft Rule Proposed to be made by the Secretary of State for the Home Department under Section 2(1) of the Prison Act, 1898, with respect to the Treatment of Offenders of the Second and Third Divisions, March 17, 1910 and Memorandum to all Local Prisons from B. H. Thomson, July 5, 1910, TNA PCOM 7/297.

77 Memorandum to all Local Prisons from B. H. Thomson, November 29, 1910, TNA PCOM 7/297.

78 Letter from E. Ruggles-Brise to Undersecretary of State, April 16, 1912, TNA PCOM 7/297.

79 Special Rule and Orders for Offenders of the Second and Third Divisions, March 20, 1913, TNA PCOM 7/297.

80 Minute from H. B. Simpson, December 6, 1900, TNA HO 45/10037/A60059.

81 *Gaols. West Indies. Copies of Correspondence Relative to the State of the Gaols in the West Indies and the British Colonies in South America; and also, of any Instructions which have been sent out from the Colonial Office relative to such Prisons*, March 30, 1831, (PP 334), pp. 48, 62, 65; Regulations for Public Gaols, Bermuda, December 27, 1834, TNA CO 37/98.

82 Saint Vincent. Consolidated Prison Rules, August, 1873, TNA CO 321/405; Report on Common Gaol, Grenada, 1877, TNA CO 321/21; Diet Tables for the Use of Various Public Institutions, TNA CO 321/52.

83 Letter to the Under Secretary of State for the Colonies from W. G. Romaine, July 31, 1868, TNA CO 137/438.

84 Letter from J. Jameson to Captain O'Toole, April 7, 1874, TNA CO 23/212.

85 Report of Izett W. Anderson to H. B. Shaw, January 13, 1882, TNA CO 137/504.

86 Letter from J. Jameson to Captain O'Toole, April 7, 1874, TNA CO 23/212.

87 Letter from Surgeon-Major Jameson to Captain O'Toole, June 11, 1874, TNA CO 23/212.

88 S. Seth, *Difference and Disease: Medicine, Race, and the Eighteenth Century British Empire* (Cambridge: Cambridge University Press, 2018); R. A. Hogarth, *Medicalizing Blackness: Making Racial Difference in the Atlantic World, 1780–1840* (Chapel Hill: University of North Carolina Press, 2017).

89 H. Cagle, *Assembling the Tropics: Science and Medicine in Portugal's Empire, 1450–1700* (Cambridge: Cambridge University Press, 2018); M. Joseph, "Military Officers, Tropical Medicine, and Racial Thought in the Formation of the West India Regiments, 1793–1802," *Journal of the History of Medicine and Allied Sciences* 72(2) (2017), 142–65.

90 Letter to the Under Secretary of State, Colonial Office from the Marquess of Hartington, March 13, 1865, TNA CO 137/397; Minute of Dr. Maclure on Surgeon-Major Jameson's letter of April 7, May 18, 1874, TNA CO 23/212; Minutes May 2, 1868 and Minute to Sir F. Roper, August 6, 1868, TNA CO 137/438.

91 *Papers Relating to the Improvement of Prison Discipline in the Colonies*, August 1875 (PP C. 1338), p. 153; Proceedings of a Commission to Enquire into the Civil Service of Jamaica, 1881, vol. 5, QQ: 314, 320, TNA CO 137/503.

92 Letter from John D. A. Dumaresq to Captain W. O'Toole, May 28, 1874, TNA CO 23/212.

93 Letter from A. Musgrave to Earl of Kimberley, January 30, 1882, Report of Izett W. Anderson to H. B. Shaw, January 13, 1882, Letter from H. B. Shaw to the Colonial Secretary, January 17, 1882, and Draft letter to the Secretary of the Admiralty, February 28 [1882], TNA CO 137/504. Some prisons skirted the issue, however, by allowing military authorities to send rations in for the use of any military prisoners. See Diet Tables for the Use of Various Public Institutions, TNA CO 321/52; Rules...for the Government of the Belize Prison, October 1897, and Rules for District Prisons, November 8, 1897, TNA CO 123/226.

94 See files on this issue in TNA CO 137/504.

95 Minute, August 19, 1868 and Draft Letter to Admiralty, August 24, 1868, TNA CO 137/438.

96 Minutes re: Dieting of Military Prisoners in Barbados, Letter to Lord Knutsford from Walter Sendall, March 29, 1890, Minute by A. H. Luck, Minute by W. E. R. Kelly, March 21, 1890, and Draft letter, May 14, 1890, TNA CO 28/227.

97 *Prison Discipline in the Colonies. Further Correspondence Respecting the Discipline and Management of Prisons in Her Majesty's Colonial Possessions* (London: HMSO, 1868) (PP 22591), p. 75.

98 Report on the Diet of Prisoners and of the Industrial and Labouring Classes in the Bombay Presidency, 1865, pp. 9, 47, British Library [hereafter BL] IOR/V/27/830/2.

99 *Prison Discipline in the Colonies*, 1868, p. 67.

100 *Improvement of Prison Discipline in the Colonies*, 1875, pp. 170–2.

101 F. Bernault, "The Shadow of Rule: Colonial Power and Modern Punishment in Africa" in F. Dikotter and I. Brown (eds.), *Cultures of Confinement: A History of the Prison in Africa, Asia and Latin America* (Ithaca: Cornell University Press, 2007), p. 75.

102 R. B. Seidman, "The Ghana Prison System: An Historical Perspective" in A. Milner (ed.), *African Penal Systems* (New York: Frederick A. Praeger, 1969), p. 467 n. 39.

103 *Improvement of Prison Discipline in the Colonies*, 1875, p. 277.

104 On meat and bread see Burnett, *Plenty and Want*; D. J. Oddy, "A Nutritional Ananlysis of Historical Evidence: The Working-Class Diet, 1880–1914" in D. Oddy and D. Miller (eds.), *The Making of the Modern British Diet* (London: Croom Helm, 1976), pp. 214–31; Barker, Oddy, and Yudkin, *Dietary Surveys*, pp. 26–34.

105 *Prison Discipline in the Colonies. Further Correspondence Respecting the Discipline and Management of Prisons in Her Majesty's Colonial Possessions, 8 August, 1870* (London: HMSO, 1871) (PP C. 228), p. 43.

106 *Prison Discipline in the Colonies*, 1870, p. 49.

107 E. Braatz, "Governing Difference: Prison and Colonial Rule on the Gold Coast, 1844–1957," Unpublished PhD dissertation, New York University (2015), pp. 126, 131.

108 *Discipline and Management of Prisons in Her Majesty's Colonial Possessions* (London: HMSO, 1871) (PP C. 355), p. 3.

109 M. Braga-Blake and Ann Ebert-Oehlers, "Where the Twain Met: Origins of Eurasian Families" in M. Braga-Blake, A. Ebert-Oehlers, and A. Pereira (eds.), *Singapore Eurasians: Memories, Hopes, and Dreams* (Singapore: World Scientific Publishing Co., 2017), pp. 39–41.

110 *Improvement of Prison Discipline in the Colonies*, 1875, p. 276.

111 F. Mouat, *Reports of Jails Visited and Inspected in Bengal, Behar, and Arracan* (Calcutta: F. Carbery, 1856), p. 176.

112 *Report on the Administration of the Jails of the Madras Presidency, 1901* (Madras: Government Press, 1902), pp. 37–40.

113 C. Mallampalli, *Race, Religion, and Law in Colonial India: Trials of an Interracial Family* (Cambridge: Cambridge University Press, 2011), pp. 42–5, 102–4, 140–2, 149–75.

114 Report on the Diet of Prisoners…in the Bombay Presidency, pp. 186–7.

115 *Prison Discipline in the Colonies. Digest and Summary of Information Respecting Prisons in the Colonies* (London: HMSO, 1867), p. 42.

116 *Improvement of Prison Discipline in the Colonies*, 1875, pp. 170–2.

117 A. J. Christopher, "'Divide and Rule': The Impress of British Separation Policies," *Area* 20(3) (1988), 233–4; S. Dubow, *Scientific Racism in Modern South Africa* (Cambridge: Cambridge University Press, 1995).

118 D. Arnold, *Colonizing the Body* (Berkeley: University of California Pres, 1993), p. 110; D. Arnold, "India: The Contested Prison" in F. Dikotter and I. Brown (eds.), *Cultures of Confinement: A History of the Prison in Africa, Asia and Latin America* (Ithaca: Cornell University Press, 2007), pp. 154–55, 163–4; C. Anderson, *The Indian Uprising of 1857–8* (London: Anthem Press, 2007), pp. 37–43; A. Yang, "Disciplining 'Natives': Prisons and Prisoners in Early Nineteenth Century India," *South Asia* 10(2) (1987), 29–45.

119 Yang, "Disciplining 'Native,'" p. 42.

120 Mouat, *Reports of Jails Visited*, pp. 63, 76–7, 155, 188, 308.

121 Report on the Diet of Prisoners…in the Bombay Presidency, pp. 55, 97, 165; Mouat, *Reports of Jails Visited*, pp. 55, 135, 151; M. K. Basu, "Food, Fatality and Deprivation in Bengal Prisons: A Study of the Santal Convicts," *Indian Historical Review* 32(2) (2005), 122–41.

122 Report on the Diet of Prisoners…in the Bombay Presidency, pp. 11, 53, 54, 118, 131.

123 R. Morrock, "Heritage of Strife: The Effects of Colonialist 'Divide and Rule' Strategy Upon the Colonized People," *Science and Society* 37(2) (1973), 129–51; S. Bayly, *Caste, Society and Politics in India from the Eighteenth Century to the Modern Age* (Cambridge: Cambridge University Press, 1999).

124 D. Arnold, "The 'Discovery' of Malnutrition and Diet in Colonial India," *Indian Economic and Social History Review* 31(1) (1994), 4.

125 *Prison Discipline in the Colonies*, 1867, p. 23; I. B. Lyon, *Food Equivalents, For Facilitating the Construction of Native Dietaries and Calculation of Food Problems Generally*, BL IOR Mss Eur F86/121; Arnold, "'Discovery' of Malnutrition," 10.

126 Surgeon-Major T. R. Lewis, A Memorandum on the Dietaries of Labouring Prisoners in Indian Jails, 1881, pp. 13–16, BL IOR/L/PJ/6/67; Memorandum by Surgeon-Major I. B. Lyons, May 7, 1877, in *East India (Famine Correspondence). Part III. Copy of Correspondence between the Secretary of State for India and the Government of India on the Subject of the Famine in Western and Southern India* (London: HMSO, 1877) (PP C. 1879), pp. 417–26.

127 Lewis, A Memorandum on the Dietaries of Labouring Prisoners, p. 13.

128 Lewis, A Memorandum on the Dietaries of Labouring Prisoners, p. 35.

129 Captain D. McCay, *Investigations on Bengal Jail Dietaries* (Simla: Government of India, 1910), pp. 159–61, 200–1, 215; Barker, Oddy, and Yudkin, *Dietary Surveys*, p. 16.

130 Major D. McCay, *Investigations into the Jail Dietaries of the United Provinces* (Calcutta: Superintendent of Government Printing, India, 1911), p. 121.

131 Lewis, A Memorandum on the Dietaries of Labouring Prisoners, pp. 17, 26–30; McCay, *Jail Dietaries of the United Provinces*, pp. 121, 189; Arnold, "'Discovery' of Malnutrition," 12.

132 Quoted in McCay, *Bengal Jail Dietaries*, p. 203.

133 McCay, *Bengal Jail Dietaries*, pp. 200–1, 209–11, 215, 221; McCay, *Jail Dietaries of the United Provinces*, pp. 189, 199; Arnold, "'Discovery' of Malnutrition," 13–16.

134 M. Sinha, *Colonial Masculinity: The "Manly Englishman" and the "Effeminate Bengali" in the Late Nineteenth Century* (Manchester: Manchester University Press, 1995).

135 H. Streets, *Martial Races: The Military, Race and Masculinity in British Imperial Culture, 1857–1914* (Manchester: Manchester University Press, 2011).

Chapter 3

1 W. Digby, *The Famine Campaign in Southern India, 1876–1878*, Vol. I (London: Longmans, Green, and Co., 1878), p. 46.

2 D. P. Nally, *Human Encumbrances: Political Violence and the Great Irish Famine* (Notre Dame: University of Notre Dame Press, 2011), p. 13; M. Davis, *Late Victorian Holocausts: El Niño Famines and the Making of the Third World* (London: Verso, 2001); S. Ambirajan, "Malthusian Population Theory and Indian Famine Policy in the Nineteenth Century," *Population Studies* 30(1) (1976), 5–14; S. Ambirajan, "Political Economy and Indian Famines," *South*

Asia 1(2) (1971), 20–8; D. Hall-Matthews, *Peasants, Famine and the State in Colonial Western India* (Houndmills: Palgrave, 2005); I. Klein, "When the Rains Failed: Famine, Relief, and Mortality in British India," *The Indian Economic and Social History Review* 21(2) (1984), 185–214.

3 R. Skinner and A. Lester, "Humanitarianism and Empire: New Research Agendas," *Journal of Imperial and Commonwealth History* 40(5) (2012), 729–47; T. Sasson and J. Vernon, "Practising the British Way of Famine: Technologies of Relief, 1770–1985," *European Review of History* 22(6) (2015), 860–72; M. Tusan, *Smyrna's Ashes: Humanitarianism, Genocide, and the Birth of the Middle East* (Berkeley: University of California Press, 2012); M. N. Barnett, *Empire of Humanity: A History of Humanitarianism* (Ithaca: Cornell University Press, 2011).

4 J. Drèze and A. Sen, *The Amartya Sen and Jean Drèze Omnibus* (Delhi: Oxford University Press, 1999).

5 R. C. Dutt, *Open Letters to Lord Curzon on Famines and Land Assessment in India* (London: Kegan, Paul, Trench, Trubner, and Co., 1900); D. Naoroji, *Poverty and Un-British Rule in India* (London: Swan Sonnenschein and Co., 1901); Arnold, *Famine*, pp. 116–18.

6 S. Devereux, *Theories of Famine* (New York: Harvester Wheatsheaf, 1993), p. 21, emphasis in original.

7 Nally, *Human Encumbrances*; B. R. Siegel, *Hungry Nation: Food, Famine, and the Making of Modern India* (Cambridge: Cambridge University Press, 2018).

8 S. Sharma, *Famine, Philanthropy and the Colonial State: North India in the Early Nineteenth Century* (Delhi: Oxford University Press, 2001), pp. ix, 135–92.

9 *Report of the Indian Famine Commission, Part I: Famine Relief* (London: HMSO, 1880) (PP C. 2591), p. 31; G. Brewis, "'Fill Full the Mouth of Famine': Voluntary Action in Famine Relief in India 1896–1901," *Modern Asian Studies* 44(4) (2010), 893; C. Ó Gráda, *Famine: A Short History* (Princeton: Princeton University Press, 2009), p. 198; A. Forth, *Barbed-Wire Imperialism: Britain's Empire of Camps, 1876–1903* (Berkeley: University of California Press, 2017), p. 47.

10 C. Kinealy, *A Death-Dealing Famine: The Great Hunger in Ireland* (London: Pluto Press, 1997), p. 71.

11 Carroll, *Science, Culture, and Modern State Formation*, p. 153.

12 On the influence of utilitarianism among the Indian civil service see E. Stokes, *The English Utilitarians and India* (Delhi: Oxford University Press, 1959).

13 Ambirajan, "Malthusian Population Theory"; Ambirajan, "Political Economy"; K. Currie, "British Colonial Policy and Famines: Some Effects and Implications of 'Free Trade' in the Bombay, Bengal and Madras Presidencies, 1860–1900," *South Asia* 14(2) (1991), 23–56; K. Edgerton-Tarpley, "Tough Choices: Grappling with Famine in Qing China, the British Empire, and Beyond," *Journal of World History* 24(1) (2013), 135–76; Forth, *Barbed-Wire Imperialism*, p. 51.

14 Sharma, *Famine, Philanthropy and the Colonial State*, pp. 164–8.

15 Davis, *Late Victorian Holocausts*, p. 9.

16 Barnett, *Empire of Humanity*, pp. 63–4.

17 Vernon, *Hunger*, pp. 17–40; A. Nag, "Managing Hunger: Famine, Science, and the Colonial State in India, 1860–1910," Unpublished PhD dissertation, University of California–Los Angeles (2010), pp. 193–247.

18 Report of the Commissioners Appointed to Inquire into the Famine in Bengal and Orissa in 1866, April 6, 1867, in *East India (Bengal and Orissa Famine). Papers and Correspondence Relative to the Famine in Bengal and Orissa, Including the Report of the Famine Commission and the Minutes of the Lieutenant Governor of Bengal and the Governor General of India, [Part I]*, May 31, 1867 (PP 335), p. 271.

19 Letter from the Collector of Ganjam to the Secretary to the Court of Wards, May 29, 1866, in *East India (Madras and Orissa Famine). Copies of Papers Relating to the Famine in the Madras Presidency in 1865–66 and Additional Papers Relating to the Famine in Orissa Subsequent to the Report of the Commission*, July 30, 1867 (PP 490), p. 17.

20 Report of the Commissioners Appointed to Inquire into the Famine in Bengal and Orissa in 1866, p. 272.

21 Report of the Commissioners Appointed to Inquire into the Famine in Bengal and Orissa in 1866, p. 272.

22 Quoted in J. C. Geddes, *Administrative Experience Recorded in Former Famines* (Calcutta: E. Bengal Secretariat Press, 1874), p. 17.

23 Minute by H. M. Durand, April 23, 1867, in *East India (Bengal and Orissa Famine), [Part I]*, p. 391.

24 *East India (Famine). Report of the East India Famine Commission, 1901 and Papers Relating Thereto* (London: HMSO, 1901) (PP Cd. 876), p. 1.

25 *Report of the Indian Famine Commission, Part I*, 1880, p. 15.

26 F. Henvey, *A Narrative of the Drought and Famine which Prevailed in the North-West Provinces during the Years 1868, 1869, and Beginning of 1870* (Allahabad: Government Press, 1871), p. 5.

27 Henvey, *Narrative of the Drought*, Appendix IV, p. XXX; *Report of the Indian Famine Commission, Part I*, 1880, p. 32.

28 Henvey, *Narrative of the Drought*, p. 125.

29 P. Gray, "Famine and Land in Ireland and India, 1845–1880: James Caird and the Political Economy of Hunger," *The Historical Journal* 49(1) (2006), 193–215.

30 Report of the Commissioners Appointed to Inquire into the Famine in Bengal and Orissa in 1866, Part III, April 20, 1867, in *East India (Bengal and Orissa Famine), [Part I]*, p. 363.

31 Sir H. B. Frere, *On the Impending Bengal Famine: How It Will Be Met and How to Prevent Future Famines in India* (London: John Murray, 1874), p. 25.

32 Letter from A. Howell to the Secretary to the Government of Bengal, February 13, 1874, in *Correspondence between the Government of India and the Secretary of State in Council Relative to the Famine in Bengal, Part I* (London: HMSO, 1874) (PP C. 955), p. 228.

33 Frere, *On the Impending Bengal Famine*, pp. 23, 50.

34 C. Bernard, Thirteenth Special Narrative of the Drought in Bengal, March 6–19, 1874, in *Further Correspondence between the Government of India and the Secretary of State in Council Relative to the Famine in Bengal, Part III* (London: HMSO, 1874) (PP C. 955-II), p. 15.

35 Sir R. Temple, *The Story of My Life*, Vol. II (London: Cassell and Co., 1896), pp. 74, 228.

36 S. Ambirajan, *Classical Political Economy and British Policy in India* (Cambridge: Cambridge University Press, 1978), p. 86.

37 Letter from the Secretary to the Government of India to Sir Richard Temple, January 16, 1877, in *East India, Part II. Copy of Correspondence between the Secretary of State for India and the Government of India on the Subject of the Threatened Famine in Western and Southern India* (London: HMSO, 1877) (PP C. 1754), p. 19; *Report of the Indian Famine Commission, Part I*, 1880, p. 33.

38 Quoted in Ambirajan, *Classical Political Economy*, p. 93.

39 Digby, *Famine Campaign*, Vol. II, pp. 55–9; Brewis, "Fill Full the Mouth of Famine," p. 896.

40 Digby, *Famine Campaign*, Vol. II, p. 55.

41 Hall-Matthews, *Peasants, Famine and the State*, p. 169.

42 Letter From the Secretary to the Government of Bombay, Public Works Department, to the Secretary to the Government of India, February 12, 1877, in *East India (Famine Correspondence), Part III*, p. 90.

43 Gray, "Famine and Land in Ireland and India."

44 Davis, *Late Victorian Holocausts*, p. 7.

45 *Report of the Indian Famine Commission, Part I*, 1880, p. 69.

46 *Report of the Indian Famine Commission, Part I*, 1880, p. 34.

47 Nag, "Managing Hunger," p. 158.

48 *Report of the Indian Famine Commission, Part I*, 1880, p. 35.

49 B. M. Bhatia, *Famines in India*, 2nd ed. (Bombay: Asia Publishing House, 1967), p. 112.

50 For the development of the Famine Codes see Nag, "Managing Hunger," pp. 156–8. A large number of the famine codes are archived at the India Office at the British Library in the series IOR/V/27/831 and P/W 87.

51 Madras Famine Code, 1883, BL IOR/V/27/831/40, p. i.

52 Letter No. 86 (Revenue) from the Government of India to Lord George F. Hamilton, November 25, 1897, in *Famine and Relief Operations in India: Further Papers Regarding the Famine and the Relief Operations in India during the Years 1896–97, No. IVA* (London: HMSO, 1898) (PP C. 8737), p. 4.

53 Statement on the Famine of 1899–1900 Made By the Governor-General in the Legislative Council Held at Simla on October 19, 1900, in *East India (Famine). Papers Regarding the Famine and the Relief Operations in India during 1900–1902, Vol. I: British Districts* (London: HMSO, 1902) (PP Cd. 1179), p. 475.

54 Quoted in Davis, *Late Victorian Holocausts*, p. 162.

55 Davis, *Late Victorian Holocausts*, p. 174; Klein, "When the Rains Failed," 189.

56 C. Blair, *Indian Famines: Their Historical, Financial and Other Aspects* (Edinburgh: William Blackwood and Sons, 1874), pp. 105, 132–3, 154.

57 R. Ahuja, "State Formation and 'Famine Policy' in Early Colonial South Asia," *The Indian Economic and Social History Review* 39(4) (2002), 367; Sharma, *Famine, Philanthropy and the Colonial State*, pp. 182–3 n. 169; H. S. Srivastava, *The History of Indian Famines 1858–1918* (Agra: Sri Ram Mehra and Co., 1968), p. 28.

58 Service Message: From Home Secretary, Simla to Secretary, Government of Bengal, May 28, 1866, in *East India (Bengal and Orissa Famine), [Part I]*, p. 12; Letter from A. Eden to the Secretary to the Board of Revenue, Lower Provinces, June 20, 1866, in *East India (Bengal and Orissa Famine), [Part I]*, p. 33; Letter from E. C. Bayley to Acting Secretary to Government of Fort St. George, June 30, 1866, in *East India (Bengal and Orissa Famine), [Part I]*, p. 41; Extract from the Annual Report of the Commissioner of Cuttack (No. 313), July 16, 1866, in *East India (Bengal and Orissa Famine), [Part I]*, p. 59.

59 R. B. Smith, *Report on the Famine of 1860–61* (Calcutta: n.p., 1861), p. 14; Revenue Letter from Madras, August 11, 1866, in *East India (Madras and Orissa Famine)*, p. 32; C. E. R. Girdlestone, *Report on Past Famines in the North-Western Provinces* (Allahabad: Government Press, 1868), p. 75; *Report on the Famine in the Panjab during 1869–70* (Lahore: Punjab Printing Company, 1870), p. 19.

60 Henvey, *Narrative of the Drought*, p. 5; Brewis, "'Fill Full the Mouth of Famine'."

61 Letter From the Government of India, Department of Revenue, Agriculture, and Commerce, to the Secretary of State for India, January 12, 1877, in *East India, Part II*, pp. 15–16; Memorandum by Mr. Bernard on the Condition and Prospects of the Salem District, as ascertained by Sir Richard Temple at his meeting with the Collector, Mr. Longley, on the 25th January in *East India (Famine Correspondence), Part III*, p. 34.

62 *Report of the Indian Famine Commission, Part I*, 1880, p. 61.

63 Smith, *Report on the Famine of 1860–61*, p. 13.

64 Narrative of Scarcity and Relief in Sarun District for the Fortnight Ending February 21, 1874, in *Further Correspondence between the Government of India and the Secretary of State in Council Relative to the Famine in Bengal, Part II* (London: HMSO, 1874) (PP C. 955-I), p. 198.

65 *Report of the Indian Famine Commission, 1898* (London: HMSO, 1898) (PP C. 9178), p. 283.

66 Smith, *Report on the Famine of 1860–61*, p. 13; Letter from A. Eden to the Secretary to the Board of Revenue, Lower Provinces, May 21, 1866, in *East India (Bengal and Orissa Famine), [Part I]*, p. 12; *Report of the Indian Famine Commission, Part III: Famine Histories* (London: HMSO, 1885) (PP C. 3086), p. 33; North-West Provinces and Oudh Famine Code, 1895 in *Famine and Relief Operations in India: Papers Regarding the Famine and the Relief Operations in India during the Year 1896* (London: HMSO, 1897) (PP C. 8302), pp. xi–xii.

67 Statements recorded by the Commissioners for Inquiring into the Famine in Bengal and Orissa in 1866 in *East India (Bengal and Orissa Famine). Papers and Correspondence Relative to the Famine in Bengal and Orissa, Including the Report of the Famine Commission and the Minutes of the Lieutenant Governor of Bengal and the Governor General of India, Part II*, July 5, 1867 (PP 335-I), p. 92.

68 Henvey, *Narrative of the Drought*, Appendix VIII, p. xxxv.

69 Notes of a Conference Held at Hoshangabad on the September 23–24, 1899 in *East India (Famine). Papers Regarding the Famine and Relief Operations in India during 1899–1900, Vol I: British Districts* (London: HMSO, 1900) (PP Cd. 205), p. 20.

70 Report of the Commissioners Appointed to Inquire into the Famine in Bengal and Orissa in 1866, Part III, p. 364.

71 Letter from A. Mackenzie to the Secretary to the Central Relief Committee; to the Commissioners of Patna, Bhaugulpore, Rajshahye, Burdwan, Chota Nagpore, and Presidency Divisions; and to the Relief Commissioner of Rajshahye, February 16, 1874, in *Further Correspondence … Relative to the Famine in Bengal, Part II*, p. 45.

72 *Report of the Indian Famine Commission, Part I*, 1880, p. 18.

73 T. W. Holderness, *Government of India. Department of Revenue and Agriculture (Famine). Narrative of the Famine in India in 1896–7* (London: HMSO, 1897) (PP C. 8812), pp. 17, 21.

74 For some famine statistics see Smith, *Report on the Famine of 1860–61*, pp. 16, 30, and Section IA, pp. 1–2; *Report of the Indian Famine Commission, Part I*, 1880, p. 24; *Report on the Famine in the Panjab*, unnumbered pages following page 49; *Report of the Indian Famine Commission, Part III*, 1885, pp. 98, 139; Government of the North-West Provinces and Oudh. Scarcity Department. Narrative and Results of the Measures Adopted for the Relief of Famine during the Years 1896 and 1897 in *Famine and Relief Operations in India: Further Papers Regarding the Famine and the Relief Operations in India during the Years 1896–97, No. V* (London: HMSO, 1898) (PP C. 8739), pp. 111–12; Letter from R. H. Craddock to the Secretary to the Government of India, Revenue and Agriculture Department, July 17, 1900, in *East India (Famine), 1900–1902, Vol I*, pp. 35, 37.

75 Letter from R. H. Craddock to the Secretary to the Government of India, Revenue and Agriculture Department, August 17, 1900, in *East India (Famine), 1900–1902, Vol I*, p. 41.

76 Kinealy, *Death-Dealing Famine*, p. 99.

77 Report of the Commissioners Appointed to Inquire into the Famine in Bengal and Orissa in 1866, Part III, p. 366; *Report of the Indian Famine Commission, 1898*, p. 286; *Report of the Indian Famine Commission, Part III*, 1885, p. 136.

78 Report of the Commissioners Appointed to Inquire into the Famine in Bengal and Orissa in 1866, p. 158; Blair, *Indian Famines*, p. 188; Letter from A. Mackenzie to the Secretary to the Central Relief Committee et al., p. 45; Letter to the Marquis of Salisbury from Northbrook, Napier of Magdala, B. H. Ellis, H. W. Norman, A. Hobhouse, E. C. Bayley, March 20, 1874, in *Further Correspondence…Relative to the Famine in Bengal, Part III*, p. 162; *Report of the Indian Famine Commission, Part III*, 1885, pp. 57, 202; *Report of the Indian Famine Commission, 1898*, p. 286; Famine Circular from R. H. Craddock to all Commissioners and Deputy Commissioners, Central Provinces, No. 53, August 14, 1900, in *East India (Famine), 1900–1902, Vol I*, p. 126.

79 Smith, *Report on the Famine of 1860–61*, pp. 14–15.

80 Geddes, *Administrative Experience*, p. 92.

81 Smith, *Report on the Famine of 1860–61*, p. 15; Srivastava, *History of Indian Famines*, pp. 39–41; Henvey, *Narrative of the Drought*, p. 92.

82 Henvey, *Narrative of the Drought*, pp. 5–6, 40.

83 Letter from H. W. Gordon to the Officiating Secretary to the Government of Bengal, Statistical Department, March 23, 1874, in *Further Correspondence between the Government of India and the Secretary of State in Council Relative to the Famine in Bengal, Part IV* (London: HMSO, 1874) (PP C. 955-III), p. 95.

84 Note of the Result of the Lieutenant-Governor's Visit to Tirhoot in *Further Correspondence...Relative to the Famine in Bengal, Part IV*, p. 35; Letter from E. E. Lowis to the Officiating Secretary to the Government of Bengal, Scarcity and Relief Department, April 6, 1874, in *Further Correspondence between the Government of India and the Secretary of State in Council Relative to the Famine in Bengal, Part V* (London: HMSO, 1874) (PP C. 955-IV), p. 106.

85 Letter from H. W. Gordon to the Officiating Secretary to the Government of Bengal, p. 95.

86 Bengal Famine Code, 1888, BL IOR V/27/831/8.

87 Bombay Famine Code, 1900, BL IOR V/27/831/22.

88 C. Bernard, Memorandum on the Condition and Prospects of Relief Affairs in the Bellary District, as Ascertained at Sir Richard Temple's Conferences with the Local Officers on the 17th and 18th January 1877, January 19, 1877, in *East India, Part II*, p. 43; Report of the Commissioners Appointed to Inquire into the Famine in Bengal and Orissa in 1866, Part III, p. 365; F. R. Cockerell, Report on the Famine in the Behar Districts and Sonthal Pergunnahs, 1866, in *East India (Bengal and Orissa Famine). Papers Relating to the Famine in Behar, Part III*, May 31, 1867 (PP 335-II), p. 36.

89 Letter From Colonel E. A. Rowlatt to the Officiating Secretary to the Government of Bengal, Scarcity and Relief Department, April 6, 1874, in *Correspondence...Relative to the Famine in Bengal, Part I*, p. 147; Memorandum Respecting the Kolar District of Mysore in *East India (Famine Correspondence), Part III*, p. 106.

90 Narrative No. 14 of the Proceedings of the Board of Revenue, and of the Several Local Offices, and Committees for the Relief of the Distress Arising from the Scarcity of Food in Orissa, and in Other parts of Bengal in *East India (Bengal and Orissa Famine), [Part I]*, pp. 96, 102, 107; Narrative No. 24, of the Proceedings of the Board of Revenue, and the Several Local Officers and Committees for the Relief of the Distress Arising from the Scarcity of Food in Orissa, and in Other Parts of Bengal, November 17, 1866, in *East India (Bengal and Orissa Famine), [Part I]*, pp. 131–2; Report of the Commissioners Appointed to Inquire into the Famine in Bengal and Orissa in 1866, pp. 293, 296; Statements Recorded by the Commissioners for Inquiring into the Famine in Bengal and Orissa in 1866, p. 35.

91 Bengal Famine Code, 1897, p. 27, BL IOR V/27/831/11; Ajmere-Merwara Famine Code, 1897, p. 27, BL IOR V/27/831/6.

92 Memorandum by Mr. Bernard...on the Condition and Prospects of the Salem District, p. 34; Memorandum by Mr. Bernard on the Condition and Prospects of the Chingleput District as Ascertained by Sir Richard Temple on his Visit of the 28th and 29th January 1877 With Notes

Regarding the Relief Camps in and Near Madras, January 30, 1877, in *East India (Famine Correspondence), Part III*, p. 42; Memorandum by Dr. Harvey, on Special Duty with Sir R. Temple, on the Physical Condition of the People in the Distressed Districts of Madras and Bombay, March 25, 1877, in *East India (Famine Correspondence), Part III*, p. 309; Notes by Dr. Townsend, Officiating Sanitary Commissioner with the Government of India, Deputed at the Request of Sir Richard Temple to Investigate and Ascertain Whether the Scale of Wages Now Given to the People Employed on the Several Famine Relief Works is Sufficient to Support them in Fair Health, April 3, 1877, in *East India (Famine Correspondence), Part III*, p. 324; Letter from the Government of India, Department of Revenue, Agriculture, and Commerce, to the Secretary of State for India, May 3, 1877, in *East India (Famine Correspondence), Part III*, p. 410; North-West Provinces and Oudh Famine Code, 1895, p. xxix; Forth, *Barbed-Wire Imperialism*, pp. 43–73.

93 Letter from the Governor-General of India, Department of Revenue, Agriculture, and Commerce (Famine), to the Secretary of State for India, September 5, 1877, in *East India (Famine Correspondence), Part IV: Copy of Correspondence between the Secretary of State for India and the Government of India on the Subject of the Famine in Western and Southern India* (London: HMSO, 1878) (PP C. 1920), p. 175; *Appendix to the Report of the Famine Commission, 1898, Vol. III: Bombay Presidency* (London: HMSO, 1899) (PP C. 9254), p. 256.

94 Memorandum by C. A. Elliott on Progress Made from the 10th to the 19th September, 1877, September 19, 1877, in *East India (Famine Correspondence), Part IV*, p. 191.

95 Letter from Governor-General to Secretary of State for India, September 5, 1877, p. 175.

96 Mysore Famine Code, 1877, in *East India (Famine Correspondence), Part IV*, pp. 223, 235.

97 Minute by Sir Richard Temple on his third visit to the North Arcot District, Vellore, March 5, 1877, in *East India (Famine Correspondence), Part III*, p. 233.

98 Ó Gráda, *Famine*, p. 206; Forth, *Barbed-Wire Imperialism*, pp. 43–73.

99 Statements Recorded by the Commissioners for Inquiring into the Famine in Bengal and Orissa in 1866, p. 91; M. S. M. Ali, *Report on the History of the Famine in His Highness the Nizam's Dominions, 1876–77, 1877–78* (Bombay: The Exchange Press, 1879), Appendix IV, p. 5; *Appendix to the Report of the Famine Commission, 1898, Vol. I: Bengal* (London: HMSO, 1899) (PP C. 9252), p. 169.

100 Smith, *Report on the Famine of 1860–61*, p. 14; Cockerell, Report on the Famine in the Behar Districts, p. 37; *Report on the Famine in the Panjab*, p. 19; Henvey, *Narrative of the Drought*, pp. 5–6, Appendix XI, p. lxiv.

101 Mysore Famine Code, 1877, p. 239; Note of the Result of the Lieutenant-Governor's Visit to Tirhoot, p. 35; *Appendix to the Report of the Famine Commission, 1898, Vol. IV: Central Provinces and Berar* (London: HMSO, 1899) (PP C. 9255), p. 115; Letter from W. Thompson to the Revenue Secretary to the Chief Commissioner, Burma, April 14,

1897, in *Famine and Relief Operations in India: Further Papers Regarding the Famine and the Relief Operations in India during the Years 1896–97, No. IV* (London: HMSO, 1897) (PP C. 8660), p. 168; *Appendix to the Report of the Famine Commission, 1898, Vol. II: Madras Presidency* (London: HMSO, 1899) (PP C. 9253), p. 28; Henvey, *Narrative of the Drought*, Appendix XI, p. lxiv.

102 Statements Recorded by the Commissioners for Inquiring into the Famine in Bengal and Orissa in 1866, p. 91; Report of the Commissioners Appointed to Inquire into the Famine in Bengal and Orissa in 1866, Part III, p. 366; Blair, *Indian Famines*, p. 190.

103 Note of the Result of the Lieutenant-Governor's Visit to Tirhoot, p. 35.

104 Letter to Sir Richard Temple from S. C. Bayley, March 6, 1874 and Letter to Sir Richard Temple from S. C. Bayley, March 13, 1874, BL IOR Mss Eur F86/121.

105 Letter from E. H. Whitfield to the Commissioner of Burdwan Division, April 6, 1874, in *Further Correspondence…Relative to the Famine in Bengal, Part V* (London: HMSO, 1874) (PP C. 955-IV), p. 127; Instructions for Sub-Committee Officers in *Further Correspondence…Relative to the Famine in Bengal, Part III*, p. 64.

106 Memorandum by Mr. Bernard on the Condition and Prospects of the Chingleput District, p. 43; Notes by Dr. Townsend, April 3, 1877, p. 324; Memorandum by Mr. Bernard Regarding the Conditions and Prospects of the Mysore Province, February 13, 1877, in *East India (Famine Correspondence), Part III*, p. 103; Memorandum Respecting the Kolar District, p. 106.

107 Letter from the Government of India…to the Secretary of State for India, May 3, 1877, p. 410.

108 D. Hall-Matthews, "Inaccurate Conceptions: Disputed Measures of Nutritional Needs and Famine Deaths in Colonial India," *Modern Asian Studies* 42(6) (2008), 1189–212.

109 *Report of the Indian Famine Commission, Part III*, 1885, p. 48; Letter from E. H. Whitfield to the Commissioner of Burdwan Division, p. 127; Report of the Commissioners Appointed to Inquire into the Famine in Bengal and Orissa in 1866, pp. 296–7; Cockerell, Report on the Famine in the Behar Districts, pp. 36–7.

110 Cockerell, Report on the Famine in the Behar Districts, p. 37.

111 Report of the Commissioners Appointed to Inquire into the Famine in Bengal and Orissa in 1866, Part III, p. 366.

112 Report of the Commissioners Appointed to Inquire into the Famine in Bengal and Orissa in 1866, Part III, p. 366.

113 Agamben, *Homo Sacer*.

114 Forth, *Barbed-Wire Imperialism*, p. 67.

115 Report of the Commissioners Appointed to Inquire into the Famine in Bengal and Orissa in 1866, Part III, p. 366.

116 For amount of food provided see Henvey, *Narrative of the Drought*, pp. 5–6, Appendix XI, p. lxiv; Instructions for Sub-Committee Officers, p. 64; Letter from E. H. Whitfield to the Commissioner of Burdwan Division, p. 127; Letter from H. W. Gordon to the Officiating Secretary

to the Government of Bengal, p. 95; Memorandum by Mr. Bernard on the Condition and Prospects of the Chingleput District, p. 43; Report by Surgeon-Major S. C. Townsend, Officiating Sanitary Commissioner with the Government of India, on the Condition of the Famine Relief Labourers in the Madras Presidency, April 3, 1877, in *East India (Famine Correspondence), Part III*, p. 321; Notes by Dr. Townsend, April 3, 1877, pp. 322–6; Memorandum by Mr. Bernard on Relief Affairs in the Worst part of the Salem District, During the Middle of April 1877, April 16, 1877, in *East India (Famine Correspondence), Part III*, p. 382; Mysore Famine Code, 1877, p. 234.

117 Hall-Matthews, "Inaccurate Conceptions," 1192.

118 Digby, *Famine Campaign*, Vol. I, p. 86.

119 W. R. Cornish, A Reply to Sir Richard Temple's Minutes of the 7th and 14th March as to the Sufficiency of a Pound of Grain as the basis of Famine Wages, in *East India (Famine Correspondence), Part III*, p. 337.

120 For a complete account of the Cornish-Temple debates see Hall-Matthews, "Inaccurate Conceptions."

121 Memorandum on the Differences in the Provincial Famine Codes in *Appendix to the Report of the Indian Famine Commission, 1898, Vol. VII: Miscellaneous* (London: HMSO, 1899) (PP C. 9258), pp. 19–23; North-West Provinces and Oudh Famine Code, 1895, p. xvii.

122 *Appendix to the Report of the Indian Famine Commission, 1898, Vol. V: North-West Provinces and Oudh* (London: HMSO, 1899) (PP C. 9256), p. 97; T. Higham, Notes on an Inspection of Famine Relief Works in the Bombay Presidency in *Famine and Relief Operations in India: Further Papers, 1897–98, No. VII* (London: HMSO, 1898) (PP C. 8823), pp. 262, 411–12, 430; *Appendix to the Report of the Indian Famine Commission, 1898, Vol. VI: Punjab* (London: HMSO, 1899) (PP C. 9257), p. 45; Instructions for the Management of Public Works Department Kitchens in *Appendix to the Report of the Famine Commission, 1898, Vol. IV*, p. 25; *Report of the Indian Famine Commission, 1898*, p. 74; F. H. S. Merewether, *Tour through the Famine Districts of India* (London: A.D. Innes and Co., 1898), p. 96.

123 *Appendix to the Report of the Famine Commission, 1898, Vol. V*, p. 38.

124 Arnold, *Famine*, p. 8; Bayly, *Caste, Society and Politics*.

125 Proceedings of the Madras Government, Revenue Department, October 10, 1866 in *East India (Madras and Orissa Famine)*, p. 152; Letter to the Marquis of Salisbury from Northbrook, et al., p. 162; Letter from E. E. Lowis to the Officiating Secretary to the Government of Bengal, p. 106.

126 Blair, *Indian Famines*, p. 198; *Appendix to the Report of the Famine Commission, 1898, Vol. II*, p. 169.

127 Mr. Kirkwood, Recovery of Caste after Partaking of Cooked Food at a Poor-House, in Geddes, *Administrative Experience*, pp. 173–7; *Report of the Indian Famine Commission, Part III*, 1885, pp. 59, 202–3.

128 Blair, *Indian Famines*, p. 199.

129 *Appendix to the Report of the Famine Commission, 1898, Vol. I*, p. 70.

130 *Appendix to the Report of the Famine Commission, 1898, Vol. V*, p. 148.

131 *Appendix to the Report of the Famine Commission, 1898, Vol. II*, p. 96.

132 *Appendix to the Report of the Famine Commission, 1898, Vol. V*, p. 123.

133 Proclamation, by the Queen in Council, to the Princes, Chiefs, and People of India (published by the Governor-General at Allahabad, November 1, 1858), BL IOR/L/PS/ 18/D154.
134 Smith, *Report on the Famine of 1860–61*, p. 14.
135 Girdlestone, *Report on Past Famines*, p. 77; The Foundling Asylum, Resolutions in *East India (Bengal and Orissa Famine)*, *[Part I]*, p. 178; Report of the Commissioners Appointed to Inquire into the Famine in Bengal and Orissa in 1866, Part III, p. 365; Statements Recorded by the Commissioners for Inquiring into the Famine in Bengal and Orissa in 1866, pp. 8, 26; Henvey, *Narrative of the Drought*, Appendix XII, p. lxvii; Blair, *Indian Famines*, p. 188; Ali, *Report on the History of the Famine*, p. 4; North-West Provinces and Oudh Famine Code, 1895, p. xxvii; Merewether, *Tour through the Famine Districts*, p. 96; Vaughan Nash, *The Great Famine and Its Causes* (London: Longmans, Green, and Co., 1900), p. 191; *Report of the Indian Famine Commission, 1880 (Appendix Part IV: Evidence)* (London: HMSO, 1885) (PP C. 3086-IV), pp. 228, 230; Memorandum of Measures Approved by the Government of India for Adoption in Times of Famine, 1868 in Geddes, *Administrative Experience*, p. 5; *Report of the Indian Famine Commission, 1898*, p. 85; Summary of the Remarks in the District Reports Accompanying Monthly Famine Statements A and B for the Month of October 1899 in *East India (Famine)*, *1899–1900*, *Vol. I*, p. 53; Minute by Sir Richard Temple, Regarding Relief Camps and Gratuitous Relief in the Ceded Districts, Madras, March 12, 1877, in *East India (Famine Correspondence)*, *Part III*, p. 259; *Report of the Indian Famine Commission*, *Part I*, 1880, p. 47; Merewether, *Tour through the Famine Districts*, pp. 224–5; *Appendix to the Report of the Famine Commission, 1898*, *Vol. I*, pp. 54, 105; *Appendix to the Report of the Famine Commission, 1898*, *Vol. II*, p. 80; *Appendix to the Report of the Famine Commission, 1898*, *Vol. III*, p. 105; *Appendix to the Report of the Famine Commission, 1898*, *Vol. IV*, p. 131; Statements recorded by the Commissioners for inquiring into the Famine in Bengal and Orissa in 1866, p. 80; *Report of the Indian Famine Commission, 1898*, p. 18.
136 Note By the Honourable Syed Ahmed Khan Bahadur on the Causes of the Unpopularity of the Poorhouses In the North-Western Provinces and Oudh during the Famine of 1878, in *Report of the Indian Famine Commission, Part III*, 1885, pp. 250–1; *Appendix to the Report of the Famine Commission, 1898*, *Vol. II*, p. 96.
137 Note By the Honourable Syed Ahmed Khan Bahadur, pp. 250–1; *Appendix to the Report of the Famine Commission, 1898*, *Vol. IV*, p. 300.
138 Digby, *Famine Campaign*, Vol. II, p. 297.
139 Letter from A. D. Younghusband to the Chief Secretary to the Chief Commissioner, Central Provinces, August 5, 1900, in *East India (Famine)*, *1900–1902*, *Vol. I*, p. 119.
140 *Appendix to the Report of the Famine Commission, 1898, Vol. II*, p. 4.
141 Note By the Honourable Syed Ahmed Khan Bahadur, p. 251; Digby, *Famine Campaign*, Vol. I, p. 349; Report of the Commissioners Appointed to Inquire into the Famine in Bengal and Orissa in 1866, p. 303; Narrative and Results of the Measures Adopted for the Relief of Famine during the

Years 1896 and 1897, p. 43; *Appendix to the Report of the Famine Commission, 1898, Vol. VI*, pp. 24, 115; Nash, *Great Famine*, p. 195; *Appendix to the Report of the Famine Commission, 1898, Vol. II*, pp. 70, 81, 96.

142 Narrative and Results of the Measures Adopted for the Relief of Famine during the Years 1896 and 1897, p. 58.

143 *Report of the Indian Famine Commission, Part III*, 1885, p. 137.

144 Narrative and Results of the Measures Adopted for the Relief of Famine during the Years 1896 and 1897, p. 58; *Appendix to the Report of the Famine Commission, 1898, Vol. IV*, p. 329.

145 Higham, Notes on an Inspection of Famine Relief Works in the Bombay Presidency, p. 430; *Appendix to the Report of the Famine Commission, 1898, Vol. III*, p. 105; Brewis, "'Fill Full the Mouth of Famine'," p. 907.

146 *Appendix to the Report of the Famine Commission, 1898, Vol. III*, p. 225.

147 P. Roy, *Alimentary Tracts: Appetites, Aversions, and the Postcolonial* (Durham: Duke University Press, 2010).

148 Arnold, *Colonizing the Body*; Forth, *Barbed-Wire Imperialism*, pp. 74–99.

149 *Appendix to the Report of the Famine Commission, 1898, Vol. I*, p. 159; Ahuja, "State Formation," p. 380; Brewis, "'Fill Full the Mouth of Famine'," p. 893; Sharma, *Famine, Philanthropy and the Colonial State*, p. 121; Nag, "Managing Hunger," p. 90.

150 Ali, *Report on the History of the Famine*, pp. 4–7; Appendix to the Report of the Famine Commission, 1898, Vol. II, p. 96; Srivastava, *History of Indian Famines*, pp. 99, 144.

151 Narrative of Scarcity and Relief in Rungtore District for the Fortnight Ending March 21, 1874, in *Further Correspondence...Relative to the Famine in Bengal Part IV*, p. 139; Memorandum by R. Porch forwarded to the Secretary to the Government of Bengal: Narrative of Scarcity and Relief in Rungpore District for the Fortnight Ending April 4, 1874, in *Further Correspondence... Relative to the Famine in Bengal, Part V*, p. 119; Statements Recorded by the Commissioners for Inquiring into the Famine in Bengal and Orissa in 1866, pp. 26, 91; C. Bernard, Twelfth Special Narrative of the Drought in Bengal, from the 20th February to the 5th March, 1874, in *Further Correspondence...Relative to the Famine in Bengal, Part II*, p. 148.

152 C. L. Novetzke, *The Quotidian Revolution: Vernacularization, Religion, and the Premodern Public Sphere in India* (New York: Columbia University Press, 2016), p. 241.

153 *Appendix to the Report of the Famine Commission, 1898, Vol. IV*, p. 285.

154 Sasson and Vernon, "Practising the British Way of Famine," p. 861; Nally, *Human Encumbrances*, pp. 15–18; M. Foucault, *The History of Sexuality, Volume 1: An Introduction* (New York: Vintage, 1990); Siegel, *Hungry Nation*, pp. 11–13.

155 A. Clark, "Humanitarianism, Human Rights, and Biopolitics in the British Empire, 1890–1902," *Britain and the World* 9(1) (2016), 96–115.

156 D. C. Zook, "Famine in the Landscape: Imagining Hunger in South Asian History, 1860–1990" in A. Agrawal and K. Sivaramakrishnan (eds.), *Agrarian Environments: Resources, Representations, and Rule in India* (Durham: Duke University Press, 2000), p. 115.

157 Forth, *Barbed-Wire Imperialism*, p. 68. Thanks to Aidan Forth for suggesting the topic of the children's kitchen to me.

158 *Appendix to the Report of the Famine Commission, 1898, Vol. IV*, p. 21; Holderness, *Narrative of the Famine*, p. 29; Letter From L. K. Lawrie to the Chief Secretary to the Chief Commissioner, Central Provinces, March 11, 1897, in *Famine and Relief Operations in India. Further Papers Regarding the Famine and the Relief Operations in India during the Years 1896–97, No. III* (London: HMSO, 1897) (PP C. 8504), p. 72; Higham, Notes on an Inspection of Famine Relief Works in the Bombay Presidency, p. 430; *Report of the Indian Famine Commission, 1898*, p. 93.

159 Letter From J. A. Bourdillon to the Secretary to the Government of Bengal Revenue Department, May 11, 1897, in *Famine and Relief Operations in India: Further Papers 1896–97 No. IV*, p. 139.

160 Letter from A. D. Younghusband to the Chief Secretary to the Chief Commissioner, Central Provinces, August 8, 1900, in *East India (Famine), 1900–1902, Vol. I*, p. 123.

161 *Narrative and Results of the Measures Adopted for the Relief of Famine during the Years 1896 and 1897*, pp. 90–1.

162 Letter From M. W. Fox-Strangways to the Deputy Secretary to the Government of India, Revenue and Agricultural Department (Famine), September 17, 1897, in *Famine and Relief Operations in India: Further Papers, 1897–98, No. VII*, p. 138.

163 Letter From Governor-General to Secretary of State, September 5, 1877, p. 174; Mysore Famine Code, 1877 p. 239; Digby, *Famine Campaign*, Vol. I, p. 138; *Report of the Indian Famine Commission, 1880 (Appendix Part IV)*, p. 234; Madras Famine Code, 1883, p. 13; Bengal Famine Code, 1892 BL IOR/V/27/831/9, p. 16.

164 Quoted in Davis, *Late Victorian Holocausts*, p. 156.

165 Nash, *Great Famine*, p. 85; Forth, *Barbed-Wire Imperialism*, p. 68.

166 A. Croll, "Starving Strikers and the Limits of the 'Humanitarian Discovery of Hunger' in Late Victorian Britain," *International Review of Social History* 56(1) (2011), 103–31.

167 E. Ross, *Love and Toil: Motherhood in Outcast London* (Oxford: Oxford University Press, 1993); A. Davin, "Imperialism and Motherhood," *History Workshop Journal* 5(1) (1978), 9–66; D. Dwork, *War Is Good for Babies and Other Young Children: A History of the Infant and Child Welfare Movement in England, 1898–1918* (London: Tavistock, 1987).

168 A rich literature exists on these topics. For a few examples see L. Mani, *Contentious Traditions: The Debate on Sati in Colonial India* (Berkeley: University of California Press, 1998); P. Levine, *Prostitution, Race and Politics: Policing Venereal Disease in the British Empire* (London: Routledge, 2003); D. Ghosh, *Sex and the Family in Colonial India: The Making of Empire* (Cambridge: Cambridge University Press, 2006); S. Sen, "The Savage Family: Colonialism and Female Infanticide in Nineteenth-Century India," *Journal of Women's History* 14(3) (2002), 53–79; P. Anagol-McGinn, "The Age of Consent Act (1891) Reconsidered: Women's Perspectives and Participation in the Child Marriage Controversy in India," *South Asia Research* 12(2) (1992), 100–18; D. J. R. Grey, "Creating the 'Problem

Hindu': *Sati, Thuggee,* and Female Infanticide in India, 1800–1860," *Gender & History* 25(3) (2013), 498–510; A. Alam, "Polygyny, Family and Sharafat: Discourses Amongst North Indian Muslims, *c.* 1870–1918," *Modern Asian Studies* 45(3) (2011), 631–68.

169 Summary of the Remarks in the District Reports to Accompany Monthly Famine Statements A and B for the Month of September 1897 in *Famine and Relief Operations in India: Further Papers, 1897–98 No. VII*, p. 184. For the term units see Letter from J. A. Bourdillon to the Secretary, p. 139; *Report of the Indian Famine Commission, 1898*, p. 214; *Appendix to the Report of the Famine Commission, 1898, Vol. VI*, p. 23.

170 For one example of this statement that appears in all the famine codes see Central Provinces Famine Code, 1896, BL IOR/V/27/831/34, p. 31.

171 *Appendix to the Report of the Famine Commission, 1898, Vol. III*, pp. 23–4.

172 *Appendix to the Report of the Famine Commission, 1898, Vol. V*, pp. 13, 123, 134, 141, 177, 207; *Appendix to the Report of the Famine Commission, 1898, Vol. IV*, pp. 255, 285; Holderness, *Narrative of the Famine*, p. 43.

173 *Appendix to the Report of the Famine Commission, 1898, Vol. IV*, p. 139; *Appendix to the Report of the Famine Commission, 1898, Vol. V*, p. 80; *Appendix to the Report of the Famine Commission, 1898, Vol. V*, p. 99.

174 *Appendix to the Report of the Famine Commission, 1898, Vol. II*, p. 178.

175 Holderness, *Narrative of the Famine*, p. 29.

176 *Narrative and Results of the Measures Adopted for the Relief of Famine during the Years 1896 and 1897*, p. 43.

177 Mysore Famine Code, 1896, p. 26, BL IOR/V/27/831/50.

178 North-West Provinces and Oudh Famine Code, 1895, pp. xvii, xxxi; *Appendix to the Report of the Famine Commission, 1898, Vol. II*, pp. 30, 33; *Appendix to the Report of the Famine Commission, 1898, Vol. IV*, p. 266.

179 North-West Provinces and Oudh Famine Code, 1895, p. xxxviii; Punjab Famine Code, 1896, Article No. 25, BL IOR/V/27/831/52.

180 T. W. Laqueur, "Bodies, Details, and the Humanitarian Narrative" in L. Hunt (ed.), *The New Cultural History* (Berkeley: University of California Press, 1989), pp. 176–204; K. Halttunen, "Humanitarianism and the Pornography of Pain in Anglo-American Culture," *American Historical Review* 100(2) (1995), 303–34.

181 *Appendix to the Report of the Famine Commission, 1898, Vol. V*, p. 9.

182 T. Higham, Notes of an Inspection of Famine Relief Works in the North-Western Provinces and Oudh in *Famine and Relief Operations in India: Further Papers, 1897–98 No. VII*, p. 263; Summary of the Remarks in the District Reports Accompanying Monthly Famine Statements A and B for the Month of January 1900 in *East India (Famine), 1899–1900, Vol. I*, p. 113.

183 *Appendix to the Report of the Famine Commission, 1898, Vol. V*, pp. 31, 56.

184 *Appendix to the Report of the Famine Commission, 1898, Vol. III*, p. 69.

185 *Appendix to the Report of the Famine Commission, 1898, Vol. IV*, pp. 4, 129–31, 139; *Report of the East India Famine Commission, 1901*, p. 41.

186 Digby, *Famine Campaign*, Vol. II, p. 285.

187 *Appendix to the Report of the Famine Commission, 1898, Vol. V*, p. 56; Holderness, *Narrative of the Famine*, p. 29; *Narrative and Results of the Measures Adopted for the Relief of Famine during the Years 1896 and 1897*, p. 91.

188 *Narrative and Results of the Measures Adopted for the Relief of Famine during the Years 1896 and 1897*, p. 38.
189 *Appendix to the Report of the Famine Commission, 1898, Vol. IV*, p. 95.
190 *Appendix to the Report of the Famine Commission, 1898, Vol. V*, p. 31.
191 *Appendix to the Report of the Famine Commission, 1898, Vol. IV*, pp. 118–19, 136, 139; *Appendix to the Report of the Famine Commission, 1898, Vol. V*, p. 56.
192 *Report of the Indian Famine Commission, 1898*, p. 286.
193 *Narrative and Results of the Measures Adopted for the Relief of Famine during the Years 1896 and 1897*, p. 38.
194 Holderness, *Narrative of the Famine*, p. 39.
195 Davin, "Imperialism and Motherhood."
196 *Report of the Indian Famine Commission, 1898*, p. 234.
197 J. Coveney, *Food, Morals and Meaning: The Pleasure and Anxiety of Eating* (London: Routledge, 2000), p. 78.
198 *Appendix to the Report of the Famine Commission, 1898, Vol. IV*, p. 266.
199 Summary of the Remarks in the District Reports to Accompany Monthly Famine Statements A and B for the Month of September 1897 in *Famine and Relief Operations in India: Further Papers, 1897–98, No. VII*, p. 184.
200 Nally, *Human Encumbrances*, p. 14.

Chapter 4

1 Forth, *Barbed-Wire Imperialism*.
2 H. Jones, *Violence against Prisoners of War in the First World War* (Cambridge: Cambridge University Press, 2011); P. Panayi, *Prisoners of Britain* (Manchester: Manchester University Press, 2012); A. Rachamimov, *POWs and the Great War: Captivity on the Eastern Front* (Oxford: Berg, 2002); M. Stibbe, *British Civilian Internees in Germany: The Ruhleben Camp, 1914–1918* (Manchester: Manchester University Press, 2008); B. K. Feltman, *The Stigma of Surrender: German Prisoners, British Captors, and Manhood in the Great War and Beyond* (Chapel Hill: University of North Carolina Press, 2015); M. Murphy, *Colonial Captivity during the First World War: Internment and the Fall of the German Empire, 1914–1919* (Cambridge: Cambridge University Press, 2017); O. Wilkinson, *British Prisoners of War in First World War Germany* (Cambridge: Cambridge University Press, 2017); A. Becker, "Captive Civilians" in J. Winter (ed.), *The Cambridge History of the First World War*, Vol. III (Cambridge: Cambridge University Press, 2014), pp. 257–81.
3 J. de Bloch, *The Future of War* (Boston: World Peace Foundation, [1899]1914), p. xvii.
4 B. J. Davis, *Home Fires Burning: Food, Politics, and Everyday Life in World War I Berlin* (Durham: University of North Carolina Press, 2000); Weinreb, *Modern Hungers*, pp. 13–39; A. Offer, *The First World War: An Agrarian Interpretation* (Oxford: Clarendon Press, 1989), p. 1; T. Proctor, *Civilians in a World at War, 1914–1918* (New York: New York University Press, 2010), p. 3; M. Richardson, *The Hunger War: Food, Rations and Rationing, 1914–1918* (Barnsley: Pen & Sword, 2015); H. Z. Veit, *Modern Food, Moral Food: Self-Control, Science, and the Rise of Modern American Eating*

in the Early Twentieth Century (Chapel Hill: University of North Carolina Press, 2013); Helstosky, *Garlic and Oil*, pp. 39–51.

5 C. Otter, *Diet for a Large Planet: Food Systems, World-Ecology, and the Making of Industrial Britain* (Chicago: University of Chicago Press, forthcoming); Y. Segers, "Food Systems in the Nineteenth Century" in Bruegel (ed.), *A Cultural History of Food*, pp. 49–66.

6 A. Kramer, "Blockade and Economic Warfare" in J. Winter (ed.), *Cambridge History of the First World War*, Vol. II (Cambridge: Cambridge University Press, 2014), pp. 473–5.

7 Davis, *Home Fires Burning*, pp. 219–36; Weinreb, *Modern Hungers*, p. 22.

8 Offer, *First World War*, p. 77; Otter, *Diet for a Large Planet*.

9 Burnett, *Plenty and Want*, p. 289; J. M. Winter, *The Great War and the British People*, 2nd ed. (Houndmills: Palgrave Macmillan, 2003); for the complexities of this see C. F. Helstosky, "The State, Health, and Nutrition" in K. F. Kiple and K. C. Ornelas (eds.), *The Cambridge World History of Food*, Vol. II (Cambridge: Cambridge University Press, 2000), pp. 1577–85.

10 G. B. Shaw, *The Complete Prefaces of Bernard Shaw* (London: Paul Hamlyn, 1965), p. 496. Thanks to Chris Otter for alerting me to this quote.

11 Weinreb, *Modern Hungers*, p. 16; V. Kellogg and A. E. Taylor, *The Food Problem* (New York: Macmillan, 1918), p. 92; C. P. Vincent, *The Politics of Hunger: The Allied Blockade of Germany, 1915–1919* (Athens: Ohio University Press, 1985), p. 20; Wilkinson, *British Prisoners of War*, p. 108; Offer, *First World War*, p. 77; Kramer, "Blockade and Economic Warfare," pp. 46–89.

12 Davis, *Home Fires Burning*.

13 Wilkinson, *British Prisoners of War*.

14 Stibbe, *British Civilian Internees*.

15 H. Jones, "A Missing Paradigm?: Military Captivity and the Prisoner of War, 1914–1918," *Immigrants & Minorities* 26(1–2) (2008), 19–48; A. Deperchin, "The Laws of War" in J. Winter (ed.), *Cambridge History of the First World War*, Vol. I (Cambridge: Cambridge University Press, 2014), pp. 615–38.

16 Wilkinson, *British Prisoners of War*, pp. 25, 65; Hansard HL Deb 31 May 1916, vol. 22 cc. 249–68; Hansard HL Deb 15 March 1915, vol. 18 cc. 745–58; I. V. Hull, *Absolute Destruction: Military Culture and the Practices of War in Imperial Germany* (Ithaca: Cornell University Press, 2005), p. 321.

17 J. W. Gerard, *My Four Years in Germany* (New York: George H. Doran, 1917), p. 162; Wilkinson, *British Prisoners of War*, pp. 47–9.

18 Military Postal Service Decree No. 42, Postal Communication to and from Prisoners of War, September 28, 1914 [Translation], TNA FO 383/19; General Post Office. Communication With Prisoners of War Interned Abroad. Postmasters No. 559, 1915, TNA FO 383/20.

19 Press Bureau. January, 1918, Serial No. O. 6359, TNA FO 383/468.

20 Note Verbale, August 30, 1915, TNA FO 383/20; Sir Bertram Blakiston Cubitt [hereafter Cubitt] to Under-Secretary of State for Foreign Affairs [hereafter USSFA], October 10, 1915, TNA FO 383/20.

21 Letter from Camilla Picton-Warlow [hereafter Picton-Warlow] to Lady Rumbold, May 21, 1915, TNA FO 383/42.

22 Letter from W. J. Thomas to USSFA, July 31, 1916, TNA FO 383/206.

23 Letter from P. D. Agnew [hereafter Agnew] to Manager, American Express, October 12, 1917, TNA FO 383/314.

24 Note Verbale, July 27, 1917, TNA FO 383/300; N. Durbach, "The Parcel Is Political: The British Government and the Regulation of Food Parcels for Prisoners of War, 1914–1918," *First World War Studies* 9(1) (2018), 93–110.

25 Jones, "A Missing Paradigm?" p. 36.

26 R. Van Emden, *Prisoners of the Kaiser: The Last POWs of the Great War* (Barnsley: Leo Cooper, 2000), pp. 113–26; M. Moynihan (ed.), *Black Bread and Barbed Wire: Prisoners in the First World War* (London: Leo Cooper, 1978), pp. xiii–xiv, 142.

27 Letter from James W. Gerard [hereafter Gerard] to Walter Hines Page [hereafter Page], November 8, 1915 and Report by Mr. Osborne on Stendal, November 9, 1915, TNA FO 383/44; Geoffrey Pyke, Report on the Note from His Excellency the American Ambassador in Berlin on the Conditions Existing at that Date (June 8th) in the Internment Camp at Ruhleben, TNA FO 383/68; Letter from Louis Mallet to Lord Robert Cecil [hereafter Cecil], September 25, 1915, Mr. Stern, Comments on Mr. G. W. Minot's Report to Gerard, June 3, 1915, and Interview with Gustav Cohen, September 10, 1915, TNA FO 383/69; Ruhleben Camp, Communicated by Sir T. Eden, August 3, 1916, TNA FO 383/142; Extracts from Reports given by Frederick Short, TNA FO 383/300.

28 Letter to Page from Gerard, November 1, 1915 TNA FO 383/44.

29 Communication from Sir Charles Lucas, June 8, 1916, and Letter from Gerard to Page, June 28, 1916, TNA FO 383/141; *Miscellaneous No. 18 (1916). Report by Doctor A. E. Taylor on the Conditions of Diet and Nutrition in The Internment Camp at Ruhleben* (London: HMSO, 1916) (PP Cd. 8259), p. 3.

30 For the term "carceral archipelago" see Michel Foucault, *Discipline and Punish: The Birth of the Prison* (New York: Vintage, 1979), p. 297.

31 Minute from Lord Newton [hereafter Newton], July 11, 1916, TNA FO 383/141.

32 Letter from USSFA to Philip Witham, June 12, 1916, TNA FO 383/193.

33 Minutes by Sir Horace Rumbold [hereafter Rumbold] on Further Report by Alonzo Taylor [hereafter Taylor] on Food at Ruhleben, June 22, 1916, TNA FO 383/141; Hansard HC Deb June 26, 1916, vol. 83 cc. 538–40.

34 *Miscellaneous No. 21 (1916). Further Correspondence Respecting the Conditions of Diet and Nutrition in the Internment Camp at Ruhleben* (London: HMSO, 1916) (PP Cd. 8262), p. 3.

35 Note Verbale, Berlin, August 31, 1916, TNA FO 383/142.

36 Letter from B. W. Young [hereafter Young] to Rumbold, December 31, 1915, and Anonymous memo, January 10, 1916, TNA FO 383/151.

37 Letter to Cecil from Sir Herbert Belfield, June 22, 1916, TNA FO 383/141.

38 Letter from Cubitt to Secretary, POWD, November 22, 1916, TNA FO 383/160.

39 Wilkinson, *British Prisoners of War*, p. 109.

40 Ruhleben Prisoners' Release Committee, The Ruhleben Prisoners: A Case for their Release, February 12, 1917, TNA FO 383/320.

41 Quoted in Van Emden, *Prisoners of the Kaiser*, p. 126.

42 A. Waugh, *The Prisoner of Mainz* (London: Chapman and Hall, 1919), pp. 118–19.

43 N. Durbach, "Comforts, Clubs, and the Casino: Food and the Perpetuation of the British Class System in First World War Civilian Internment Camps," *Journal of Social History* 53(2) (2019) 487–507.

44 Letter from A. Law to Secretary of the Admiralty, April 14, 1915, and Minute from E. G., March 31, 1915, TNA FO 383/40.

45 Draft Letter from Foreign Office to Sir F. Bertie and Sir G. Buchanan, April, 1915, TNA FO 383/40.

46 Jones, *Violence*, p. 264.

47 Minute by Rumbold re: Diet at Ruhleben, July 11, 1916, TNA FO 383/141.

48 J. D. Ketchum, *Ruhleben: A Prison Camp Society* (Toronto: University of Toronto Press, 1965), p. 163.

49 Helstosky, "The State, Health, and Nutrition," pp. 1580–2; Barry Supple, "War Economies" in J. Winter (ed.), *Cambridge History of the First World War*, Vol. II (Cambridge: Cambridge University Press, 2014), pp. 295–324.

50 E. M. H. Lloyd, *Experiments in State Control at the War Office and the Ministry of Food* (Oxford: Clarendon Press, 1924).

51 J. Harris, "Bureaucrats and Businessmen in British Food Control, 1916– 19" in K. Burk (ed.), *War and the State: The Transformation of British Government, 1914–1919* (London: George Allen & Unwin, 1982), pp. 135–56; L. M. Barnett, *British Food Policy during the First World War* (Boston: George Allen & Unwin, 1985), pp. 94–124.

52 D. French, "The Rise and Fall of 'Business as Usual,'" in K. Burk (ed.), *War and the State* (London: George Allen & Unwin, 1982), pp. 7–31.

53 F. Trentmann, *Free Trade Nation* (Oxford: Oxford University Press, 2008), pp. 18, 192–3.

54 A. Gregory, *The Last Great War: British Society and the First World War* (Cambridge: Cambridge University Press, 2008), pp. 213–16; Trentmann, *Free Trade Nation*, pp. 195–9.

55 Barnett, *British Food Policy*, p. 216.

56 N. Gullace, *"The Blood of Our Sons": Men, Women, and the Renegotiation of British Citizenship during the Great War* (Houndmills: Palgrave, 2002).

57 Francis Gribble, The Conditions at Ruhleben, TNA FO 383/69.

58 Letter to Neil Primrose from R. Meade, March 22, 1915, Letter from Gerard to Page forwarded to Sir Edward Grey [hereafter Grey], March 25, 1915, Letter to Page from Grey, March 20, 1915, and Minute from E.G. to Y.E., April, 1915, TNA FO 383/40; Letter from Young to Rumbold, December 31, 1915, and Anonymous memo, January 10, 1916, TNA FO 383/151.

59 Gerard, *My Four Years*, p. 179; Minutes of a Conference Held at the Prisoners of War Department January 2 to Discuss Compensation of British POWs and Interned Civilians, TNA FO 383/542; Hansard HC Deb 5 March 1917, vol. 91 cc. 32–3.

60 Letter from Page to Grey, March 17, 1915, and Letter from Page to Grey, March 23, 1915, TNA FO 383/40; Letter from Secretary of State for Foreign Affairs [hereafter SSFA] to US Ambassador, September 9, 1915, TNA FO 383/44; Hansard HC Deb March 10, 1915, vol. 70 cc. 1518–31; Letter from Gerard to Page, October 16, 1915, TNA FO 383/69; Ketchum, *Ruhleben*, p. 121; Hansard HL Deb July 11, 1916, vol. 22 cc. 608–9.

61 Durbach, "The Parcel Is Political."

62 C. Hoffman, *In the Prison Camps of Germany* (New York: Association Press, 1920), p. 73.

63 Hansard HL Deb July 5, 1916, vol. 22 cc. 578–96; Report on the Directorate of Prisoners of War, 1920, pp. 5–6, TNA HO 45/11025/410118; P. Panayi, *The Enemy in Our Midst: Germans in Britain during the First World War* (Oxford: Berg, 1991), pp. 83–4; N. Durbach, "The Politics of Provisioning: Feeding South Asian Prisoners during the First World War," *War & Society* 37(2) (2018), 75–90.

64 J. C. Drummond and A. Wilbraham, *The Englishman's Food: Five Centuries of English Diet*, rev. ed. (London: Pimlico, 1991), p. 431.

65 [Report on Internment Camps in the UK by Repatriated Austro-Hungarian], November 12, 1917, TNA FO 383/359.

66 D. Simmons, "Starvation Science: From Colonies to Metropole" in A. Nützenadel and F. Trentmann (eds.), *Food and Globalization: Consumption, Markets and Politics in the Modern World* (Oxford: Berg, 2008), p. 174.

67 Letter from John Pedder to the Secretary, POWD, August 13, 1917, TNA FO 383/247; Minute by John Pedder, June 29, 1918, and Letter from Arthur Friedel to Swedish Legation, February 28, 1918, TNA HO 45/10835/329066; Minutes of the Second Conference, February 14, 1917, TNA FO 383/295; Cullather, "Foreign Policy of the Calorie"; Vernon, *Hunger*, pp. 83–91.

68 M. Teich, "Science and Food during the Great War: Britain and Germany" in H. Kamminga and A. Cunningham (eds.), *Science and Culture of Nutrition, 1840–1940* (Amsterdam: Rodopi, 1995), p. 229; Barnett, *British Food Policy*, pp. 97–8, 217; D. F. Smith, "Nutrition Science and the Two World Wars" in D. F. Smith (ed.), *Nutrition in Britain: Science, Scientists and Politics in the Twentieth Century* (London: Routledge, 1997), pp. 142–9.

69 Vernon, *Hunger*, p. 44.

70 Minute from H.B.S., December 6, 1900, TNA HO 45/10037/A60059.

71 Letter from SSFA to Swedish Minister, June 12, 1918, TNA FO 383/360.

72 F. Schwyzer to M. Gaston Carlin [hereafter Carlin], Report on Hospital for Prisoners of War at Belmont, July 26, 1917, and A. L. Vischer to Carlin, Report on Knockaloe, November 29, 1917, TNA FO 383/277.

73 War Prisoners' Rations. The Revised Scale, TNA FO 383/360.

74 Letter from SSFA to Swedish Minister, May 18, 1918, TNA HO 45/10835/329066; Letter to Secretary, POWD from Edward Troup, October 11, 1918, TNA FO 383/360.

75 Minute from J.P., June 18, 1918, TNA HO 45/10835/329066; Memorandum on the Swiss Legation Reports on Douglas and Knockaloe, TNA HO 45/10947/266042.

76 R. W. Branthwaite to Sir William Byrne, Douglas Camp Visited September 30, 1916, TNA HO 45/10946/266042.

77 Minutes of a Conference Held at the War Office February 8, 1917 to Consider the Question of Rations for Prisoners of War, and Parcels of Food Received by Prisoners of War from Friends in the United Kingdom in View of the Recent Recommendations of the Food Controller, TNA FO 383/295.

78 F. Schwyzer to Carlin, Report on Prisoners of War Camp at Leigh, October 10, 1917, TNA FO 383/277.

79 Letter to Secretary, POWD from Cubitt, February 28, 1918, TNA FO 383/432.

80 J. C. Bird, *Control of Enemy Alien Civilians in Great Britain, 1914–1918* (New York: Garland, 1986), pp. 149, 161; P. Cohen-Portheim, *Time Stood Still: My Internment in England, 1914–1918* (New York: E. P. Dutton & Co., 1932), p. 74; Barnett, *British Food Policy*, p. 117; Minutes on Rations for Prisoners Engaged in Heavy Manual Work, June 21, 1918, TNA NATS 1/570.

81 Reply to Statement of Complaints Transmitted with Note Verbale, November 12, 1917, TNA FO 383/432; Report to Page from Taylor on the Diet of the Prisoner of War Camp at Dorchester, August 20–26, September 23, 1916, and Report to Page from Taylor on the Diet of the Prisoner of War Camp at Knockaloe, August 31–September 6, 1916, September 28, 1916, TNA FO 383/164; Minute from Owen Monk to Robert Vansittart [hereafter Vansittart], September 12, 1916, TNA FO 383/157.

82 Statement Concerning the Principles Observed in the Housing, Feeding, and Clothing as well as the Postal Traffic, of Officers and Men held Prisoners of War in Germany, February 28, 1915, TNA FO 383/40.

83 Letter from Cecil to Gerard, November 27, 1915, TNA FO 383/45.

84 Letter to Cecil from Gerard, December 7, 1915, Report from B. W. Caldwell [hereafter Caldwell] to Gerard, November 21, 1915, and Report from Caldwell to Gerard, November 29, 1915, TNA FO 383/45.

85 Letter to Rumbold from C. P. Lucas, August 25, 1916, TNA FO 383/142.

86 Statement Concerning the Principles Observed in the Housing, Feeding, and Clothing as well as the Postal Traffic, of Officers and Men held Prisoners of War in Germany, February 28, 1915, TNA FO 383/40.

87 Note Verbale, Berlin, April 11, 1918, TNA FO 383/432.

88 Memorandum by the Prisoners of War Department on the Question of Reducing the Food Rations Despatched to Prisoners of War in Germany, [March 20, 1917], TNA FO 383/354.

89 Cullather, "Foreign Policy of the Calorie," pp. 340–44; Vernon, *Hunger*, pp. 81–117; R. Duffett, *The Stomach for Fighting: Food and the Soldiers of the Great War* (Manchester: Manchester University Press, 2012), p. 35; Offer, *First World War*, p. 41.

90 Biltekoff, *Eating Right in America*, p. 15.

91 Scale of Daily Rations Per Man [for Austro-Hungarian Civilian POWs at Oldcastle], TNA FO 383/247; A. Rabinbach, *The Human Motor: Energy, Fatigue, and the Origins of Modernity* (Berkeley: University of California Press, 1990), p. 263.

92 Duffett, *Stomach for Fighting*, p. 30; U. Thoms, "The Innovative Power of War: The Army, Food Sciences and the Food Industry in Germany in the Twentieth Century" in R. Duffett, I. Zweiniger-Bargielowska, and A. Drouard (eds.), *Food and War in Twentieth Century Europe* (Farnham: Ashgate, 2011), pp. 247–62; Vernon, *Hunger*, p. 90.

93 For some examples see Letter from Albert H. Michelson to Gerard, May 4, 1915, TNA FO 383/42; Letter from Sir Timothy Eden to Mrs. Cottrell Dormer, December 22, 1916, TNA FO 383/312; Letter from Annie Struckmeyer to POWD, June 10, 1917, TNA FO 383/313; Report to Page from Taylor on the Diet of the Prisoner of War Camp at Dorchester, August 20–26, September 23, 1916, TNA FO 383/164.

94 For some examples see Reports by Mr. Jackson on Visits to Detention Camps, August 26, 1915, TNA FO 383/44; Letter from Netherland Legation at Berlin (British Section) to British Legation at the Hague, October 10, 1917, TNA FO 383/314; Leland H. Littlefield, Boylston A. Beal, and W. H. Buckler, Report of Inspection of POW Internment Camp at Knockaloe, April 29–May 1, 1916, TNA FO 383/163; Francis E. Brantingham to Irwin Laughlin, Report of the Visit of Inspection to the Place of Internment for Prisoners of War at Leigh, September 8, 1916, TNA FO 383/164; John B. Jackson, Report on Visit to Detention Camp at Furstenberg i/Mecklenburg, August 22, 1916, TNA FO 383/158.

95 Letter from George H. Murphy to the Governor General of the Union of South Africa, May 27, 1916, TNA FO 383/163.

96 Standing Committee on Medical and Nutritional Problems. Welfare Foods Concentrated Orange Juice. Memorandum by the Ministry of Food on Supply and Distribution, TNA FD 1/2386; Davis, *Home Fires Burning*, p. 49.

97 *Misc. No. 18*, pp. 3–4.

98 Letter from Taylor to Gerard, July 26, 1916, TNA FO 383/157; Knockaloe and Douglas Detention Camps Dietary, July 23, 1917, TNA FO 383/247; Drummond and Wilbraham, *Englishman's Food*, p. 439.

99 Robert Dolbey, A Report on the Medical Conditions of the Prisoners of War at Sennelager bei Paderborn from December 12, 1914, to March 6, 1915, July 20, 1915, TNA FO 383/44; Report on the Conditions of the Camp for Prisoners of War at Sennelager during the First Eight Months of the War, TNA FO 383/155; E. M. Middleton, Statement Regarding Condition of British Soldiers Prisoners in Germany, July 16, 1915, TNA FO 383/43.

100 W. R. Cornish, *Observations on the Nature of the Food of the Inhabitants of Southern India and on Prison Dietaries in the Madras Presidency* (Madras: Gantz Brothers, 1864), pp. 36–7; Report by Captain Middleton, August 10, 1915, TNA FO 383/43.

101 J. L. Notter and R. H. Firth, *The Theory and Practice of Hygiene*, 3rd ed. (London: J & A Churchill, 1908), p. 233.

102 Notter and Firth, *Theory and Practice*, p. 240; Extract from the *Journal Officiel*, October 21, 1915, TNA FO 383/44; Letter from Charles Walker to Secretary, POWD, September 18, 1918, TNA FO 383/443; *Misc. No. 18*, pp. 3–4; R. W. Branthwaite to Sir William Byrne, Douglas Camp Visited September 30, 1916, TNA HO 45/10946/266042.

103 Letter to Cecil from Gerard, December 7, 1915, Report from Caldwell to Gerard, November 21, 1915, and Report from Caldwell to Gerard, November 29, 1915, TNA FO 383/45.

104 *Misc. No. 21*, p. 2.; Vincent, *Politics of Hunger*, p. 128.

105 Draft letter to Netherlands Legation at Berlin from POWD, April, 1918, TNA FO 383/390.

106 Letter from Cubitt to Secretary, POWD, March 19, 1918, TNA FO 383/389.

107 Letter from Charles Walker to Secretary, POWD, September 18, 1918, TNA FO 383/443.

108 Notter and Firth, *Theory and Practice*, pp. 237–8.

109 Letter from Cubitt to Secretary, POWD, March 19, 1918, TNA FO 383/389; P. Lummel, "Food Provisioning in the German Army of the First World War" in R. Duffet, I. Zweiniger-Bargielowska, and A. Drouard (eds.), *Food and War in Twentieth Century Europe* (Farnham: Ashgate, 2011), p. 20.

110 *Prison Commission for Scotland*, p. 130.

111 Barnett, *British Food Policy*, p. 148.

112 Cullather, "Foreign Policy of the Calorie," p. 338.

113 Arthur W. May, Memorandum, July 29, 1916, TNA FO 383/142.

114 *Misc. No. 18*, p. 5.

115 *Misc. No. 18*, pp. 3–4, 10–12; Gerard, *My Four Years*, p. 184.

116 *Misc. No. 18*, pp. 8–12.

117 *Misc. No. 18*, pp. 5–6; Letter from Taylor to Gerard, June 20, 1916, TNA FO 383/141.

118 Hoffman, *In the Prison Camps*, p. 70.

119 Jones, "A Missing Paradigm?" p. 36; Wilkinson, *British Prisoners of War*, pp. 105–12.

120 Letter from Taylor to Gerard, June 20, 1916, TNA FO 383/141.

121 Hansard HL Deb July 5, 1916, vol. 22 cc. 578–96.

122 Letter from Cubitt to Secretary, POWD, March 19, 1918, TNA FO 383/389.

123 Cullather, "Foreign Policy of the Calorie," p. 338.

124 Hansard HC Deb February 19, 1917, vol. 90 cc. 981–2.

125 H. E. Belfield, "The Treatment of Prisoners of War," *Transactions of the Grotius Society* 9 (1923), 138; Lummel, "Food Provisioning in the German Army," p. 20.

126 An Agreement between the British and German Governments Concerning Combatant Prisoners of War and Civilians [June 1918], TNA FO 383/417; Belfield, "Treatment of Prisoners of War," p. 139.

127 Written Answers June 24, 1918, and Minute to John Pedder, June 18, 1918, TNA HO 45/10835/329066; Lummel, "Food Provisioning in the German Army," p. 15.

128 Davis, *Home Fires Burning*, p. 180.
129 Draft letter to Netherlands Legation at Berlin from POWD, April 1918, Letter from SSFA to Swiss Minister, May 11, 1918, and Letter to Cubitt from POWD, April 26, 1918, TNA FO 383/390; Burnett, *Plenty and Want*, p. 249.
130 Barnett, *British Food Policy*, p. 217.
131 *Misc. No. 18*, pp. 3–4.
132 Ellis Loring Dresel, Report on the Civilian Internment Camp for British Prisoners at Ruhleben, July 22, 1916, TNA FO 383/142.
133 Letter from USSFA to Philip Witham, June 12, 1916, and Draft Press Notice, Foreign Office, June, 1916 TNA FO 383/193.
134 C. Hamlin, "Could you Starve to Death in England in 1839?" *American Journal of Public Health* 85(6) (1995), 856–66.
135 *Miscellaneous No. 19 (1915). Correspondence with the United States Ambassador Respecting the Treatment of British Prisoners of War and Interned Civilians in Germany* (London: HMSO, 1915) (PP Cd. 8108), p. 52; D. J. McCarthy, *The Prisoner of War in Germany: The Care and Treatment of the Prisoner of War with History of the Development of the Principle of Neutral Inspection and Control* (New York: Moffat, Yard and Company, 1918), p. 35; Taylor and Daniel J. McCarthy [hereafter McCarthy], Report on Visit to Detention Camp at Wahn, July 11, 1916, and Letter from Taylor to Gerard, July 28, 1916, TNA FO 383/157.
136 Letter to Agnew from G. R. Warner, February 16, 1917, TNA FO 383/295.
137 Hansard HL Deb May 31, 1916, vol. 22 cc. 249–68; Newspaper clipping enclosed in Letter to Newton from Edith Grant Duff, June 6, 1916, TNA FO 383/193.
138 Durbach, "The Parcel Is Political"; Wilkinson, *British Prisoners of War*, pp. 247–8; Feltman, *Stigma of Surrender*, pp. 79–80; Ketchum, *Ruhleben*, pp. 158, 309, 359.
139 Letter to Page from Gerard, July 10, 1915, TNA FO 383/43; Wilkinson, *British Prisoners of War*, p. 107.
140 Report of an Inspection at the Detention Camp at Hameln by Taylor and McCarthy on May 20, 1916, and Report by McCarthy and Taylor [on the camp at Schneidemuhl, June 2, 1916], TNA FO 383/155; Taylor, Ration Adapted for British P.O.W. – Germany, enclosed in Letter to G. R. Warner from W. H. Buckler, September 18, 1916, TNA FO 383/158; *Miscellaneous No. 26 (1916) Further Correspondence with the United States Ambassador Respecting the Treatment of British Prisoners of War and Interned Civilians in Germany* (London: HMSO, 1916) (PP Cd. 8297), p. 34.
141 Report by Mr. Osborne on Visit to Detention Camp at Stendal, November 9, 1915, TNA FO 383/44; Draft Suggestions Regarding the Action to be Taken by the Government, September 19, 1916, TNA FO 383/243.
142 Letter from Arthur Dodd to Cooper and Co., June 15, 1916, TNA FO 383/206; Extracts from Reports Given by Capt M. C. C. Harrison, TNA FO 383/300; Report by McCarthy and Taylor [on the camp at Schneidemuhl, June 2, 1916], TNA FO 383/155; Ketchum, *Ruhleben*, p. 160; Stibbe, *British Civilian Internees*, p. 69; Wilkinson, *British Prisoners of War*, p. 129.

143 Statement Concerning the Principles Observed in the Housing, Feeding, and Clothing as well as the Postal Traffic, of Officers and Men Held Prisoners of War in Germany, February 28, 1915, TNA FO 393/40; Report by the German Military Authorities in Reply to the Enquiries of the British Government About the Treatment of Prisoners, Officers and Men, in Germany, [July 1915], TNA FO 383/43.

144 Letter from Gerard to Page, April 9, 1915, TNA FO 393/40.

145 Letter from John B. Jackson to Grey, March 31, 1915, TNA FO 393/40.

146 *Misc. No. 19*, p. 56; Interviews with Privates Returned from Limburg, c. November, 1915, TNA FO 383/44; Letter from Gerard to Page, April 9, 1915, TNA FO 393/40.

147 Report Given by Lieut. Gerald Featherstone Knight, September 16, 1917, TNA FO 383/272.

148 *Misc. No. 18*, p. 6.

149 P. Rozin, "The Psychology of Food and Food Choice" in K. F. Kiple and K. C. Ornelas (eds.), *Cambridge World History of Food*, Vol. II (Cambridge: Cambridge University Press, 2000), p. 1479.

150 "The Treatment of Prisoners of War," *British Medical Journal*, January 23, 1915, p. 172.

151 Extracts from Manuscript book "From Within the Barbed-Wire Enclosure" by Jeno Herczy, March 15, 1916, TNA HO 45/10946/266042. Emphasis in original.

152 *British Medical Journal*, January 23, 1915, p. 172.

153 Report to Page from Taylor on the Diet of the Prisoner of War Camp at Dorchester, August 20–26, September 23, 1916, TNA FO 383/164; Letter from Assistant Director of Army Contracts to Under-Secretary of State for the Home Office, August 14, 1917, and Letter from H. Barlow for Director of Army Contacts to Under-Secretary of State for the Home Office, June 25, 1917, TNA HO 45/10835/329066.

154 Letter from Boylston A. Beal to Page, March 13, 1916 in *Miscellaneous No. 30 (1916). Reports of Visits of Inspection Made by Officials of the United States Embassy to Various Internment Camps in the United Kingdom* (London: HMSO, 1916) (PP Cd. 8324).

155 Report to Page from Taylor on the Diet of the Prisoner of War Camp at Dorchester, August 20–26, September 23, 1916, TNA FO 383/164.

156 Panayi, *Enemy in Our Midst*, p. 114; H. Teuteberg, "Food Provisioning on the German Home Front, 1914–1918" in R. Duffet, I. Zweiniger-Bargielowska, and A. Drouard (eds.), *Food and War in Twentieth Century Europe* (Farnham: Ashgate, 2011), p. 66; A. Drouard, "Horsemeat in France" in R. Duffet, I. Zweiniger-Bargielowska, and A. Drouard (eds.), *Food and War in Twentieth Century Europe* (Farnham: Ashgate, 2011), pp. 233–46.

157 Letter from Vansittart to Secretary to Army Council, June 28, 1918, and Letter from Newton to Carlin, August 7, 1918, TNA FO 383/432.

158 Letter from Vansittart to Secretary to Army Council, June 28, 1918, TNA FO 383/432.

159 Notter and Firth, *Theory and Practice*, p. 235.

160 Duffett, *Stomach for Fighting*, p. 146.

161 Confidential Report from A. M. D. Hughes, May, 1915, TNA FO 383/42; Letter to Mansfeldt de C. Findlay from H. Yarde Buller, February 5, 1918, TNA FO 383/449.
162 *Misc. No. 18*, p. 6.
163 Ross, *Love and Toil*, pp. 27–55.
164 Grimsby Fishermen in Germany, Statement by William Savory, June 8, 1916, TNA FO 383/156.
165 Davis, *Home Fires Burning*, pp. 65–70.
166 Edward Vicars, Report on the Treatment of Prisoners in Germany, March 31, 1915, TNA FO 393/40; Ketchum, *Ruhleben*, pp. 324–5; Report on Inspection of Soltau, August 31, 1917, TNA FO 383/272; Quoted in Van Emden, *Prisoners of the Kaiser*, p. 195; Letter from Page to Cecil, October 29, 1915, TNA FO 383/44; Extracts from Reports Given by Captain John A. Mott, TNA FO 383/300; Report on the Conditions of the Camp for Prisoners of War at Doeberitz during the First Eight Months of the War, Appendix E. 2, TNA FO 383/155; Letter from Charles J. King to the Editor of the *Morning Post*, May 25, 1916, TNA FO 383/141.
167 Letter to the Camp Commandant from W. G. A. Kennedy, December 15, 1915, TNA FO 383/212; Letter to Mansfeldt de C. Findlay from H. Yarde Buller, February 5, 1918, TNA FO 383/449.
168 Letter from W. G. A. Kennedy to the British Legation, Christiania, January 7, 1918, TNA FO 383/449.
169 Letter to Mansfeldt de C. Findlay from H. Yarde Buller, February 5, 1918, TNA FO 383/449; Knockaloe and Douglas Detention Camps Dietary, April 13, 1917, TNA HO 45/10835/329066; Proctor, *Civilians*, p. 225; Report of the Directorate of Prisoners of War, p. 15.
170 Draft Letter to the Secretary, Army Council from Vansittart, August, 1918, TNA FO 383/443.
171 Letter from J. R. Brooke to Secretary, POWD, July 30, 1918, TNA FO 383/443; Duffett, *Stomach for Fighting*, p. 92.
172 *Miscellaneous No. 15 (1915). Further Correspondence With the United States Ambassador Respecting the Treatment of British Prisoners of War and Interned Civilians in Germany* (London: HMSO, 1915) (PP Cd. 7961), p. 15.
173 Letter from Angus Watson and Co. to A. Ryan, July 13, 1917, TNA FO 383/300.
174 Letter from the Assistant Director of Army Contracts to the Secretary, POWD, July 14, 1917, TNA FO 383/300.
175 Duffett, *Stomach for Fighting*, pp. 47–8; Burnett, *Plenty and Want*, p. 121; C. Otter, "Liberty and Ecology: Resources, Markets, and the British Contribution to the Global Environmental Crisis" in S. Gunn and J. Vernon (eds.), *The Peculiarities of Liberal Modernity in Imperial Britain* (Berkeley: University of California Press, 2011), pp. 191–2.
176 Ella Scarlett Synge, Report of Inspection of Wittenberg Prisoners of War Camp, December 17, 1915, TNA FO 383/153; K. Jensen, "Volunteers, Auxiliaries, and Women's Mobilization: The First World War and Beyond (1914–1939)" in B. C. Hacker and M. Vining (eds.), *A Companion to Women's Military History* (Leiden: Brill, 2012), p. 195.

177 Interview with Alfred Wood, TNA FO 383/69; Extracts from Reports Given by Captain John A. Mott and Extracts from Reports Given by Pte. J. D. Harrison, TNA FO 383/300; Report on the Conditions of the Camp for Prisoners of War at Sennelager during the First Eight Months of the War, TNA FO 383/155; Evidence of Richard Edward Thompson, April 3, 1918, TNA FO 383/390; "Interned Civilians at Ruhleben. Restricted Food and Overcrowding. Infirm and Aged Prisoners," *The Times*, March 13, 1915, TNA FO 393/40; Vincent, *Politics of Hunger*, p. 127.

178 Letter from Arthur Keane to Capt. Donelan, July 25, 1916, TNA FO 383/142.

179 *Misc. No. 18*, p. 6.

180 *Misc. No. 26*, p. 32.

181 Letter from USSFA to Brecknell, Munro & Rogers, April 20, 1915, TNA FO 393/40; Teuteberg, "Food Provisioning," p. 63; Davis, *Home Fires Burning*, pp. 28–9.

182 Report on the Conditions of the Camp for Prisoners of War at Friedrichsfeld during the First Eight Months of the War, Appendix E, TNA FO 383/155.

183 Letter to Grey from Ernest B. Maxse, September 27, 1915, TNA FO 383/44.

184 Letter from Picton-Warlow to Cecil, June 27, 1916, TNA FO 383/141.

185 Report by McCarthy and Taylor [on the camp at Schneidemuhl, June 2, 1916], and Report on the Conditions of the Camp for Prisoners of War at Sennelager during the First Eight Months of the War, Appendix E.2, TNA FO 383/155; Trentmann, *Free Trade Nation*, p. 214.

186 Burnett, *Plenty and Want*, p. 253 n. 10.

187 K. Palmer, "Ruhleben Concentration Camp for British Civilian Prisoners of War," Imperial War Museum, London.

188 Ruhleben Prisoners' Release Committee, The Ruhleben Prisoners: A Case for Their Release, February 12, 1917, TNA FO 383/320; Letter to Robert P. Skinner, June 21, 1916, TNA FO 383/141.

189 H. P. Picot, *The British Interned in Switzerland* (London: Edward Arnold, 1919), pp. 57–9; E.G.D., The British Section of the Bureau de Secours aux Prisonniers de Guerre, December 31, 1915, TNA FO 383/45; Letter to Grey from Evelyn Grant Duff, October 19, 1915, TNA FO 383/44; Lord Northcliffe, "Berne. The Bread. Our Prisoners in Germany. Some of Their Views," *The Times*, August 31, 1916, TNA FO 383/349; Edith Grant Duff, British Section of the Bureau de Secours Aux Prisonniers De Guerre, July 26, 1916, TNA FO 383/157.

190 E.G.D., The British Section of the Bureau de Secours aux Prisonniers de Guerre, December 31, 1915, TNA FO 383/45; Letter to Grey from Evelyn Grant Duff, October 19, 1915, TNA FO 383/44.

191 Lord Northcliffe, "Berne. The Bread. Our Prisoners in Germany. Some of their Views," *The Times*, August 31, 1916, TNA FO 383/349; Ellis Loring Dresel, Report on the Civilian Internment Camp for British Prisoners at Ruhleben, July 22, 1916, TNA FO 383/142; Telegram from H.M. Minister in Berne, January 1, 1916, TNA FO 383/151; Edith Grant Duff, British Section of the Bureau de Secours Aux Prisonniers De Guerre, July 26, 1916, TNA FO 383/157.

192 Report of the British Section of the Bureau de Secours Aux Prisonniers de Guerre, December 10, 1916, TNA FO 383/354; Quoted in J. Yarnall, *Barbed Wire Disease: British and German Prisoners of War, 1914–19* (Stroud: The History Press, 2011), p. 112.

193 Letter from USSFA to Horace Cocker, June 1, 1916, TNA FO 383/192; Prisoners of War Help Committee, June 8, 1916, TNA FO 383/155; Letter to Picton-Warlow from Secretary, POWD, January 18, 1917, TNA FO 383/352; Supplementary Report Covering the Work Done by the British Section of the Bureau de Secours Aux Prisonniers de Guerre, January 1–June 1, 1917, TNA FO 383/354.

194 Picton-Warlow, Bread Fund for Prisoners of War, TNA FO 383/155.

195 Picton-Warlow, Circular Letter, undated, TNA FO 383/352.

196 Letter from Thora Deane to the British Legation, Copenhagen, May 24, 1915, and Letter to USSFA from Young, May 28, 1915, TNA FO 383/42.

197 Letter from Picton-Warlow to Cecil, June 27, 1916, TNA FO 383/141.

198 Letter to Newton from Edith Grant Duff, June 6, 1916, TNA FO 383/193.

199 Official Memorandum, CPOWC, June 13, 1917, TNA FO 383/313; Letter to Grey from Sir Ralph Paget [hereafter Paget], September 2, 1916, TNA FO 383/158; Letter from Agnew to the Secretary, POWD, February 22, 1917, TNA FO 383/349; Letter to the Secretary, War Office, from Agnew, June 9, 1917, and Letter to the Secretary, POWD, from Agnew, July 18, 1917, TNA FO 383/354; *Report of the Joint Committee to Inquire into the Organisation and Methods of the Central Prisoners of War Committee* (London: HMSO, 1917) (PP Cd. 8615), p. 7.

200 Letter from Agnew to the Secretary, POWD, February 22, 1917, TNA FO 383/349; Official Memorandum, CPOWC, June 13, 1917, TNA FO 383/313; Minutes of a Conference Held July 23, 1917 to Consider the Report of the Joint Committee on the CPOWC, TNA FO 383/352; Telegram from Paget to Secretary, CPOWC, April 4, 1917, Telegram from Paget to Sir Starr Jameson, April 17, 1917, Letter from Agnew to Secretary, POWD, June 14, 1917, Letter to the Secretary, War Office, from Agnew, June 9, 1917, Letter from Marcus Slade to Agnew, April 30, 1917, Letter to Marcus Slade, April 24, 1917, Letter from Secretary, POWD, to Secretary, CPOWC, June 23, 1917, Minute from Owen Monk, July 6, 1917, Telegram from Paget, July 12, 1917, Letter to the Secretary, POWD, from Agnew, July 18, 1917, Letter from Agnew to Secretary, POWD, May 3, 1917, and Translation of a Letter from Copenhagen Bakers to Mr. Abrahamson, July 26, 1917, TNA FO 383/354.

201 Minutes of a Conference Held July 23, 1917 to Consider the Report of the Joint Committee on the CPOWC, TNA FO 383/352; Lord Northcliffe, "Berne. The Bread. Our Prisoners in Germany. Some of Their Views," *The Times*, August 31, 1916, TNA FO 383/349.

202 Letter from Agnew to the Secretary, War Office, August 31, 1917, Letter from Secretary, POWD to Secretary, CPOWC, September 10, 1917, and Letter from J. Corcoran to Secretary, CPOWC, September 6, 1917, TNA FO 383/354.

203 Hansard HC Deb October 10, 1916, vol. 86 cc. 18–21; Letter from Vansittart to Secretary, Commission Internationale de Ravitaillement, September 10, 1917, Letter from M. A. Abrahamson to Agnew, September 13, 1917, Letter from Secretary, Commission Internationale de Ravitaillement, to Secretary POWD, October 10, 1917, and Letter to Agnew from O. Pelly Dick, October 6, 1917, TNA FO 383/354.
204 Letter to G. R. Warner from W. A. Bulkeley-Evans, January 10, 1918, Telegram from Sir W. Townley, January 16, 1918, Letter from Cubitt to the Secretary, POWD, January 23, 1918, Letter to Sir W. Townley from W. Langley, for SSFA, February 19, 1918, and Telegram from Sir W. Townley, March 29, 1918, TNA FO 383/443; Letter to R. A. Hawley, 10 August, 1917, TNA FO 383/351.

Chapter 5

1 J. Vernon, "The Ethics of Hunger and the Assembly of Society: The Techno-Politics of the School Meal in Modern Britain," *American Historical Review* 110(3) (2005), 693–725; Vernon, *Hunger*, pp. 124–8.
2 Vernon, "Ethics of Hunger," 724.
3 J. Belchem, *Popular Radicalism in Nineteenth Century Britain* (Houndmills: Palgrave, 1996), pp. 166–83.
4 [6 Edw. 7] *Education (Provision of Meals) Act, 1906* [CH 57], Section 4; L. Andrews, "The School Meals Service," *British Journal of Educational Studies* 20 (1) (1972), 74.
5 B. B. Gilbert, *The Evolution of National Insurance in Great Britain* (London: Michael Joseph, 1966), p. 112.
6 *Special Report and Report From the Select Committee on the Education (Provision of Meals) Bill, 1906; and the Education (Provision of Meals) (Scotland) Bill, 1906* (London: HMSO, 1906) (PP 205), p. viii.
7 *The Health of the School Child. Annual Report of the Chief Medical Officer of the Board of Education for the Year 1935* (London: HMSO, 1936), p. 40; Letter from Cecil Maudslay [hereafter Maudslay] to W. A. Brockington, December 4, 1937, TNA ED 123/112.
8 M. E. Green, *School Feeding in England and Wales* (London: Children's Minimum Council, 1938), p. 13; Report on Special Services. Cheshire, October, 1936, TNA ED 123/12; Provision of Meals. County Borough of Wakefield, July 6–7, 1938, TNA ED 123/276.
9 Green, *School Feeding*, p. 11; J. Alison Glover [hereafter Glover], "The History of the School Meals," Address to Conference of School Meals Organisers. Reprinted in "School Canteens," Special Section of "Education," September 13, 1946, TNA ED 158/171.
10 Extract from the School Medical Officer's Report, Stoke-on-Trent, 1934, TNA ED 123/272; H. R. Bennett, Value for Money: Free Meals for School Children, March 9, 1937, TNA ED 123/282.
11 Minute from J.S.S. to Miss Kennedy, December 17, 1938, TNA ED 123/243.

12 Report on Special Services. Farnworth, March 27, 1935, TNA ED 123/95.

13 Birkenhead. School Feeding: Elementary Schools, February 19, 1938, TNA ED 123/209.

14 Minute from J.S.S. to Miss Kennedy, December 17, 1938, TNA ED 123/243.

15 Sunderland. Report on Nutrition of School Children and Provision of Meals, January 28, 1929, TNA ED 50/66; Mansfield. Provision of Meals, March 2–3, 1939, TNA ED 123/142; Minute to Dr. Alford from P. R. Odgers, February 14, 1939, TNA ED 123/293A; Interview Memorandum. Ashton-Under-Lyne. Provision of Meals, January 23, 1935, TNA ED 123/86.

16 Interview Memorandum. Monmouthshire. Provision of Meals, November 11, 1936, TNA ED 123/290A; Maudslay, The Selection of Children for Free Meals and Milk, March 18, 1939, TNA ED 50/216.

17 E. M. Langley [hereafter Langley], Stockton-on-Tees Borough. Provision of School Meals, May 12, 1938, TNA ED 123/43.

18 Oldham. Provision of Meals, January 26–7, 1939, TNA ED 123/254.

19 Unemployment Assistance Board. Note on the Treatment of Meals Provided at School by Local Education Authorities, TNA AST 7/685; South Wales Coal Mining Areas. Investigation into the Physique of School Children, January 11, 1928, and Note by R.S.W., January 25, 1928, TNA ED 50/83; Minute to Fawkes from Gahl, December 7, 1921, Hebburn. Investigation into the Incidence of Malnutrition among School Children, January 29, 1929, Jarrow. Investigation into the Incidence of Malnourishment in School Children, January 29, 1929, Workington. Report on Nutrition of School Children and Provision of Meals, October 16, 1929, and Minute to Mr. Lowndes from Maudslay, October 28, 1932, TNA ED 50/77; Report on Special Services. Ilkeston, March 22, 1938 TNA ED 123/29; Report on Special Services. Farnworth, March 27, 1935, TNA ED 123/95; Interview Memorandum. Blackburn, September 24, 1934, TNA ED 123/211.

20 K. Jones, *The Making of Social Policy in Britain: From the Poor Law to New Labour*, 3rd ed. (London: Athlone Press, 2000), p. 100.

21 *The Health of the School Child: Annual Report of the Chief Medical Officer of the Board of Education for the Year 1931* (London: HMSO, 1932), p. 147; Minute to Mr. Todhunter from Maudslay, March 25, 1938, and Letter from Mr. Todhunter to B. Kenyon, March 30, 1938, TNA ED 50/214; Interview Memorandum. Manchester, Provision of Meals, May 2, 1935, TNA ED 123/248; Report on Special Services. Birmingham, March 2–5, 8–12, 16–17, 1937, TNA ED 123/210.

22 Middlesbrough Education Committee. Report by Director of Education on Provision of Meals For Necessitous School Children, January, 1933, TNA ED 123/249; E. W. Woodhead, Norwich Education Committee. Provision of Meals. Report of Director, May 20, 1935, TNA ED 123/252; Bennett, Value for Money.

23 Glover, "The History of the School Meals"; F. Le Gros Clark, *Social History of the School Meals Service* (London: London Council of Social Service, 1948), p. 14.

24 Interview Memorandum. Portsmouth. Provision of Meals, February 21, 1935, TNA ED 123/258; Interview Memorandum. Sheffield. Provision of Meals, January 17, 1935, TNA ED 123/265; Letter to Secretary, Board of Education from S. Childs, February 18, 1935, TNA ED 123/266.

25 D. J. Oddy, *From Plain Fare to Fusion Food: British Diet from the 1890s to the 1990s* (Woodbridge: The Boydell Press, 2003), pp. 115–32; M. W. Weatherall, "The Foundation and Early Years of the Dunn Nutritional Laboratory" and S. M. Horrocks, "Nutrition Science and the Food and Pharmaceutical Industries in Inter-War Britain," in D. F. Smith (ed.), *Nutrition in Britain: Science, Scientists and Politics in the Twentieth Century* (London: Routledge, 1997), pp. 29–52, 53–74.

26 Vernon, *Hunger*, pp. 96–117; M. Worboys, "The Discovery of Colonial Malnutrition between the Wars" in D. Arnold (ed.), *Imperial Medicine and Indigenous Societies* (Manchester: Manchester University Press, 1988), pp. 208–25; Arnold, "The 'Discovery' of Colonial Malnutrition"; B. Harris, *The Health of the School Child: A History of the School Medical Service in England and Wales* (Buckingham: Open University Press, 1995), pp. 127–130.

27 *The Health of the School Child. Annual Report of the Chief Medical Officer of the Board of Education for the Year 1933* (London: HMSO, 1934), p. 16; J. A. Glover, A. P. Hughes Gibb, and James Pearse, Inquiry into the Present Conditions in Regards the Effects of Continued Unemployment on Health in Certain Distressed Areas. Report on Investigations in Certain Districts of Tyneside, April 26, 1934, TNA ED 50/53.

28 R. Weaver, Cumberland. Provision of Meals, March 22, 1939, TNA 123/22.

29 Milk and Human Health. Memorandum by the Secretary of the Medical Research Council, March 19, 1934, TNA ED 24/1374; Glover, Gibb, and Pearse, Inquiry Into the Present Conditions...Tyneside; *Health of the School Child...1935*, p. 31; Burnett, *Plenty and Want*, pp. 266–88.

30 McCollum, *The Newer Knowledge of Nutrition*.

31 Green, *School Feeding*, p. 1.

32 Davin, "Imperialism and Motherhood"; J. Stewart, "'This Injurious Measure': Scotland and the 1906 Education (Provision of Meals) Act," *Scottish Historical Review* 78(1) (1999), 77–9; W. J. Reese, "After Bread, Education: Nutrition and Urban School Children, 1890–1920," *Teachers College Record* 81(4) (1980), 512–13; J. Hurt, "Feeding the Hungry Schoolchild in the First Half of the Twentieth Century" in D. J. Oddy and D. S. Miller (eds.), *Diet and Health in Modern Britain* (London: Croom Helm, 1985), pp. 179–80; Dwork, *War Is Good for Babies*, pp. 167–74; J. Burnett, "The Rise and Decline of School Meals in Britain, 1860–1990" in J. Burnett and D. J. Oddy (eds.), *The Origins and Development of Food Policies in Europe* (Leicester: Leicester University Press, 1994), pp. 61–2.

33 Andrews, "The School Meals Service," 72–3; *Report of the Inter-Departmental Committee on the Medical Inspection and Feeding of Children Attending Public Elementary Schools* (London: HSMO, 1905) (PP Cd. 2779); *Report of the Inter-Departmental Committee on Physical Deterioration* (London: HMSO, 1904) (PP Cd. 2175); Summary of Evidence Given Before the Physical Deterioration Committee on the Question of the Feeding of School Children, TNA ED 24/106.

34 *The Health of the School Child. Annual Report of the Chief Medical Officer of the Board of Education for the Year 1922* (London: HMSO, 1923), p. 120.

35 *The Health of the School Child. Annual Report of the Chief Medical Officer of the Board of Education for the Year 1938* (London: HMSO, 1940), p. 21.

36 J. V. A. Simpson, Memorandum on Milk and Meals in School, July 25, 1939, TNA ED 123/33.

37 "Fruit for Malnourished Children," *The Medical Officer*, September 12, 1936, p. 117.

38 E. Rathbone, "Introduction" to B. Drake, *Nutrition: A Policy of National Health* (London: New Fabian Research Bureau, 1936), p. 2.

39 D. J. Dutton, "Wood, Edward Frederick Lindley, First Earl of Halifax (1881–1959)," *Oxford Dictionary of National Biography*, January 6, 2011.

40 *Health of the School Child...1933*, p. 29.

41 Maudslay, The Selection of Children.

42 The School Meals Service. Dinner at School, TNA ED 158/171.

43 Minute from J.R.W. to A. H. Wood, November 3, 1921, and Memorandum by Mr. Branch Relating to the Limitation of Expenditure on Which the Provision of Meals Grant will be Payable in Respect of the Year 1922–3, January 26, 1923, TNA ED 24/1373.

44 Harris, *Health of the School Child*, p. 95.

45 Memorandum by Mr. Branch Relating to the Limitation of Expenditure.

46 Minute to A. H. Wood and Sir George Newman [hereafter Newman] from Sir Lewis Amherst Selby-Bigge, January 28, 1924, TNA ED 50/77.

47 Minute to Sir Lewis Amherst Selby-Bigge from Newman, January 29, 1924, TNA ED 50/77.

48 Board of Education (Special Services) Regulations 1925, in Walsall Education Committee. Provision of Meals. Report of Education Committee to the Town Council, February 9, 1934, Appendix, TNA ED 123/277.

49 J. Welshman, "School Meals and Milk in England and Wales," *Medical History* 41 (1997), 14.

50 Harris, *Health of the School Child*, pp. 96–7, 124; C. Webster, "The Health of the School Child During the Depression" in N. Parry and D. McNair (eds.), *The Fitness of the Nation: Physical and Health Education in the Nineteenth and Twentieth Centuries* (Leicester: History of Education Society of Great Britain, 1983), p. 77.

51 Interview Memorandum. Lancashire. Provision of Meals, March 7, 1935, TNA ED 123/84.

52 Milk and Human Health; Valenze, *Milk*, pp. 235–78.

53 P. Atkins, "The Milk in Schools Scheme, 1934–45: 'Nationalization' and Resistance," *History of Education* 34(1) (2005), 1–21; P. Atkins, "School Milk in Britain, 1900–1934," *Journal of Policy History* 19(4) (2007), 398–9, 404–7, 419; Hurt, "Feeding the Hungry Schoolchild," 186.

54 S. Levine, *School Lunch Politics: The Surprising History of America's Favorite Welfare Program* (Princeton: Princeton University Press, 2008); A. R. Ruis, *Eating to Learn, Learning to Eat: The Origins of School Lunch in the United States* (New Brunswick: Rutgers University Press, 2017).

55 Minute to E.N. Strong from H.M., February 13, 1935, TNA ED 123/56; Folkestone Borough Education Committee. Thirtieth Annual Report of the School Medical Officer, December 31, 1937, TNA ED 123/75; Report on Special Services. Kettering, April 13, 1937, TNA ED 123/135; Minute from A. F. Birch-Jones to E. R. Turnbull, June 15, 1934, and Minute from E. H. Pelham [hereafter Pelham] to Parliamentary Secretary and President, July 10, 1934, TNA ED 123/278; Marshall, Note, May 2, 1935, TNA ED 123/282. See also the school meals files for Harwich: TNA ED 123/38; Banbury: TNA ED 123/145; Sutton Coldfield: TNA ED 123/180; and Oldbury: TNA ED 123/188.

56 *The Health of the School Child. Annual Report of the Chief Medical Officer of the Board of Education for the Year 1932* (London: HMSO, 1933), pp. 168–9. These figures do not include breakfasts and teas, which tended to be provided to those also receiving dinners in most areas that furnished these meals.

57 *The Health of the School Child. Annual Report of the Chief Medical Officer of the Board of Education for the Year 1936* (London: HMSO, 1937), p. 127.

58 Minute from A. F. Birch-Jones, May 30, 1934, TNA ED 123/139.

59 Provision of Milk for School Children, Board of Education Circular 1437, September 5, 1934, TNA AST 7/685.

60 Letter from E. R. Turnbull to Blyth LEA, August 8, 1935, TNA ED 123/138; Minute from E.N. Strong to Maudslay, June 27, 1935, TNA ED 123/123.

61 *The Health of the School Child. Annual Report of the Chief Medical Officer of the Board of Education for the Year 1934* (London: HMSO, 1935), p. 26.

62 Harris, *Health of the School Child*, pp. 131–2.

63 British Medical Association, "Report of Committee on Nutrition," Supplement to the *British Medical Journal*, November 25, 1933, p. 2.

64 London Council of Social Service, School Meals in Greater London, 1938, TNA ED 50/214.

65 *Health of the School Child...1935*, pp. 12–13.

66 Letter from Percival Sharp to Secretary, Board of Education, October 31, 1934, TNA ED 50/78; S. Pedersen, *Family, Dependence, and the Origins of the Welfare State: Britain and France, 1914–1945* (Cambridge: Cambridge University Press, 1993), p. 321; S. Pedersen, *Eleanor Rathbone and the Politics of Conscience* (New Haven: Yale University Press, 2004), pp. 234–7.

67 The Children's Minimum Council. For the Improvement of Child Nutrition. An Appeal, TNA ED 50/216; Interview Memorandum. Note of Discussion with the Association of Education Committees About the Board's Policy with Regard to Medical Selection, September 19, 1935, Interview Memorandum. Note of Discussion with Representatives of the Association of Education Committees on the Draft Circular in Regard to the Provision of Meals for School Children, October 18, 1935, Minute from Pelham to Secretary, November 23, 1935, and Minute to Secretary and President from H.R., July 19, 1935, TNA ED 50/78.

68 *Health of the School Child...1934*, p. 29; The Provision of Meals for Children Attending Public Elementary Schools. Board of Education. Circular 1443, December 16, 1935, TNA AST 7/685.

69 Annual Report to the City of Birmingham Education Committee of the School Medical Officer, December 31, 1937, TNA ED 123/210; G. C. M. M'Gonigle and J. Kirby, *Poverty and Public Health* (London: Victor Gollancz, 1936), p. 40; British Medical Association, "Report of Committee on Nutrition," p. 2.

70 Minute to Maudslay from Glover, November 2, 1936, TNA ED 50/216.

71 For available tests see *Health of the School Child…1932*, pp. 126–7; *Health of the School Child…1934*, p. 30; Glover, Cumberland. Provision of Meals and Nutrition, June 28, 1939, TNA ED 123/22; Extract from School Medical Officer's Report 1934, Derbyshire, TNA ED 123/25; James Deeny, "The Assessment of Nutrition," *Ulster Medical Journal* 7 (1938), 206–14; W. R. Dunstan, "Functional Tests for Nutrition," *The Medical Officer*, March 6, 1937, pp. 97–8.

72 M'Gonigle and Kirby, *Poverty and Public Health*, p. 144.

73 Letter to Kenneth Fraser from Glover, May 26, 1939, TNA ED 123/22.

74 Glover, Cumberland.

75 Minute from J.L. to P. R. Odgers and Gosling, June 7, 1939, TNA ED 123/20.

76 Minute from Maudslay to Underwood and Glover, November 3, 1938, TNA ED 123/293A.

77 Letter from Henry Herd to Glover, April 17, 1935, and Manchester School Medical Service. Classifications of Nutrition Expressed as Percentages from January to March, 1935, TNA ED 123/248.

78 *The Health of the School Child. Annual Report of the Chief Medical Officer of the Board of Education for the Year 1937* (London: HMSO, 1938), p. 19; Children's Minimum Council, Statement on School Meals and Milk Submitted to the President of the Board of Education, March, 1939, TNA ED 50/216.

79 M. E. Green, *Malnutrition among School Children* (London: Children's Minimum Council, 1938), p. 8.

80 School Attendance and Medical Service Sub-Committee, January 17, 1939. Notes on Malnutrition and School Meals by Thomas C. Lonie, and Thomas C. Lonie, School Attendance and Medical Service Sub-Committee, March 21, 1939, TNA ED 123/63.

81 Interview Memorandum. Leyton, May 23, 1935, TNA ED 123/50; Dudley. Provision of Meals, September 4, 1934, TNA ED 123/231.

82 Extract from School Medical Officer's Report. Derbyshire, 1934, TNA ED 123/25; Extract from School Medical Officer's Report. London County Council [hereafter LCC], 1934, TNA ED 123/118.

83 Somerville Hastings, *A National Physiological Minimum* (London: The Fabian Society, 1934), p. 7.

84 Children's Minimum Council, Statement on School Meals and Milk.

85 Manchester Education Committee. Report of the Education Committee on the Arrangements for the Provision of Milk and of Free Meals for School Children, Arising out of Correspondence with the Board of Education, February 18, 1935, TNA ED 123/248.

86 Interview Memorandum. Portsmouth. Provision of Meals, February 21, 1935, TNA ED 123/258; Dr. H. Paul, Medical Inspection of Children in the Smethwick Public Elementary and Secondary Schools. Annual

Report, 1934, TNA ED 123/266; London Council of Social Service, School Meals in Greater London; Extract from School Medical Officer's Report. LCC, 1934, TNA ED 123/118.

87 Letter from E. O. Taylor to Secretary, Board of Education, June 5, 1935, TNA ED 123/123.

88 Quoted in Hastings, *A National Physiological Minimum*, p. 8.

89 Minute from Maudslay to Arthur MacNalty, June 25, 1935, TNA ED 123/266. Emphasis in original.

90 Minute to Glover from Maudslay, October 15, 1934, Minute to Glover from J. E. Underwood, October 17, 1934, Minute to Glover from R.P.W., October 22, 1934, and Minute to Maudslay from Glover, November 14, 1934, TNA ED 50/78; Minute from Glover to C.M.O., June 26, 1935, TNA ED 123/266.

91 Minute from Arthur MacNalty to Maudslay, June 26, 1935, TNA ED 123/266.

92 Minute from E.N. Strong to Maudslay, March 22, 1935, TNA ED 123/228.

93 Interview Memorandum. Ashton-Under-Lyne. Provision of Meals, January 23, 1935, TNA ED 123/86.

94 Minute to Secretary and President from H.R., July 19, 1935, TNA ED 50/78.

95 Letter from T. J. Rees to Secretary, Welsh Department, Board of Education, December 19, 1934, TNA ED 123/294B; Interview Memorandum. Lancashire. Provision of Meals, March 7, 1935, TNA ED 123/84; Interview Memorandum. Portsmouth. Provision of Meals, February 21, 1935, TNA ED 123/258.

96 Note on Dr. Mellanby's Memorandum, TNA ED 24/1374; Welshman, "School Meals and Milk," 18.

97 Minute from Maudslay to W. P. Wheldon, December 21, 1934, TNA ED 123/294B.

98 *Special Report and Report from the Select Committee*, p. v; Minutes on Feeding of Children to Mr. Birrell from Pelham, February 26, 1906, TNA ED 24/107.

99 Minute from Newman to President, Board of Education, March 25, 1914, TNA ED 31/198.

100 Green, *Malnutrition*, p. 1.

101 Quoted in D. Smith, "The Social Construction of Dietary Standards: The British Medical Association-Ministry of Health Advisory Committee on Nutrition Report of 1934" in D. Maurer and J. Sobal (eds.), *Eating Agendas: Food and Nutrition as Social Problems* (New York: Aldine de Gruyter, 1995), p. 280.

102 *Annual Report for 1908 of the Chief Medical Officer of the Board of Education* (London: HMSO, 1910), p. 44.

103 A. W. Forrest, Report by the School Medical Officer on Nutritional Surveys in School (Minute 1094), March 6, 1935, TNA ED 123/50.

104 D. Smith and M. Nicolson, "Nutrition, Education, Ignorance and Income: A Twentieth-Century Debates" in H. Kamminga and A. Cunningham (eds.), *Science and Culture of Nutrition, 1840–1940* (Amsterdam: Rodopi, 1995), p. 300.

105 D. N. Paton and L. Findlay, *Medical Research Council. Child Life Investigations. Poverty, Nutrition and Growth: Studies of Child Life in Cities and Rural Districts of Scotland* (London: HMSO, 1926), p. 303.

106 D. Smith and M. Nicolson, "The 'Glasgow School' of Paton, Findlay and Cathcart: Conservative Thought in Chemical Physiology, Nutrition and Public Health," *Social Studies of Science* 19(2) (1989), 201.

107 Paton and Findlay, *Poverty, Nutrition and Growth*, p. 304; Smith and Nicolson, "Glasgow School," 216–17.

108 *The Health of the School Child. Annual Report of the Chief Medical Officer of the Board of Education for the Year 1926* (London: HMSO, 1927), p. 16; Smith and Nicolson, "Nutrition, Education, Ignorance," 297–8.

109 Hamlin, "Could you Starve to Death?"

110 Smith and Nicolson, "Glasgow School," 220–1; Smith and Nicolson, "Nutrition, Education, Ignorance," 288–318.

111 Minute from Pelham to Maudslay, December 17, 1934, TNA ED 50/78.

112 James Fairlely, Isle of Wight County Council. Health (Education) Sub-Committee. Report on the State of Nutrition of Certain School Children, September, 1936, TNA ED 123/64; *Health of the School Child...1931*, p. 108; Newspaper clipping, March 23, 1936, TNA ED 123/194.

113 Whitwood District. Provision of Meals. Reports by School Medical Inspector, TNA ED 123/194.

114 Inquiry into the Present Conditions in Regards the Effects of Continued Unemployment on Health in Certain Distressed Areas. Interim Report on Certain Distressed Areas in the Coalfields of Glamorgan and Monmouth Counties, TNA ED 50/53.

115 Glover, Gibb, and Pearse, Inquiry Into the Present Conditions...Tyneside.

116 James Fairlely, Report on the State of Nutrition of Certain School Children.

117 "Smethwick Education Committee," *Smethwick Telephone*, May 18, 1935, TNA ED 123/266.

118 Nutritional Condition of Elementary School Children, October 21, 1938, TNA ED 123/137.

119 Interview Memorandum. H.M., July 13, 1935, TNA ED 123/22; Interview Memorandum. Mossley: Special Services, July 14, 1939, TNA ED 123/105; Letter from F.N. Tribe to Maudslay, May 9, 1935, TNA ED 50/78; "The Remedy for Malnutrition," *The Medical Officer*, January 26, 1935, p. 39.

120 Investigation of Special Areas. County Borough of South Shields, October 10–14, 1938, TNA ED 123/270.

121 Interview Memorandum. H.M., July 13, 1935, TNA ED 123/22; Notes from Investigation of Special Areas by Doctor Pearse. Whitehaven, February 22–March 5, 1937, TNA ED 123/23; East Ham. Nutrition Surveys, October 22, 1935, TNA ED 123/233.

122 Cumberland. Report on Nutrition of School Children, November 2, 1929, TNA ED 123/22.

123 Interview Memorandum. H.M., July 13, 1935, TNA ED 123/22.

124 Inquiry into the Present Conditions...Glamorgan and Monmouth Counties.

125 Minute to Maudslay from Glover, November 3, 1938, TNA ED 123/293A.

126 J. E. Underwood, Report on the Conditions of Health, Nutrition, Clothing and Boots of School Children in the South Wales Colliery Districts, c. December 1930, TNA ED 50/83.

127 *The Health of the School Child. Annual Report of the Chief Medical Officer of the Board of Education for the Year 1930* (London: HMSO, 1931), p. 46.

128 *Health of the School Child...1938*, p. 17; G. A. Auden, "Nutrition of School Children," *The Medical Officer*, November 30, 1935, p. 225; J. F. Galloway, "Free Meals," *The Medical Officer*, May 23, 1936, p. 208.

129 Ministry of Health Advisory Committee on Nutrition. *Memorandum to the Minister of Health on the Criticism and Improvement of Diets* (London: HMSO, 1932); British Medical Association, "Report on Nutrition"; Smith, "Social Construction," pp. 279–303; Oddy, *From Plain Fare*, pp. 122–4; Vernon, *Hunger*, pp. 124–5; M. Mayhew, "The 1930s Nutrition Controversy," *Journal of Contemporary History* 23(3) (1988), 445–64.

130 For similar debates in France see D. Simmons, *The Vital Minimum* (Chicago: University of Chicago Press, 2015).

131 Oddy, *From Plain Fare*, p. 122; Smith, "Social Construction," p. 285.

132 British Medical Association, "Report on Nutrition."

133 M'Gonigle and Kirby, *Poverty and Public Health*, pp. 123–9.

134 J. B. Orr, *Food, Health and Income* (London: Macmillan and Co., 1936), p. 21; M'Gonigle and Kirby, *Poverty and Public Health*, p. 191.

135 Smith, "Social Construction."

136 Children's Minimum Council, Statement on School Meals and Milk; South Wales and Monmouthshire Conference on Child Nutrition, December 4, 1937, TNA ED 50/217; Memorandum on the Provision of Free Solid Meals to Children Attending Public Elementary Schools and Grant Earning Secondary Schools on an Economic Basis of Selection, March 16, 1939, TNA ED 50/217; Green, *Malnutrition*, pp. 12–13; M'Gonigle and Kirby, *Poverty and Public Health*, p. 142.

137 Walsall Education Committee. Provision of Meals. Report of Education Committee to the Town Council, February 9, 1934, TNA ED 123/277.

138 Children's Minimum Council. Points to be Put Before the Parliamentary Secretary to the Board of Education, July 29, 1936, TNA ED 50/214; Interview Memorandum. Note of Discussion [with Children's Minimum Council], July 29, 1936, TNA ED 50/214; Children's Minimum Council, Statement on School Meals and Milk.

139 London Council of Social Service, School Meals in Greater London; J. V. A. Simpson, Memorandum on Milk and Meals in School; Notes on Malnutrition and School Meals by Thomas C. Lonie; Letter to Secretary Board of Education from John Orton, December 15, 1934 TNA ED 123/205; "Health of Ipswich Schoolchildren," *Ipswich Evening Star*, July 13, 1937, TNA ED 123/242; Letter to the Secretary, Board of Education from Sydney E. Allen, December 5, 1934, TNA ED 123/258.

140 J. V. A. Simpson, Memorandum on Milk and Meals in School.

141 Letter from the Director of Education, Preston to Secretary, Board of Education, December 18, 1934, TNA ED 123/259.

142 Pedersen, *Family*, p. 54.

143 Standing Joint Committee of Industrial Women's Organisations, TNA
    AST 7/685; Children's Minimum Council, Statement on School Meals and
    Milk; Memorandum. Proposal for the Repetition in South Wales, Upon a
    Wider Scale, of the Experimental Scheme for the Distribution of Foodstuffs
    Recently Carried Out in Bishop Auckland by the Potato Marketing Board,
    October 21, 1935, TNA ED 50/78; London Council of Social Service, School
    Meals in Greater London; Interview Memorandum. London Council of
    Social Services, October 26, 1938, TNA ED 50/214; Cumberland County
    Public Assistance Committee. Unemployment Act, 1934, TNA ED 123/22;
    Letter from L. H. Kaufman and G. Ashbee to Great Yarmouth LEA,
    June 23, 1936, TNA ED 123/237; Extract from School Medical Officer's
    Report, Stoke-on-Trent, 1934, TNA ED 123/272; Interview Memorandum.
    Abertillery, September 26, 1934, TNA ED 123/292.
144 Interview Memorandum. Manchester. Provision of Meals, May 2, 1935,
    TNA ED 123/248.
145 Interview Memorandum. Hastings. Provision of Meals, October 22, 1934,
    TNA ED 123/240; Note by H.H., July 16, 1935; Interview Memorandum.
    Children's Minimum Committee, January 31, 1935, TNA ED 50/214;
    Letter from Lesley Byrde to Lord De La Warr, November 22, 1938, TNA ED
    50/214; Interview Memorandum. Manchester. Provision of Meals, May 2,
    1935, TNA ED 123/248; Interview Memorandum. Gosport, May 14,
    1935, TNA ED 123/56; Minute from Maudslay to Secretary, December
    31, 1934, TNA ED 123/228; Letter to Secretary, Board of Education from
    F. C. Smithard, March 5, 1935, TNA ED 123/228; Interview Memorandum.
    Liverpool, January 24, 1935, TNA ED 123/247.
146 "Health of Ipswich Schoolchildren."
147 Glover, Gibb, and Pearse, Inquiry Into the Present Conditions…Tyndeside;
    South Wales Coal Mining Areas. Investigation into the Physique of School
    Children; Minute from Newman to Secretary and President, January 17,
    1928, TNA ED 50/83; Northumberland. Report on Investigation into
    Incidence of Malnutrition in School Children, February 1, 1929, and
    Whitehaven. Report on Nutrition of School Children, October 17, 1929,
    TNA ED 50/77; Minute to Maudslay from Glover, November 14, 1934,
    and Minute from Maudslay to Secretary, November 19, 1934, TNA ED
    50/78; Minute from H.M. to Maudslay, October 24, 1938, TNA ED 50/214.
148 Minute from J.R. to His Majesty's Inspector, December 3, 1935, TNA
    ED 123/41; Letter to F. P. Armitage from K. W. Elliott [hereafter Elliott],
    August 12, 1938, TNA ED 123/245; Letter to J. E. Holden from Elliott,
    June 2, 1938, TNA ED 123/261.
149 Minute from Glover to Maudslay, March 22, 1935, TNA ED 123/84;
    Report on Special Services. Oldham, October 23–4, November 6–7, 1934,
    TNA ED 123/254; Abertillery. Provision of Meals. Nutrition Survey,
    November 22–5, 1938, TNA ED 123/292.
150 Welshman, "School Meals and Milk," 21.
151 Oddy, *From Plain Fare*, p. 130.
152 Minute to Secretary from Newman, July 6, 1934, TNA ED 123/278;
    Letter from H. Marshall to West Hartlepool LEA, January 19, 1939, TNA
    ED 123/281.

153 Extract from the School Medical Officer's Report for 1934, LCC, TNA ED 123/118.

154 Provision of Meals. Summer Menu, 1938 [Bedfordshire], TNA ED 123/1.

155 Report by the School Medical Officer on Provision of School Meals, January 25, 1938, TNA ED 123/50.

156 Minute to Sir Lewis Amherst Selby-Bigge from Newman, January 29, 1924, TNA ED 50/77.

157 Glover, "The History of the School Meals"; Report on Special Services. Cheshire, October, 1936, TNA ED 123/12.

158 Rochdale. Provision of Meals. Dinners – Feeding Centres, May 10–11, 1939, TNA ED 123/261.

159 Minute from H. E. Magee to Dr. Hamill, June 2, 1934, Minute from H. E. Magee to H. Marshall, November 29, 1934, and Provision of Free Meals for Children Attending Public Elementary Schools. Glossop, 1938, TNA ED 123/28; Letter from T. Foreman to Secretary, Board of Education, May 6, 1938, Minute from G.S. to H. Marshall, May 12, 1938, Minute to Glover from A. H. Gale [hereafter Gale], May 19, 1938, Minute to Gale from Glover, May 19, 1938, Letter from T. Foreman to Secretary, Board of Education, July 11, 1938, Minute from Langley to Gale, July 15, 1938, Letter to A. J. Smyth from Gale, July 20, 1938, Letter to Glover from A. J. Smyth, July 21, 1938, Letter to A. J. Smyth from Glover, July 23, 1938, Cutting from *Cambridge Daily News*, April 28, 1938, Minute from Glover to Dr. Llewellin and Langley, July 10, 1940, and Letter to Glover from Mr. Godfrey, July 9, 1940, TNA ED 123/11; Provision of Meals. Ipswich, July 20, 1939, TNA ED 123/242; Harris, *Health of the School Child*, p. 129.

160 Special Services Sub-Committee Report, LCC, January 17, 1938, TNA ED 123/118.

161 Minute from Langley to Glover, February 7, 1938, TNA ED 123/118; Letter to Kenneth Fraser from Glover, May 26, 1939, TNA ED 123/22; *Health of the School Child…1938*, pp. 24–6.

162 Letter to Newton from Maudslay, February 11, 1938, and Minute from Maudslay to Mr. Flemming, August 14, 1939, TNA ED 123/118; Letter from Elliott to Cornwall LEA, August 15, 1939, TNA ED 123/19; Letter to Isle of Ely LEA from Elliott, July 18, 1939, TNA ED 12/63; Letter to Shropshire LEA from Elliott, August 19, 1939, TNA ED 123/147.

163 Welshman, "School Meals and Milk," 16.

164 Minute to Glover from Maudslay, March 11, 1938, TNA ED 50/217; Ebbw Vale. Provision of Meals. Nutrition Survey, November 29–December 2, 1938, TNA ED 123/293A.

165 Mansfield. Provision of Meals, March 2–3, 1939, TNA ED 123/142.

166 Sunderland. Provision of Meals, December 15–16, 1938, TNA ED 123/273.

167 *Health of the School Child…1931*, p. 96.

168 Report on Special Services. Stockton-on-Tees B, April 2–3, 1936, TNA ED 123/43; Report on Special Services. Birmingham, March 2–5, 8–12, and 16–17, 1937, TNA ED 123/210.

169 Letter to Secretary, Board of Education from John Cox, October 3, 1938, TNA ED 123/213.

170 Minute from N. D. Bosworth Smith to Maudslay, May 17, 1939, TNA ED 50/219.
171 Draft Extract from Board of Education Report for 1938, TNA ED 50/216; Extract from School Medical Officer's Report, Walthamstow, 1933, TNA ED 123/51; Letter to Secretary, Board of Education from W. J. O. Newton, January 19, 1938, TNA ED 123/118.
172 Provision of Meals. Report by Langley, April 4, 1939, TNA ED 50/219.
173 Vernon, "Ethics of Hunger," 722; Vernon, *Hunger*, pp. 174–5.
174 *The Health of the School Child. Fifty Years of the School Health Service. Report of the Chief Medical Officer of the Ministry of Education for the Years 1956 and 1957* (London: HMSO, 1958), p. 69.
175 Welshman, "School Meals and Milk," 25–7; Harris, *Health of the School Child*, p. 159.
176 Welshman, "School Meals and Milk," 24.
177 Quoted in Green, *Malnutrition*, p. 7.

Chapter 6

1 Answering You II, July 17, 1941, Mass Observation [hereafter MO] File Report 792. All MO sources are from the Mass Observation Online database.
2 British Restaurants, undated draft memo, *c.* 1943, and Wartime Meals Division, March, 1943, TNA MAF 152/55.
3 Day to Day Feeding. British Restaurants, TNA MAF 83/382.
4 W. J. O. Newton [hereafter Newton], Meals Service. Conference at the Ministry of Health, September 12, 1940, LMA LCC/RC/GEN/01/002.
5 P. J. Atkins, "Communal Feeding in War Time: British Restaurants, 1940–1947" in R. Duffet, I. Zweiniger-Bargielowska, and A. Drouard (eds.), *Food and War in Twentieth Century Europe* (Farnham: Ashgate, 2011), p. 151; Oddy, *From Plain Fare*, p. 159; Extract from *Birmingham Post*, August 18, 1943, MAF 99/1734.
6 F. Trentmann and F. Just, "Introduction" in F. Trentmann and F. Just (eds.), *Food and Conflict in Europe in the Age of the Two World Wars* (Houndmills: Palgrave, 2006), p. 2.
7 Vernon, *Hunger*, pp. 118–39; Ministry of Food, *How Britain Was Fed in War Time* (London: HMSO, 1946), p. 46; "National Food Policy," *British Medical Journal*, July 16, 1938, pp. 139–41.
8 J. B. Orr and D. Lubbock, *Feeding the People in War-Time* (London: Macmillan, 1940), p. 1.
9 J. B. Orr, et al., "The Wage-earner's Diet: Risk of Malnutrition," *British Medical Journal*, July 6, 1940, p. 29.
10 Collingham, *Taste of War*, pp. 11–12, 141–54.
11 Provision of Cheap Food for the Poorer Classes, June 24, 1940, TNA MAF 99/1580.
12 Vernon, *Hunger*, pp. 180–2; Barnett, *British Food Policy*, p. 151.
13 War Cabinet. Food Policy Committee. Memorandum by the Minister of Food. Communal Feeding, July 3, 1940, TNA MAF 99/1580.
14 J. C. Drummond [hereafter Drummond], Memorandum on Meals for Collective Feeding, August 11, 1940, TNA MAF 156/282.

15 Letter to Sir Russell Scott [hereafter Scott] from H. L. French [hereafter French], September 21, 1940, TNA MAF 128/565.

16 Howard Marshall, Notes on Communal Feeding Memorandum to the Minister, August 5, 1940, TNA MAF 99/1578. On morale, see D. Ussishkin, *Morale: A Modern British History* (Oxford: Oxford University Press, 2017).

17 Answering You II; F. Solomon and B. Litvinoff, *A Woman's Way* (New York: Simon and Schuster, 1984), pp. 160–1, 179–80; R. Calder, *Carry on London* (London: The English Universities Press, 1941), p. 73.

18 National Restaurants, July 30, 1940, TNA MAF 99/1794.

19 Minute to Secretary from H. G. Vincent, July 30, 1940, TNA MAF 99/1578; S. Ward, *Unemployment and the State in Britain: The Means Test and Protest in 1930s South Wales and North-East England* (Manchester: Manchester University Press, 2013).

20 Letter to E. C. H. Salmon from S. W. Hood, September 5, 1940, LMA LCC/RC/GEN/01/002.

21 R. Farmer, *The Food Companions: Cinema and Consumption in Wartime Britain, 1939–45* (Manchester: Manchester University Press, 2011), p. 3.

22 Calder, *Carry on London*, p. 67.

23 Solomon and Litvinoff, *A Woman's Way*, pp. 182–5.

24 Ministry of Food. Wartime Meals Division. Circular Letter from E. G. Harwood to Local Authorities Responsible for British Restaurants. British Restaurants: Amortisation of Capital Expenditure, TNA MAF 99/1801. Interest was charged only if a Local Authority wished to take full responsibility for the financial operation of its British Restaurants, becoming responsible for its losses as well as retaining its profits.

25 Extract from Draft Conclusion of Lord President's Committee on Air Raid Damage, September 24, 1940, TNA MAF 128/565; Hansard HC Deb October 1, 1941, vol. 374 cc. 599–600W.

26 Minute from J. J. Llewellin to Prime Minister, May 18, 1945, TNA MAF 99/1736.

27 British Restaurants. Brief for Minister's Press Conference, c. February, 1945, TNA MAF 99/1762.

28 R. J. Hammond, *Food, Volume II: Studies in Administration and Control* (London: HMSO, 1956), pp. 391–2.

29 Letter from D. Watson [hereafter Watson] to R. H. Murray, March 22, 1943, and Letter from W. B. Chrimes [hereafter Chrimes] to R. H. Murray, June 29, 1942, TNA MAF 99/1748.

30 Letter to Magnus Pyke [hereafter Pyke] from C. F. Strong, February 23, 1944, and Report on Diet at British Restaurants. Memo From Public Health Department, Grays to Essex Epidemiological Committee, July 15, 1942, TNA MAF 98/61; Minute from Watson to Chrimes, September 28, 1942, TNA MAF 99/1706.

31 Turnover of Broken Boxes of Margarine. Ministry of Food. Wartime Meals Division. Circular CMFE 40, October 24, 1941, TNA MAF 99/1797.

32 Memorandum on British Restaurants, TNA MAF 83/382; Teleprint Message From W. J. M. Menzies [hereafter Menzies] to Damerell,

O'Brien, and Chrimes, January 10, 1942, and Priority Arrangements. British Restaurants, TNA MAF 99/1644.

33 Wartime Meals Division, March, 1943, TNA MAF 152/55.

34 Memorandum on the Provision of British Restaurants and Emergency Meals Centres, June 11, 1941, TNA MAF 99/1797.

35 Hammond, *Food*, pp. 397–8.

36 Letter to Scott from French, September 21, 1940, TNA MAF 128/565.

37 E. Leopold, "LCC Restaurants and the Decline of Municipal Enterprise" in A. Saint (ed.), *Politics and the Peoples of London: The London County Council, 1889–1965* (London: Hambledon Press, 1989), pp. 202–3.

38 Provision of Cheap Food for the Poorer Classes; London County Council [hereafter LCC]. Meals Services. Origins of the Service, LMA LCC/RC/GEN/01/001.

39 Communal Feeding. Letter from Menzies to all District Food Officers. Ministry of Food, Circular CF 58, TNA MAF 99/1797.

40 Community Kitchens: Notes for Divisional Food Officers. Ministry of Food, Circular CMF 1, November 21, 1940, TNA MAF 99/1797.

41 Chatham, September, 1941, MO File Report 877.

42 Orr and Lubbock, *Feeding the People*. See also G. Walworth, *Feeding the Nation in Peace and War* (London: George Allen & Unwin, 1940).

43 Hammond, *Food*, p. 383.

44 Community Kitchens: Notes for Divisional Food Officers.

45 Ministry of Food. Divisional Food Officers' Conference, November 22–3, 1940, TNA MAF 74/49.

46 Note of an Interview between Newton and Chrimes, November 13, 1940, LMA LCC/RC/GEN/01/002; Report by the Chief Officer of Meals Service, LCC, Civil Defence and General Purposes Committee, April 21, 1943, TNA MAF 99/1765.

47 Letter from Watson to H. Fieldhouse, July 23, 1941, Letter to Watson from H. Fieldhouse, August 2, 1941, and Letter from Watson to H. Fieldhouse, August 20, 1941, TNA AST 7/524.

48 Community Kitchens: Notes for Divisional Food Officers; Newspaper Clipping, 1940, LMA LCC/RC/GEN/01/002; Notes on Wartime Community Feeding Centres, TNA MAF 99/1797.

49 Collingham, *Taste of War*, p. 395.

50 Newton, Conference on Communal Meals Service at the Ministry of Food, September 26, 1940, LMA LCC/RC/GEN/01/002; Calder, *Carry on London*, p. 64.

51 Ministry of Food. Divisional Food Officers' Conference, November 22–3, 1940.

52 British Restaurants and Cooking Depots Trading Results, 1944, TNA MAF 99/1797.

53 Newspaper Clipping, 1940, LMA LCC/RC/GEN/01/002.

54 Fenn Diary, October 25, 1941, MO Topics Collections, TC 75 Industry 1940–55, Box 3, 75-3-H; "A War-Time Index of Social Change: British Restaurants," *The Times*, August 22, 1942, TNA, MAF 152/55; Hansard HC Deb January 28, 1942, vol. 377 cc. 717–18. For critiques that British Restaurants were still too expensive for the working poor, see MO

Diarist 5427, December 3, 1941; Blaina, November, 1942, MO File Report 1498, p. 19.

55 Ministry of Food. Wartime Meals Division. Circular CMF 19, to all District Food Officers, from Menzies, May 24, 1941, TNA MAF 99/1797.

56 Report by the Chief Officer of Meals Service, LCC, April 21, 1943.

57 Community Feeding Division. Memorandum on Draft Order Giving Power to Local Authorities to Carry on Catering Trade at Community Kitchens. Orders Committee Doc. 344, January 10, 1941, Letter to French from T. S. Quintin Hill, December 3, 1940, Memo to E. Twentyman from T. S. Quintin Hill, November 27, 1940, and Memo to Menzies from W. Bankes Amery, January 14, 1941, TNA MAF 154/421; Minute from French to the Minister, January 20, 1941, MAF 99/1638.

58 Orr and Lubbock, *Feeding the People*, p. 36.

59 National Restaurants, July 30, 1940, TNA MAF 99/1794; Letter from John Maude to Scott, June 27, 1940, TNA MAF 128/565; Minute to Secretary from H. G. Vincent, July 30, 1940, TNA MAF 99/1578; Communal Feeding. Ministry of Food Circular CF 58; Notes on Wartime Community Feeding Centres.

60 Howard Marshall, Notes on Communal Feeding.

61 *Daily Mail*, March 26, 1941, p. 5.

62 Wartime Social Survey. Inquiry for the Ministry of Food. Community Feeding in Glasgow, March 14, 1941, TNA INF 1/275.

63 Ministry of Food. Community Feeding. To all District Food Officers West and South East Scotland from Menzies, November 15, 1940, TNA MAF 99/1796; Letter from Newton to Watson, November 28, 1940; Note of an Interview between Newton and Chrimes.

64 Women's Voluntary Service, *Community Feeding in Wartime*, 2nd ed. (London: HMSO, 1941).

65 "Standardization in Communal Feeding," *British Medical Journal*, March 6, 1943, pp. 293–4.

66 Solomon and Litvinoff, *A Woman's Way*, p. 185.

67 Answering You II.

68 H. L. Mencken, "War Words in England," *American Speech* 19(1) (1944), 3; *Daily Mail*, March 29, 1941, p. 2; Wartime Social Survey. Inquiry for the Ministry of Food. Community Feeding in Harrow, February 18, 1941, MO File Report 594B, p. 35.

69 M. Gilbert (ed), *The Churchill War Papers: The Ever-Widening War, 1941* (New York: Norton, 2000), p. 376.

70 Ministry of Food. Community Feeding Division. Circular CMF 11, to all District Food Officers from Menzies, April 7, 1941, TNA MAF 99/1797; Note of an Interview between Newton and Chrimes.

71 J. Burnett, *England Eats Out, 1830–Present* (Harlow: Pearson, 2004); R. Rich, *Bourgeois Consumption: Food, Space, and Identity in London and Paris, 1850–1914* (Manchester: Manchester University Press, 2011); B. Assael, "Gastro-cosmpolitanism and the Restaurant in Late Victorian and Edwardian London," *The Historical Journal* 56(3) (2013), 681–706.

72 National Council of Social Service [hereafter NCSS], *British Restaurants: An Inquiry Made by the National Council of Social Service* (Oxford: Oxford

University Press, 1946), p. 19; N. Durbach, "British Restaurants and the Gender Politics of the Wartime Midday Meal" in M. J. Crowley and S. T. Dawson (eds.), *Home Fronts: Britain and the Empire at War, 1939–45* (Woodbridge: The Boydell Press, 2017), pp. 19–36.
73 Letter from John Maude to Scott.
74 Solomon and Litvinoff, *A Woman's Way*, p. 179.
75 London Council of Social Service [hereafter LCSS], *The Communal Restaurant: A Study of the Place of Civic Restaurants in the Life of the Community* (London: LCSS, 1943), p. 19.
76 Ministry of Food. Wartime Meals Division. Circular CMF 37. Wireless Sets in British Restaurants, October 31, 1941, TNA MAF 99/1797.
77 Farmer, *Food Companions*, pp. 98, 105–6.
78 Wilt, *Food For War*, pp. 215–22; Smith, "Nutrition Science and the Two World Wars," p. 161.
79 Atkins, "Communal Feeding," pp. 144, 149–50.
80 Letter from Pyke to C. L. Jones, December 9, 1942, TNA MAF 98/61.
81 Oxford Nutritional Survey. Survey of Mid-day Meals Served in the Municipal Restaurant at the Town Hall, Oxford, during September and October 1942, TNA MAF 98/94; The Nutritive Value of Communal Meals, Scientific Advisor's Division, Ministry of Food, February 16, 1943, TNA MAF 99/1583; Letter from Pyke to Marion Ratcliffe, February 18, 1943, TNA MAF 98/61; Report by the Chief Officer of Meals Service, LCC, April 21, 1943.
82 Drummond, Memorandum on Meals for Collective Feeding.
83 Control of the Nutritive Value of Communal Meals, Memo from Pyke to Dr. Needham, February 4, 1943, TNA MAF 98/61.
84 *How Britain Was Fed in War Time*, p. 47.
85 Drummond, Memorandum on Meals for Collective Feeding; Letter to Watson from Newton, July 20, 1942, TNA MAF 99/1581.
86 Minute from Menzies to E. Twentyman, October 31, 1940, TNA MAF 99/1582.
87 M. C. Broatch, Diet, December 3, 1943, LMA LCC/RC/GEN/01/001.
88 Day to Day Feeding. British Restaurants; LCSS, *Communal Restaurant*, p. 24.
89 Ministry of Food, Canteen Catering, TNA, MAF 223/25.
90 LCC. Meals Service. Serial Note No. 33/44, LMA LCC/RC/GEN/04/25.
91 Hansard HC Deb June 10, 1941, vol. 372 c. 51W; British Restaurants. Ministry of Food. Public Relations Division: Information Branch, September 3, 1943, TNA MAF 74/49; Ministry of Food. Meals in Community Kitchens. Menus and Recipes Suggested for Use in Scotland. Menus. Memorandum No. 3, TNA MAF 99/1794; Ministry of Food, Canteen Catering.
92 Newton, The Londoners' Meals Service. Serial Note No. 44, LMA LCC/RC/GEN/04/23; Letter from Pyke to H. M. Sinclair, June 18, 1942, TNA MAF 98/94. For other communal feeding arrangements for the Jewish population, see Survey of Voluntary and Official Bodies during Bombing of the East End, September, 1940, MO File Report 431, p. 61; Evacuation Problems and their Effect on Local Trade, MO File Report 565A.

93 Ministry of Food. Nutritional Section. Food Advice Division, TNA MAF 98/55; Extract from *Evening Standard*, August 8, 1943, and Letter to Mr. Holroyd from H. Hardman [hereafter Hardman], August 16, 1943, TNA MAF 99/1762.
94 See files in TNA MAF 98/110.
95 LCSS, *Communal Restaurant*, p. 19.
96 www.stonehousehistorygroup.org.uk/page69.html; www.wringtonsomer set.org.uk/history/bullenwar/wringtonwar12.htm; www.burtonlatimer.info/war/britishrestaurant.html
97 Letter from C. F. Strong to Pyke, August 31, 1943, TNA MAF 98/61; West Green British Restaurant – Tottenham, October 2, 1942, TNA MAF 98/106; Report on Diet at British Restaurants, July 15, 1942.
98 Letter from C. F. Strong to Pyke, February 11, 1944, TNA MAF 98/61.
99 Letter to Watson from H. G. Houghton, November 24, 1942, TNA MAF 99/1581.
100 [Report on Nutrition of Sheffield Municipal Restaurant and Sheffield Educational Settlement], April 1942, TNA MAF 98/61.
101 Notes on British Restaurants, TNA MAF 98/61.
102 LCSS, *Communal Restaurant*, p. 21; Letter to Chrimes from Newton, June 29, 1942, TNA MAF 99/1745; M.C Broatch, Diet.
103 Notes on British Restaurants.
104 Talk to Birmingham Canteen Supervisors and Caterers.
105 Ministry of Food, Canteen Catering; Ministry of Food. Nutrition Section. Food Advice Division.
106 Menus and Recipes Suggested for Use in Scotland; Notes on British Restaurants.
107 Report of Conference of Wartime Meals Advisers, September 18, 1942, TNA MAF 99/1725.
108 Collingham, *Taste of War*, p. 495; MO Diarist 5236, January, 1942; MO Diarist 5408, September, 1943; MO Diarist 5399, December 16, 1943; MO Diarist 5282, September, 1942; MO Diarist 5176, December 10, and 16–23, 1942, and April 29, 1943; MO Diarist 5446, January 2, 1943; MO Diarist 5205, September 14, 1942; MO Diarist 5132; Eighth Weekly Report, July, 1941, MO File Report 802, pp. 16–18; MO Diarist 5199, October 1, 1942; MO Diarist 5240, November 16, 1943; MO Diarist 5455, November 20, 1945; MO Diarist 5035, December, 1942; MO Diarist 5192, May, 1942; MO Diarist 5390, May 22, 1942; MO Diarist 5176, April 13, 1943; MO Diarist 5039.2, May 20, 1942; MO Diarist 5410, September 21, 1942.
109 Quoted in C. Driver, *The British At Table, 1940–1980* (London: Chatto and Windus, 1983), p. 35; Derek Milton, Sound Recording 11451, and Peter Bruce Saunders, Sound Recording 18748, Imperial War Museum, London.
110 Chatham, September 1941, p. 8; Newton, Meals Service. Conference at the Ministry of Health, September 12, 1940.
111 Newton, Londoners' Meals Service, October 23, 1940, LMA LCC/RC/GEN/01/002; Letter from Magdalen E. Macdonald to Annette Snapper, August 10, 1943, TNA MAF 99/1612; NCSS, *British Restaurants*, p. 45; "A War-Time Index of Social Change"; Barnett, *British Food Policy*, p. 151.

112 Quoted in K. Price, "Changes on the 'Kitchen Front': The Case of British Restaurants in World War Two," *North East Labour History* 22 (1988), 13; P. Fussell, *Wartime: Understanding and Behavior in the Second World War* (Oxford: Oxford University Press, 1989), p. 204.

113 A. Calder, *The People's War: Britain 1939–1945* (New York: Pantheon, 1969), pp. 138–9.

114 Communal Feeding Centres, MO Topic Collection, TC 17, Box 11, 17-11-G.

115 MO Diarist 5233, January, 1942.

116 MO Diarist 5423, January 19, 1942.

117 Menzies, Memorandum: Communal Feeding, October 19, 1940, TNA MAF 156/282.

118 Letter from Dorothy Green to Lord Woolton [hereafter Woolton], January 14, 1942, TNA MAF 99/1589.

119 Reply by Watson to Memo Regarding Monthly Report to the War Cabinet for February 1941. Community Feeding, February 15, 1941, TNA MAF 156/282.

120 Monthly Report to the War Cabinet for June 1941. British Restaurants, TNA MAF 156/282.

121 People in Production, July, 1942, MO File Report 1344, pp. 270, 272.

122 City of Birmingham. Reconstruction Committee. British Restaurant Inquiry, September 11–October 6, 1944, TNA MAF 99/1734.

123 NCSS, *British Restaurants*, p. 3; LCSS, *The Communal Restaurant*, pp. 10–14, 24.

124 Minute from French to Harwood, October 13, 1941, TNA MAF 99/1645.

125 Memorandum on the Provision of British Restaurants and Emergency Meals Centres.

126 Letter from Woolton to the Heads of Local Authorities, November 5, 1940, TNA MAF 99/1797.

127 *Eating Out With Tommy Trinder*, Ministry of Information, 1941, www.you tube.com/watch?v=1YnFGx1rv20; Farmer, *Food Companions*; pp. 103–7.

128 Calder, *Carry On London*, p. 91.

129 Minute from Menzies to T. S. Quintin Hill, January 30, 1941, TNA MAF 99/1638.

130 Hansard HC Deb June 25, 1941, vol. 372 c. 1066W.

131 People in Production, pp. 270, 272; Hansard HC Deb September 11, 1942, vol. 383 c. 513.

132 Hansard HC Deb February 3, 1942, vol. 377 cc. 1061–2W.

133 Minute from Woolton to Wheeldon, October 4, 1942, TNA MAF 99/1759.

134 Establishment of British Restaurants, TNA MAF 99/1759.

135 Establishment of British Restaurants.

136 Atkins, "Communal Feeding," p. 144.

137 Calder, *People's War*, p. 138.

138 Hansard HC Deb September 11, 1942, vol. 383 cc. 513–14; British Restaurants: Priority for Workers with Limited Meal Periods. Ministry of Food, Circular DO 40, CMF 80, September 19, 1942, TNA MAF 99/1801; British Restaurants. Ministry of Food, Public Relations Division.

139 Day to Day Feeding. British Restaurants; Memorandum on British Restaurants.

140 Memorandum on Communal Feeding, TNA MAF 152/55.
141 British Restaurants, undated draft memo, *c.* 1943.
142 Letter from Menzies to Drummond, May 7, 1941, TNA MAF 98/270.
143 Letter from E. Wightman to Menzies, August 17, 1942, TNA MAF 99/1645; LCC. Meals Service. Serial Note No. 176, LMA LCC/RC/GEN/04/23.
144 LCSS, *Communal Restaurant*, p. 19; Eighth Weekly Report, pp. 16–18.
145 Notes on British Restaurants.
146 MO Diarist 5271, November, 1942.
147 N. Longmate, *How We Lived Then* (London: Hutchinson and Co., 1971), p. 175.
148 Letter from E. G. Houghton to Pyke, June 5, 1943, TNA MAF 98/112.
149 Notes on British Restaurants.
150 Letter from Newton to Watson, October 23, 1941, TNA MAF 99/1610.
151 Memorandum from the Chief Officer, Meals Services to the Chairman of the Civil Defence and General Purposes Committee, Second Draft, July 12, 1945, LMA RCC/GEN/01/026.
152 Eighth Weekly Report, pp. 16–18.
153 Mass Observation Diarist 5271, November, 1942.
154 Imperial War Museum, London, Images D10680, D10681.
155 Imperial War Museum, London, Image D12268.
156 LCSS, *Communal Restaurant*, p. 14.
157 MO Diarist 5157, August 6, 1942.
158 MO Diarist 5271, February, 1943.
159 MO Diarist 5307, September, 1942.
160 British Restaurants. Diary. Housewife, October 23, 1941, MO Topics Collections, TC 75 Industry 1940–55, Box 3, 75-3-H.
161 MO Diarist 5240, December, 1941; Communal Feeding Centres, MO Topic Collection, TC 17, Box 11, 17-11-G.
162 LCSS, *Communal Restaurant*, p. 8.
163 Memorandum on Model Plan for Communal Feeding Centres, TNA MAF 99/1797.
164 Farmer, *Food Companions*, p. 105; Durbach, "British Restaurants," pp. 28–32.
165 M. Barsley, *Common Man and Colonel Bogus* (London: Pilot Press, 1944), p. 24.
166 Calder, *Carry On London*, p. 91.
167 Quoted in J. Davies, *The Wartime Kitchen and Garden* (London: BBC Books, 1993), p. 198. See also MO Diarist 5390, May 22, 1942; Memorandum from the Chief Officer, Meals Services to the Chairman of the Civil Defence and General Purposes Committee, September, 1945, LMA RCC/GEN/01/027; MO Diarist 5192, November 25, 1941, January 21, 1942, May 22, 1942, September 14, 1942; Eighth Weekly Report.
168 Answering You II.
169 NCSS, *British Restaurants*, p. 34.
170 MO Diarist 5192, November 25, 1941, January 21, 1942, May 22, 1942, September 14, 1942.
171 Communal Feeding Centres, MO Topic Collection, TC 17, Box 11, 17-11-G.
172 Wartime Social Survey. Inquiry for the Ministry of Food. Community Feeding in Nottingham, March 10, 1941, TNA INF 1/275.

173 MO Day Survey Respondent 5455, November 20, 1945.
174 NCSS, *British Restaurants*, p. 34.
175 MO Diarist 5236, January, 1942; People in Production, p. 273.
176 Annette M. Snapper, "British Restaurants," TNA MAF 99/1734.
177 Public Feeling About Wartime Reforms, December, 1941, MO File Report 990, p. 2.
178 Eighth Weekly Report, pp. 16–18.
179 MO Diarist 5199, October 1, 1942.
180 Imperial War Museum, London, Image D 10676.
181 LCSS, *Communal Restaurant*, p. 12.
182 Borough of Stetford. Investigation Regarding the Use Made of British Restaurants, TNA MAF 98/112.
183 J. R. Walkowitz, *Nights Out: Life in Cosmopolitan London* (New Haven: Yale University Press, 2012), pp. 194–201.
184 S. Rose, *Which People's War?: National Identity and Citizenship in Britain, 1939–1945* (Oxford: Oxford University Press, 1993); P. Goodman, "'Patriotic Femininity': Women's Morals and Men's Morale during the Second World War," *Gender & History* 10(2) (1998), 278–93.
185 Durbach, "British Restaurants," pp. 19–36.
186 NCSS, *British Restaurants*, p. 73.
187 Hansard HC Deb October 2, 1941, vol. 374 cc. 762–3.
188 Housewive's [sic] Feelings About Food, April, 1942, MO File Report 1224.
189 Housewive's [sic] Feelings About Food.
190 Calder, *Carry on London*, p. 63.
191 Hansard HC Deb March 3, 1942, vol. 378 cc. 540–1.
192 City of Birmingham. Reconstruction Committee. British Restaurant Inquiry.
193 "60 per cent Would Like British Restaurants After the War," *News Chronicle*, January 5, 1945, TNA MAF 99/1734.
194 NCSS, *British Restaurants*, pp. 63–6.
195 NCSS, *British Restaurants*, pp. 5, 20; LCSS, *Communal Restaurant*, p. 19.
196 Barbara Ward, "Young Britain," *Foreign Affairs* 21(4) (1943), 621.
197 C. McNab Shaw, "Communal Feeding," *The Labour Woman*, March, 1941, TNA MAF 99/1589.
198 Beatrice Gomberg, "British Food Control," *Antioch Review* 4(2) (1944), 228.
199 Let Us Face the Future: A Declaration of Labour Policy for the Consideration of the Nation, TNA MAF 99/1736; Minute by Hardman, April 23, 1945, TNA MAF 99/1789.
200 Hansard HL Deb August 15, 1945, vol. 137 cc. 8–12.
201 S. Fielding, P. Thompson, and N. Tiratsoo, *England Arise!: The Labour Party and Popular Politics in 1940s Britain* (Manchester: Manchester University Press, 1995), pp. 108–10.
202 See MAF 99/1706 and MAF 99/1705.
203 Leopold, "LCC Restaurants," p. 203.
204 Minute from Woolton, August 21, 1941, TNA MAF 99/1705.
205 LCSS, *Communal Restaurant*, pp. 6, 25.
206 *Daily Mail*, February 27, 1943, p. 3.

207 Hammond, *Food*, p. 401; Ministry of Food. Statement on British Restaurants, April 10, 1945, TNA MAF 152/55; Cabinet. Lord President's Committee. Conclusions of Meeting held November 16, 1945, TNA MAF 99/1760. Whether the LCC restaurants were profitable is much harder to gauge as many of them also undertook the extra expenses involved in the quarter-mastering of emergency food stocks and supplies. These accounts were not kept separate from the day-to-day feeding responsibilities of the LMS and were estimated at £90,000 per annum. See LMA RCC/GEN/01/028.

208 Caterers Protests. Statement of Representations Received, TNA MAF 99/1644.

209 Letter to Minister of Food from E. Thorpe, June 12, 1941, and Letter to Minister of Food from E. Thorpe, June 14, 1941, TNA MAF 99/1644.

210 Incorporated Association of Purveyors of Light Refreshments, British Restaurants, TNA MAF 99/1737.

211 NCSS, *British Restaurants*, pp. 40, 42.

212 Communal Feeding. Note of a Meeting in the Minister's Room at Great Westminster House, July 9, 1940, TNA MAF 99/1580.

213 LCSS, *Communal Restaurant*, p. 11.

214 Annette M. Snapper, "British Restaurants."

215 *Daily Mirror*, December 11, 1945, TNA MAF 99/1736.

216 Calder, *People's War*, p. 386; Burnett, *England Eats Out*, p. 260.

217 "His 'Bait' – Fresh Salmon," *Daily Mail*, January, 1945, LMA RCC/GEN/01/026.

218 NCSS, Report of the Conference "The Future of the Communal Restaurants," September 7, 1944, TNA MAF 99/1734.

219 Memorandum from the Chief Officer, Meals Services to the Chairman of the Civil Defence and General Purposes Committee, Second Draft.

220 Morale, 1943, January, 1943, MO File Report 1579, p. 9; NCSS, *British Restaurants*, pp. 18–19, 50.

221 Blaina, p. 19.

222 General Department. Informal Post-War Plans Committee. Sub-Committee on Nutritional Policy. Communal Feeding, November 26, 1943, TNA MAF 152/55.

223 Letter to J. M. L. Watson from Hardman, January 2, 1945, TNA MAF 99/1770; British Restaurants. Supplementary Notes for Press Conference, February 13, 1945, TNA MAF 99/1762; Minute by Hardman, April 23, 1945, TNA MAF 99/1789.

224 Minute by Hardman, April 23, 1945, and Minutes by S. W. Hood, April 25, 1945, TNA MAF 99/1789.

225 Minute from French to C. H. Blagburn, May 15, 1945, and Minute from French to Damerell, May 18, 1945, TNA MAF 99/1735; P. Addison, *The Road to 1945: British Politics and the Second World War* (London: Jonathan Cape, 1975), p. 265.

226 M. Roberts, "Private Kitchens, Public Cooking" in J. Boys et al. (eds.), *Making Space: Women and the Man Made Environment* (Sydney: Pluto Press, 1984), p. 113.

227 British Restaurants. Memorandum by Minister of Food to Lord President's Committee, November 2, 1945, TNA MAF 99/1760.

228 Leopold, "LCC Restaurants," p. 206.
229 British Restaurants, TNA MAF 99/1738.
230 Civic Restaurants in Operation during 8 Weeks Ended January 3, 1948. Statistics and Intelligence Division (Catering), TNA CAB 102/747.
231 Hansard HC Deb June 30, 1950, vol. 476 c. 262W; Hansard HC Deb July 23, 1951, vol. 491 c. 5W; Leopold, "LCC Restaurants," pp. 209–11; Hansard HC Deb Feb 11, 1976, vol. 905 c. 550.
232 Hammond, *Food*, p. 412.
233 I. Zweiniger-Bargielowska, "Fair Shares? The Limits of Food Policy in Britain During the Second World War" in R. Duffet, I. Zweiniger-Bargielowska, and A. Drouard (eds.), *Food and War in Twentieth Century Europe* (Farnham: Ashgate, 2011), p. 125; Vernon, *Hunger*, p. 194; M. Roodhouse, *Black Market Britain, 1939–1955* (Oxford: Oxford University Press, 2013).
234 D. Morgan and M. Evans, *The Battle for Britain: Citizenship and Ideology in the Second World War* (London: Routledge, 1993), pp. 161–3; R. M. Titmuss, *Problems of Social Policy* (London: HMSO, 1950), p. 533.
235 Leopold, "LCC Restaurants," p. 212; Atkins, "Communal Feeding," p. 149.
236 Burnett, *England Eats Out*, pp. 248–9, 263.
237 G. Cross, *Time and Money: The Making of Consumer Culture* (London: Routledge, 1993), pp. 184–212; S. Todd, *The People: The Rise and Fall of the Working Class, 1910–2010* (London: John Murray, 2014), pp. 155–6, 199–212; K. Bradley, "Rational Recreation in the Age of Affluence: The Café and Working-Class Youth in London, c. 1939–1965" and K. Moure, "Prosperity for All? Britain and Mass Consumption in Western Europe after World War II" in M. J. Crowley, S. T. Dawson, and E. D. Rappaport (eds.), *Consuming Behaviors: Identity, Politics and Pleasure in Twentieth Century Britain* (London: Bloomsbury, 2015), pp. 71–86, 213–36.
238 P. Gould, *The Unfinished Revolution: How the Modernisers Saved the Labour Party* (London: Little, Brown, and Company, 1998), p. 4.

Chapter 7

1 Occasionally this was referred to as the Welfare Food Service.
2 Levine, *School Lunch Politics*.
3 P. Chapman, *Bananas: How the United Fruit Company Shaped the World* (Edinburgh: Canongate, 2007); C. D. Kepner, Jr. and J. H. Soothill, *The Banana Empire* (New York: The Vanguard Press, 1935); J. Soluri, *Banana Cultures: Agriculture, Consumption, and Environmental Change in Honduras and the United States* (Austin: University of Texas Press, 2005).
4 L. Jacobson, "Beer Goes to War: The Politics of Beer Promotion and Production in the Second World War," *Food, Culture & Society* 12(3) (2009), 275–312; R. D. Apple, *Vitamania: Vitamins in American Culture* (New Brunswick: Rutgers University Press, 1996), pp. 9–11.
5 Pyke, *Food and Society*, p. 7.

6 Smith, "Nutrition Science and the Two World Wars," p. 161; Collingham, *Taste of War*, pp. 10, 353.
7 Collingham, *Taste of War*, p. 389.
8 G. Bourne, *Nutrition and the War* (Cambridge: Cambridge University Press, 1940), pp. 28–9; Orr and Lubbock, *Feeding the People*, p. 1.
9 "Food Facts No. 72," *The Times*, December 2, 1941, p. 2.
10 Titmuss, *Problems of Social Policy*, p. 514.
11 C. Webster, "Government Policy on School Meals and Welfare Foods, 1939–1970" in D. F. Smith (ed.), *Nutrition in Britain: Science, Scientists and Politics in the Twentieth Century* (London: Routledge, 1997), pp. 190–213.
12 Letter to W. T. Jarrett from F. D. Proctor, October 13, 1941, TNA MAF 86/232; Draft Letter to A. S. Marre, TNA MH 110/12.
13 Collingham, *Taste of War*, p. 67.
14 Welfare Milk, Orange Juice, Cod Liver Oil, and Vitamin Tablets, TNA T 227/1176.
15 "Milk and Juices for Children," *The Times*, March 16, 1942, p. 2.
16 "Haliborange Advertisement," *The Times*, February 19, 1940, p. 9.
17 Minute to the Secretary from C. H. Blagburn, December 4, 1945, TNA MAF 101/530; Minute from F. N. Tribe to Minister, November 27, 1945, TNA MAF 101/530.
18 To Clerk of the Council or Town Clerk from Ministry of Health. Welfare Foods Scheme. Circular 152/46, July 16, 1946, TNA MH 56/413; Welfare Foods Scheme. Application for Free Benefit, TNA MH 110/5.
19 Teleprint Message from F. Hollins to G. E. F. Chilver, Distribution of Fruit Juices and Cod Liver Oil to Infants and Young Children, TNA MAF 86/232; Titmuss, *Problems of Social Policy*, p. 512.
20 Letter to Drummond from M. P. Renner, September 8, 1943, TNA MAF 98/59; Hansard HC Deb March 8, 1944, vol. 397 cc. 2079–166; "Vitamins Offer Ignored," *Daily Mail*, December 3, 1942, p. 3; "A Parental Duty," *The Times*, December 5, 1942, p. 5.
21 Welfare Foods Scheme. Average Weekly Quantity Issued and Percentage Uptake in the United Kingdom, April 13, 1948, TNA CAB 102/747.
22 Standing Committee on Medical and Nutritional Problems. Welfare Foods Concentrated Orange Juice. Memorandum by the Ministry of Food on Supply and Distribution, TNA FD 1/2386.
23 Clipping from *News Chronicle*, January 8, 1942 and other clippings in TNA, MH 55/1550.
24 Clipping from *Daily Mirror*, January 8, 1942, TNA, MH 55/1550.
25 "Vitamin Foods," *The Times*, December 19, 1942, p. 2; "Distribution of Vitamin Foods," *The Times*, December 23, 1942, p. 2; "Vitamin Foods for Children," *The Times*, December 15, 1942, p. 2; J. Garnett Harper, "Letter to the Editor of the Times," *The Times*, December 12, 1942, p. 5; Ursula Benoy, "Letter to the Editor of the Times," *The Times*, December 10, 1942, p. 5; Anne Hopkinson, "Letter to the Editor of the Times," *The Times*, April 15, 1943, p. 2; "Points from Letters," *The Times*, August 29, 1945, p. 8; Clipping from *Daily Mirror*, January 13, 1942, TNA MH 55/1550.

26 "Milk and Juices for Children," *The Times*, March 16, 1942, p. 2; "Food Ration Changes," *The Times*, January 16, 1943, p. 2; "Vitamins at War Factories," *The Times*, July 19, 1943, p. 2; "Protective Foods for Winter," *The Times*, October 6, 1943, p. 8; Letter from E. Preston to Dorothy Taylor, January 2, 1943, and National Milk and Vitamins Scheme. Ministry of Health Circular 2609, March 17, 1942, TNA MH 56/413; Ministry of Food. Welfare Foods Service. R.F.O. Bulletin, April, 1951, TNA MH 110/6; "Food Facts, No. 207A," *The Times*, June 20, 1944, p. 3; "Food Facts, No. 372," *The Times*, August 25, 1947, p. 2; "Food Facts, No. 392," *The Times*, January 12, 1948, p. 7.

27 Keeping in Touch, No. 24, August, 1947, TNA MH 55/1561.

28 Keeping in Touch, No. 18, January, 1947, Photograph of Reading Welfare Food Babies, Letter to Dr. W. A. Lethem from E. Hughes, January 29, 1949, Minute to Mr. Rowland from G. I. Brodie, February 11, 1948, Minute to Dr. Taylor from Eric Donaldson, December 23, 1947, Letter from R. A. Smart to G. I. Brodie, August 18, 1947, and Baby Shows, TNA MH 55/1561.

29 Farmer, *Food Companions*, p. 89.

30 "Food Facts, No. 171," *Sunday Times*, October 10, 1943, p. 7, emphasis in original.

31 Family Planning 1944–49, Survey # 365, MO 3–1–C Surveys (Topic Collection); The Effect of the War on Health and Happiness, February 11, 1942, MO File Report 1086; Anne Blythe, "Article by a Mother of 5," *Daily Mail*, March 23, 1944, p. 2; Rhona Churchill, "Mme. Morin's Third Baby," *Daily Mail*, December 28, 1944, p. 2; Ann Temple, "Mothers Say the War Babies Don't Suffer," *Daily Mail*, May 25, 1943, p. 2; Charles J. Martin, Harriette Chick, and E. Margaret Hume, "Letter to the Editor of the Times," *The Times*, November 14, 1944, p. 5.

32 How Britain Eats, January 1, 1942, MO File Report 1022.

33 Hansard HC Deb March 3, 1942, vol. 378 cc. 541–2, and June 9, 1944, vol. 400 cc. 1666–7; Minute from J. R. Bellerby to A. Feavearyear, September 10, 1945, TNA MAF 101/513.

34 Hansard HC Deb June 9, 1944, vol. 400 cc. 1667.

35 Ministry of Food. Actual Arrivals of Concentrated Orange Juice during the Period 1947–1950 and Estimated Arrivals in 1951, TNA T 227/1173.

36 Post-War Food Policy. Maintenance of Special Provisions for Supplying Milk and Vitamin Preparations to Expectant and Nursing Mothers and to Infants, TNA MAF 101/513. On the rhetoric of and schemes to "develop" Palestine see S. Seikaly, *Men of Capital: Scarcity and Economy in Mandate Palestine* (Stanford: Stanford University Press, 2015).

37 Long Term Contract with the West Indies for Supplies of Concentrated Orange Juice, TNA MH 110/18; Letter to C. Eastwood from R. Herbert, January 5, 1950, TNA CO 852/1153/12.

38 Vernon, *Hunger*, pp. 104–17; Worboys, "Discovery of Colonial Malnutrition"; Arnold, "The 'Discovery' of Malnutrition and Diet."

39 Colonial Primary Products Committee Interim Report, TNA MAF 83/2310.

40 Colonial Primary Products Committee Interim Report, Revised Draft, November 8, 1947, TNA MAF 83/2310; Colonial Primary Products Committee Meeting, March 11, 1948, TNA CO 1002/2.
41 Colonial Primary Products Committee Interim Report.
42 Colonial Primary Products Committee. Minutes of the First Meeting, May 29, 1947, TNA MAF 83/2310.
43 J. Darwin, "Was There a Fourth British Empire?" in M. Lynn (ed.), *The British Empire in the 1950s: Retreat or Revival?* (Houndmills: Palgrave, 2006), p. 25.
44 L. J. Butler, "The Ambiguities of British Colonial Development Policy, 1938–48" in A. Gorst, L. Johnman, and W. Scott Lucas (eds.), *Contemporary British History, 1931–61: Politics and the Limits of Policy* (London: Pinter, 1991), pp. 119–40; D. J. Morgan, *The Official History of Colonial Development. Volume II: Developing British Colonial Resources, 1945–1951* (Atlantic Highlands: Humanities Press, 1980), pp. 4–17.
45 A. Hinds, *Britain's Sterling Colonial Policy and Decolonization, 1939–1958* (Westport: Greenwood Press, 2001), pp. 47–51.
46 Seikaly, *Men of Capital*, pp. 77–102; N. Cullather, *The Hungry World: America's Cold War Battle Against Poverty in Asia* (Cambridge: Harvard University Press, 2010), pp. 4–8. See also J. M. Hodge, *Triumph of the Expert: Agrarian Development and the Legacies of British Colonialism* (Athens: Ohio University Press, 2007), pp. 208, 236; M. Cowen and R. Shenton, "The Origin and Course of Fabian Colonialism in Africa," *Journal of Historical Sociology* 4(2) (1991), 143; L. J. Butler, *Britain and Empire: Adjusting to a Post-Imperial World* (London: I.B. Tauris, 2002), p. 83.
47 J. Bailkin, *The Afterlife of Empire* (Berkeley: University of California Press, 2012). See also J. Vernon, "The Local, the Imperial, and the Global: Repositioning Twentieth-Century Britain and the Brief Life of Its Social Democracy," *Twentieth-Century British History* 21(3) (2010), 417.
48 Memorandum, April 28, 1948, TNA, T 227/1173.
49 Cable from Foreign Office to Cairo, November 13, 1948, and Purchase of Citrus Fruit from Palestine, TNA FO 371/68684B; Overseas Negotiations Committee. Working Party on Palestine. Note on Proceedings of First Meeting, September 7, 1948, TNA T 227/1173; Colonial Primary Products Committee Meeting, March 11, 1948. See also documents in MAF 83/2333.
50 Letter from Stafford Cripps to John Strachey, August 14, 1948, and Letter to G. R. Oake from L. C. Pickering, August 23, 1948, TNA MH 110/18; Letter from H. E. Magee [hereafter Magee] to Norman Wright, May 5, 1948; Minute to Dr. Dorothy Taylor from Magee, September 6, 1950, TNA MH 56/413.
51 Letter to C. Eastwood from R. Herbert, February 10, 1950, TNA CO 852/1153/12.
52 Hansard HC Deb February 21, 1946, vol. 419 cc. 292–3W; G. T. Shipston, "The Preparation of Antiscorbutic Concentrates," *Journal of the Society of Chemical Industry* 45 (1926), 1002.
53 Letter from P. G. R. Whalley to John Bodinnar, November 20, 1943, MAF 86/232; Hansard HC Deb February 21, 1946, vol. 419 cc. 293W;

D. C. Sackman, *Orange Empire: California and the Fruits of Eden* (Berkeley: University of California Press, 2005), p. 291.

54 Commonwealth Relations Office. Purchase of Orange Juice Concentrate from Jamaica and British Honduras, September 6, 1962, TNA DO 200/25.

55 Letter to J. W. Seymour from B. J. Crisp, January 21, 1971, TNA MH 156/335; Caribbean Commission Central Secretariat, *Caribbean Market Survey: Citrus* (Port-of-Spain: Caribbean Commission, 1956), p. 14.

56 Hansard HC Deb July 13, 1948, vol. 453 cc. 1156–64.

57 On West Indian immigrants and the Welfare State see V. A. Noble, *Inside the Welfare State: Foundations of Policy and Practice in Post-War Britain* (London: Routledge, 2009), pp. 91–120; Bailkin, *Afterlife of Empire*.

58 Letter to H. L. Jenkyns from E. Melville, September 24, 1948, TNA T 227/1173.

59 "Area Council Delegates Approve Changes in Articles of Citrus Assocn.," *The Daily Gleaner*, August 6, 1948, p. 8.

60 Letter to H. L. Jenkyns from H. F. Heinemann, October 15, 1948, TNA MH 110/18.

61 Letter to H. L. Jenkyns from H. F. Heinemann, October 15, 1948, TNA MH 110/18.

62 Telegram from Secretary of State for the Colonies to all West Indian Colonies (except Bermuda), October 25, 1948, TNA MH 110/12.

63 Long Term Contract With the West Indies for Supplies of Concentrated Orange Juice.

64 "House of Commons Monday, Nov. 29," *The Times*, November 30, 1948, p. 6; "Citrus Men Get 10 Year Contract," *The Daily Gleaner*, November 30, 1948, p. 1.

65 "Orange Juice Price at 30/- Again," *The Daily Gleaner*, August 7, 1951, p. 1.

66 Long Term Contract With the West Indies for Supplies of Concentrated Orange Juice; Memorandum. Purchases of 65 Brix Concentrated Orange Juice by Ministry of Health from Jamaica and British Honduras, June 21, 1965, TNA CO 852/2429; *Caribbean Market Survey*, p. 14.

67 Concentrated Orange Juice. Maximum and Minimum Availability Over 1950–1951 Season, TNA T 227/1173.

68 Letter to P. M. Johnson from B. Donaldson, October 23, 1950, and Ministry of Food Memorandum: Supplies and Distribution of Orange Juice Concentrate, Rationing and Welfare Foods Division, September 15, 1950, TNA MH 110/16; Standing Committee on Medical and Nutritional Problems. Welfare Foods Concentrated Orange Juice. Memorandum by the Ministry of Food on Supply and Distribution, TNA FD 1/2386; Minute to Dr. Dorothy Taylor from Magee, September 6, 1950, TNA MH 56/413; Letter from Ministry of Food to Treasury, November 21, 1949, TNA MH 110/18.

69 "Infant Princess Named," *The Times*, August 30, 1950, p. 4; "Princess Anne is the Name," *Daily Mail*, August 30, 1950, p. 3.

70 Let Us Win Through Together: A Declaration of Labour Policy for the Consideration of the Nation, http://politicsresources.net/area/uk/man/lab50.htm.

71 On the interwar "Buy Empire Goods" campaign see Trentmann, *Free Trade Nation*, pp. 228–40.

72 J. M. Lee, *Colonial Development and Good Government* (Oxford: Clarendon Press, 1967), p. 134; Morgan, *Official History of Colonial Development. Volume II*, pp. 226–319; M. Havinden and D. Meredith, *Colonialism and Development: Britain and Its Tropical Colonies, 1850–1960* (London: Routledge, 1993), pp. 276–83, 292, 304–5.

73 M. Hill, *The Welfare State in Britain: A Political History Since 1945* (Aldershot: Edward Elgar, 1993), p. 46; T. F. Lindsay and M. Harrington, *The Conservative Party, 1918–1979*, 2nd ed. (Basingstoke: Macmillan, 1979), p. 173.

74 H. Jones, "The Cold War and the Santa Claus Syndrome: Dilemmas in Conservative Social Policy-Making, 1945–57" in M. Francis and I. Zweiniger-Bargielowska (eds.), *The Conservatives and British Society, 1880–1990* (Cardiff: University of Wales Press, 1996), pp. 240–54; K. Jeffreys, *Retreat from New Jerusalem: British Politics, 1951–64* (New York: St. Martin's Press, 1997), pp. 131–53.

75 Assessment of Risks to the West Indian Citrus Industry, Appendix A, Draft, TNA MH 110/12.

76 *Caribbean Market Survey*, p. 45.

77 Concentrated Orange Juice. Contract, Prices, and Values, TNA MH 110/11.

78 Pyke, *Food and Society*, pp. 91, 93; Bourne, *Nutrition and the War*, p. 37; M. Joseph and M. Nestle, "Food and Politics in the Modern Age: 1920–2012" in A. Bentley (ed.), *A Cultural History of Food in the Modern Age* (London: Bloomsbury, 2016), pp. 99–102.

79 Standing Committee on Medical and Nutritional Problems. Concentrated Orange Juice for Children and Mothers: Medical Aspects, Ministry of Health, September 1950, TNA FD 1/2386.

80 Minute to Magee from E. R. Bransby, January 9, 1953, and Minute from Magee to Enid Russell-Smith [hereafter Russell-Smith], January 10, 1953, TNA MH 56/535.

81 E. R. Bransby and J. E. Fothergill, "The Diets of Young Children," *British Journal of Nutrition* 8(3) (1954), 195–204.

82 Sackman, *Orange Empire*, pp. 107–14.

83 Minute to Magee from E. R. Bransby, January 9, 1953, and Magee, National Vitamin Schemes, August 7, 1953, TNA MH 56/535.

84 Minute from Magee to Russell-Smith, January 10, 1953, TNA MH 56/535.

85 Minute from E. R. Bransby to Magee, March 30, 1953, TNA MH 56/535.

86 Minute from Magee to D. Emery and Beattie, March 31, 1953, TNA MH 56/535.

87 Minute from D. Emery to Russell-Smith, April 10, 1953, TNA MH 56/535.

88 Clipping from *Daily Express*, April 7, 1953, TNA MH 56/535.

89 Letter from Norman Wright to Sir John Charles, April 8, 1953, and Letter from D. Emery to W. Donaldson, April 10, 1953, TNA MH 56/535.

90 Note of the Proposed Discontinuance of Welfare Food Orange Juice Concentrate to Children in the 2–5 Age Group, TNA MH 56/535.

91 Letter from Gwilym Lloyd-George, November 13, 1953, TNA MH 56/535; National Food Survey Figures. Changes in Earnings, Prices and Expenditure of Food, 1950–55, TNA MH 134/109.

92 Review of Welfare Foods, January, 1956, TNA MH 55/2358.

93 Chapman Pincher, "Cut-price Orange Juice – the Facts Come Out, 33,000,000 Bottles of Lost Cash," *Daily Express*, January 26, 1955, TNA MH 56/535; Bransby and Fothergill, "Diets of Young Children," pp. 195–204.

94 Draft Letter to Moss from Ministry of Health re: Consumption of Welfare Foods, August, 1955, and Notes on Uptake of Welfare Foods, TNA MH 55/2354.

95 Note of an Informal Talk With Representatives of S&S Services Ltd. About the Ministry's Next Purchase of Concentrated Orange Juice, June 11, 1954, TNA MH 110/12.

96 *Caribbean Market Survey*, p. 31; Morgan, *Official History of Colonial Development. Volume III*, p. 131.

97 Minute from R. E. Stedman to E. C. Harwood re: Concentrated Orange Juice – British West Indies, January 12, 1955, TNA MH 110/12.

98 Minute from R. E. Stedman to John Roberts, January 14, 1955, TNA MH 110/12.

99 West Indian Citrus Industry. Report of Fact-Finding Mission. Summary of Conclusions and Prospects of Industry, Draft, General Economic Background of Citrus-Growing Territories c. 1955, and Assessment of Risks to the West Indian Citrus Industry, Appendix A, Draft, TNA MH 110/12.

100 Assessment of Risks to the West Indian Citrus Industry.

101 West Indian Citrus Industry. Report of Fact-Finding Mission; C. Leubuscher, *Bulk Buying from the Colonies* (Oxford: Oxford University Press, 1956), p. 114, ftnt 3.

102 "Citrus Mission Report Out," *The Daily Gleaner*, April 8, 1955, pp. 1, 3, 5.

103 Letter to W. B. L. Monson from F. Hollins, May 19, 1955, TNA MH 110/12.

104 Extract from Estimates 1956/57 Class V4 England and Wales. Welfare Foods Service, TNA MH 56/535.

105 Minute to Pater from N. Teller, September 18, 1970, TNA MH 156/335; Collingham, *Taste of War*, p. 396.

106 Supply of Concentrated Orange Juice from Jamaica and British Honduras in 1955, September 19, 1955, TNA MH 110/12.

107 "Sir Robert Kirkwood, Philanthropist, is Dead," *The Daily Gleaner*, May 9, 1984, p. 1.

108 Supply of Concentrated Orange Juice from Jamaica and British Honduras in 1955.

109 Background Note on Proposals for Assistance to West Indian Citrus Industry Other Than the Price Assistance Scheme, TNA CO 1029/148; Morgan, *Official History of Colonial Development. Volume III*, pp. 130–1; Butler, *Britain and Empire*, p. 107.

110 Note for the Secretary of State on the West Indian Citrus Delegation's Letter of July 13, TNA CO 1029/148. For more on the Colonial Development and Welfare Funds see E. Wallace, *The British Caribbean: From the Decline of*

Colonialism to the End of the Federation (Toronto: University of Toronto Press, 1977), pp. 48–52; Lee, *Colonial Development*; Morgan, *Official History of Colonial Development.Volumes II and III*; Hinds, *Britain's Sterling Colonial Policy*; H. Johnson, "The West Indies and the Conversion of the British Official Classes to the Development Idea," *Journal of Commonwealth and Comparative Politics* 15(1) (1977), 55–83; Havinden and Meredith, *Colonialism and Development*.

111 Minute from E. C. U. Wilson to J. Roberts, August 20, 1955, TNA MH 110/12.

112 Letter from R. L. M. Kirkwood to John Roberts, August 9, 1955, emphasis in original, and Note of a Meeting held at Great Westminster House on August 5, 1955: Concentrated Orange Juice from Jamaica, August 12, 1955, TNA MH 110/12.

113 Supply of Concentrated Orange Juice from Jamaica and British Honduras in 1955.

114 Note of a Meeting held in Mr. Harwood's Room at 10 Whitehall Place on September 29, 1955, TNA MH 110/12.

115 Minute from A. Lennox-Boyd to N. Manley and A. Gomes, September 29, 1955, TNA MH 110/12.

116 *Caribbean Market Survey*, p. 30.

117 *Caribbean Market Survey*, p. 4.

118 Memorandum: Comments of the British Caribbean Citrus Association on the Secretary of State's Letter of September 29, TNA MH 110/12.

119 Letter from N. W. Manley to Alan Lennox-Boyd, October 4, 1955, TNA MH 110/12.

120 West Indian Citrus Negotiations, and Colonial Office, Notes on Agreed Price Assistance Scheme, October 7, 1955, TNA MH 110/12.

121 Note on a Suggestion to Cut Down the Subsidy on "Welfare" Orange Juice, TNA MH 110/16; Minute to Turnbull, Marshall, and Painter from R. L. Workman, February 14, 1956, TNA T 227/1178; Minute re: Supply of Welfare Foods by Local Authorities. To Mr. Turnbull and Mr. Painter from R. L. Workman, November 8, 1955, TNA T 227/1182.

122 Hansard HC Deb June 5, 1946, vol. 423 c. 324–5W.

123 Minute to Turnbull, Marshall, and Painter from R. L. Workman, February 14, 1956, TNA T 227/1178; Minute from the Minister of Health to the Secretary, January 9, and Letter to Russell-Smith from T. D. Haddow, January 5, 1956, TNA MH 55/2358.

124 Copy of a Letter from the Ministry of Health to Sir Henry Cohen, and Minute to the Chief Medical Officer and Secretary from Russell-Smith, January 3, 1956, TNA MH 55/2358.

125 Central Health Services Councils (England and Scotland). Standing Medical Advisory Committees. Joint Sub-Committee on Welfare Foods. Minutes of Meeting Held June 11, 1956, TNA MH 55/2358.

126 Need for Welfare Food Supplements. Ministry of Health Paper for Joint Sub-Committee, TNA MH 55/2358.

127 Joint Sub-Committee on Welfare Foods. Minutes of Meeting Held June 11, 1956; Central Health Services Councils (England and Scotland). Standing Medical Advisory Committees. Joint Sub-Committee on Welfare Foods. Interim Report on Orange Juice, TNA MH 55/2358.

128 Draft Paper for Home Affairs Committee by the Parliamentary Secretary to the Ministry of Health and Secretary of State for Scotland. Welfare Foods, TNA T 227/1176; E. McKenzie, Welfare Food Service. Changes Recommended in Provision of Welfare Orange Juice, May 14, 1957, TNA MH 55/2358.

129 Minute to Turnbull from G. R. Ashford, July 25, 1957, TNA T 227/1176.

130 Note on a Suggestion to Cut Down the Subsidy on "Welfare" Orange Juice.

131 Memorandum by the Secretary of State for the Colonies to the Home affairs Committee of the Cabinet re: Welfare Foods, July 26, 1957, TNA PREM 11/1986.

132 "Macmillan: My Political Philosophy," *Sunday Times*, July 10, 1966, p. 22.

133 P. Hennessy, *Having It So Good: Britain in the Fifties* (London: Allen Lane, 2006), pp. 533–4.

134 Personal Minute from Harold Macmillan to Chancellor of the Exchequer, August 3, 1957, TNA PREM 11/1986.

135 "July 20, 1957: Britons 'Have Never Had It So Good'" http://news.bbc.co.uk/onthisday/hi/dates/stories/july/20/newsid_3728000/3728225.stm

136 C.C. (57) 63rd Conclusions Minute 1: Welfare Orange Juice, August 27, 1957, TNA PREM 11/1986; Cable to Jamaica and British Honduras from Secretary of State Colonies, September 27, 1957, TNA MH 110/13.

137 Letter from David to John Hare re: Welfare Orange Juice Contract, June 4, 1959, TNA MAF 255/910.

138 Minute from M.W., July 27, 1959, and Minute from J.H., July 27, 1959, TNA MH 110/19.

139 Minute from G. S. Bishop, July 27, 1959 to Secretary, TNA MH 110/19.

140 Purchases of Orange Juice From the West Indies. Memorandum by the Minister of Agriculture, Fisheries and Food, July 23, 1959, TNA MH 110/19.

141 *Our Jamaican Problem*, January 17, 1955, British Pathé newsreels, www.britishpathe.com/video/our-jamaican-problem; Hennessy, *Having It So Good*, pp. 223–4.

142 Letter from British Caribbean Citrus Association to Minister of State for Colonial Affairs, July 20, 1960, TNA MAF 255/910.

143 Draft Statement of Intent. Purchases of Concentrated Orange Juice from the British West Indies, and Purchase of Concentrated Orange Juice from West Indies, 1960–61, MK 4597, TNA MAF 255/910.

144 R. M. Page, *Revisiting the Welfare State* (Maidenhead: Open University Press, 2007), pp. 51–4; R. Lowe, *The Welfare State in Britain Since 1945*, 3rd ed. (Houndmills: Palgrave, 2005), p. 95.

145 Jeffreys, *Retreat From New Jerusalem*, pp. 70–1.

146 Letter to B. D. Fraser from W. L. Gorell Barnes, November 23, 1960, and Extract from Note of Meeting held in the Chancellor's Room in the House of Commons on November 17, 1960, TNA MH 134/126; Minute to the Minister of Health, Proposed Economies in Estimates 1961–2, TNA MH 134/126.

147 Hansard HC Deb February 8, 1961, vol. 634 c. 438.

148 Uptake of Welfare Foods-Quantities, TNA MH 156/94.

149 West Indian Welfare Orange Juice – Publicity. Note of a Meeting of the Informal Group held at the Commonwealth Relations Office, September 25, 1962, TNA DO 200/26.
150 Note for the Record. Jamaican Orange Juice Concentrate, August 1, 1962, TNA DO 200/25.
151 Minute from L. B. Walsh Atkins to J. J. Saville Garner [hereafter Garner], August 10, 1962, and Letter from Garner to Hilton Poynton, August 13, 1962, TNA DO 200/25.
152 Purchase of Orange Juice Concentrate from Jamaica and British Honduras, September 6, 1962.
153 Jamaican Orange Juice, TNA DO 200/25.
154 Minute from L. B. Walsh Atkins to Garner, August 10, 1962, TNA DO 200/25.
155 Talking Points on Jamaican Orange Juice, TNA DO 200/25.
156 Minute to L. B. Walsh Atkins from Garner, August 3, 1962, TNA DO 200/25.
157 Letter to C. E. Diggines from E. L. Sykes [hereafter Sykes], September 14, 1962, TNA DO 200/25.
158 Minute from Duke of Devonshire to Secretary of State, September 12, 1962, TNA DO 200/25.
159 Letter to Enoch Powell from Duncan Sandys, August 16, 1962, and Ministry of Health's Purchases of Concentrated Orange Juice from Jamaica and British Honduras for the UK Welfare Foods Scheme, August 1, 1962, TNA DO 200/25.
160 Talking Points on Jamaican Orange Juice.
161 S. Mawby, *Ordering Independence: The End of Empire in the Anglophone Caribbean, 1947–1969* (Houndmills: Palgrave, 2012), pp. 72–94.
162 Draft Letter from Duke of Devonshire to Minister of Health, TNA DO 200/25.
163 Draft Letter from Duke of Devonshire to Minister of Health.
164 Minute from Duke of Devonshire to Secretary of State, September 12, 1962.
165 Chapman, *Bananas*.
166 Telegram from Kingston to Commonwealth Relations Office, September 28, 1962, Letter from Sykes to C. E. Diggines, October 22, 1962, Letter from Sykes to R. M. K. Slater, October 22, 1962, and Letter to Sykes from C. E. Diggines, November 2, 1962, TNA DO 200/26.
167 Purchase of Orange Juice Concentrate from Jamaica and British Honduras, September 6, 1962.
168 The figures have to be inferred for British Honduras by reading these files against each other as figures are primarily for Jamaica, the larger of the two suppliers: Purchases of 65 Brix Concentrated Orange Juice; Appendix to "History," TNA BN 13/186; Letter to F. D. Milne from B. J. Crisp, October 28, 1969, TNA FCO 67/100.
169 Purchase of Orange Juice Concentrate from Jamaica and British Honduras, September 6, 1962.
170 Purchases of 65 Brix Concentrated Orange Juice.

171 Hansard HC Deb March 23, 1964, vol. 692 cc. 28–9, and July 29, 1964, vol. 699 cc. 1420–2; Letter from F. J. Farrell to D. A. Shepherd, February 6, 1964, TNA CO 852/2429.

172 Unsigned Memo to Mr. Mayston and Mr. John, July, 1965, and Suggested Reply to High Commissioner, August 10, 1965, TNA CO 852/2429.

173 Elizabeth Pakenham, "Penal Reform in the Nursery," *Sunday Times*, April 24, 1960, p. 22.

174 T. E. Oppe, et al., "Committee on Medical Aspects of Food Policy. Panel on Cariogenic Foods: First Report," *British Dental Journal*, March 18, 1969, pp. 273–80.

175 J. F. Burton, "Dangers of Fortified Syrups," *British Dental Journal*, July 4, 1967, p. 6; "Vitamin Supplements," *British Dental Journal*, July 18, 1967, pp. 65–6; M. R. Shaw, "Dangers of Fortified Syrups," *British Dental Journal*, July 18, 1967, p. 70; E. B. D. Jones, "Dangers of Fortified Syrups," *British Dental Journal*, August 1, 1967, p. 119; W. T. C. Berry, "Vitamin Supplements," *British Dental Journal*, September 5, 1967, p. 199; David Lindsey, "Vitamin Supplements," *British Dental Journal*, September 5, 1967, p. 199; W. T. C. Berry, "Vitamin Supplements," *British Dental Journal*, September 19, 1967, p. 265; Alan Edwards, "Vitamin Supplements," *British Dental Journal*, October 17, 1967, p. 365; C. H. Rubra, "Vitamin Supplements," *British Dental Journal*, November 7, 1967, pp. 416–17; Rosemary Simon, "Drawback of Cheaper Sweets," *The Times*, July 27, 1967, p. 7.

176 Letter to J. W. Seymour from B. J. Crisp, January 21, 1971, and Withdrawal of Welfare Orange Juice form the Welfare Food Service, TNA MH 156/335; Minute to Mr. Gallagher and Mr. Williams from G. S. Whitehead, Welfare Orange Juice, TNA FCO 44/238; Welfare Foods Service. New Vitamin (A, C, and D) Preparation, November, 1970, TNA BN 13/186.

177 M. Donnelly, *Sixties Britain* (Harlow: Longman, 2005), pp. 139–42; D. Vincent, *Poor Citizens: The State and the Poor in Twentieth-Century Britain* (London: Longman, 1991), p. 164.

178 Minute to Gordon from R. A. Owen, September 4, 1968, TNA MH 156/328; Department of Health and Social Security, Your Right to Free Welfare Milk and Foods, Leaflet W11, February, 1971, Minute from E. L. Mayston to Mr. Collier and Mr. Betts, February 23, 1971, and Welfare Foods Service. New Vitamin (A, C, and D) Preparation, November, 1970, TNA BN 13/186; Minute to Ferry from A. S. Marre, January 16, 1969, TNA MH 156/328; Withdrawal of Welfare Orange Juice from the Welfare Food Service.

179 Letter to Lord Shepherd from Dick Crossman, August 22, 1969, TNA FCO 44/238.

180 "Are Baby Clinics Needed? Ask GPs," *Daily Mail*, April 16, 1966, p. 3. See also Elizabeth Good, "Wide-Awake Ideas," *Sunday Times*, February 3, 1963, p. 31; Rodney Tyler, "Why I Can't Get into Top Gear...," *Daily Mail*, November 19, 1970, p. 8.

181 "The Voice of Youth," *Daily Mail*, November 30, 1967, p. 1.

182 Peter Black, "Teleview," *Daily Mail*, March 9, 1962, p. 3.

183 "Mr. Muggeridge and the A-levels Road to Paradise," *The Times*, February 17, 1967, p. 12.

184 Ian Church, "Callaghan Insulted," *The Times*, June 9, 1970, p. 1; Donnelly, *Sixties Britain*, pp. 154–5.

185 The WFS continued without the orange juice through 2006 when it was replaced with the Healthy Start Scheme, which provided vouchers for infant formula, cow's milk, fruit and vegetables to pregnant women and children under 4 who met certain qualifications. See H. Lambie-Mumford, *Hungry Britain: The Rise of Food Charity* (Bristol: Policy Press, 2017), p. 28.

186 Hansard HL Deb March 11, 1971, vol. 316 cc.197–204, and March 22, 1971, vol. 316 cc. 646–8.

187 B. J. Crisp, Concentrated Orange Juice. Note of Visit to Jamaica and British Honduras, January/February 1971, February 15, 1971, TNA BN 13/186.

188 S. R. Ashton, "Keeping Change Within Bounds: A Whitehall Reassessment" in M. Lynn (ed.), *The British Empire in the 1950s: Retreat or Revival?* (Houndmills: Palgrave, 2006), p. 41; Nicole Longpré, "'An Issue That Could Tear Us Apart': Race, Empire, and Economy in the British (Welfare) State," *Canadian Journal of History* 46(1) (2011), 87–9.

Conclusion

1 Hamlin, "Could You Starve to Death?"

2 Minute from H. W. S. Francis, July 19, 1929, TNA MH 55/486; Letter from S. P. Vivian to A. N. Rucker, July 29, 1929, TNA RG 26/13; Vernon, *Hunger*, pp. 81–3.

3 See TNA RG 26/13, MH 55/485, and MH 55/486.

4 Foucault, *Discipline and Punish*, pp. 135–69.

5 Lambie-Mumford, *Hungry Britain*.

Bibliography

Archival Sources

British Library
Imperial War Museum, London
Lancashire Archives
London Metropolitan Archives
The National Archives, United Kingdom

Digital Collections

Hansard, https://hansard.parliament.uk/
Mass Observation Online, http://www.massobs.org.uk/

Films

Eating Out with Tommy Trinder. Ministry of Information, 1941.
Our Jamaican Problem. British Pathé, 1955.

Parliamentary Papers and Government Publications

1835: Gaols, Copies of All Reports and of Schedules (B), February 17, 1836. (PP 31).
Annual Report for 1908 of the Chief Medical Officer of the Board of Education. London: HMSO, 1910.
Appendix to the Report of the Famine Commission, 1898, Vol. I: Bengal. London: HMSO, 1899. (PP C. 9252).
Appendix to the Report of the Famine Commission, 1898, Vol. II: Madras Presidency. London: HMSO, 1899. (PP C. 9253).
Appendix to the Report of the Famine Commission, 1898, Vol. III: Bombay Presidency. London: HMSO, 1899. (PP C. 9254).
Appendix to the Report of the Famine Commission, 1898, Vol. IV: Central Provinces and Berar. London: HMSO, 1899. (PP C. 9255).
Appendix to the Report of the Famine Commission, 1898, Vol. V: North-West Provinces and Oudh. London: HMSO, 1899. (PP C. 9256).
Appendix to the Report of the Famine Commission, 1898, Vol. VI: Punjab. London: HMSO, 1899. (PP C. 9257).

Appendix to the Report of the Indian Famine Commission, 1898, Vol. VII: Miscellaneous. London: HMSO, 1899. (PP C. 9258).

Convict Prison Dietaries: Copy of the Reports of a Committee Appointed to Inquire into the Dietaries of Convict Prisons, July 8, 1864. (PP 467).

Copy of the Rules for the Dietaries of the Prisons in England and Wales, March 18, 1878. (PP 93).

Correspondence between the Government of India and the Secretary of State in Council Relative to the Famine in Bengal, Part I. London: HMSO, 1874. (PP C. 955).

Dietaries for Convicts, &c. Returns of the Dietaries Sanctioned by the Government for Convicts at Gibraltar, Bermuda, and the Different Convict Establishments of Every Class in England, Wales, and Ireland, March 21, 1857. (PP 154).

Dietaries in Prisons (England and Wales) (Acts 1865 and 1877). Copy of the Report of the Committee Appointed to Inquire into the Dietaries of the Prisons in England Wales Subject to the Prison Acts 1865 and 1877, with the Memorandum of Instruction of the Prison Commissioners, March 19, 1878. (PP 95).

Discipline and Management of Prisons in Her Majesty's Colonial Possessions. London: HMSO, 1871. (PP C. 355).

Dudley Union: Copy of Correspondence between the Guardians of Dudley Union and the Poor-Law Commissioners Respecting the Disallowance of the Money Paid for the Last Christmas-day Dinner Given to the Paupers, 1847. (PP 276).

East India (Bengal and Orissa Famine): Papers and Correspondence Relative to the Famine in Bengal and Orissa, Including the Report of the Famine Commission and the Minutes of the Lieutenant Governor of Bengal and the Governor General of India, Part I, May 31, 1867. (PP 335).

East India (Bengal and Orissa Famine): Papers and Correspondence Relative to the Famine in Bengal and Orissa, Including the Report of the Famine Commission and the Minutes of the Lieutenant Governor of Bengal and the Governor General of India, Part II, July 5, 1867. (PP 335-I).

East India (Bengal and Orissa Famine): Papers Relating to the Famine in Behar, Part III, May 31, 1867. (PP 335-II).

East India (Famine Correspondence), Part III: Copy of Correspondence between the Secretary of State for India and the Government of India on the Subject of the Famine in Western and Southern India. London: HMSO, 1877. (PP C. 1879).

East India (Famine Correspondence), Part IV: Copy of Correspondence between the Secretary of State for India and the Government of India on the Subject of the Famine in Western and Southern India. London: HMSO, 1878. (PP C. 1920).

East India (Famine): Papers Regarding the Famine and Relief Operations in India during 1899–1900, Vol. I: British Districts. London: HMSO, 1900. (PP Cd. 205).

East India (Famine): Papers Regarding the Famine and the Relief Operations in India during 1900–1902, Vol. I: British Districts. London: HMSO, 1902. (PP Cd. 1179).

East India (Famine): Report of the East India Famine Commission, 1901 and Papers Relating Thereto. London: HMSO, 1901. (PP Cd. 876).

East India (Madras and Orissa Famine): Copies of Papers Relating to the Famine in the Madras Presidency in 1865–66 and Additional Papers Relating to the Famine in Orissa Subsequent to the Report of the Commission, July 30, 1867. (PP 490).

East India, Part II: Copy of Correspondence between the Secretary of State for India and the Government of India on the Subject of the Threatened Famine in Western and Southern India. London: HMSO, 1877. (PP C. 1754).

Eight Report from the Select Committee on the Poor Law Amendment Act, 1837. (PP 278).

Famine and Relief Operations in India: Further Papers Regarding the Famine and the Relief Operations in India during the Years 1896–97, No. IV. London: HMSO, 1897. (PP C. 8660).

Famine and Relief Operations in India: Further Papers Regarding the Famine and the Relief Operations in India during the Years 1896–97, No. IVA. London: HMSO, 1898. (PP C. 8737).

Famine and Relief Operations in India: Further Papers Regarding the Famine and the Relief Operations in India during the Years 1896–97, No. V. London: HMSO, 1898. (PP C. 8739).

Famine and Relief Operations in India: Further Papers, 1897–98, No. VII. London: HMSO, 1898. (PP C. 8823).

Famine and Relief Operations in India: Papers Regarding the Famine and the Relief Operations in India during the Year 1896. London: HMSO, 1897. (PP C. 8302).

Famine and Relief Operations in India: Further Papers Regarding the Famine and the Relief Operations in India during the Years 1896–97, No. III. London: HMSO, 1897. (PP C. 8504).

Fourteenth Report of the Poor Law Commissioners, Appendix A, 1847–48. (PP 960).

Further Correspondence between the Government of India and the Secretary of State in Council Relative to the Famine in Bengal, Part II. London: HMSO, 1874. (PP C. 955-I).

Further Correspondence between the Government of India and the Secretary of State in Council Relative to the Famine in Bengal, Part III. London: HMSO, 1874. (PP C. 955-II).

Further Correspondence between the Government of India and the Secretary of State in Council Relative to the Famine in Bengal, Part IV. London: HMSO, 1874. (PP C. 955-III).

Further Correspondence between the Government of India and the Secretary of State in Council Relative to the Famine in Bengal, Part V. London: HMSO, 1874. (PP C. 955-IV).

Gaols, West Indies: Copies of Correspondence Relative to the State of the Gaols in the West Indies and the British Colonies in South America; and Also, of Any Instructions Which Have Been Sent Out from the Colonial Office Relative to Such Prisons, March 30, 1831. (PP 334).

Hammond, R.J. Food, Volume II: Studies in Administration and Control. London: HMSO, 1956.

The Health of the School Child: Annual Report of the Chief Medical Officer of the Board of Education for the Year 1922. London: HMSO, 1923.

The Health of the School Child: Annual Report of the Chief Medical Officer of the Board of Education for the Year 1926. London: HMSO, 1927.

The Health of the School Child: Annual Report of the Chief Medical Officer of the Board of Education for the Year 1931. London: HMSO, 1932.

The Health of the School Child: Annual Report of the Chief Medical officer of the Board of Education for the Year 1932. London: HMSO, 1933.

The Health of the School Child: Annual Report of the Chief Medical officer of the Board of Education for the Year 1933. London: HMSO, 1934.

The Health of the School Child: Annual Report of the Chief Medical Officer of the Board of Education for the Year 1934. London: HMSO, 1935.

The Health of the School Child: Annual Report of the Chief Medical Officer of the Board of Education for the Year 1935. London: HMSO, 1936.

The Health of the School Child: Annual Report of the Chief Medical Officer of the Board of Education for the Year 1936. London: HMSO, 1937.

The Health of the School Child: Annual Report of the Chief Medical Officer of the Board of Education for the Year 1937. London: HMSO, 1938.

The Health of the School Child: Annual Report of the Chief Medical Officer of the Board of Education for the Year 1938. London: HMSO, 1940.

The Health of the School Child: Fifty Years of the School Health Service. Report of the Chief Medical Officer of the Ministry of Education for the Years 1956 and 1957. London: HMSO, 1958.

Holderness, T.W. *Government of India: Department of Revenue and Agriculture (Famine). Narrative of the Famine in India in 1896–7.* London: HMSO, 1897.

Instructions to be Followed in the Carrying Out of the Rules Approved by the Secretary of State for the Home Department for the Government of Convict Prisons. London: HMSO, 1896.

Jebb, Colonel Joshua. *Report on the Discipline of the Convict Prisons for 1856 and 1857.* London: HMSO, 1858.

Jebb, Sir Joshua. *General Report on the Convict Prisons, 1860–1.* London: HMSO, 1862.

Metropolitan Workhouses, 1850. (PP 133).

Ministry of Food. *How Britain Was Fed in War Time.* London: HMSO, 1946.

Ministry of Health Advisory Committee on Nutrition. *Memorandum to the Minister of Health on the Criticism and Improvement of Diets.* London: HMSO, 1932.

Minutes of Evidence Taken by the Departmental Committee on Prisons. London: HMSO, 1895. (PP C. 7702 – I).

Miscellaneous No. 15 (1915). Further Correspondence with the United States Ambassador Respecting the Treatment of British Prisoners of War and Interned Civilians in Germany. London: HMSO, 1915. (PP Cd. 7961).

Miscellaneous No. 18 (1916). Report by Doctor A.E. Taylor on the Conditions of Diet and Nutrition in the Internment Camp at Ruhleben. London: HMSO, 1916. (PP Cd. 8259).

Miscellaneous No. 19 (1915). Correspondence with the United States Ambassador Respecting the Treatment of British Prisoners of War and Interned Civilians in Germany. London: HMSO, 1915. (PP Cd. 8108).

Miscellaneous No. 21 (1916). Further Correspondence Respecting the Conditions of Diet and Nutrition in the Internment Camp at Ruhleben. London: HMSO, 1916. (PP Cd. 8262).

Miscellaneous No. 26 (1916). Further Correspondence with the United States Ambassador Respecting the Treatment of British Prisoners of War and Interned Civilians in Germany. London: HMSO, 1916. (PP Cd. 8297).

Miscellaneous No. 30 (1916). Reports of Visits of Inspection Made by Officials of the United States Embassy to Various Internment Camps in the United Kingdom. London: HMSO, 1916. (PP Cd. 8324).

Ninth Report from the Select Committee on the Poor Law Amendment Act, 1837. (PP 296).

Papers Relating to the Improvement of Prison Discipline in the Colonies, August 1875. (PP C. 1338).

Paton, D. Noel and Leonard Findlay. *Medical Research Council. Child Life Investigations. Poverty, Nutrition and Growth: Studies of Child Life in Cities and Rural Districts of Scotland.* London: HMSO, 1926.

Prison Commission for Scotland: Report on Prison Dietaries by James Craufurd Dunlop. London: HMSO, 1899. (PP C. 9514).

Prison Dietaries (Scotland): Rules Made by the Secretary of State for Scotland under the Prisons (Scotland) Act, 1877, Establishing New Rates of Dietaries for the Several Classes of Prisoners, June 15, 1900. (PP 205).

Prison Dietaries Committee: Report of the Departmental Committee on Prison Dietaries. London: HMSO, 1899. (PP C. 9166).

Prison Discipline: Copies of Correspondence between the Secretary of State for the Home Department and the Inspector of Prisons Relating to the Report of a Select Committee of the House of Lords on Prison Discipline; and of the Report of a Committee Appointed by the Secretary of State to Inquire into the Dietaries of County and Borough Prisons, May 20, 1864. (PP 313).

Prison Discipline in the Colonies: Digest and Summary of Information Respecting Prisons in the Colonies. London: HMSO, 1867.

Prison Discipline in the Colonies: Further Correspondence Respecting the Discipline and Management of Prisons in Her Majesty's Colonial Possessions. London: HMSO, 1868.

Prison Discipline in the Colonies: Further Correspondence Respecting the Discipline and Management of Prisons in Her Majesty's Colonial Possessions, August 8, 1870. London: HMSO, 1871. (PP C. 228).

Prison Rules (Convict Prisons): Draft of Rules Proposed to Be Made under the Prison Act, 1898, March 1901. London: HMSO, 1901.

Prison Rules (Convict Prisons): Draft of Rules Proposed to Be Made under the Prison Act, 1898. London: HMSO, 1898. (PP C. 8771).

Prisons (Rules for Local Prisons): Draft of Rules Proposed to Be Made By the Secretary of State for the Home Department under the Prison Act, 1898, with Regard to the Dietary of Prisoners, May 16, 1901. (PP 187).

Report from the Select Committee of the House of Lords on the Present State of Discipline in Gaols and Houses of Correction Together with the Proceedings of the Committee, Minutes of Evidence, Appendix and Index, July 24, 1863. (PP 49).

Report from the Select Committee on the Andover Union, 1846. (PP 663).

Report of the Commissioners Appointed to Inquire into the Acts Relating to Transportation and Penal Servitude, Vol. I. London: HMSO, 1863.

Report of the Commissioners Appointed to Inquire into the Management of Millbank Prison, January 20, 1847. (PP 8).

Report of the Indian Famine Commission, 1880 (Appendix Part IV: Evidence). London: HMSO, no date. (PP C. 3086-IV).

Report of the Indian Famine Commission, 1898. London: HMSO, 1898. (PP C. 9178).

Report of the Indian Famine Commission, Part I: Famine Relief. London: HMSO, 1880. (PP C. 2591).

Report of the Indian Famine Commission, Part III: Famine Histories. London: HMSO, 1885. (PP C. 3086).

Report of the Inter-Departmental Committee on Physical Deterioration. London: HMSO, 1904. (PP Cd. 2175).

Report of the Inter-Departmental Committee on the Medical Inspection and Feeding of Children Attending Public Elementary Schools. London: HSMO, 1905. (PP Cd. 2779).

Report of the Joint Committee to Inquire into the Organisation and Methods of the Central Prisoners of War Committee. London: HMSO, 1917. (PP Cd. 8615).

Report Relative to the System of Prison Discipline &c. by the Inspectors of Prisons. London: HMSO, 1843.

Smith, Richard Baird. *Report on the Famine of 1860–61*. Calcutta: n.p., 1861.

Special Report and Report from the Select Committee on the Education (Provision of Meals) Bill, 1906; and the Education (Provision of Meals) (Scotland) Bill, 1906. London: HMSO, 1906. (PP 205).

Titmuss, Richard M. *Problems of Social Policy*. London: HMSO, 1950.

Women's Voluntary Service, *Community Feeding in Wartime*, 2nd ed. London: HMSO, 1941.

Published Primary Sources

Ali, Maulavi Saiad Mahdi. *Report on the History of the Famine in His Highness the Nizam's Dominions, 1876–77, 1877–78*. Bombay: The Exchange Press, 1879.

Barsley, Michael. *Common Man and Colonel Bogus*. London: Pilot Press, 1944.

Baxter, G.R. Wythen. *The Book of the Bastiles: Or, the History of the Working of the New Poor Law*. London: John Stephens, 1841.

Belfield, Herbert E. "The Treatment of Prisoners of War." *Transactions of the Grotius Society* 9 (1923): 131–47.

Blair, Charles. *Indian Famines: Their Historical, Financial and Other Aspects*. Edinburgh: William Blackwood and Sons, 1874.

Bourne, Geoffrey. *Nutrition and the War*. Cambridge: Cambridge University Press, 1940.

Calder, Ritchie. *Carry on London*. London: The English Universities Press, 1941.

Caribbean Commission Central Secretariat. *Caribbean Market Survey: Citrus*. Port-of-Spain: Caribbean Commission, 1956.

Cohen-Portheim, Paul. *Time Stood Still: My Internment in England, 1914–1918*. New York: E.P. Dutton & Co., 1932.

Cornish, William Robert. *Observations on the Nature of the Food of the Inhabitants of Southern India and on Prison Dietaries in the Madras Presidency*. Madras: Gantz Brothers, 1864.

de Bloch, Jean. *The Future of War*. Boston: World Peace Foundation, 1914 [1899].

Dickens, Charles. *A Christmas Carol*. London: Bradbury & Evans, 1858 [1843].

Oliver Twist, Vol. I, 2nd ed. London: Richard Bentley, 1839.

Digby, William. *The Famine Campaign in Southern India, 1876–1878*. London: Longmans, Green, and Co., 1878.

Drake, Barbara. *Nutrition: A Policy of National Health*. London: New Fabian Research Bureau, 1936.

Dutt, Romesh C. *Open Letters to Lord Curzon on Famines and Land Assessment in India*. London: Kegan, Paul, Trench, Trubner, and Co., 1900.

Frere, Sir H. Bartle. *On the Impending Bengal Famine: How It Will Be Met and How to Prevent Future Famines in India*. London: John Murray, 1874.

Geddes, J.C. *Administrative Experience Recorded in Former Famines*. Calcutta: E. Bengal Secretariat Press, 1874.

Gerard, James W. *My Four Years in Germany*. New York: George H. Doran, 1917.

Girdlestone, C.E.R. *Report on Past Famines in the North-Western Provinces*. Allahabad: Government Press, 1868.

Green, Marjorie E. *Malnutrition among School Children*. London: Children's Minimum Council, 1938.

School Feeding in England and Wales. London: Children's Minimum Council, 1938.

Hastings, Somerville. *A National Physiological Minimum*. London: The Fabian Society, 1934.

Henvey, Frederick. *A Narrative of the Drought and Famine which Prevailed in the North-West Provinces During the Years 1868, 1869, and Beginning of 1870*. Allahabad: Government Press, 1871.

Hodgson, George B. *The Borough of South Shields: From the Earliest Period to the Close of the Nineteenth Century*. Newcastle: A. Reid, 1903.

Hoffman, Conrad. *In the Prison Camps of Germany*. New York: Association Press, 1920.

Kellogg, Vernon and Alonzo E. Taylor. *The Food Problem*. New York: Macmillan, 1918.

Ketchum, J. Davidson. *Ruhleben: A Prison Camp Society*. Toronto: University of Toronto Press, 1965.

Le Gros Clark, F. *Social History of the School Meals Service*. London: London Council of Social Service, 1948.

Leubuscher, Charlotte. *Bulk Buying from the Colonies*. Oxford: Oxford University Press, 1956.

Lloyd, E.M.H. *Experiments in State Control at the War Office and the Ministry of Food*. Oxford: Clarendon Press, 1924.

London Council of Social Service. *The Communal Restaurant: A Study of the Place of Civic Restaurants in the Life of the Community*. London: London Council of Social Service, 1943.

M'Gonigle, G. C. M. and J. Kirby. *Poverty and Public Health*. London: Victor Gollancz, 1936.

Maltbie, Milo Roy. *English Local Government of Today*. New York: Columbia University Press, 1897.

Mayhew, Henry and John Binny. *The Criminal Prisons of London and Scenes of Prison Life*. London: Frank Cass and Co., 1968 [1862].

McCarthy, Daniel J. *The Prisoner of War in Germany: The Care and Treatment of the Prisoner of War with History of the Development of the Principle of Neutral Inspection and Control.* New York: Moffat, Yard and Company, 1918.

McCay, Captain D. *Investigations on Bengal Jail Dietaries.* Simla: Government of India, 1910.

McCay, Major D. *Investigations into the Jail Dietaries of the United Provinces.* Calcutta: Superintendent of Government Printing, India, 1911.

McCollum, Elmer Verner. *The Newer Knowledge of Nutrition: The Use of Food for the Preservation of Vitality and Health.* New York: Macmillan, 1919.

Mencken, H.L. "War Words in England." *American Speech* 19(1) (1944): 3–15.

Merewether, F.H.S. *A Tour through the Famine Districts of India.* London: A.D. Innes and Co, 1898.

Mouat, Frederic. *Reports of Jails Visited and Inspected in Bengal, Behar, and Arracan.* Calcutta: F. Carbery, 1856.

Naoroji, Dadabhai. *Poverty and Un-British Rule in India.* London: Swan Sonnenschein and Co., 1901.

Nash, Vaughan. *The Great Famine and Its Causes.* London: Longmans, Green, and Co., 1900.

National Council of Social Service. *British Restaurants: An Inquiry Made by the National Council of Social Service.* Oxford: Oxford University Press, 1946.

Nicholls, George. *A History of the English Poor Law*, Vol. II. London: P.S. King & Son, 1898.

Notter, James Lane and Sir Robert Hammill Firth. *The Theory and Practice of Hygiene*, 3rd ed. London: J & A Churchill, 1908.

Orr, John Boyd. *Food, Health and Income.* London: Macmillan and Co., 1936.

Orr, John Boyd and David Lubbock. *Feeding the People in War-Time.* London: Macmillan, 1940.

Picot, H.P. *The British Interned in Switzerland.* London: Edward Arnold, 1919.

Pyke, Magnus. *Food and Society.* London: John Murray, 1968.

Report on the Administration of the Jails of the Madras Presidency, 1901. Madras: Government Press, 1902.

Report on the Famine in the Panjab during 1869–70. Lahore: Punjab Printing Company, 1870.

Ruggles-Brise, Evelyn. *The English Prison System.* Maidstone: H.M. Convict Prison, 1921.

Shaw, George Bernard Shaw. *The Complete Prefaces of Bernard Shaw.* London: Paul Hamlyn, 1965.

Sims, George R. *How the Poor Live and Horrible London.* London: Chatto & Windus, 1889.

Smith, Edward. "Gaol Dietary: The Operations of the Recent Committee." *Journal of the Society of Arts,* September 2, 1864.

——— "Gaol Dietary: The Operations of the Recent Committees (continued)." *Journal of the Society of Arts,* September 9, 1864.

——— "On the Principles Involved in a Scheme of Prison Dietary." In *Transactions of the National Association for the Promotion of Social Science, 1857.* London: John W. Parker and Son, 1858.

Smith, Edward and W.R. Milner. "Report on the Action of Prison Diet and Discipline on the Bodily Functions of Prisoners, Part I." In *Report of the Thirty-First Meeting of the British Association for the Advancement of Science, September, 1861.* London: John Murray, 1862.

Solomon, Flora and Barry Litvinoff. *A Woman's Way.* New York: Simon and Schuster, 1984.

Steedman, Carolyn Kay. *Landscape for a Good Woman: A Story of Two Lives.* New Brunswick: Rutgers University Press, 1987.

Temple, Sir Richard. *The Story of My Life,* Vol. II. London: Cassell and Co., 1896.

Walworth, George. *Feeding the Nation in Peace and War.* London: George Allen & Unwin, 1940.

Waugh, Alec. *The Prisoner of Mainz.* London: Chapman and Hall, 1919.

Wilkinson, Robert. *The Law of Prisons in England and Wales.* London: Knight and Co., 1878.

Secondary Sources

Addison, Paul. *The Road to 1945: British Politics and the Second World War.* London: Jonathan Cape, 1975.

Agamben, Giorgio. *Homo Sacer: Sovereign Power and Bare Life.* Trans. Daniel Heller-Roazen. Stanford: Stanford University Press, 1998.

Ahuja, Ravi. "State Formation and 'Famine Policy' in Early Colonial South Asia." *The Indian Economic and Social History Review* 39(4) (2002): 351–80.

Alam, Asiya. "Polygyny, Family and Sharafat: Discourses amongst North Indian Muslims, c. 1870–1918." *Modern Asian Studies* 45(3) (2011): 631–68.

Ambirajan, S. *Classical Political Economy and British Policy in India.* Cambridge: Cambridge University Press, 1978.

"Malthusian Population Theory and Indian Famine Policy in the Nineteenth Century." *Population Studies* 30(1) (1976): 5–14.

"Political Economy and Indian Famines." *South Asia* 1(2) (1971): 20–8.

Anagol-McGinn, Padma. "The Age of Consent Act (1891) Reconsidered: Women's Perspectives and Participation in the Child Marriage Controversy in India." *South Asia Research* 12(2) (1992): 100–18.

Anderson, Benedict. *Imagined Communities,* Revised ed. London: Verso, 1991.

Anderson, Clare. *The Indian Uprising of 1857–8.* London: Anthem Press, 2007.

Andrews, L. "The School Meals Service." *British Journal of Educational Studies* 20 (1) (1972): 70–5.

Anstruther, Ian. *The Scandal of the Andover Workhouse.* London: Bles, 1973.

Apple, Rima D. *Vitamania: Vitamins in American Culture.* New Brunswick: Rutgers University Press, 1996.

Armstrong, Neil. *Christmas in Nineteenth-Century England.* Manchester: Manchester University Press, 2010.

Arnold, David. *Colonizing the Body.* Berkeley: University of California Press, 1993.

"The 'Discovery' of Malnutrition and Diet in Colonial India." *Indian Economic and Social History Review* 31(1) (1994): 1–26.

Famine: Social Crisis and Historical Change. Oxford: Basil Blackwell, 1988.

"India: The Contested Prison." In *Cultures of Confinement: A History of the Prison in Africa, Asia and Latin America,* edited by Frank Dikotter and Ian Brown, 147–84. Ithaca: Cornell University Press, 2007.

Ashton, S. R. "Keeping Change within Bounds: A Whitehall Reassessment." In *The British Empire in the 1950s: Retreat or Revival?,* edited by Martin Lynn, 32–52. Houndmills: Palgrave, 2006.

Assael, Brenda. "Gastro-cosmopolitanism and the Restaurant in Late Victorian and Edwardian London." *The Historical Journal* 56(3) (2013): 681–706.

Atkins, Peter. J. "Communal Feeding in War Time: British Restaurants, 1940–1947." In *Food and War in Twentieth Century Europe,* edited by Rachel Duffett, Ina Zweiniger-Bargielowska, and Alain Drouard, 139–54. Farnham: Ashgate, 2011.

"The Milk in Schools Scheme, 1934–45: 'Nationalization' and Resistance." *History of Education* 34(1) (2005): 1–21.

"School Milk in Britain, 1900–1934." *Journal of Policy History* 19(4) (2007): 395–427.

Auerbach, Sascha. "'Some Punishment Should Be Devised': Parents, Children, and the State in Victorian London." *The Historian* 71(4) (2009): 757–79.

Bailkin, Jordanna. *The Afterlife of Empire.* Berkeley: University of California Press, 2012.

Barker, Theodore Cardwell, Derek J. Oddy, and John Yudkin, *The Dietary Surveys of Dr. Edward Smith, 1862–3: A New Assessment.* London: University of London Department of Nutrition, 1970.

Barnett, L. Margaret. *British Food Policy during the First World War.* Boston: George Allen & Unwin, 1985.

Barnett, Michael N. *Empire of Humanity: A History of Humanitarianism.* Ithaca: Cornell University Press, 2011.

Basu, Mrinal Kumar. "Food, Fatality and Deprivation in Bengal Prisons: A Study of the Santal Convicts." *Indian Historical Review* 32(2) (2005): 122–41.

Bayly, Susan. *Caste, Society and Politics in India from the Eighteenth Century to the Modern Age.* Cambridge: Cambridge University Press, 1999.

Becker, Annette. "Captive Civilians." In *The Cambridge History of the First World War,* Vol. III, edited by Jay Winter, 257–82. Cambridge: Cambridge University Press, 2014.

Belchem, John. *Popular Radicalism in Nineteenth Century Britain.* Houndmills: Palgrave, 1996.

"Republicanism, Popular Constitutionalism and the Radical Platform in Early Nineteenth-Century England." *Social History* 6(1) (1981): 1–32.

Bentley, Amy. *Eating for Victory: Food Rationing and the Politics of Domesticity.* Urbana: University of Illinois Press, 1998.

Bernault, Florence. "The Shadow of Rule: Colonial Power and Modern Punishment in Africa." In *Cultures of Confinement: A History of the Prison in Africa, Asia and Latin America,* edited by Frank Dikotter and Ian Brown, 55–94. Ithaca: Cornell University Press, 2007.

Bhatia, B.M. *Famines in India,* 2nd ed. Bombay: Asia Publishing House, 1967.

Biltekoff, Charlotte. *Eating Right in America: The Cultural Politics of Food and Health.* Durham: Duke University Press, 2013.

Bird, J.C. *Control of Enemy Alien Civilians in Great Britain, 1914–1918.* New York: Garland, 1986.

Bradley, Kate. "Rational Recreation in the Age of Affluence: The Café and Working-Class Youth in London, c. 1939–1965." In *Consuming Behaviors: Identity, Politics and Pleasure in Twentieth Century Britain,* edited by Mark J. Crowley, Sandra Trudgen Dawson, and Erika D. Rappaport, 71–86. London: Bloomsbury, 2015.

Braga-Blake, Myrna and Ann Ebert-Oehlers. "Where the Twain Met: Origins of Eurasian Families." In *Singapore Eurasians: Memories, Hopes, and Dreams,* edited by Myrna Braga-Blake, Ann Ebert-Oehlers, and Alexius Pereira, 33–50. Singapore: World Scientific Publishing Co., 2017.

Brears, Peter. "Bastille Soup and Skilly: Workhouse Food in Yorkshire." In *Food for the Community: Special Diets for Special Groups,* edited by C. Anne Wilson, 116–50. Edinburgh: Edinburgh University Press, 1993.

Brewis, Georgina. "'Fill Full the Mouth of Famine': Voluntary Action in Famine Relief in India 1896–1901." *Modern Asian Studies* 44(4) (2010): 887–918.

Brown, Alyson. *English Society and the Prison.* Woodbridge: Boydell Press, 2003.

Bruegel, Martin. "Introduction: Locating Foodways in the Nineteenth Century." In *A Cultural History of Food in the Age of Empire,* edited by Martin Bruegel, 1–26. London: Bloomsbury, 2016.

Brundage, Anthony. *England's 'Prussian Minister': Edwin Chadwick and the Politics of Government Growth.* University Park: Penn State University Press, 1988.

The English Poor Laws, 1700–1930. Houndmills: Palgrave, 2002.

"The Landed Interest and the New Poor Law: A Reappraisal of the Revolution in Government." *The English Historical Review* 87(342) (1972): 27–48.

The Making of the New Poor Law: The Politics of Inquiry, Enactment, and Implementation, 1832–1839. New Brunswick: Rutgers University Press, 1978.

Burnett, John. *England Eats Out, 1830–Present.* Harlow: Pearson, 2004.

Plenty and Want: A Social History of Food in England from 1815 to the Present Day, 3rd ed. London: Routledge, 1989.

"The Rise and Decline of School Meals in Britain, 1860–1990." In *The Origins and Development of Food Policies in Europe,* edited by John Burnett and Derek J. Oddy, 55–69. Leicester: Leicester University Press, 1994.

Butler, L.J. "The Ambiguities of British Colonial Development Policy, 1938–48." In *Contemporary British History, 1931–61: Politics and the Limits of Policy,* edited by A. Gorst, L. Johnman and W. Scott Lucas, 119–40. London: Pinter, 1991.

Britain and Empire: Adjusting to a Post-Imperial World. London: I.B. Tauris, 2002.

Bynum, Carolyn Walker. *Holy Feast and Holy Fast: The Religious Significance of Food to Medieval Women.* Berkeley: University of California Press, 1988.

Cagle, Hugh. *Assembling the Tropics: Science and Medicine in Portugal's Empire, 1450–1700.* Cambridge: Cambridge University Press, 2018.

Calder, Angus. *The People's War: Britain 1939–1945.* New York: Pantheon, 1969.

Carney, Judith. *In the Shadow of Slavery: Africa's Botanical Legacy in the Atlantic World.* Berkeley: University of California Press, 2010.

Carpenter, Kenneth J. "Nutritional Studies in Victorian Prisons." *Journal of Nutrition* 136(1) (2006): 1–8.

Carroll, Patrick E. "Medical Police and the History of Public Health." *Medical History* 46 (2002): 461–94.
  Science, Culture, and Modern State Formation. Berkeley: University of California Press, 2006.

Chandler, J.A. *Explaining Local Government: Local Government in Britain since 1800*. Manchester: Manchester University Press, 2007.

Chapman, Peter. *Bananas: How the United Fruit Company Shaped the World*. Edinburgh: Canongate, 2007.

Charlesworth, Lorie. *Welfare's Forgotten Past: A Socio-Legal History of the Poor Law*. London: Routledge, 2010.

Christopher, A.J. "'Divide and Rule': The Impress of British Separation Policies." *Area* 20(3) (1988): 233–40.

Claeys, Gregory. "Political Thought." In *A Companion to Nineteenth-Century Britain*, edited by Chris Williams, 189–202. Oxford: Blackwell, 2004.

Clark, Anna. "Humanitarianism, Human Rights, and Biopolitics in the British Empire, 1890–1902." *Britain and the World* 9(1) (2016): 96–115.

Cody, Lisa Forman. "The Politics of Illegitimacy in an Age of Reform: Gender, Reproduction and Political Economy in England's New Poor Law of 1834." *Journal of Women's History* 11(4) (2000): 131–56.

Colley, Linda. *Britons: Forging the Nation, 1707–1837*. New Haven: Yale University Press, 1992.

Collingham, Lizzie. *The Taste of War: World War II and the Battle for Food*. New York: Penguin Press, 2012.

Connelly, Mark. *Christmas: A Social History*. London: I.B. Tauris, 1999.

Coveney, John. *Food, Morals and Meaning: The Pleasure and Anxiety of Eating*. London: Routledge, 2000.

Cowen, Michael and Robert Shenton. "The Origin and Course of Fabian Colonialism in Africa." *Journal of Historical Sociology* 4(2) (1991): 143–74.

Cowherd, Raymond G. *Political Economists and the English Poor Laws*. Athens: Ohio University Press, 1977.

Crawford, E.M. "The Irish Workhouse Diet, 1840–90." In *Food, Diet and Economic Change Past and Present*, edited by Catherine Geissler and Derek J. Oddy, 83–100. Leicester: Leicester University Press, 1993.

Cressy, David. *Bonfires and Bells: National Memory and the Protestant Calendar in Elizabethan and Stuart England*. Berkeley: University of California Press, 1989.

Croll, Andy. "Starving Strikers and the Limits of the 'Humanitarian Discovery of Hunger' in Late Victorian Britain." *International Review of Social History* 56(1) (2011): 103–31.

Cromwell, Valerie. "Interpretations of Nineteenth-Century Administration: An Analysis." *Victorian Studies* 9(3) (1966): 245–55.

Cronon, William. *Nature's Metropolis: Chicago and the Great West*. New York: W. W. Norton, 1991.

Crook, Tom. *Governing Systems: Modernity and the Making of Public Health in England, 1830–1910*. Berkeley: University of California Press, 2016.

Cross, Gary. *Time and Money: The Making of Consumer Culture*. London: Routledge, 1993.

Crowther, M.A. *The Workhouse System, 1834–1929*. London: Batsford, 1981.

Cullather, Nick. "The Foreign Policy of the Calorie." *American Historical Review* 112(2) (2007): 337–64.

The Hungry World: America's Cold War Battle against Poverty in Asia. Cambridge: Harvard University Press, 2010.

Currie, Kate. "British Colonial Policy and Famines: Some Effects and Implications of 'Free Trade' in the Bombay, Bengal and Madras Presidencies, 1860–1900." *South Asia* 14(2) (1991): 23–56.

Darwin, John. "Was There a Fourth British Empire?" In *The British Empire in the 1950s: Retreat or Revival?*, edited by Martin Lynn, 16–31. Houndmills: Palgrave, 2006.

Davies, Jennifer. *The Wartime Kitchen and Garden*. London: BBC Books, 1993.

Davin, Anna. "Imperialism and Motherhood." *History Workshop Journal* 5(1) (1978): 9–66.

Davis, Belinda J. *Home Fires Burning: Food, Politics, and Everyday Life in World War I Berlin*. Chapel Hill: University of North Carolina Press, 2000.

Davis, Mike. *Late Victorian Holocausts: El Niño Famines and the Making of the Third World*. London: Verso, 2001.

Deperchin, Annie. "The Laws of War." In *The Cambridge History of the First World War*, Vol. I, edited by Jay Winter, 615–38. Cambridge: Cambridge University Press, 2014.

Devereux, Stephen. *Theories of Famine*. New York: Harvester Wheatsheaf, 1993.

Digby, Anne. *Pauper Palaces*. London: Routledge & Kegan Paul, 1978.

Diner, Hasia. *Hungering for America: Italian, Irish, and Jewish Foodways in the Age of Migration*. Cambridge: Harvard University Press, 2003.

Donnelly, Mark. *Sixties Britain*. Harlow: Longman, 2005.

Drewnowski, Adam. "Poverty and Obesity: The Role of Energy Density and Energy Costs." *American Journal of Clinical Nutrition* 79(1) (2004): 6–16.

Drèze, Jean and Amartya Sen. *The Amartya Sen and Jean Drèze Omnibus*. Delhi: Oxford University Press, 1999.

Driver, Christopher. *The British at Table, 1940–1980*. London: Chatto & Windus, 1983.

Driver, Felix. *Power and Pauperism: The Workhouse System, 1834–1884*. Cambridge: Cambridge University Press, 1993.

Drouard, Alain. "Horsemeat in France." In *Food and War in Twentieth Century Europe*, edited by Rachel Duffett, Ina Zweiniger-Bargielowska, and Alain Drouard, 233–46. Farnham: Ashgate, 2011.

Drummond, J.C. and Anne Wilbraham. *The Englishman's Food: Five Centuries of English Diet*. Revised ed. London: Pimlico, 1991.

Dubow, Saul. *Scientific Racism in Modern South Africa*. Cambridge: Cambridge University Press, 1995.

Duffett, Rachel. *The Stomach for Fighting: Food and the Soldiers of the Great War*. Manchester: Manchester University Press, 2012.

Dunkley, Peter. "The 'Hungry Forties' and the New Poor Law: A Case Study." *The Historical Journal* 17(2) (1974): 329–46.

"Whigs and Paupers: The Reform of the English Poor Laws, 1830–34." *Journal of British Studies* 20(2) (1981): 124–49.

Durbach, Nadja. *Bodily Matters: The Anti-Vaccination Movement in England, 1853–1907.* Durham: Duke University Press, 2005.

"British Restaurants and the Gender Politics of the Wartime Midday Meal." In *Home Fronts: Britain and the Empire at War, 1939–45*, edited by Mark J. Crowley and Sandra Trudgen Dawson, 19–36. Woodbridge: The Boydell Press, 2017.

"Comforts, Clubs, and the Casino: Food and the Perpetuation of the British Class System in First World War Civilian Internment Camps." *Journal of Social History* 53(2) (2019): 487-507.

"The Parcel Is Political: The British Government and the Regulation of Food Parcels for Prisoners of War, 1914–1918." *First World War Studies* 9(1) (2018): 93–110.

"The Politics of Provisioning: Feeding South Asian Prisoners during the First World War." *War & Society* 37(2) (2018): 75–90.

Dutton, D.J. "Wood, Edward Frederick Lindley, First Earl of Halifax (1881– 1959)." *Oxford Dictionary of National Biography*, January 6, 2011.

Dwork, Deborah. *War Is Good for Babies and Other Young Children: A History of the Infant and Child Welfare Movement in England, 1898–1918.* London: Tavistock, 1987.

Eastwood, David. "'Amplifying the Province of the Legislature': The Flow of Information and the English State in the Early Nineteenth Century." *Historical Research* 62(149) (1989): 276–94.

Edgerton-Tarpley, Kathryn. "Tough Choices: Grappling with Famine in Qing China, the British Empire, and Beyond." *Journal of World History* 24(1) (2013): 135–76.

Edsall, Nicholas C. *The Anti-Poor Law Movement, 1834–44.* Manchester: Manchester University Press, 1971.

Englander, David. *Poverty and Poor Law Reform in Nineteenth Century Britain, 1834–1914.* London: Pearson, 1998.

Epstein, James. *Radical Expression: Political Language, Ritual, and Symbol in England, 1790–1850.* Oxford: Oxford University Press, 1994.

Farmer, Richard. *The Food Companions: Cinema and Consumption in Wartime Britain, 1939–45.* Manchester: Manchester University Press, 2011.

Feltman, Brian K. *The Stigma of Surrender: German Prisoners, British Captors, and Manhood in the Great War and Beyond.* Chapel Hill: University of North Carolina Press, 2015.

Fiddes, Nick. *Meat: A Natural Symbol.* London: Routledge, 1991.

Fielding, Steven, Peter Thompson, and Nick Tiratsoo. *England Arise!: The Labour Party and Popular Politics in 1940s Britain.* Manchester: Manchester University Press, 1995.

Finer, Herman. *English Local Government*, 4th ed. London: Methuen and Co., 1950.

Finlayson, Geoffrey. *Citizen, State, and Social Welfare in Britain, 1830–1990.* Oxford: Clarendon Press, 1994.

Fletcher, David. "Government Boundary Mapping and the Knowledge Apparatus of the British State, 1841–1889." *Journal of Policy History* 25(4) (2013): 512–37.

Forsythe, W.J. *Penal Discipline, Reformatory Projects and the English Prison Commission, 1895–1939*. Exeter: University of Exeter Press, 1991.

The Reform of Prisoners, 1830–1900. New York: St. Martin's Press, 1987.

Forth, Aidan. *Barbed-Wire Imperialism: Britain's Empire of Camps, 1876–1903*. Berkeley: University of California Press, 2017.

Foucault, Michel. *Discipline and Punish: The Birth of the Prison*. New York: Vintage, 1979.

The History of Sexuality, Volume 1: An Introduction. New York: Vintage, 1990.

Fraser, Derek. "The Poor Law as a Political Institution." In *The New Poor Law in the Nineteenth Century*, edited by Derek Fraser, 111–27. London, 1976.

French, David. "The Rise and Fall of 'Business as Usual.'" In *War and the State: The Transformation of British Government, 1914–1919*, edited by Kathleen Burk, 7–31. London: George Allen & Unwin, 1982.

Fussell, Paul. *Wartime: Understanding and Behavior in the Second World War*. Oxford: Oxford University Press, 1989.

Geddes, J.F. "Culpable Complicity: The Medical Profession and the Forcible Feeding of Suffragettes, 1909–1914." *Women's History Review* 17(1) (2008): 79–94.

Ghosh, Durba. *Sex and the Family in Colonial India: The Making of Empire*. Cambridge: Cambridge University Press, 2006.

Gilbert, Bentley B. *The Evolution of National Insurance in Great Britain*. London: Michael Joseph, 1966.

Gilbert, Martin, ed. *The Churchill War Papers: The Ever-Widening War, 1941*. New York: W. W. Norton, 2000.

Golby, J.M. and A.W. Purdue. *The Making of the Modern Christmas*. Athens: University of Georgia Press, 1986.

Goodman, Phil. "'Patriotic Femininity': Women's Morals and Men's Morale during the Second World War." *Gender & History* 10(2) (1998): 278–93.

Goody, Jack. *Cooking, Cuisine, and Class*. Cambridge: Cambridge University Press, 1982.

Gould, Philip. *The Unfinished Revolution: How the Modernisers Saved the Labour Party*. London: Little, Brown, and Company, 1998.

Grant, Kevin. "British Suffragettes and the Russian Method of Hunger Strike." *Comparative Studies in Society and History* 53(1) (2011): 113–43.

Gray, Peter. "Famine and Land in Ireland and India, 1845–1880: James Caird and the Political Economy of Hunger." *The Historical Journal*, 49 (1) (2006): 193–215.

Gray, Robert. *The Factory Question and Industrial England, 1830–1860*. Cambridge: Cambridge University Press, 1996.

Green, David R. "Pauper Protests: Power and Resistance in Early Nineteenth-Century London Workhouses." *Social History* 31(2) (2006): 137–59.

Gregory, Adrian. *The Last Great War: British Society and the First World War*. Cambridge: Cambridge University Press, 2008.

Grey, Daniel J.R. "Creating the 'Problem Hindu': Sati, Thuggee, and Female Infanticide in India, 1800–1860." *Gender & History* 25(3) (2013): 498–510.

Gullace, Nicoletta. *"The Blood of Our Sons": Men, Women, and the Renegotiation of British Citizenship during the Great War.* Houndmills: Palgrave, 2002.

Gunn, Simon and James Vernon, eds. *The Peculiarities of Liberal Modernity in Imperial Britain.* Berkeley: University of California Press, 2011.

Gutchen, Robert M. "Local Improvements and Centralization in Nineteenth-Century England." *The Historical Journal* 4(1) (1961): 85–96.

Guy, Kolleen M. *"Food Representations."* In *A Cultural History of Food in the Age of Empire,* edited by Martin Bruegel, 181–97. London: Bloomsbury, 2016.

Hadley, Elaine. *Living Liberalism: Practical Citizenship in Mid-Victorian Britain.* Chicago: University of Chicago Press, 2010.

Hall-Matthews, David. "Inaccurate Conceptions: Disputed Measures of Nutritional Needs and Famine Deaths in Colonial India." *Modern Asian Studies* 42(6) (2008): 1189–212.

   Peasants, Famine and the State in Colonial Western India. Houndmills: Palgrave, 2005.

Halttunen, Karen. "Humanitarianism and the Pornography of Pain in Anglo-American Culture." *American Historical Review* 100(2) (1995): 303–34.

Hamlin, Christopher. "Could You Starve to Death in England in 1839?" *American Journal of Public Health* 85(6) (1995): 856–66.

   "The 'Necessaries of Life' in British Political Medicine, 1750–1850." *Journal of Consumer Policy* 29(2006): 373–97.

   "Nuisances and Community in Mid-Victorian England: The Attractions of Inspection." *Social History* 38(3) (2013): 346–79.

   Public Health and Social Justice in the Age of Chadwick: Britain, 1800–1854. Cambridge: Cambridge University Press, 1998.

Hardy, Anne. "Development of the Prison Medical Services, 1774–1895." In *The Health of Prisoners,* edited by Richard Creese, W.F. Bynum, and J. Bearn, 59–82. Amsterdam: Rodopi, 1995.

Hargrove, James L. "History of the Calorie in Nutrition." *Journal of Nutrition* 136(12) (2006): 2957–61.

Harling, Philip. *The Modern British State: An Historical Introduction.* Cambridge: Polity, 2001.

   "The Power of Persuasion: Central Authority, Local Bureaucracy and the New Poor Law." *The English Historical Review* 107(422) (1992): 30–53.

Harris, Bernard. *The Health of the School Child: A History of the School Medical Service in England and Wales.* Buckingham: Open University Press, 1995.

Harris, Jose. "Bureaucrats and Businessmen in British Food Control, 1916–19." In *War and the State: The Transformation of British Government, 1914–1919,* edited by Kathleen Burk, 135–56. London: George Allen & Unwin, 1982.

Hasluck, E.L. *Local Government in England.* Cambridge: Cambridge University Press, 1936.

Havinden, Michael and David Meredith. *Colonialism and Development: Britain and Its Tropical Colonies, 1850–1960.* London: Routledge, 1993.

Hay, D. "Property, Authority, and the Criminal Law." In *Albion's Fatal Tree: Crime and Society in Eighteenth Century England,* edited by D. Hay, Peter Linebaugh, John G. Rule, E.P. Thompson, and Cal Winslow, 17–63. London: Allen Lane, 1975.

Helstosky, Carol. *Garlic and Oil: Food and Politics in Italy*. Oxford: Berg, 2004.
"The State, Health, and Nutrition." In *The Cambridge World History of Food*, Vol. II, edited by Kenneth F. Kiple and Kriemhild C. Ornelas, 1577–85. Cambridge: Cambridge University Press, 2000.
Hennessy, Peter. *Having It So Good: Britain in the Fifties*. London: Allen Lane, 2006.
Henriques, Ursula. "How Cruel Was the Victorian Poor Law?" *The Historical Journal* 11(2) (1968): 365–71.
Higginbotham, Peter. *The Prison Cookbook*. Stroud: The History Press, 2010.
Higgs, Edward. *The Information State in England*. Houndmills: Palgrave, 2004.
Hill, Michael. *The Welfare State in Britain: A Political History since 1945*. Aldershot: Edward Elgar, 1993.
Hinds, Allister. *Britain's Sterling Colonial Policy and Decolonization, 1939–1958*. Westport, Greenwood Press, 2001.
Hobsbawm, Eric and Terence O. Ranger, eds. *The Invention of Tradition*. Cambridge: Cambridge University Press, 1983.
Hodge, Joseph Morgan. *Triumph of the Expert: Agrarian Development and the Legacies of British Colonialism*. Athens: Ohio University Press, 2007.
Hogarth, Rana A. *Medicalizing Blackness: Making Racial Difference in the Atlantic World, 1780–1840*. Chapel Hill: University of North Carolina Press, 2017.
Horrocks, Sally M. "Nutrition Science and the Food and Pharmaceutical Industries in Inter-War Britain." In *Nutrition in Britain: Science, Scientists and Politics in the Twentieth Century*, edited by David F. Smith, 53–74. London: Routledge, 1997.
Howlett, Caroline. "Writing on the Body? Representation and Resistance in British Suffragette Accounts of Forcible Feeding." *Genders* 23 (1996): 3–41.
Hull, Isabel V. *Absolute Destruction: Military Culture and the Practices of War in Imperial Germany*. Ithaca: Cornell University Press, 2005.
Hurt, John. "Feeding the Hungry Schoolchild in the First Half of the Twentieth Century." In *Diet and Health in Modern Britain*, edited by Derek J. Oddy and Derek S. Miller, 178–206. London: Croom Helm, 1985.
Ignatieff, Michael. *A Just Measure of Pain: The Penitentiary in the Industrial Revolution, 1750–1850*. New York: Pantheon, 1978.
Innes, Joanna. "Changing Perceptions of the State in the Late Eighteenth and Early Nineteenth Centuries." *Journal of Historical Sociology* 15(1) (2002): 107–13.
Jacobson, Lisa. "Beer Goes to War: The Politics of Beer Promotion and Production in the Second World War." *Food, Culture & Society* 12(3) (2009): 275–312.
Jeffreys, Kevin. *Retreat from New Jerusalem: British Politics, 1951–64*. New York: St. Martin's Press, 1997.
Jensen, Kimberley. "Volunteers, Auxiliaries, and Women's Mobilization: The First World War and Beyond (1914–1939)." In *A Companion to Women's Military History*, edited by Barton C. Hacker and Margaret Vining, 189–231. Leiden: Brill, 2012.
Johnes, Martin. *Christmas and the British: A Modern History*. London: Bloomsbury, 2016.

Johnson, Howard. "The West Indies and the Conversion of the British Official Classes to the Development Idea." *Journal of Commonwealth and Comparative Politics* 15(1) (1977): 55–83.

Johnston, Valerie J. *Diet in Workhouses and Prisons 1835–1895*. New York: Garland, 1985.

Jones, Gareth Stedman. *Languages of Class: Studies in English Working Class History, 1832–1982*. Cambridge: Cambridge University Press, 1983.

Jones, Harriet. "The Cold War and the Santa Claus Syndrome: Dilemmas in Conservative Social Policy-Making, 1945–57." In *The Conservatives and British Society, 1880–1990*, edited by Martin Francis and Ina Zweiniger-Bargielowska, 240–54. Cardiff: University of Wales Press, 1996.

Jones, Heather. "A Missing Paradigm?: Military Captivity and the Prisoner of War, 1914–1918." *Immigrants & Minorities* 26(1–2) (2008): 19–48.

Violence against Prisoners of War in the First World War. Cambridge: Cambridge University Press, 2011.

Jones, Kathleen. *The Making of Social Policy in Britain: From the Poor Law to New Labour*, 3rd ed. London: Athlone Press, 2000.

Joseph, Maya and Marion Nestle. "Food and Politics in the Modern Age: 1920–2012." In *A Cultural History of Food in the Modern Age*, edited by Amy Bentley, 87–110. London: Bloomsbury, 2016.

Joseph, Michael. "Military Officers, Tropical Medicine, and Racial Thought in the Formation of the West India Regiments, 1793–1802." *Journal of the History of Medicine and Allied Sciences* 72 (2) (2017): 142–65.

Joyce, Patrick. "The Constitution and the Narrative Structure of Victorian Politics." In *Re-Reading the Constitution: New Narratives in the Political History of England's Long Nineteenth Century*, edited by James Vernon, 179–203. Cambridge: Cambridge University Press, 1996.

The Rule of Freedom: Liberalism and the Modern City. London: Verso, 2003.

Kamminga, Harmke and Andrew Cunningham, eds. *The Science and Culture of Nutrition, 1840–1940*. Amsterdam: Rodopi, 1995.

Kepner, Jr., Charles David and Jay Henry Soothill. *The Banana Empire*. New York: The Vanguard Press, 1935.

Kidd, Alan. *State, Society and the Poor in Nineteenth-Century England*. Houndmills: Palgrave Macmillan, 1999.

Kinealy, Christine. *A Death-Dealing Famine: The Great Hunger in Ireland*. London: Pluto Press, 1997.

Klein, Ira. "When the Rains Failed: Famine, Relief, and Mortality in British India." *The Indian Economic and Social History Review* 21(2) (1984): 185–214.

Kramer, Alan. "Blockade and Economic Warfare." In *The Cambridge History of the First World War*, Vol. II, edited by Jay Winter, 460–90. Cambridge: Cambridge University Press, 2014.

Lambie-Mumford, Hannah. *Hungry Britain: The Rise of Food Charity*. Bristol: Policy Press, 2017.

Langer, Gary F. *The Coming of Age of Political Economy, 1815–1825*. New York: Greenwood Press, 1987.

Laqueur, Thomas W. "Bodies, Details, and the Humanitarian Narrative." In *The New Cultural History*, edited by Lynn Hunt, 176–204. Berkeley: University of California Press, 1989.

Lee, J.M. *Colonial Development and Good Government*. Oxford: Clarendon Press, 1967.

Lees, Lynn Hollen. *The Solidarity of Strangers: The English Poor Laws and the People, 1700–1948*. Cambridge: Cambridge University Press, 1998.

Leopold, Ellen. "LCC Restaurants and the Decline of Municipal Enterprise." In *Politics and the Peoples of London: The London County Council, 1889–1965*, edited by Andrew Saint, 199–213. London: Hambledon Press, 1989.

Lévi-Strauss, Claude. *Totemism*. Trans. Rodney Needham. Boston: Beacon Press, 1963.

Levine, Philippa. *Prostitution, Race and Politics: Policing Venereal Disease in the British Empire*. London: Routledge, 2003.

Levine, Susan. *School Lunch Politics: The Surprising History of America's Favorite Welfare Program*. Princeton: Princeton University Press, 2008.

Levine-Clark, Marjorie. "Engendering Relief: Women, Ablebodiedness, and the New Poor Law in Early Victorian England." *Journal of Women's History* 11(4) (2000): 107–30.

Lindsay, T.F. and Michael Harrington. *The Conservative Party, 1918–1979*, 2nd ed. Basingstoke: Macmillan, 1979.

Longmate, Norman. *How We Lived Then*. London: Hutchinson and Co., 1971.

Longpré, Nicole. "'An Issue That Could Tear Us Apart': Race, Empire, and Economy in the British (Welfare) State." *Canadian Journal of History* 46(1) (2011): 63–96.

Lowe, Rodney. *The Welfare State in Britain since 1945*, 3rd ed. Houndmills: Palgrave, 2005.

Lummel, Peter. "Food Provisioning in the German Army of the First World War." In *Food and War in Twentieth Century Europe*, edited by Rachel Duffett, Ina Zweiniger-Bargielowska, and Alain Drouard, 13–26. Farnham: Ashgate, 2011.

MacDonagh, Oliver. *Early Victorian Government*. London: Weidenfeld and Nicolson, 1977.

"The Nineteenth-Century Revolution in Government: A Reappraisal." *The Historical Journal* 1(1) (1958): 52–67.

Mackay, Robert. *The Test of War: Inside Britain, 1939–1945*. London: Routledge, 1999.

Mallampalli, Chandra. *Race, Religion, and Law in Colonial India: Trials of an Interracial Family*. Cambridge: Cambridge University Press, 2011.

Mani, Lata. *Contentious Traditions: The Debate on Sati in Colonial India*. Berkeley: University of California Press, 1998.

Mauss, Marcel. *The Gift*. Trans. W.D. Halls. New York: Routledge, 1990.

Mawby, Spencer. *Ordering Independence: The End of Empire in the Anglophone Caribbean, 1947–1969*. Houndmills: Palgrave, 2012.

Mayhew, Madeline. "The 1930s Nutrition Controversy." *Journal of Contemporary History* 23(3) (1988): 445–64.

McCollum, Elmer Verner. *A History of Nutrition*. Boston: Houghton Mifflin, 1957.

McConville, Sean. *A History of English Prison Administration*, Vol. I. London: Routledge & Kegan Paul, 1981.

McCord, Norman. "The Poor Law and Philanthropy." In *The New Poor Law in the Nineteenth Century*, edited by Derek Fraser. Basingstoke: Macmillan 1976.

Miller, Ian. "Feeding in the Workhouse: The Institution and the Ideological Functions of Food c. 1834–1870." *Journal of British Studies* 52(4) (2013): 940–62.

"Food, Medicine, and Institutional Life in the British Isles, c. 1790–1900." In *The Routledge History of Food*, edited by Carol Helstosky, 200–19. London: Routledge, 2015.

"A Prostitution of the Profession? Forcible Feeding, Prison Doctors, Suffrage and the British State, 1909–1914." *Social History of Medicine* 26(2) (2013): 225–45.

Mintz, Sidney W. *Sweetness and Power: The Place of Sugar in Modern History*. Harmondsworth: Penguin, 1985.

Moore, Tara. "Starvation in Victorian Christmas Fiction." *Victorian Literature and Culture* 36(2) (2008): 489–505.

Morgan, D.J. *The Official History of Colonial Development. Volume II: Developing British Colonial Resources, 1945–1951*. Atlantic Highlands: Humanities Press, 1980.

The Official History of Colonial Development. Volume III: A Reassessment of British Aid Policy, 1951–1965. Atlantic Highlands: Humanities Press, 1980.

Morgan, David and Mary Evans. *The Battle for Britain: Citizenship and Ideology in the Second World War*. London: Routledge, 1993.

Morrock, Richard. "Heritage of Strife: The Effects of Colonialist 'Divide and Rule' Strategy upon the Colonized People." *Science and Society* 37(2) (1973): 129–51.

Moure, Kenneth. "Prosperity for All? Britain and Mass Consumption in Western Europe after World War II." In *Consuming Behaviors: Identity, Politics and Pleasure in Twentieth Century Britain*, edited by Mark J. Crowley, Sandra Trudgen Dawson, and Erika D. Rappaport, 213–36. London: Bloomsbury, 2015.

Moynihan, Michael, ed. *Black Bread and Barbed Wire: Prisoners in the First World War*. London: Leo Cooper, 1978.

Muldrew, Craig. *Food, Energy and the Creation of Industriousness: Work and Material Culture in Agrarian England, 1550–1780*. Cambridge: Cambridge University Press, 2011.

Murphy, Mahon. *Colonial Captivity during the First World War: Internment and the Fall of the German Empire, 1914–1919*. Cambridge: Cambridge University Press, 2017.

Nally, David P. *Human Encumbrances: Political Violence and the Great Irish Famine*. Notre Dame: University of Notre Dame Press, 2011.

National Child Measurement Programme, England 2015–16 School Year, NHS Digital, November 3, 2016: https://digital.nhs.uk/services/national-child-measurement-programme/.

Newby, Howard, Colin Bell, David Rose, and Peter Saunders. *Property, Paternalism and Power: Class and Control in Rural England*. Madison: University of Wisconsin Press, 1978.

Noble, Virginia A. *Inside the Welfare State: Foundations of Policy and Practice in Post-War Britain*. London: Routledge, 2009.

Novetzke, Christian Lee. *The Quotidian Revolution:Vernacularization, Religion, and the Premodern Public Sphere in India*. New York: Columbia University Press, 2016.

Nützenadel, Alexander and Frank Trentmann. "Introduction: Mapping Food and Globalization." In *Food and Globalization: Consumption, Markets and Politics in the Modern World*, edited by Alexander Nützenadel and Frank Trentmann, 1–18. Oxford: Berg, 2008.

Ó Gráda, Cormac. *Famine: A Short History*. Princeton: Princeton University Press, 2009.

Oddy, Derek J. *From Plain Fare to Fusion Food: British Diet from the 1890s to the 1990s*. Woodbridge: The Boydell Press, 2003.

"A Nutritional Analysis of Historical Evidence: The Working-Class Diet, 1880–1914." In *The Making of the Modern British Diet*, edited by Derek Oddy and Derek Miller, 214–31. London: Croom Helm, 1976.

Offer, Avner. *The First World War: An Agrarian Interpretation*. Oxford: Clarendon Press, 1989.

Otter, Chris. "The British Nutrition Transition and Its Histories." *History Compass* 10 (11) (2012): 812–25.

"Feast and Famine: The Global Food Crisis." *Origins* 3(6) (2010): http://origins.osu.edu/article/feast-and-famine-global-food-crisis/page/0/1.

"Liberty and Ecology: Resources, Markets, and the British Contribution to the Global Environmental Crisis." In *The Peculiarities of Liberal Modernity in Imperial Britain*, edited by Simon Gunn and James Vernon, 182–98. Berkeley: University of California Press, 2011.

Page, Robert M. *Revisiting the Welfare State*. Maidenhead: Open University Press, 2007.

Panayi, Panikos. *The Enemy in Our Midst: Germans in Britain during the First World War*. Oxford: Berg, 1991.

Prisoners of Britain. Manchester: Manchester University Press, 2012.

Parris, Henry. "The Nineteenth-Century Revolution in Government: A Reappraisal Reappraised." *The Historical Journal* 3(1) (1960): 17–37.

Pedersen, Susan. *Eleanor Rathbone and the Politics of Conscience*. New Haven: Yale University Press, 2004.

Family, Dependence, and the Origins of the Welfare State: Britain and France, 1914–1945. Cambridge: Cambridge University Press, 1993.

Pelling, Henry. *The Origins of the Labour Party, 1880–1900*. Oxford: Clarendon Press, 1965.

Pennybacker, Susan. *A Vision for London 1889–1914: Labour, Everyday Life, and the LCC Experiment*. London: Routledge, 1995.

Perren, Richard. *The Meat Trade in Britain 1840–1914*. London: Routledge & Kegan Paul, 1978.

Pilcher, Jeffrey M. *Que Vivan Los Tamales!: Food and the Making of Mexican Identity*. Albuquerque: University of New Mexico Press, 1998.

Pimlott, J.A.R. *The Englishman's Christmas*. Hassocks: Harvester Press, 1978.

Pitts, Martin, Charles Pattie, and Danny Dorling. "Christmas Feasting and Social Class." *Food, Culture & Society* 10(3) (2007): 407–24.

Poovey, Mary. *A History of the Modern Fact: Problems of Knowledge in the Sciences of Wealth and Society*. Chicago: University of Chicago Press, 1998.

Powell, David. "The New Liberalism and the Rise of Labour, 1886–1906." *The Historical Journal* 29(2) (1986): 369–93.

Poynter, J.R. *Society and Pauperism: English Ideas on Poor Relief, 1795–1834.* London: Routledge & Kegan Paul, 1969.

Price, Kath. "Changes on the 'Kitchen Front': The Case of British Restaurants in World War Two." *North East Labour History* 22 (1988): 4–19.

Proctor, Tammy M. *Civilians in a World at War, 1914–1918.* New York: New York University Press, 2010.

Rabinbach, Anson. *The Human Motor: Energy, Fatigue, and the Origins of Modernity.* Berkeley: University of California Press, 1990.

Rachamimov, Alon. *POWs and the Great War: Captivity on the Eastern Front.* Oxford: Berg, 2002.

Rappaport, Erika. *A Thirst for Empire: How Tea Shaped the Modern World.* Princeton: Princeton University Press, 2017.

Reese, William J. "After Bread, Education: Nutrition and Urban School Children, 1890–1920." *Teachers College Record* 81(4) (1980): 496–525.

Rich, Rachel. *Bourgeois Consumption: Food, Space, and Identity in London and Paris, 1850–1914.* Manchester: Manchester University Press, 2011.

Richardson, Matthew. *The Hunger War: Food, Rations and Rationing, 1914–1918.* Barnsley: Pen & Sword, 2015.

Richardson, Stanley I. *A History of the Edmonton Poor Law Union, 1837–1854.* Edmonton Hundred Historical Society, Occasional Papers, New Series Number 8, n.d.

Roberts, David. "How Cruel Was the Victorian Poor Law?" *The Historical Journal* 6(1) (1963): 97–107.

   Paternalism in Early Victorian England. New Brunswick: Rutgers University Press, 1979.

Roberts, Marion. "Private Kitchens, Public Cooking." In *Making Space: Women and the Man Made Environment,* edited by Jos Boys et al., 106–19. Sydney: Pluto Press, 1984.

Rogers, Ben. *Beef and Liberty: Roast Beef, John Bull and the English Nation.* New York: Vintage, 2004.

Roodhouse, Mark. *Black Market Britain, 1939–1955.* Oxford: Oxford University Press, 2013.

Rose, Michael E. *The Relief of Poverty, 1834–1914.* Houndmills: Macmillan, 1986.

Rose, Sonya. *Which People's War?: National Identity and Citizenship in Britain, 1939–1945.* Oxford: Oxford University Press, 1993.

Ross, Ellen. *Love and Toil: Motherhood in Outcast London.* Oxford: Oxford University Press, 1993.

Roy, Parama. *Alimentary Tracts: Appetites, Aversions, and the Postcolonial.* Durham: Duke University Press, 2010.

Rozin, Paul. "The Psychology of Food and Food Choice." In *The Cambridge World History of Food,* Vol. II, edited by Kenneth F. Kiple and Kriemhild C. Ornelas, 1476–86. Cambridge: Cambridge University Press, 2000.

Ruis, A.R. *Eating to Learn, Learning to Eat: The Origins of School Lunch in the United States.* New Brunswick: Rutgers University Press, 2017.

Sackman, Douglas Cazaux. *Orange Empire: California and the Fruits of Eden.*
   Berkeley: University of California Press, 2005.
Sasson, Tehila and James Vernon. "Practising the British Way of Famine:
   Technologies of Relief, 1770–1985." *European Review of History* 22(6)
   (2015): 860–72.
Savage, Gail. *The Social Construction of Expertise: The English Civil Service and
   its Influence, 1919–39.* Pittsburgh: University of Pittsburgh Press, 1996.
Segers, Yves. "Food Systems in the Nineteenth Century." In *A Cultural History
   of Food in the Age of Empire*, edited by Martin Bruegel, 49–66. London:
   Bloomsbury, 2016.
Seidman, Robert B. "The Ghana Prison System: an Historical Perspective."
   In *African Penal Systems*, edited by Alan Milner, 59–87. New York:
   Frederick A. Praeger, 1969.
Seikaly, Sherene. *Men of Capital: Scarcity and Economy in Mandate Palestine.*
   Stanford: Stanford University Press, 2015.
Sen, Satadru. "The Savage Family: Colonialism and Female Infanticide in
   Nineteenth-Century India." *Journal of Women's History* 14(3) (2002): 53–79.
Seth, Suman. *Difference and Disease: Medicine, Race, and the Eighteenth Century
   British Empire.* Cambridge: Cambridge University Press, 2018.
Shapin, Steven. "'You Are What You Eat': Historical Changes in Ideas About
   Food and Identity." *Historical Research* 87(237) (2014): 385–9.
Sharma, Sanjay. *Famine, Philanthropy and the Colonial State: North India in the
   Early Nineteenth Century.* Delhi: Oxford University Press, 2001.
Showalter, Elaine. *The Female Malady: Women, Madness, and English Culture,
   1830–1980.* New York: Pantheon, 1985.
Siegel, Benjamin Robert. *Hungry Nation: Food, Famine, and the Making of
   Modern India.* Cambridge: Cambridge University Press, 2018.
Sim, Joe. "The Prison Medical Service and the Deviant, 1895–1948."
   In *The Health of Prisoners*, edited by Richard Creese, W.F. Bynum, and
   J. Bearn, 102–17. Amsterdam: Rodopi, 1995.
Simmons, Dana. "Starvation Science: From Colonies to Metropole." In *Food
   and Globalization: Consumption, Markets and Politics in the Modern World*,
   edited by Alexander Nützenadel and Frank Trentmann, 173–91. Oxford:
   Berg, 2008.
   The Vital Minimum: Need, Science, and Politics in Modern France. Chicago:
   University of Chicago Press, 2015.
Sinha, Mrinalini. *Colonial Masculinity: The "Manly Englishman" and the
   "Effeminate Bengali" in the Late Nineteenth Century.* Manchester:
   Manchester University Press, 1995.
Skinner, Rob and Alan Lester. "Humanitarianism and Empire: New Research
   Agendas." *Journal of Imperial and Commonwealth History* 40(5) (2012): 729–47.
Smith, David F. "Nutrition Science and the Two World Wars." In *Nutrition in
   Britain: Science, Scientists and Politics in the Twentieth Century*, edited by
   David F. Smith, 142–65. London: Routledge, 1997.
   "The Politics of Food and Nutrition Policies." In *The Handbook of Food
   Research*, edited by Anne Murcott, Warren Belasco, and Peter Jackson,
   398–409. London: Bloomsbury, 2013.

"The Social Construction of Dietary Standards: The British Medical Association – Ministry of Health Advisory Committee on Nutrition Report of 1934." In *Eating Agendas: Food and Nutrition as Social Problems*, edited by Donna Maurer and Jeffery Sobal, 279–304. New York: Aldine de Gruyter, 1995.

Smith, David and Malcolm Nicolson. "The 'Glasgow School' of Paton, Findlay and Cathcart: Conservative Thought in Chemical Physiology, Nutrition and Public Health." *Social Studies of Science* 19(2) (1989): 195–238.

"Nutrition, Education, Ignorance and Income: A Twentieth-Century Debates." In *The Science and Culture of Nutrition, 1840–1940*, edited by Harmke Kamminga and Andrew Cunningham, 288–318. Amsterdam: Rodopi, 1995.

Soluri, John. *Banana Cultures: Agriculture, Consumption, and Environmental Change in Honduras and the United States*. Austin: University of Texas Press, 2005.

Spang, Rebecca L. *The Invention of the Restaurant: Paris and Modern Gastronomic Culture*. Cambridge: Harvard University Press, 2000.

Srivastava, Hari Shanker. *The History of Indian Famines 1858–1918*. Agra: Sri Ram Mehra and Co., 1968.

Stallybrass, Peter and Allon White. *The Politics and Poetics of Transgression*. Ithaca: Cornell University Press, 1986.

Stewart, John. "'This Injurious Measure': Scotland and the 1906 Education (Provision of Meals) Act." *Scottish Historical Review* 78(1) (1999): 76–94.

Stibbe, Matthew. *British Civilian Internees in Germany: The Ruhleben Camp, 1914–1918*. Manchester: Manchester University Press, 2008.

Stokes, Eric. *The English Utilitarians and India*. Delhi: Oxford University Press, 1959.

Streets, Heather. *Martial Races: The Military, Race and Masculinity in British Imperial Culture, 1857–1914*. Manchester: Manchester University Press, 2011.

Supple, Barry. "War Economies." In *The Cambridge History of the First World War*, Vol. II, edited by Jay Winter, 295–324. Cambridge: Cambridge University Press, 2014.

Taylor, Miles. "John Bull and the Iconography of Public Opinion in England c. 1712–1929." *Past and Present* 134 (1992): 93–128.

Teich, Mikuláš. "Science and Food during the Great War: Britain and Germany." In *The Science and Culture of Nutrition, 1840–1940*, edited by Harmke Kamminga and Andrew Cunningham, 213–34. Amsterdam: Rodopi, 1995.

Teuteberg, Hans-Jurgen. "Food Provisioning on the German Home Front, 1914–1918." In *Food and War in Twentieth Century Europe*, edited by Rachel Duffett, Ina Zweiniger-Bargielowska, and Alain Drouard, 59–72. Farnham: Ashgate, 2011.

Thane, Pat. "Women and the Poor Law in Victorian and Edwardian England." *History Workshop Journal* 6(1) (1978): 29–51.

Thompson, E.P. *Customs in Common*. New York: The New Press, 1993.

Thompson, Noel. *Political Economy and the Labour Party*. London: UCL Press, 1996.

Thoms, Ulrike. "The Innovative Power of War: The Army, Food Sciences and the Food Industry in Germany in the Twentieth Century." In *Food and War in Twentieth Century Europe*, edited by Rachel Duffett, Ina Zweiniger-Bargielowska, and Alain Drouard, 247–62. Farnham: Ashgate, 2011.

Tickner, Lisa. *The Spectacle of Women*. Chicago: University of Chicago Press, 1988.

Todd, Selina. *The People: The Rise and Fall of the Working Class, 1910–2010*. London: John Murray, 2014.

Trentmann, Frank. "Bread, Milk and Democracy: Consumption and Citizenship in Twentieth-Century Britain." In *Politics of Consumption: Material Culture and Citizenship in Europe and America*, edited by Martin Daunton and Matthew Hilton, 129–63. Oxford: Berg, 2001.

Free Trade Nation. Oxford: Oxford University Press, 2008.

Trentmann, Frank and Flemming Just. "Introduction." In *Food and Conflict in Europe in the Age of the Two World Wars*, edited by Frank Trentmann and Flemming Just, 1–12. Houndmills: Palgrave, 2006.

Tucker, Richard P. *Insatiable Appetite: The United States and the Ecological Degradation of the Tropical World*. Berkeley: University of California Press, 2000.

Tusan, Michelle. *Smyrna's Ashes: Humanitarianism, Genocide, and the Birth of the Middle East*. Berkeley: University of California Press, 2012.

Twigg, Julia. "Vegetarianism and the Meanings of Meat." In *The Sociology of Food and Eating*, edited by Anne Murcott, 18–30. Aldershot: Gower, 1983.

Ussishkin, Daniel. *Morale: A Modern British History*. Oxford: Oxford University Press, 2017.

Valenze, Deborah. *Milk: A Local and Global History*. New Haven: Yale University Press, 2011.

Van Emden, Richard. *Prisoners of the Kaiser: The Last POWs of the Great War*. Barnsley: Leo Cooper, 2000.

Veit, Helen Zoe. *Modern Food, Moral Food: Self-Control, Science, and the Rise of Modern American Eating in the Early Twentieth Century*. Chapel Hill: University of North Carolina Press, 2013.

Vernon, James. *Distant Strangers: How Britain Became Modern*. Berkeley: University of California Press, 2014.

"The Ethics of Hunger and the Assembly of Society: The Techno-Politics of the School Meal in Modern Britain." *American Historical Review* 110(3) (2005): 693–725.

Hunger: A Modern History. Cambridge: Harvard University Press, 2007.

"The Local, the Imperial, and the Global: Repositioning Twentieth-Century Britain and the Brief Life of Its Social Democracy." *Twentieth-Century British History* 21(3) (2010): 404–18.

"Notes Towards an Introduction." In *Re-Reading the Constitution: New Narratives in the Political History of England's Long Nineteenth Century*, edited by James Vernon, 1–21. Cambridge: Cambridge University Press, 1996.

Politics and the People: A Study in English Political Culture, c.1815–1867. Cambridge: Cambridge University Press, 1993.

Vincent, C. P. *The Politics of Hunger: The Allied Blockade of Germany, 1915–1919*. Athens: Ohio University Press, 1985.

Vincent, David. *Poor Citizens: The State and the Poor in Twentieth-Century Britain*. London: Longman, 1991.

Walkowitz, Judith R. *Nights Out: Life in Cosmopolitan London*. New Haven: Yale University Press, 2012.

——— *Prostitution and Victorian Society: Women, Class, and the State*. Cambridge: Cambridge University Press, 1980.

Wallace, Elisabeth. *The British Caribbean: From the Decline of Colonialism to the End of the Federation*. Toronto: University of Toronto Press, 1977.

Ward, Stephanie. *Unemployment and the State in Britain: The Means Test and Protest in 1930s South Wales and North-East England*. Manchester: Manchester University Press, 2013.

Warde, Alan. *Consumption, Food and Taste: Culinary Antinomies and Commodity Culture*. London: Sage, 1997.

Weatherall, Mark W. "The Foundation and Early Years of the Dunn Nutritional Laboratory." In *Nutrition in Britain: Science, Scientists and Politics in the Twentieth Century*, edited by David F. Smith, 29–52. London: Routledge, 1997.

Webb, Sidney and Beatrice Webb. *English Poor Law History. Volume II: The Last Hundred Years*. Hamden: Archon, 1963.

——— *English Poor Law Policy*. Hamden: Archon, 1963.

Webster, Charles. "Government Policy on School Meals and Welfare Foods, 1939–1970." In *Nutrition in Britain: Science, Scientists and Politics in the Twentieth Century*, edited by David F. Smith, 190–213. London: Routledge, 1997.

——— "The Health of the School Child during the Depression." In *The Fitness of the Nation: Physical and Health Education in the Nineteenth and Twentieth Centuries*, edited by Nicholas Parry and David McNair, 70–85. Leicester: History of Education Society of Great Britain, 1983.

Weiler, Peter. *The New Liberalism: Liberal Society Theory in Great Britain, 1889–1914*. New York: Garland, 1982.

Weinreb, Alice. *Modern Hungers: Food and Power in Twentieth-Century Germany*. Oxford: Oxford University Press, 2017.

Welshman, John. "School Meals and Milk in England and Wales." *Medical History* 41 (1997): 6–29.

Wiener, Martin J. "The Health of Prisoners and the Two Faces of Benthamism." In *The Health of Prisoners*, edited by Richard Creese, W.F. Bynum, and J. Bearn, 44–58. Amsterdam: Rodopi, 1995.

——— *Reconstructing the Criminal: Culture, Law, and Policy in England, 1830–1914*. Cambridge: Cambridge University Press, 1990.

Wilkinson, Oliver. *British Prisoners of War in First World War Germany*. Cambridge: Cambridge University Press, 2017.

Williams, Karel. *From Pauperism to Poverty*. London: Routledge & Kegan Paul, 1981.

Wilt, Alan F. *Food for War: Agriculture and Rearmament in Britain before the Second World War*. Oxford: Oxford University Press, 2001.

Winter, J.M. *The Great War and the British People*, 2nd ed. Houndmills: Palgrave Macmillan, 2003.

Wood, Peter. *Poverty and the Workhouse in Victorian Britain*. Stroud: Sutton, 1991.

Worboys, Michael. "The Discovery of Colonial Malnutrition between the Wars." In *Imperial Medicine and Indigenous Societies*, edited by David Arnold, 208–25. Manchester: Manchester University Press, 1988.

Wylie, Diana. *Starving on a Full Stomach: Hunger and the Triumph of Cultural Racism in Modern South Africa*. Charlottesville: University Press of Virginia, 2001.

Yang, Anand. "Disciplining 'Natives': Prisons and Prisoners in Early Nineteenth Century India." *South Asia* 10(2) (1987): 29–45.

Yarnall, John. *Barbed Wire Disease: British and German Prisoners of War, 1914–19*. Stroud: The History Press, 2011.

Zedner, Lucia. *Women, Crime, and Custody in Victorian England*. Oxford: Clarendon, 1991.

Zook, Darren C. "Famine in the Landscape: Imagining Hunger in South Asian History, 1860–1990." In *Agrarian Environments: Resources, Representations, and Rule in India*, edited by Arun Agrawal and K. Sivaramakrishnan, 107–31. Durham: Duke University Press, 2000.

Zweiniger-Bargielowska, Ina. *Austerity in Britain: Rationing, Controls, and Consumption, 1939–1955*. Oxford: Oxford University Press, 2000.

"Fair Shares? The Limits of Food Policy in Britain during the Second World War." In *Food and War in Twentieth Century Europe*, edited by Rachel Duffett, Ina Zweiniger-Bargielowska, and Alain Drouard, 125–38. Farnham: Ashgate, 2011.

Unpublished Secondary Sources

Braatz, Erin. "Governing Difference: Prison and Colonial Rule on the Gold Coast, 1844–1957." Unpublished PhD dissertation, New York University (2015).

Nag, Anindita. "Managing Hunger: Famine, Science, and the Colonial State in India, 1860–1910." Unpublished PhD dissertation, University of California–Los Angeles (2010).

Otter, Chris. *Diet for a Large Planet: Food Systems, World-Ecology, and the Making of Industrial Britain*. Chicago: University of Chicago Press, forthcoming.

Index

Atwater, Wilbur O., 53, 130

Beveridge Report, 10, 205, 217
biopolitics, 83, 105–9, 113, 246–47
bread, 144, 189, 208
  in British prison diets, 51, 55, 59, 60,
    61, 80
  in British Restaurant meals, 184, 189,
    191
  as central to British diet, 26, 73, 140
  in colonial prison diets, 70, 72–73, 74,
    75, 76, 80
  and famine feeding, 97
  in prisoner of war diets, 120, 126,
    131–32, 137, 139–45, 250
  and racial theories, 80
  in school meals, 161, 171, 172–73
  in workhouse diets, 26, 35
  in working-class diets, 151
British Honduras. See West Indies
British Restaurants, 4, 15, 178–210, 211,
  212, 213, 247, 250
  cash-and-carry services, 183, 185–86

calories, 1, 2, 138, 139
  in British civilian diet during World
    War I, 134
  in British Restaurant meals, 188–90
  in German civilian diet during World
    War I, 134
  in German diet before World War I, 116
  interwar disputes over, 167–68
  in military diets, 138
  in prison diets, 53
  in prisoner of war diets, 124, 130–34,
    135, 139, 164
  in school meals, 151, 172, 174
  theorization of, 53–54, 128,
    144, 248
  in working-class diet, 172
caste, 4, 77, 93, 101–3, 247, 250

Central Prisoners of War Committee,
  123, 141–42, 143
Chadwick, Edwin, 22, 23, 25–26, 164
children, 142, 185, 249
  and British Restaurants, 194, 201
  and famine relief, 82, 83, 171
    justifications for, 14, 92–93, 105–13,
      166, 170, 177, 211, 246
    parental fears surrounding, 104
    special foods, 97
  illegitimate, 39
  in prisons, 51, 56–57, 58, 62
  schoolchildren, 3, 15, 146–77, 189, 247,
    248, 250
  and Welfare Foods Service, 3, 16,
    211–43, 248, 249, 250
  in workhouses, 21, 35, 41, 46
Children's Minimum Council, 158, 169
Christmas, 27, 29–35, 47, 249
Churchill, Winston, 179, 180, 223, 226
  and famine policy, 179
  and naming of British Restaurants,
    178, 187
  and postwar food policy, 208–9
  and suffragettes, 66–67
class, 3, 42, 46, 152. See also
  maternalism; paternalism
  and British Restaurants, 4, 15, 179–82,
    183–86, 187–88, 189–210, 246,
    250
  conflict, 7, 8, 29–30, 31, 37, 48
  diets of working class during World
    War II, 179–84, 189–91
  diets of working class in interwar
    period, 146, 151, 172, 248, 249
  diets of working class in nineteenth
    century, 25, 26, 130
  diets of working class in pre-industrial
    period, 27
  and discourses of rights, 8, 25, 28–29,
    31, 33, 34, 37–38
  and Reform Act of 1832, 19–20

Woolton, Lord, 180, 181, 182, 205, 206
and clientele of British Restaurants,
193, 195–96
and justification for British
Restaurants, 194, 205
and naming of British Restaurants,
186, 187
and Welfare Foods Service, 213
during World War I, 185
workhouses. *See* poor laws

World War I, 9, 14, 53, 114–45, 185. *See
also* morale; nutritional sciences;
prisoners of war; rationing
aftermath of, 146, 152, 213, 245
and communal feeding, 180, 192
World War II, 9–10, 178–210, 212–17,
219, 248, 250. *See also* British
Restaurants; Ministry of Food;
nutritional sciences; rationing;
school meals